IFLA Publications

Edited by
Janine Schmidt

International Federation of Library Associations and Institutions
Fédération Internationale des Associations de Bibliothécaires et des Bibliothèques
Internationaler Verband der bibliothekarischen Vereine und Institutionen
Международная Федерация Библиотечных Ассоциаций и Учреждений
Federación Internacional de Asociaciones de Bibliotecarios y Bibliotecas
国际图书馆协会与机构联合会　الاتحاد الدولي لجمعيات ومؤسسات المكتبات

Volume 176

Public Library Governance

International Perspectives

Edited on behalf of IFLA by Edward Abbott-Halpin
and Carolynn Rankin

DE GRUYTER
SAUR

ISBN 978-3-11-053076-6
e-ISBN (PDF) 978-3-11-053332-3
e-ISBN (EPUB) 978-3-11-053092-6
ISSN 0344-6891

Library of Congress Control Number: 2020939073

Bibliografische Information der Deutschen Nationalbibliothek
The Deutsche Nationalbibliothek lists this publication in the Deutsche Nationalbibliografie;
detailed bibliographic data is available on the internet at http://dnb.dnb.de.

www.degruyter.com

Contents

About IFLA — VII

Edward Abbott-Halpin and Carolynn Rankin
Acknowledgements — 1

Edward Abbott-Halpin and Carolynn Rankin
Foreword — 3

Edward Abbott-Halpin and Carolynn Rankin
Introduction: Public Library Governance and Wicked Problems — 5

Part 1: Historical, Philosophical and Ethical Perspectives

Alistair Black
1   Governance and History: The Direction of Public Libraries in the UK since
     the Second World War — 19

Joe Pateman and John Pateman
2   Marx Meets Maslow: An Analytical Framework for Managing Cultural Change
     in Public Libraries — 41

David McMenemy
3   Governance of Public Library Services: How Philosophical Approaches to
     Service Delivery Impact on Practice — 63

Simon Robinson
4   Corporate Governance and Public Libraries — 78

Part 2: Practitioner Views and Public Policy

John Dolan
5   The Dilemmas of Governance — 103

Jenny Bossaller and Jenna Kammer
6   The Power of Public Space: Equal Access in an Era of Fear
     and Austerity — 125

Bill Irwin
7   Public Library Board Trustees: Policy Makers, Policy Takers,
    or Policy Fakers? —— 152

Ian Anstice
8   Trusting in Others: The Experience of Councils Transferring Libraries to
    Other Organisations Since 2010 —— 166

Part 3: International Perspectives

Marian Koren
9   Library Governance in View of the Rights of the Child: The Sustainable
    Development Goals as Catalyst —— 187

John Abdul Kargbo
10 The Public Library and Good Governance: Perspectives from
    Sierra Leone —— 237

Umut Al and Seda Öz
11 The Role of Municipal Public Libraries in the E-Transformation
    of Turkey —— 265

Irhamni Ali
12 Public Library Development Policy in Indonesia: The Present and the
    Future —— 283

Part 4: Impact and Evaluation

Anne Goulding
13 The Impact of Evaluation: The Use of Evidence for Decision-Making and
    Service Development in Public Libraries —— 315

David Streatfield, Sharon Markless and Jeremy Paley
14 Measuring Performance and Evaluating Impact of Public Libraries from a
    Governance Perspective —— 335

Jan Richards
15 Public Libraries – A Global Vision —— 356

Contributors —— 375

About IFLA

www.ifla.org

IFLA (The International Federation of Library Associations and Institutions) is the leading international body representing the interests of library and information services and their users. It is the global voice of the library and information profession. IFLA provides information specialists throughout the world with a forum for exchanging ideas and promoting international cooperation, research, and development in all fields of library activity and information service. IFLA is one of the means through which libraries, information centres, and information professionals worldwide can formulate their goals, exert their influence as a group, protect their interests, and find solutions to global problems.

IFLA's aims, objectives, and professional programme can only be fulfilled with the co-operation and active involvement of its members and affiliates. Currently, approximately 1400 associations, institutions and individuals, from widely divergent cultural backgrounds are working together to further the goals of the Federation and to promote librarianship on a global level. Through its formal membership, IFLA directly or indirectly represents some 500,000 library and information professionals worldwide.

IFLA pursues its aims through a variety of channels, including the publication of a major journal, as well as guidelines, reports and monographs on a wide range of topics. IFLA organises workshops and seminars around the world to enhance professional practice and increase awareness of the growing imporRefenbtance of libraries supporting their communities and society in the digital age. All this is done in collaboration with a number of other non-governmental organisations, funding bodies and international agencies such as UNESCO and WIPO. The Federation's website is a prime source of information about IFLA, its policies and activities: www.ifla.org

Library and information professionals gather annually at the IFLA World Library and Information Congress, held in August each year in cities around the world. IFLA was founded in Edinburgh, Scotland, in 1927 at an international conference of national library directors. IFLA was registered in the Netherlands in 1971. The Koninklijke Bibliotheek (Royal Library), the national library of the Netherlands, in The Hague, generously hosts IFLA's headquarters. Regional offices are located in Buenos Aires, Argentina; Pretoria, South Africa; and Singapore.

https://doi.org/10.1515/9783110533323-202

Acknowledgement

The editors would like to offer sincere thanks to:
- Ian Johnson who initially encouraged us to develop ideas for the book
- Naomi Colhoun who provided expert administrative assistance at the outset of the project
- The panel of reviewers: Briony Birdi, Judy Broady-Preston, Christine Browne, Tony Bryant, Lo Claesson, Premila Gamage, Anne Goulding, Leikny H. Indergaard, Bill Irwin, Simon Robinson and Paul Sturges
- The ever-helpful staff in the reading room at the British Library in Boston Spa
- Last, but not least, all the contributing authors who are helping to continue the debate on public library governance.

Edward Abbott-Halpin and Carolynn Rankin

https://doi.org/10.1515/ 9783110533323-001

Foreword

As this book: *Public Library Governance: International Perspectives* goes to press, the world we know is in the grip of a global pandemic caused by the Coronavirus. To reduce the spread of the Covid-19 infections and to protect both staff and the users they serve, many public libraries have had to temporarily close their doors or reduce services. The impact of Covid-19 is a global challenge and a local challenge, and decision makers are faced with a multiplicity of wicked problems. This is a time of tough issues and uncertain answers. What will be the aftermath? Will there be a default to the old normal, or a new direction? Many contributing authors question the neoliberal approach to library governance. Will there be other challenges to the orthodoxy? If so, what will this mean for the public library, at the heart of communities, as place and space?

Edward Abbott-Halpin and Carolynn Rankin
June 2020

https://doi.org/10.1515/ 9783110533323-002

Edward Abbott-Halpin and Carolynn Rankin

Introduction: Public Library Governance and Wicked Problems

Abstract: Major changes in public libraries throughout the world have led to an increased focus on governance issues, and to debate about the decision-making and the decision makers involved in this governance process. The introductory chapter to this book highlights such issues and outlines the various perspectives to be presented on the topic, with a wide range of views provided by prominent figures from the public library community throughout the world. This chapter creates a space in which to reflect on the challenges and wicked problems facing the public library sector. The context is described, the role of public libraries explored, the topic of governance introduced, and the concept of wicked problems used to explain some of the complex challenges faced.

Keywords: Corporate governance; Public libraries; Public administration; Social problems – Government policy; Wicked problems

The Context

> A library is a mandated and facilitated space supported by the community, stewarded by librarians, and dedicated to knowledge creation. (Lankes 2016, 95)

In recent years, within the UK context, but also internationally, there have been marked changes in the provision of public library services. In the UK this has been signalled by the closure of many libraries and the movement to pass some libraries into voluntary or not-for-profit management. The journey to this book started in research undertaken by the editors in relation to determining the value and impact of public libraries which was published in the article *Measuring the Value of Public Libraries in the Digital Age: What the Power People Need to Know* (Abbott-Halpin et al. 2015). Left open was the question of who the power people are and more importantly what they needed to know. We suggest that there is a need to address the power people, but who are they? Are they just the policy makers or are they the people who take and make the day-to-day decisions, governance and agency in action?

We see this book as a valuable and insightful resource for practitioners, policy makers, researchers and students who are interested in future paradigms of the public library. We hope to move the debates concerning public libraries

https://doi.org/10.1515/9783110533323-003

forward and offer new voices to address the challenges before us, and provide a space in which experienced practitioners and academics share their knowledge about strategies to address such challenges. The aim is to open up discussion on the wicked problems in both policy and practice, engage in debate and encourage difficult conversations, and thereby afford opportunities for solutions to be advanced. To situate the topic, it is worth considering the historical development and governance of the public library, and past key players and concepts.

This book provides a broad range of thinking on the contexts of governance from the perspectives of leaders, practitioners, researchers, and decision makers, offering differing views on current and future library provision and usage. Included are examination of the political and policy making governance of public library provision, professional decision-making in planning and implementing delivery and various practitioner and professional practice issues associated with provision of public libraries. The chapters of the book address real and present challenges of the connections and disconnections between policy and practice, and values and ethics. The contributors address the challenges of policy and decision-making, but also the daily decisions on implementation and practice in the public library world.

Public Libraries are Good for Society – Perspectives and Challenges

Public libraries are an international phenomenon although they differ in policies, practices and governance. It is evident there is a need for a new approach to governance as the policy and implementation of this public service is undergoing rapid and radical change around the world. There is much evidence in the professional literature supporting the premise that public libraries are good for society, taking on essential roles in ensuring access to information and digital inclusion for all members of their communities. Lankes makes the case for the public library service saying,

> It is one of the few civic institutions that span the range of a geographic community. The library provides a connective tissue between young and old, rich and poor. The children of the white collar sit with the children of the blue to listen to story hour. The library is open to banker and beggar alike. (Lankes 2011, 9)

The *IFLA Public Library Guidelines* (Koontz and Gubbin 2010) state that the public library is the prime community access point designed to respond to a multitude of ever-changing information needs, signalling the complexity of the service. William Sieghart, commissioned by the UK government to review the public library service in England, reported in 2014 that

> Libraries are... a golden thread throughout our lives. Despite the growth in digital technologies, there is still a clear need and demand within communities for modern, safe, non-judgemental, flexible spaces, where citizens of all ages can mine the knowledge of the world for free, supported by the help and knowledge of the library workforce. (UKDCMS 2014, 5)

Goulding's (2006) research into public libraries found that discourses around partnership working were very strong. There was recognition that libraries are operating in a cross-cutting policy environment and that partnership can assist them in explicitly connecting with important political priorities, placing them at the heart of local, regional and national activities.

Challenges of Governance Ideologies

Despite the evidence base supporting the value of public library provision to their communities, there are apparent problems of resourcing and provision. Mathieson (2013) posits that as a result of the global economic turndown, many local and national governments are disinvesting in public libraries and argues that governments have an obligation to create and fund public libraries, because access to a public library is a human right. The value and purpose are not always recognised, and Jaeger, Taylor and Gorman (2015, 83) suggest that libraries have often failed to define these essential roles in a way that resonates with policy makers who are primarily concerned with the economic contributions of public services. Jaeger et al. (2014) note that the successes of public libraries in recent years such as e-government, emergency response, digital literacy, technology access and community partnerships have not given them a greater role in the policy process. Although the authors are discussing the issues in the context of the US, it is pertinent elsewhere. The shortcoming is echoed by Lankes with the challenging view that "All too often librarians talk a good game on democracy and empowerment, but most of their time is devoted to technology and procedure. We need to do a better job connecting our values, our work, and our communities into the policy conversations" (Lankes 2011, 127).

Our view in this introductory chapter is that there is abundant evidence of the value of providing public library service for the benefit of communities. It is demonstrated in the evidence of outcomes, the value of interventions and benefits to local communities. However, it must be recognised that other public institutions can make the same claims and having a public library voice in policy conversations is vitally important. Jaeger and others raise the challenge that "Regardless of libraries' demonstrations of success and contribution, their lack of voice is predetermined by governance ideologies that are based on the belief that public goods are always inferior to private efforts" (Jaeger 2014, 62). McCook (2000, 37) notes that while libraries and librarians build community, this fact is not recognised in the broad literature of community building. Libraries are viewed by the broader community building movement as partners on various projects, not as integral components of comprehensive community change.

The introductory chapter provides general perspectives on governance and how it might be defined. The concept of "wicked problems" in relation to public libraries is introduced and initial thoughts presented. Concluding thoughts, questions and challenges in the future life and governance of the public library, whether locally, nationally, or internationally, are offered.

Defining Governance

Many authors confirm that defining governance is difficult. For example, the two major handbooks on governance, *The SAGE Handbook of Governance* (Bevir 2011) and *The Oxford Handbook of Governance* (Levi-Faur 2014), reflect on the complexity of governance issues in the reform of the state and on various aspects of democratic governance. Defining governance in relation to public libraries seems to be equally difficult, with seemingly few specific references to governance, whilst there are many to policy, practice, service delivery and planning. In the United Kingdom, the Libraries Taskforce (https://www.gov.uk/government/groups/libraries-taskforce) has been charged with implementing the Independent Library Report for England (https://www.gov.uk/government/publications/independent-library-report-for-england), providing leadership and helping to reinvigorate public library services. It might well be claimed that the work of the Libraries Taskforce is designed to respond to the need for changes in public library governance.

The variety of responses delivered by the various authors in this book provides distinctive views on the topic of public library governance giving cause for further reflection. The chapters provide a range of perspectives from practitioners and academics that both reflect on broad definitions and approaches to governance in public libraries and offer insights into current trends. We will not attempt to offer a single definition of governance in this book, but rather reflections on the current thinking of some leading academics.

In introducing *The Sage Handbook of Governance*, Bevir suggests that "At the most general level, governance refers to theories and issues of social coordination and the nature of all patterns of rule" (Bevir 2013, 1), whilst Lynn (2014, 49), in *The Oxford Handbook of Governance* (Levi-Faur 2014) offers a paraphrasing that defines governance as "the action or manner of governing, that is, of directing, guiding, or regulating individuals, organisations, nations, or multinational associations – public or private, or both – in the conduct of actions". There remains much debate and dispute about the development of the term governance, some claiming that it originates in the 1950s or 1960s, whilst the root perhaps goes back to a Greek word *kybernan*, which can be translated to mean pilot or steer (Levi-Faur 2014, 5). There appears to be consensus that from the 1950s onwards, governance has become an increasingly significant issue to the social and political sciences. Levi-Faur suggests that the emergence of the importance of governance coincides with a rapidly evolving and changing society and new roles of state and government as they respond to such changes. Levi-Faur goes on to evidence this in an observation on what are described as shifts: "The shifts are conceptualised in three different directions: upward (to the regional, transnational, intergovernmental and global), downward (to the local, regional, and metropolitan), and horizontally (to private and civil spheres of authority)" (Levi-Faur 2014, 7).

Levi-Faur describes how the relationship of authority has changed, including moves from central political, market, and social hierarchies to decentred markets, partnerships and networks. In the relationship changes it might be said that there is a move from what has been called or described as Big Government to Small Government, though this in itself is perhaps a simplification of the changes that occurred from the late 1970s onwards, and in particular to the directional changes of the 1980s to what has been described as New Public Management.

New Public Management

New Public Management (NPM) is associated with a neo-liberal model of the state and has emerged as a new approach to management of public sector organisations through the use of private sector management techniques. It has variously been considered as a necessary change to modernise government and services; an opportunity to seek greater effectiveness and efficiency in the public sector; a space for the private sector to bring skills and knowledge to a state sector that needed reform; or an opportunity to reduce cost and privatise services, at the same time reshaping them and often reducing them. Jaeger and others consider this in terms of public library provision:

> ...austerity provided a means to justify deeper cuts into public goods and services that cannot articulate an economically quantified value and/or that are deemed morally objectionable under the neoconservative ideology. As the language of value is based on economic contributions rather than public good, the terms of austerity are clearly biased against educational and cultural institutions like public libraries (Jaeger et al 2014, 66)

The development of public-private partnerships and contracting has over the years become a significant component of the landscape of government and the dominant governance paradigm, although in the UK for example the collapse of a very major provider, Carillion (as widely reported in the press), has raised new questions about the relationship between the public and private sectors. Some public library changes in the UK have seen a rise in a volunteerism where in some instances private provision was not seen as a viable alternative to public provision. These developments speak of new relationships between stakeholders. Those who are now described as consumers of the services are taking on new roles. These relationships are said to empower end-users, but also serve to replace existing democratic processes and to move direct accountability from the elected representatives to bodies that oversee or act as arbiters or regulators, at a step removed from the state apparatus. This brings us to the vexed questions of who are the power people and how are decisions really made now. These questions are relevant to the public library service where we are seeing the changes from direct provision, and of closure or refinement, to allow volunteer provision replace a direct government provision. Occurrences in the UK are mirrored elsewhere in the world, although direct government provision and direction of libraries are observed in other parts of the world.

If there are power people, who are they today, national or regional government, local government, autonomous task forces, professional bodies, the volunteers in communities, the public library users? The chapters in this book offer insights into some of these issues, but who will make or is making the decisions driving the direction and governance of public libraries? Is the frame of reference broad, taking into account direct and indirect impacts of the public libraries, or narrow and confined to cost of the specific delivery? As we can see in the chapters presented here, and from the wide literature on public libraries, the role is not confined to direct impact, but has social, economic, educational, and community impact well beyond the immediate role that is often understood. Within the complexity is the concept of wicked problems which we discuss in the next section.

Wicked Problems and Public Libraries

To engage in the debate, we suggest that public libraries, and the communities they serve, are facing wicked problems, so-called because they have complex interdependencies and are intertwined in the social, economic, and cultural fabric of society. A problem whose solution requires many people to change their mindsets and behaviour is likely to be a wicked problem. Wicked problems cannot be solved through strategic planning and data-gathering. Dealing with wicked problems involves engaging stakeholders in a robust and healthy process of making sense of the problem's dimensions. The term wicked in this context is used not in the sense of evil or bad, but to denote an issue highly resistant to resolution. The term was originally proposed by Rittel and Webber (1973), professors of design and urban planning at the·University of California at Berkeley.

Wicked problems are socially complex and difficult to define clearly. The various stakeholders may not be able to agree on what the definition of the problem should be, let alone on what the solution is. Camillus, Bidanda and Mohan (2017) have stated that wicked problems defy description and are viewed differently by diverse stakeholders. We have already noted the range of challenges facing public libraries and the policy debates around funding and provision of services to the communities they serve. The nature and extent of any problem depends on who has been consulted. Different stakeholders will have different versions of what the problem is. Who, for example, determines the level and quality of provision? Some key ingredients in solving or at least managing complex policy problems include working successfully across both internal and external organisational boundaries and engaging citizens and stakeholders in policy making and implementation (APSC 2007). Developing a shared understanding of contentious issues among relevant stakeholders and organisations will encourage collaboration and engagement. However, as Conklin (2006, 42) attests, shared understanding is not the same as consensus. Stakeholders do not necessarily agree with each other but know about each other's concerns and goals.

We have identified that wicked problems are complex, and according to Head and Alford (2015, 719) traditional hierarchical forms of public administration have not been conducive to grappling productively with wicked problems. Public sector managers can be constrained in their efforts to tackle wicked problems by the structure and processes of government administration. Head and Alford posit that the conventional structures and processes of administration of the public sector are not scoped to address the tasks of conceptualising, mapping and responding to wicked problems. New ways of thinking, leading, managing and organising are needed. Collaboration offers one way of recognising the complexity of problems and engaging the multiplicity of actors affecting the wickedness of a problem. Librarians are recognised as being effective in building partnerships and working collaboratively, but it may be difficult to establish and sustain robust collaboration in a public sector context subject to turbulence and strict accountability rules.

Agency is the capacity for human beings to make choices. Governance theory is mainly occupied with institutional change and it involves human agency (Kjaer 2004, 10). A reassessment of some of the traditional ways of working and solving problems may help to successfully tackle wicked policy problems and this offers potential for innovative and proactive public library managers who can challenge traditional approaches to governance.

Structure of the Book

In exploring public library governance from a range of perspectives, the book is organised into four parts:
- Part 1. Historical, Philosophical and Ethical Perspectives
- Part 2. Practitioner Views and Public Policy
- Part 3. International Perspectives
- Part 4. Impact and Evaluation.

Key aspects of public library governance are examined including the following themes:
- Using the past to inform the future
- The impact of philosophical approaches to service delivery on practice
- Influences of corporate governance
- Influences of New Public Management theory
- Influences of the politics of the place
- Governance, interpretations of policy and implementation
- Sustainable Development Goals and the public library
- Human rights and the library
- Structures of management and control
- Responsibility and duty
- Care and transparency
- NGO perspectives.

Part 1: Historical, Philosophical and Ethical Perspectives

Part 1 examines governance from historical, philosophical and ethical perspectives. In Chapter 1, library historian Alistair Black sets the historical context by examining governance issues in public libraries in the UK since the Second World War. Chapter 2 by Joe and John Pateman synthesises the ideas of Karl Marx and Abraham Maslow into an analytical framework for the purpose of critically analysing public libraries. One of the key challenges faced by public services is how the prevailing political philosophy influences governance regimes. In Chapter 3, David McMenemy explores over time the impact on public libraries and their governance of changing political philosophies, and how an understanding of the phenomenon contributes to effective advocacy. Governance, especially corporate governance, has held the headlines for several decades. Chapter 4 by Simon Robinson offers reflections on corporate governance and implications for the public library sector.

Part 2: Practitioner Views and Public Policy

The second part of the book presents the perspectives of practitioners and those concerned with public policy. The contributors critically examine some of the current political and philosophical drivers of public library development and delivery particularly in the context of North America and the UK, but also with relevance internationally in respect of prevailing public policy and political thinking. An experienced UK practitioner, John Dolan, provides in Chapter 5 a personal reflective account of the dilemmas of governance based on his extensive experience as a senior library manager and innovator. Chapter 6 is predicated on the belief that librarians need to be careful to preserve and promote the library as a public space. In this chapter, Jenny Bossaller and Jenna Kammer explore the belief that libraries should promote themselves as public spaces that need funding. The wicked problem they are tackling here is the dissonance between neoliberal conceptions of public space and the ideology of the common good, especially in relation to public libraries. The tactics that public bodies, and in particular public libraries, take in the development and delivery of policy is central in determining the authenticity of their approach to governance.

The primary focus of Chapter 7 by Bill Irwin is to further the understanding of the impact of decision makers' values on the design of public policy. The author addresses the challenging issue of who gets to set the policy direction for the public library. In Chapter 8, Ian Anstice provides an account of the experience of councils in England transferring libraries to other organisations since 2010.

There has been more change to the governance of English public libraries in the last decade than in the previous century and Anstice shows the wide variety of models of governances present in the United Kingdom today.

Part 3: International Perspectives

Part 3 offers valuable insights into settings around the world in which public libraries are developing their own responses to particular societal needs. With the United Nations Sustainable Development Goals and human rights in mind, a general oversight of international policy is provided, together with responses from various countries including Sierra Leone, Turkey and Indonesia. Chapter 9 by international law and human rights expert Marian Koren provides an international lens and observations on the relationship of human rights and libraries. Apart from the central right of freedom of expression, which includes the right of access to information, there are other rights with implications for library governance, policy and practice. The author focuses on the Rights of the Child, its international Convention, and the rights especially relevant for public libraries. In the next three chapters we have the opportunity to examine the situation in particular countries. In Chapter 10, John Abdul Kargbo offers a contribution to the ongoing debate on good governance and the role of the public library with particular reference to Sierra Leone. In Chapter 11, Umut Al and Seda Öz discuss the role of municipal public libraries in the e-transformation of Turkey. Chapter 12 by Irhamni Ali provides an overview of current and future public library development policy in Indonesia.

Part 4: Impact and Evaluation

The concluding section affords a critical examination of ways of envisioning the impact and evaluation of public libraries today, with the final chapter providing a vision of the future by the current Chair of the IFLA Public Libraries Section. Anne Goulding has a particular interest in how library and information services demonstrate the impact of their programmes and services and Chapter 13 explores the role of evaluation of public library services in governance and discusses the situation in New Zealand. In Chapter 14 David Streatfield, Sharon Markless, and Jeremy Paley examine measuring performance and evaluating impact of public libraries from a governance perspective. Chapter 15 gives the last words to Jan Richards, a strong advocate for the International Federation of Library and

Information Associations (IFLA) and Chair of the IFLA Public Libraries Section Standing Committee. She outlines a global vision for public libraries.

Conclusion

In conclusion, this book addresses the wicked problems of governance that are faced by all public libraries and which must be tackled in delivering the public library of the future. Libraries are part of a multi-stakeholder society and it is appropriate to end this introductory chapter with a quotation from the 2013 IFLA 2013 *Statement on Libraries and Development*.

> Libraries work effectively with many different stakeholder groups in varied situations. They deliver programmes and services alongside local and national governments, community groups, charities, funding organisations, and private and corporate enterprises. Librarians are agile actors who are able to work alongside others in governments, civil society, business, academia and the technical community to help deliver policy goals. (IFLA 2013).

This is positive affirmation of the significance of governance, yet there are still challenges, such as McCook's view that "As agencies of local governments, libraries are not generally perceived by community builders as potential participants in comprehensive community initiatives" (McCook 2000, 37). We hope that the contributions of the wide range of authors bring a variety of perspectives providing both scope for debate and the opportunity to develop fresh and innovative solutions to the governance of public libraries.

References

Abbott-Halpin, E., C. Rankin, E. Chapman, and C. Walker. "Measuring the Value of Public Libraries in the Digital Age: What the Power People Need to Know." *Journal of Librarianship and Information Science* 47, no. 1 (2015): 30–42.

Australian Public Service Commission (APSC). *Tackling Wicked Problems: A Public Policy Perspective*. Canberra: Australian Public Service Commission, 2007. http://www.enablingchange.com.au/wickedproblems.pdf

Bevir, M. ed. *The SAGE Handbook of Governance*. London: SAGE Publications Ltd., 2013.

Camillus, J.C., B. Bidanda, and N.C. Mohan. *The Business of Humanity: Strategic Management in the Era of Globalization, Innovation, and Shared Value*. New York: Routledge, Taylor Francis Group, 2017.

Conklin, E.J. *Wicked Problems and Social Complexity*. Napa, CA: CogNexus Institute, 2001–2010. http://cognexus.org/wpf/wickedproblems.pdf

Conklin, E.J. *Dialogue Mapping. Building Shared Understanding of Wicked Problems.* Hoboken, NJ: Wiley, 2006.

Goulding, A. *Public Libraries in the 21st Century: Defining Services and Debating the Future.* Farnham: Ashgate, 2006.

Head, B. W., and J. Alford. "Wicked Problems Implications for Public Policy and Management." *Administration & Society* 47, no. 6 (2015): 711–739.

IFLA. IFLA Statement on Libraries and Development. International Federation of Library Associations and Institutions. 2013. https://www.ifla.org/publications/ifla-statement-on-libraries-and-development

Jaeger, P.T., U. Gorham, J.S. Bertot, and L.C. Sarin. *Public Libraries, Public Policies, and Political Processes Serving and Transforming Communities in Times of Economic and Political Constraint.* Lanham, MD: Rowman & Littlefield, 2014.

Jaeger, P.T., N.G. Taylor, and U. Gorham. *Libraries, Human Rights and Social Justice. Enabling Access and Promoting Inclusion.* Lanham, MD: Rowman and Littlefield, 2015.

Kjaer, A.M. *Governance: Key Concepts.* Cambridge: Polity Press, 2004.

Koontz, C., and B. Gubbin. eds. *IFLA Public Library Service Guidelines.* 2nd edition. IFLA Publications Series 147. Berlin: De Grutyer Saur, 2010.

Lankes, R.D. *The Atlas of New Librarianship.* London: MIT Press, 2011.

Lankes, R.D. *The New Librarianship Field Guide.* Cambridge, Mass.: MIT Press, 2016.

Levi-Faur, D. ed. *The Oxford Handbook of Governance.* Oxford: Oxford University Press, 2012.

Lynn, L.E. "The Many Faces of Governance: Adaptation? Transformation? Both? Neither?" In *The Oxford Handbook of Governance*, edited by D. Levi-Faur, 49–64. Oxford: Oxford University Press, 2012.

McCook, K. de la Peña. *A Place at the Table: Participating in Community Building.* Chicago: American Library Association, 2000.

Mathiesen, K. "The Human Right to a Public Library." *Journal of Information Ethics* 22, no. 1 (2013): 60–79. Also available at SSRN: https://ssrn.com/abstract=2081178

Rittel, H., and M. Webber. "Dilemmas in a General Theory of Planning." *Policy Sciences* 4, no. 2 (1973): 155–169.

UK Department for Culture, Media and Sport (DCMS). *Independent Library Report for England.* Presented by William Sieghart and an expert panel. London: DCMS, 2014. https://www.gov.uk/government/uploads/system/uploads/attachment_data/file/388989/Independent_Library_Report-_18_December.pdf

Part 1: **Historical, Philosophical and Ethical Perspectives**

Alistair Black

1 Governance and History: The Direction of Public Libraries in the UK since the Second World War

Abstract: In order to develop strategic visions designed to anticipate and accommodate change well into the future, this chapter argues that stakeholders, both leaders and participants, should ideally possess an understanding of the historical purposes and past practices that have defined the institutions they serve or use. Looking back through time, being time conscious, contributes to an understanding of the present and to planning the future effectively. Knowing the past helps govern the future. Without a clear and persuasive strategic direction, the future of the public library as the great public sphere institution it has proved itself to be in the past is in great jeopardy. The approaches to public library governance and the role of the public library in the UK are tracked and the various perspectives from government, practitioners and users presented. There is a lack of clarity and consensus regarding a desired role of the public library in the twenty-first century.

Keywords: Public libraries – Great Britain; Public libraries – History; Corporate governance

Introduction

Any exploration of the relationship between library governance and history first requires an identification of the constituent elements of governance *per se*. According to Graham, Amos and Plumptre (2003), governance encompasses five core principles:
- Legitimacy, based on input (direct and indirect) into decision-making
- Accountability, including appropriate levels of transparency
- Performance, involving issues of effectiveness, efficiency and responsiveness
- Fairness, founded on legal frameworks and rule-based practices
- Direction, otherwise referred to as strategic vision.

A comprehensive study of the history of UK public library governance would necessitate an investigation of each of these principles over the public library's long history, dating back to the institution's inception in 1850. Some key questions forming the basis of such a study would be:

https://doi.org/10.1515/ 9783110533323-004

- What have been the central legislative and local government democratic arrangements that have bestowed legitimacy on the publicly funded free municipal library, from the permissive inaugural legislation of 1850 to legislation in 1964, still in force, making provision by local authorities compulsory?
- In which ways have public library professionals and managers been held accountable to local citizens and central government, from early plebiscites of local taxpayers on the question of opening a local library, the emergence of the phenomenon of the library committee and the overarching context of local government reform and re-organization to the establishment of local libraries by councillor vote only after 1892, the imposition of default ministerial oversight after 1964, the appearance in some places in the late twentieth century of readers' committees and the emergence of the voluntary community library in recent years?
- What various instruments have been employed to measure performance, from the early analysis of collections and borrowing patterns by type of literature, and of readers categorised by age, gender or occupation, to today's mass surveys, academic studies and detailed reports by central government?
- To what extent has the public library operated a regime of fairness through its multifarious rule-based practices, from censorship, selection and lending to access, charging and the question of professional ethics?

Answers to such questions, and there are many more, are beyond the scope of this single book chapter. They could, of course, be systematically excavated from the large number of histories of the public library published in recent decades (Black 1996; 2000; Hendry 1974; Kelly 1977; Morris 1977; Munford 1951; Murison 1988; Pemberton 1977; Snape 1995). That would be a large task. Therefore, in advance of any attempt to mount a full-scale study of the history of public library governance, it would be profitable to undertake a case study based on one of governance's five core principles, direction, akin to the concept of long-term strategic vision. What might be the reason for selecting this particular dimension?

The concept of governance has the ring of immediacy, of liminality and of practical importance to the good functioning of institutions today and in the immediate, foreseeable future. At first glance, governance barely possesses a time dimension. Yet, upon further inspection, it becomes clear that one of its core principles, direction, is especially time-rich. In order to develop strategic visions designed to anticipate and accommodate change well into the future, stakeholders, both leaders and participants, should possess an understanding of the historical purposes and past practices that have defined the institutions they run or use. Looking back through time, being time conscious helps in both understanding the present and planning the future. Good governance demonstrates a sensitivity towards history, harnessing statements about the future to directions formulated and followed in the past (Inayatullah 2014).

Envisioning Library Futures

In the middle of the twentieth century, looking forward was a fairly common pastime, prompted by a pervasive sense of hope, in contrast to today's deep-seated sense of uncertainty about the future. The optimism of the post-war era reached a crescendo in the sun-drenched decade of the 1960s (Sandbrook 2006) and often coalesced with the excitement that a new millennium was just around the corner (Grimshaw 1975; Jordan 1975). This produced a heady mix of social, political and technological confidence.

Heightened expectations regarding the future, including the future of libraries, found expression in a wave of futurology. In 1962, in his book *Profiles of the Future*, the British futurist Arthur C. Clarke predicted that scientists would soon develop a memory device in a six-foot cube that could store all information recorded during the last 10,000 years containing not only every book ever printed but everything ever written in any language on paper, papyrus, parchment or stone. He also predicted that by the early twentieth century a global library would be in existence. An authentic world brain, he predicted, would not arrive until the end of the twenty-first century (Clarke 1974[1962], 235, 251-252). Breathtaking information and communication futures were also glimpsed by the magazine *Popular Mechanics*. In 1959, the magazine predicted that within twenty years there would be an information-retrieval machine that could "hunt through memory drums on which the complete texts of millions of documents might be stored"; the machine would "set aside all references to a desired subject, then assemble the facts from each reference and present them in smooth sentences" (Benford 2010, 99).[1]

Mid-twentieth century librarians were given to flights of imagination regarding the future of their institutions. In 1968, at a conference of fellow professionals entitled *The Shape of Things to Come*, the City Librarian of Southampton, Eric Clough, addressed the question of the future of public libraries. Envisaging the public library fifty years ahead, in 2018, he mused that it would be "staffed by computer managers and facsimile-transmission specialists who work a few hours each day in a splendid building from which the public are excluded"; in

---

1 The most famous library futurology of this period was produced in the United States, by J.C.R. Licklider (1965), a communications engineer.

this building "requests for information would be assessed and the answers duly retrieved" (Clough 1968, 22).[2]

Admitting that H.G. Wells had been a big influence on him in his youth, Clough presented a quote from Wells' *The Work, Wealth and Happiness of Mankind* (1932): "In England we have come to rely upon a comfortable time-lag of fifty years or a century intervening between the perception that something ought to be done and a serious attempt to do it" (Clough 1968, 23).[3]

In the middle of the twentieth century there certainly was, to echo Wells' words, a perception that something significant ought to be done, that fresh visions needed to be created regarding the trajectory of the public library, an institution that in many respects owed more to its Victorian origins than to the twenty-first century destination that many had started to imagine. It is appropriate from a twenty-first century vantage point to look back over the period since the end of the Second World War to examine how arguably the most important element of public library governance, direction, developed through several identifiable phases.

Recreational and Educational Roles

Since the inception of the public library in Britain in the middle of the nineteenth century, questions have continuously been raised regarding the type of books, information and services the public library should provide and the social groups it should serve. In short, there has been an unceasing debate about the institution's evolving mission. In the conference presentation highlighted above, Eric Clough went straight to the heart of a question that had dominated public library debate from the outset: should the institution's serious, educational purpose take preference over its recreational and entertainment function, notwithstanding the fact that the two are by no means mutually exclusive? Clough argued that it

---

2 Other library futures were discussed in Finsberg (1955), Batty (1966), Grimshaw (1975), Jordan (1975) and Bamber (1978).

3 Clough's science fiction imagination appears to have tapped into a futurist tradition in librarianship. One of the more interesting essays published in *The Wicket*, the staff magazine of Sheffield Public Libraries, was entitled *Looking Forward*. The anonymous author, a member of the library staff, imagined the public library a hundred years into the future, in 2031. By that time, the author conjectured, travel in cities would be by airship, with passengers alighting on rooftops. On one dream trip, the author wrote that he alighted at the public library where he found books were issued by taking the borrower's fingerprints; in the news room the latest news was broadcast over loudspeakers (*Looking Forward* 1931, 3).

was sentimental to conceptualise the public library as primarily a recreational service; to do so, he suggested, would be to imitate the now ineffectual commercial subscription library. The W.H. Smith Library, the Times Book Club and the Boots Book Lovers' Library disappeared, in 1961, 1965 and 1966 respectively. The alternative, said Clough, especially at a time of increasing scrutiny of public spending, was to demonstrate an educational purpose: "I believe that public libraries have a tremendous potential as an educational force – far greater than has yet been realised", he surmised (Clough 1968, 36). He was especially keen to emphasise the importance of cooperation to build a nationwide network of libraries to complement Britain's strident scientific and technological advance. He had high praise, for example, for the new National Lending Library for Science and Technology, which had been established in 1962 at Boston Spa, Yorkshire (Clough 1968, 23-25; Houghton 1972). For Clough, and others, public libraries had a serious mission to fulfil.

However, Clough's desire to see a resolution to the tension between recreational and educational roles in favour of the latter attracted opposition from some in his audience. Aware that their bread was buttered on the popular side, two local councillors were vocal supporters of recreational services. The chair of Haringey's library committee argued that local authorities had a duty to provide recreational reading in line with the rise of a leisure society; librarians, in his opinion, were becoming too specialist to meet general recreational needs, a thought echoed by a representative of Hillingdon's library committee who said that ordinary people, who clearly wanted recreational services, thought differently to librarians.[4] In fact, there is a great deal of evidence to suggest that mid-twentieth century librarians did indeed think differently to ordinary people, thereby placing in sharp relief any mission statements librarians might have issued.

The public library's serious, rational educational-scientific side, what Jones (1971, 76) referred to as the grand tradition of the public library,[5] had received a real boost in the Second World War. Despite library use being promoted as a relief from wartime stress, the library establishment took the opportunity presented by the war to underpin the public library's credentials as essentially an educational force for democratic civilization and citizenship, the very thing the Allies were defending in the face of fascist aggression. Full of high-flown, Churchillian lan-

---

4 The chair of Haringey's library committee was D. Clark; the member of Hillingdon's library committee was L. Sherman.
5 The grand tradition of the public library might be defined as the philosophy whereby the institution sustains an open society by serving and nurturing the rational, truth-seeking citizen for the purpose of individual and social progress.

guage, the famous 1942 report on the state of public libraries in Britain authored by librarian Lionel McColvin sought to reinforce the institution's civilizing, democratic mission. "We admit our indebtedness to education", wrote McColvin (9), adding that the main purpose of libraries was to help make "individuals better able to contribute to and benefit from the constructive life of the community, the nation and the world" (195). In line with this serious stance, shortly after the war, along with others (Lamb 1955), McColvin welcomed the fact that more attention was being paid to reference and information work, "and especially... to making the public library, in close association with research organisations, a better medium for the wide dissemination of scientific and technical information" (McColvin 1953, 527).

In 1950, the Library Association celebrated the centenary of the British public library movement (Jefcoate 1999). Part of the celebrations included the publication of a booklet, *A Century of Public Library Service: Where Do We Stand To-day?* (Library Association 1950). While it was admitted in the booklet that too many library services were inadequate and ill-supported, it was also stressed that there had been a century of worthwhile achievement by a "democratic institution of which we can all be proud" (3, 6). A serious note was struck in imbuing the public library with the potential to improve productivity, assist the manufacturer and "help the country in its export drive" (17). The appeal to seriousness was underlined by an attack on the public library's recreational tendencies: "Despite the protestations of the ostrich-headed, the best test of a library is the percentage of non-fiction issued from its lending departments" (24). Yet, this loudly shouted statement seemed to be at odds with what the Library Association identified as the enduring philosophy of the public library, namely, that the public library was an essential instrument for democracy, providing "an adequate opportunity for all, subject to no limitation, censorship, partisanship or ulterior motives"' (7). If the public library was truly a democratic institution, surely its professionals, managers and high-level supporters would not express dissatisfaction at the overwhelming demand for recreational reading? For over a century, however, the institution's leaders had done just that, while at the same time, hypocritically, some might say, supplying recreational reading in great quantities to satisfy demand. A similar story regarding the United States has been told by Wiegand (2012).

Despite the historic reluctance of public librarianship to outwardly support recreational and entertainment roles, it would nonetheless be an exaggeration to view librarians as members of what Pierre Bourdieu called a cultural nobility[6]. This is not to say that librarians did not claim to invest, to invoke Bourdieu again,

---

6 Unlike, as Hung (2015) has pointed out, in the case of many professionals working in the BBC.

in elite cultural capital and occupy a highbrow cultural habitus (Grenfell 2014). Librarians' cultural elitism was linked to the fact that the post-war Left was, counter-intuitively, conservative in cultural matters, while most public librarians were broadly progressive in their politics. A major characteristic of post-war British cultural policy was its tendency towards exclusivity which manifested itself in the financial and intellectual backing of traditional art forms as well as in its lack of empathy with popular culture (Black 2003; Mulgan 1996, 201). In essence, Left culturalism amplified the ideology of welfare-capitalism that had taken shape in the 1940s, that everyone should have the opportunity to share the good things that elites had customarily enjoyed. These things included economic security, education, healthcare, decent housing and good culture (Sinfield 1997, 243).

As one library educator put it in 1974, the continuing and implicit objective of the post-war public library was "to put readers on the road to high culture... rather than positively to encourage the emergent plural culture" (Jones 1974, 77). In short, librarians of the early welfare state seemed more interested in Debussy than in Dylan. A good example of this highbrow trajectory is the programme of film shows offered in 1956 and 1957 by the central library in Stepney, one of London's poorest districts. An average audience of ninety-five people watched a series of so-called continental films. Partly to promote the gramophone library, film biographies of Chopin, Strauss and Caruso were preceded by performances of their music (Metropolitan Borough of Stepney 1957, 12-13). Perhaps tinged by guilt that they were out of step with the cultural revolution of the time, some librarians came to admit that the cultural services they were offering were class partial (Wilson 1970, 191-3). Halliwell (1975) sensed that many of the non-book cultural services offered by libraries were essentially for a small and influential section of the community (26).

The Reaction to Conservatism

Looking forward to the new millennium, in the mid-1960s the library educator Roy Stokes hoped that by that time the profession would be vastly different to that of the mid-twentieth century. With the previous generation, the speed of change in librarianship, he argued, had lagged behind social change. Librarianship had successfully resisted innovation and maintained the status quo (Stokes 1966, 35). This was an astute observation, in keeping with the point made about the cultural stances of librarians in this chapter. To summarise, in the mid-twentieth century librarians can be found openly pursuing a recreational role for their institutions, often articulated in the rise of the library as cultural centre (Joliffe 1962). However, the strongest enthusiasm they displayed in this regard resided in the realm of traditional and high culture; meanwhile, culture that might be deemed mere entertainment, from romances to the Rolling Stones, from westerns to The Who, received much less attention and was tolerated rather than encouraged.

The seemingly Victorian attitude to culture dispensed by public libraries was eventually worn down by what Marwick (1998) has described as a cultural revolution. Brought about in part by the philosophies of a new generation of university-trained librarians following the rapid growth in postgraduate courses in librarianship in the 1960s (Bramley 1981), the 1970s witnessed a notable reaction to the public library's highbrow cultural preferences. "Perhaps by A.D. 2000 we will be less puritanical about recreation, particularly as leisure time is likely to be greater than at present", said the library educator Peter Jordan in 1975 (17). It is not just that the emergence of the postmodern condition (Harvey 1989) involved the growth of cultural relativism, permitting Mills and Boon light fiction to exist on the same plane as the novels of Jane Austen; it is also that relativism's emphasis on pluralism, and the activism that went with it, appeared to render both the public library's reliance on the middling sort and its historic embrace of political neutrality anachronistic. The increasing attraction of middle-class readers to the public library accelerated after the Second World War.

In welfare-state Britain, middle-class users of the public library, as in many other areas of post-war social, cultural and welfare provision, benefited proportionately more than groups further down the social scale. A survey of public library readers in Tottenham just after the war had shown how little compared with the middle class (in terms of the proportion of the population they represented) the working class made use of the public library (Mass-Observation Archive 1947). In addressing the Library Association in 1966, the library historian Thomas Kelly noted there was a real "danger of converting libraries into purely middle-class institutions" (Kelly, 251). "When and by whom was it decided that public libraries should cater primarily for the middle classes?" asked a contributor to the *Assistant Librarian* in 1975 (Halliwell 1975, 25). In 1978, a government report, *The Libraries' Choice*, observed that in the 1950s and 1960s, "libraries went from strength to strength... attracting the middle classes in ever-increasing numbers". The report noted that the middle classes, who made up less than 20% of the population, accounted for 50% of library membership (Great Britain Department of Education and Science 1978, 6-7). There was a growing feeling that the institution had become over-responsive to middle-class tastes and demands. The attachment of the public library to its middle-class readers (though there were of course geographical variations to the general pattern) became stronger in the 1960s and 1970s and goes a long way to explaining the forcefulness of the push-back in the 1970s and 1980s against the cultural conservatism of the public library.

The mounting awareness of the increasing middle-class orientation of public libraries led a growing band of socially aware librarians and library educators to call for the abandonment of middle-class domination of the public library and a return to what they saw as the institution's primary heritage as a popular institution. This perception of the public library's past was, and remains, simplistic as libraries, especially institutions, in many ways originated as much in the interests of an emerging middle class as for the increasingly literate lower orders (Black 1996).[7] Priority in service provision, as had been advocated in the United States in respect of segments of the population described as unserved and the information poor (Childers and Post 1975), had to be given to the socially deprived and those seeking alternative culture. "Library services to the disadvantaged" (Martin, 1975) became the clarion call of a new movement which eventually took the name community librarianship (Black and Muddiman 1997; Martin 1989; O'Kelley 1975; Vincent 1986).

Community librarianship discriminated in favour of the socially and economically marginalised, including ethnic minorities (Clough and Quarmby 1978). It was a mode of service which embodied, in the words of the librarian Barry Totterdell (1981, 39-40) "a recognition that public library services are for all, not only for the better educated, more affluent middle class minority from whom the service has tended to draw its clientele, but also for the less literate, the disadvantaged, those who are perhaps less book-oriented but whose need for information and for life-enrichment may be greater". It entailed a focusing of resources on the vulnerable and the needy, not least the rising army of unemployed (Astbury 1985). Moreover, authentic community librarianship demanded not only sophisticated, qualitative research into the complexion and needs of local communities (community profiling), but also the proactive involvement of librarians in these communities, along the lines of contemporary practice in community work.

In 1972 Geoffrey Smith, the County Librarian of Leicestershire, captured this growing radical strain of public librarianship when he urged professionals to get involved "at the grass roots and in the dusty streets". Librarians, argued Smith, needed to get out into communities and liaise closely with local groups; only in

---

7 Despite this qualification, it should be recognised that in the nineteenth century, libraries overwhelmingly served a working-class readership. In fact, their wash-house image was one of the main reasons local tax-payers often rejected proposals to establish a local library (Kelly 1966, 248). The key issue to consider, however, is whether or not middle-class users of libraries, including the increasingly numerous lower-middle class white-collar workers, were in any particular locality disproportionately represented in respect of their presence in the population.

this way could services be brought to the needy in the community. Librarians, he added, needed to study the people they were serving, substituting the scientific profiling of communities for the hunch factor previously prevalent in developing services in relation to needs. This user-oriented philosophy, he argued, would replace the largely redundant supplier-oriented approach that in the past had prioritised the educational and cultural goals of librarians rather than local people (Smith 1972).

Conservatism Rallies

In the mid-1980s, however, the community librarianship movement began to lose momentum.[8] Against the backdrop of political hostility and cuts in public services, many librarians began to believe that its expense could not be justified. Further, criticised as a vehicle for political correctness, its ethos was questioned by the library establishment on the grounds that it had infringed the noble tradition of neutrality in librarianship. As one London librarian announced angrily in 1984, "libraries... are being used as a noticeboard for a political controlling group" (The Privatisation of Reading 1984, 6).

Community librarianship also required a reorientation of the librarian towards community work, a trend which some viewed as a threat to professional status. "There is no doubt that some of the activities engaged in by librarians in the course of community librarianship were not entirely appropriate", remarked one of the pioneers of services to the disadvantaged in the early 1990s (Coleman 1992, 301). Further, the targeting of the disadvantaged in preference to other user groups appeared to counter the welfarist creed of universalism to which many public librarians felt deeply attached. While equality of opportunity had always been an unassailable tenet of public library philosophy, community librarianship's pursuit of equality of outcome, where intervention was based on positive discrimination in an attempt to raise the disadvantaged to a level and quality of use commensurate with that experienced by middle-class users, was difficult for many to swallow.[9]

Resistance to the political objectives that community librarianship had formulated also came from outside the profession, from traditionalists emboldened

---

8 The emphasis here is on momentum, for community and social justice perspectives have continued to re-surface: see Pateman and Vincent (2016) and Pateman and Williment (2016).

9 Positive discrimination in community information services was advocated, for example, by Ward (1974, 595).

by the advance of the neo-liberal project. In 1986, a report by the Adam Smith Institute, *Ex-Libris*, decried the fact that, as the Institute saw it, "the bulk of library *customers* [my emphasis] use the service as a publicly funded provider of free romantic fiction" (21). Moreover, this subsidisation of the reading of pulp fiction consumed by those who, it was suggested, could afford to pay for it was, the Institute argued, at the expense of the provision of library and reference facilities serving an educational role and of the need to "move with the quickening pace of information technology" (42).

The back to basics philosophy of the Major government between 1992 and 1997 drew in cultural policy and thus libraries. Towards the end of the government's term, the Department of National Heritage published a report on public libraries, *Reading the Future* (1997). The report was unequivocal in its belief, as well as in its dismay, that there had been "a shift away from high seriousness towards entertainment", adding that information technology offered the opportunity to reverse this trend (Great Britain Department of National Heritage 1997, 3), a policy proposition with a ring of authenticity to it given the prohibition of the use of email by the public in many libraries at the time. It was a philosophy that found resonance in the campaign to preserve the public library's serious, reference role with the early 1990s witnessing a heated reaction to the weeding of historic scholarly collections built up over a century and, in many cases, more (West 1989).

Popular Culture Embraced

However, the attempted turn to seriousness, though helping to blunt politicised community librarianship, did little to negate the public library's recreational role. Arguments promoting the public library as essentially an educational force made little headway. Instead, the winds of popular culture filled the sails of the public library service, which became increasingly defined, to the chagrin of traditionalists, by growing collections of audio and video cassettes, CDs, DVDs and, eventually, by provision of access to the World Wide Web and other digital services[10].

In the last decade and a half of the twentieth century, the de-politicised approach to public librarianship began to reassert itself. In the new commercialised environment created by Thatcherite neo-liberalism, users and readers, as evidenced in the statement from the Adam Smith Institute quoted above, became mere customers. Further, all that was really needed, it was proposed,

---

10 On changing use and users, see Goulding (2006).

was good ongoing marketing of the public library. This would include a rebranding of the institution, not least through a renaissance in library design, epitomized by the award-winning Peckham Library, winner of the Stirling Prize for Architecture in 2000. As McMenemy (2016, 17) has put it, addressing the needs of the modern citizen in an infrastructural way "in practice often involves a re-imagining of environment and location for many public library authorities who feel that the old way of doing things no longer sustains enough interest with the public".

Rebranding took a drastic shift in nomenclature away from the ancient word "library". In various locations, public libraries became hives whose members, like bees, contribute to the common good; hubs to which people gravitate to associate; living rooms in the city where, like members of a family, citizens congregate informally; civic public squares wherein freedom of thought and expression thrive; and idea stores in which individuals transfer their commonly held skills as consumers to the consumption of cultural goods. Other rebranding operating today includes: media lounge; library café; learning zone; discovery centre; learning pod; resource centre; and postmodern terms like explore, as in the renaming of the York Central Library, York Explore, where signifier and signified appear disconnected. Serving as an umbrella concept for all these new terms was the proposition that the public library was first and foremost a place of social interaction. More specifically, the public library was rebranded as an informal third place, one that is not the home and not work, where, either online or physically, people could connect to knowledge or network with others (Buschman and Lecki 2007; Oldenburg 2001).

The New Public Library and the Critique of Universal Access

Conceptualising the public library as a third place drew on the institution's egalitarian, public-sphere credentials, and nowhere were these credentials more strongly touted than in the arrival in the late 1990s of the library without walls, branded the people's network. In its plan for a revitalised public library, spelled out in *New Library: The People's Network* (Library and Information Commission 1997), the newly elected Labour government under Tony Blair, who the previous year had published his plan for a better future for the country under the title *New Britain: My Vision of a Young Country*, placed a large amount of faith in the ability of new ICTs, especially the World Wide Web, to bring about change on a scale not seen since the Industrial Revolution.[11]

In an emergent digital, networked, information society (Webster 2014; Castells 1996), free access to new ICTs facilitated by institutions like the public library would encourage, it was predicted, the "nurturing [of] social cohesion through fostering a politically and culturally informed society (Great Britain Library and Information Commission 1997, 2). Poignantly, this vision echoed the claim made by supporters of the early public library movement in the mid-nineteenth century that the institution could help corrode social class differences, and that social harmony would inevitably arise when equality of opportunity, through the public library and other self-help mechanisms, was provided. Fast forward a century and a half and the same simplistic appeal to, and faith in, equality of access can be found in the late 1990s new library prescription for a reformed public library. The panacea it contained promised that: "Tomorrow's new library will remain open and accessible to all, without precondition" (Great Britain Library and Information Commission 1997, 2).

Muddiman et al. (2000) have identified the danger in adopting an approach focused primarily on access, a concept which is inherent in the notion of a universal wired library, notwithstanding the presumption that everyone has the skills to exploit digital platforms, which is by no means the case. While providing equality of access is a core component of a truly egalitarian service, if it is established merely on a standardised take it or leave it basis then exclusion is bound to ensue. Equal access amounts to little if what is provided, or the way it is provided, is not relevant to, or efficacious for, everyone. In short, in an ideal world equality of outcome trumps equality of access. Of course, this rarely happens in practice. Even in the context of the supposedly new library, services have tended to be utilised, as in the past, more heavily by the middle classes, social groups already included in society's mainstream. Public library modernisation, Muddiman et al. (2000) have asserted, has meant relatively little to the disadvantaged and deprived who, ideally, require targeted, tailored modes of service provision to compensate for their exclusion. Thus, the poverty, specifically the marginality and short-termism, of initiatives that are proactive and interventionist, and based on community-development and social justice principles, means that the twenty-first century public library is only superficially open to all.

---

11 Precise plans for the network were set out the following year (Library and Information Commission, 1998). These initiatives came in the wake of an extensive independent, academic review of public library services conducted under the auspices of Aslib (1995), led by the Sheffield University public library expert Bob Usherwood.

Of course, community initiatives helpful to marginalised groups are far from absent from the range of services offered by today's public library. A lot of good outreach and extension work is undertaken (Peachey 2014). There is good evidence that the vast majority of librarians seek to connect with people outside of the physical library space, extending their presence in the community by visiting schools, engaging in local events and liaising with local services (Axiell 2017). Given the long record that the public library can point to in reaching out to readers and in extending what they do beyond the provision of reading, it would be surprising if this was not the case. In the nineteenth and early twentieth centuries, libraries were already keen to develop extra-book services like public lectures, educational classes, exhibitions, music libraries and wireless listening clubs. In 1892 in Bradford, described by its deputy librarian, M.E. Hartley (1906, 23), as a go-ahead city, the central library purchased eighty volumes in Braille type, and it enhanced this service to the blind and partially sighted readers by borrowing stocks of Braille books from the National Incorporated Lending Library for the Blind and the Manchester and Salford Blind Aid Society. Providing such reading was seen as a "matter of the highest human interest and civic duty" (Hartley 1906, 16). Ten years later a travelling library service was inaugurated. Stocks of approximately four hundred books were deposited in outlying districts, in premises such as Sunday Schools. Changed periodically, these travelling collections were open on two evenings a week (Hartley 1906, 21).

Pop Culture Supermarket and Existential Social Centre

The tradition of reaching out to society and going beyond the core service of book provision has continued into the twenty-first century. However, such an orientation is difficult to maintain, as late-twentieth century community librarianship attempted with its ideology of redistribution, let alone enhance in a climate of austerity and increasing doubt as to the value of public services in general; and, it has been pointed out, with a workforce that is increasingly voluntary and non-professional.[12] Today's public library is caught between a rock and a hard

---

12 Most library users believe volunteers should not replace staff in a library, though many think they had a role to play (Peachy 2017, 49). The number of volunteers in public libraries now vastly outweighs the number of paid staff whose numbers, especially qualified librarians, have been declining rapidly (Barnett, 2018; Page 2018). Research has suggested that volunteers can enhance the library service in certain ways, including using existing ties to assist community

place. Unable to develop fully the range of imaginative services that a different economic and ideological climate might have encouraged, the institution has taken on the role, according to some, of a pop culture, or leisure, supermarket. According to former Secretary of State for Culture Andy Burnham, public libraries need an "image re-vamp", entailing the provision of such recreational facilities as coffee franchises, film centres and bookshops, that would shake off their popular image as "solemn and sombre places patrolled by fearsome and formidable staff" (quoted in Akbar 2009). It has been observed that in some of the new, especially large, public libraries "the consumer is king" and as such libraries tend to "market themselves as one-stop community centres, catering more to the needs of children and entertainment than serious learning (Sherriff 2005, 210). Giving libraries names other than the word "library" has been seen as part of a silent conspiracy to turn them into entertainment centres, ostensibly to justify their public expense (Usherwood 2007, 2).

The former bookshop entrepreneur Tim Coates, a loud and, even if some disagree with him, important voice in stimulating debate on the future of public libraries, has pushed the idea of returning to a core raison d'être. Libraries should, he has argued, be re-emphasising the importance of their book collections (Coates 2004), which would necessarily, if libraries are to boost their popularity, mean investing heavily in recreational reading that is easily available for borrowing. Coates has amplified the fairly widespread perception that libraries should stick to what has been their overwhelmingly central concern for over a century and a half: books. As he told a Parliamentary inquiry in 2005: "Greengrocers do not improve or modernise by selling ice cream just because they perceive that is what children like to eat. The service should have modernised by improving, not diversifying... The policy of diversification has been a catastrophe" (House of Commons 2005, 1-2). This view was echoed by the Reading Agency at the same inquiry: "During the last 20 years libraries have spread themselves very thinly, feeling they must be all things to all people and running the risk of neglecting one of their main audiences – readers" (House of Commons 2005, 6).

Other visions stress the social aspect of the public library ethos, pitching the institution as a place where self-realisation is achieved through "sharing", even if the community in which one is participating is partly "imagined" (Anderson 1991). Accordingly, the public library has been branded as the perfect "makerspace", a physical location where people gather to co-create, benefit from shared resources and knowledge, work on projects, network, and "build" (Libraries and Makerspaces 2017) – a place of culture, self-help and endeavour where people

---

engagement. (Casselden, Pickard and McLeod 2015) The consensus, however, is that volunteer systems are no match for operations that are run by professional staff.

can get everyday stuff done, whether that may be doing homework, photocopying a personal document, filling in a benefit claim online, attending a class, or taking a child to a learning disability group. The public library has been marketed as the ideal venue for events and initiatives arising from partnerships with other agencies. Far from being a diversion from the bread and butter provision that some think the public library should be about, such "beyond the book" offerings fit ideally, it has been suggested, with the institution's historic self-improvement ethos (Matarasso 1998, 55).

The book-warehouse image of the public library may well have grown faint, but this does not mean that the impression of the library as physical place has similarly paled. If anything, the library as physical place has undergone a renaissance. There is much to commend the notion of today's public library as a "home in a public place". The increasingly domestic feel of library spaces, arising out of the continuing mid-twentieth century revolution in contemporary, Scandinavian-inspired interior design, has to a significant degree helped change the way people have used, and thought of, libraries (Comedia, 1993, 32).

Further, conjuring up notions of Puginian medieval social stability and responsibility (Pugin 1841[1836]) and what has become known as the experience economy (Pine and Gilmore 1998), as well as drawing on third place characteristics of the public library, the journalist and historical author Simon Jenkins believes the local library should be marketed as a place of congregation: "It should combine coffee shop, book exchange, playgroup, art gallery, museum and performance. It must be the therapist of the mind. It must be what medieval churches once were" (Jenkins 2016). This prescription for a type of existential social centre was played out in the evolution of the strategic plan for the new Library of Birmingham, Europe's largest public library, opened in 2013 (Clawley 2016). The library was charged with a mission to transform public perceptions of libraries. New features included a flexible studio theatre, a British Film Institute Médiathèque, and a purpose-built, state-of-the-art exhibition space for Birmingham's internationally significant archives and heritage collections. Among the new additions was a teenage zone for young people to relax, meet friends and chill out, and a contemplation room for prayer and quiet thought (Clawley 2016).

Thus, if this vision of the future direction of the public library is correct then, notwithstanding its continuing function as an important source of informed citizenship (Kerslake and Kinnell 1998, 164-166), as well as the many facets of the public library that still satisfy educational needs (one only has to think of provision for local studies in this regard), it would appear that the institution's social-recreational role, about which librarians had been so hesitant for so long, has finally triumphed over its historic image as a place of serious learning.[13] The displacement (not replacement, note) of education and learning has happened without a commensurate deepening of the professional guilt that accompanied earlier fulfilment of the recreational function.

Conclusion

Knowing our history helps us govern our future. This chapter has concentrated on the most history-rich aspect of governance, direction, in order to examine the post-war history of the public library in the UK.[14] Dictated by the interplay of trajectory that is planned and social change that is mostly unpredictable, since 1945 the public library's strategic vision has followed a number of twists and turns on its journey from mid-twentieth century hope to twenty-first century uncertainty.

Post-war strategy was initially informed by the enduring Victorian vision of educational seriousness, political responsibility and good citizenship, as opposed to a mere entertainment/recreational function, even if this function had in fact always been dominant, yet denied. Despite claims in the 1960s that the public library had metaphorically entered the space age, with the appearance of a swathe of new, modernist library buildings housing a wide range of cultural facilities and communication technologies, librarians retained an attachment to cultural conservatism that chimed with the highbrow and middlebrow preferences of its majority middle-class clientele. As postmodern forms took hold, however, conservatism in the institution was challenged by the rise of community librarianship, a new mode of service delivery driven by the political objective of redistributing wealth and opportunity, as well as by an interest in popular and alternative cultural forms. In reaction, uneasy about the retreat from neutrality and the lurch towards popular and other culture, the library and political establishments called for a return to core purpose and practice. This proved fruitless, however, in the face of a pop culture tsunami enhanced by powerful new digital information and communication technologies, an enhancement that belied the earlier assumption that these technologies would primarily fuel educational seriousness.

In the digital age of the early twenty-first century public libraries, notwithstanding the large differences between them, the continuing resilience of the book and the provision of life-chance information so important to needy sections

---

13 Today, learning tends to be conceptualised in terms of services for upskilling, assistance to basic learners and provision for early learners (Goulding 2006, 261-294).
14 Space has not permitted analysis of direction of specific services such as children's, reference and local studies.

of the population, have taken on the role of the digitally inflected, third place social centre where self-realisation, self-help and personal spiritual enrichment are achieved through participation in a community that is intuitively viewed as highly supportive of public services and free access. Recognition of the public library as a thoroughly public good will no doubt continue to inform debates about the direction in which the institution should travel; but whether the public good concept in the context of the public library will endure in an age of strengthening neo-liberalism and an impoverished public library profession is another matter. Certainly, without a clear and persuasive strategic direction the future of the public library as the great public sphere institution it has proved itself to be in the past is in great jeopardy. There is lack of clarity and consensus regarding a desired role of the public library in the twenty-first century, or as Goulding (2006, 347) has put it, "the social purpose and position of the contemporary public library service is still being negotiated". Unfortunately, there may not be enough time left for such negotiations to reach fruition, which would obviously render academic the question of what constitutes good public library governance.

References

Adam Smith Institute. *Ex-Libris*. London: Adam Smith Institute, 1986.

Akbar, A. "The Big Question: How Are Public Libraries Changing, and What Does Their Future Hold?" *The Independent/Culture* September 28 2009. Accessed June 25, 2019. https://www.independent.co.uk/arts-entertainment/books/features/the-big-question-how-are-public-libraries-changing-and-what-does-their-future-hold-1794725.html

Anderson, B. *Imagined Communities: Reflections on the Origin and Spread of Nationalism*. London: Verso, 1991.

Aslib. *Review of the Public Library Service in England and Wales for the Department of National Heritage*. London: Aslib, 1995.

Astbury, R. *Libraries and the Unemployed: Needs and Responses*. London: Special Community Services Sub-Committee of the Library Association, 1983.

Axiell. *A Review of UK Public Libraries in 2017: A Guide for Delivering Sustainable, Community-Centric Services*. Nottingham: Axiell, 2017. Accessed April 2, 2020. https://wwwaxiellcom.cdn.triggerfish.cloud/uploads/sites/3/2019/05/axiell-report-a-review-of-uk-libraries-in-2017.pdf.

Bamber, A.L. *Public Libraries – The Future?* London: Public Libraries Group of the Library Association, 1978.

Batty, C.D. "The Library of Tomorrow." In *The Library and the Machine*, edited by C.D. Batty, 37-52. Scunthorpe: North Midland Branch of the Library Association, 1966.

Benford, G. *The Wonderful Future That Never Was*. New York: Hearst Books, 2010.

Black, A. *A New History of the English Public Library: Social and Intellectual Contexts, 1850-1914*. London: Leicester University Press, 1996.

Black, A. *The Public Library in Britain, 1914–2000*. London: The British Library, 2000.

Black, A. and D. Muddiman. 1997. *Understanding Community Librarianship: The Public Library in Post-modern Britain*. Aldershot: Avebury, 1997.

Black, L. 2003. *The Political Culture of the Left in Affluent Britain, 1951–1964: Old Labour, New Britain*. Basingstoke: Palgrave Macmillan.

Blair, T. *New Britain: My Vision of a Young Country*. London: Fourth Estate, 1996.

Bramley, G. *Apprentice to Graduate: A History of Library Education in the United Kingdom*. London: Bingley, 1981.

Buschman, J.E. and G.J. Leckie. eds. *The Library as Place: History, Community, and Culture*. Westport, Connecticut and London: Libraries Unlimited, 2007.

Casselden, B., A.J. Pickard and J. McLeod. "The Challenges Facing Public Libraries in the Big Society: The Role of Volunteers, and the Issues that Surround Their Use in England." *Journal of Librarianship and Information Science* 47, No. 3 (2015): 187–203.

Castells, M. *The Rise of the Network Society*. Oxford: Blackwell, 1996.

Childers, T., and J. A. Post. *The Information Poor in America*. Metuchen, NJ: Scarecrow Press, 1975.

Clarke, A.C. *Profiles of the Future: An Inquiry into the Limits of the Possible*. London: Victor Gollancz, 1974 [1962].

Clawley, A. *Library Story: A History of Birmingham Central Library*. Birmingham: The Author, 2016.

Clough, E.A. "The Future of Public Libraries." In *The Shape of Things to Come*, edited by T.D.F. Barnard, 22–40. London: London & Homes Counties Branch of the Library Association, 1968.

Clough, E., and J. Quarmby. *A Public Library Service for Ethnic Minorities in Great Britain*. London: The Library Association, 1978.

Coates T. *Who's in Charge: Responsibility for the Public Library Service*. London: The Libri Trust, 2004.

Coleman, P. "Past to Future – The Public Library's Changing Role." In *Informing Communities: The Role of Libraries and Information Services*, edited by M. Kinnell, 297–313. Newcastle, Staffordshire: Community Services Group of the Library Association, 1992.

Comedia. *Borrowed Time? The Future of Public Libraries in the UK*. Bournes Green: Comedia, 1993.

Finsberg, G. "Libraries and the Future: A Personal View." In *Requirements for a National Library Service*, edited by K.M. Newbury, 30–34. Eastbourne: London & Home Counties Branch of the Library Association, 1955.

Goulding, A. *Public Libraries in the 21st Century: Defining Services and Debating the Future*. Aldershot: Ashgate, 2006.

Graham, J., B. Amos and T. Plumptre. *Principles for Good Governance in the 21st Century*. Policy Brief No. 15. Ottawa, Canada: Institute on Governance, 2003. Accessed June 25 2019. https://iog.ca/research-publications/publications/iog-policy-brief-no-15-principles-for-good-governance-in-the-21st-century/.

Great Britain Department of Education and Science. *The Libraries' Choice: [Report / by a Working Party of the Library Advisory Council for England]*. London: HMSO, 1978.

Great Britain Department of National Heritage. *Reading the Future*. London: HMSO, 1997.

Great Britain Library and Information Commission. *Building the New Library Network: A Report to Government*. London: Library and Information Commission, 1998.

Great Britain Library and Information Commission. *New Library: The People's Network*. London: Library and Information Commission, 1997.

Grenfell, J.G. *Pierre Bourdieu: Key Concepts*. 2nd edition. Abingdon: Routledge, 2014.

Grimshaw, R.E. "Towards A.D. 2000: New Directions for the Public library Service (1)." In *Proceedings, Papers and Summaries of Discussions at the Public Libraries Conference held at Eastbourne, 13th September – 18th September 1975*, 12–15. London: The Library Association, 1975.

Halliwell, P. "Plea for a Public Library." *Assistant Librarian* 68, no. 2 (February 1975): 25–26.

Hartley, M.E. *A Survey of the Public Library Movement in Bradford*. Aberdeen: Aberdeen University Press, 1906.

Harvey, D. *The Condition of Postmodernity: An Inquiry into the Origins of Cultural Change*. Oxford: Blackwell, 1989.

Hendry, J.D. *A Social History of Branch Library Development; With Special Reference to the City of Glasgow*. Glasgow: The Scottish Library Association, 1974.

Houghton, B. *Out of the Dinosaurs: The Evolution of the National Lending Library for Science and Technology*. London: Clive Bingley, 1972.

House of Commons Culture, Media and Sport Committee. *Public Libraries: Third Report of Session 2004–5, Vol II: Oral and Written Evidence*, HC 81–II. London: The Stationery Office, 2005.

Hung, M. *The Popularisation of Public Libraries, c. 1930–70*. PhD diss., Leeds Metropolitan University, 2015.

Inayatullah, S. "Library Futures." *The Futurist* (November–December 2014): 25–28.

Jefcoate, G. "Democracy at Work: The Library Association's 'Centenary Assessment' of 1950." *Library History* 15 (November 1999): 99–111.

Jenkins, S. "Libraries are Dying – But it's not About the Books." *The Guardian* (December 22 2016). Accessed June 25, 2019. https://www.theguardian.com/commentisfree/2016/dec/22/libraries-dying-books-internet.

Jolliffe, H. *Public Library Extension Activities*. London: Library Association, 1962.

Jones, K.H. "Towards a Re-interpretation of Public Library Purpose." *New Library World* 73, no. 855 (September 1971): 76–79.

Jordan, P. "Towards A.D. 2000: New Directions for the Public library Service (2)." In *Proceedings, Papers and Summaries of Discussions at the Public Libraries Conference held at Eastbourne, 13th September – 18th September 1975*, 16–19. London: The Library Association, 1975.

Kelly, T. *A History of Public Libraries in Great Britain, 1845–1975*, 2nd edition. London: The Library Association, 1977.

Kelly, T. "Public Libraries and Public Opinion." *Library Association Record* 68, No. 7 (July 1966): 246–251.

Kerslake, E., and M. Kinnell. "Public Libraries, Public Interest and the Information Society." *Journal of Librarianship & Information Science* 30, no. 3 (1998): 159–167.

Lamb, J.P. *Commercial and Technical libraries*. London: The Library Association, 1955.

"Libraries and Makerspaces." *Designing Libraries* News Archive. 2017. Accessed June 25, 2019. http://www.designinglibraries.org.uk/index.asp?PageID=1437.

Library Association. *A Century of Public Library Service: Where Do We Stand To-day?* London: Library Association, 1950.

Licklider, J. C. R. *Libraries of the Future*. Cambridge, MA: M.I.T. Press, 1965.

"Looking Forward". *The Wicket: Staff Magazine of the Sheffield Public Libraries* 2 (April 1931): 3–4.

Martin, W.J. *Community Librarianship: Changing the Face of Public Libraries*. London: Clive Bingley, 1989.

Martin, W.J. ed. *Library Services to the Disadvantaged*. London: Clive Bingley, 1975.

Marwick, A. *The Sixties: Cultural Revolution in Britain, France, Italy, and the United States c.1958–c.1974*. Oxford: Oxford University Press, 1998.

Mass-Observation Archive, University of Sussex. *Reading in Tottenham*. File Report 2537 November, 1947. http://www.massobservation.amdigital.co.uk/Documents/Details/READING-IN-TOTTENHAM/FileReport-2537

Matarasso, F. *Beyond Book Issues: The Social Potential of Library Projects*. London: British Library Research and Innovation Centre; and Comedia, 1998.

McColvin, L. "English Public Libraries." *Library Trends* 1, no. 4 (Spring 1953): 522–530.

McMenemy, D. *The Public Library*. London: Facet, 2008.

Metropolitan Borough of Stepney. *Annual Report of the Borough Librarian, 1956–1957*. 1957.

Morris, R.J.B. *Parliament and the Public Libraries*. London: Mansell Information Publishing, 1977.

Muddiman, D., S. Durrani, M. Dutch, R. Linley, J. Pateman and J. Vincent. *Open to All? The Public Library and Social Exclusion. Volume 1: Overview and Conclusions*. London: Resource: The Council for Museums, Archives and Libraries, 2000.

Mulgan, G. "Culture." In *The Ideas That Shaped Post-war Britain*, edited by D. Marquand and A. Seldon, 195–213. London: Fontana, 1996.

Munford, W.A. *Penny Rate: Aspects of British Public Library History, 1850–1950*. London: The Library Association, 1951.

Murison, W.J. *The Public Library: Its Origins, Purpose and Significance*. 3rd edition. London: Clive Bingley, 1988.

O'Kelley, J. *The Political Role of Public Libraries*. Brighton: Smoothie Publications, 1975.

Oldenburg, R. *Celebrating the Third Place: Inspiring Stories About the 'Great Good Places' at the Heart of Our Communities*. New York: Marlow & Co., 2001.

Page, B. "Latest CIPFA Statistics Reveal Yet More Library Closures and Book Loan Falls." *The Bookseller* (7 December 2018). Accessed October 21, 2019. https://www.thebookseller.com/news/cipfa-records-yet-more-library-closures-and-book-loan-falls-911061.

Pateman, J., and J. Vincent. *Public Libraries and Social Justice*. 2nd edition. Abingdon: Routledge, 2016.

Pateman, J., and K. Williment. *Developing Community-Led Public Libraries: Evidence from the UK and Canada*. Abingdon: Routledge, 2016.

Peachey, J. "Four of the UK's Most Innovative Libraries." *The Guardian* (September 1 2014). Accessed June 26, 2017. https://www.theguardian.com/public-leaders-network/2014/sep/01/four-of-the-uks-most-innovative-libraries.

Peachy, J. *Shining a Light: How People in the UK and Ireland Use Public Libraries: Data Booklet*. Dunfermline: Carnegie United Kingdom Trust, 2017. Accessed October 17, 2019. https://d1ssu070pg2v9i.cloudfront.net/pex/carnegie_uk_trust/2017/04/LOW-RES-2867-Libraries-Main-Report-Complete-1.pdf

Pemberton, J.E. *Politics and Public Libraries in England and Wales, 1850–1970*. London: The Library Association, 1977.

Pine, B.J., and J.H. Gilmore. "Welcome to the Experience Economy." *Harvard Business Review* 76, no. 4 (1998): 97–105.

Pugin, A.W. *Contrasts*. London: C. Dolman, 1841[1836]. https://archive.org/details/contrastsorparal00pugi/page/n4/mode/2up

Sandbrook, D. *White Heat: A Story of Britain in the Swinging Sixties*. London: Abacus, 2006.

Sinfield, A. *Literature, Politics and Culture in Post-war Britain*. London: Athlone Press, 1997.

Smith, G. "At the Grass Roots and in the Dusty Streets: Some Thoughts on the Library in the Community." In *The New Public Libraries: Integration and Innovation*, edited by F. Hallworth, 32–40. London: Library Association County Libraries Group, 1972.

Snape, R. *Leisure and the Rise of the Public Library*. London: The Library Association, 1995.

Stokes, R. "Professional Education." In *Library Staffs: Today and Tomorrow*, edited by P. Davies, 21–35. London: Association of Assistant Librarians, Greater London Division, 1966.

"The Privatisation of Reading." *City Limits* (July 13–19 1984): 6–7.

Totterdell, B. "Public Libraries in a Changing Society." In *Public Library Policy*, edited by K.C. Harrison, 37–42. Munich: K.G. Saur, 1981.

Usherwood, B. *Equity and Excellence in the Public Library: Why Ignorance is Not Our Heritage*. London: Routledge, 2007.

Vincent, J. *An Introduction to Community Librarianship*. Newcastle under Lyme: Association of Assistant Librarians, 1986.

Ward, J. "Equality of Information." *Municipal Journal* 82, no. 20 (May 17 1974): 595.

Webster, F. *Theories of the Information Society*. 4th edition. London: Routledge, 2014.

West, W. J. *The Strange Rise of Semi-literate England: Dissolution of the Libraries*. London: Gerald Duckworth & Co., 1989.

Wiegand, W. *Main Street Public Library: Community Places and Reading Spaces in the Rural Heartland, 1876–1956*. Iowa City: Iowa University Press, 2012.

Wilson, A. "Practical Implications of a Permanent Programme." In *Libraries and the Arts*, edited by D. Gerard, 165–196. London: Clive Bingley, 1970.

Joe Pateman and John Pateman

2 Marx Meets Maslow: An Analytical Framework for Managing Cultural Change in Public Libraries

Abstract: The superstructure of the public library includes its prevailing culture and its way of doing things in addition to the behaviour, personal beliefs and attitudes of its staff and patrons. Just as the economic base of society determines its ideological and political superstructure, so too does the economic base of the public library determine its ideological and cultural superstructure. In this chapter, the ideas of Karl Marx and Abraham Maslow are synthesised into an analytical framework for critically analysing public libraries and assessing and managing cultural change in public libraries. The Thunder Bay Public Library on the shores of Lake Superior in Canada is presented as an example of the strategy development process for public libraries. Ideas and arguments from metaphysics and dialectics are drawn on to track differences between the traditional public library, the needs-based public library and the community-led public library. The framework presented can be used to assess and manage cultural change in public libraries.

Keywords: Public libraries; Public libraries – Canada; Cultural change

Overview

Part one outlines Maslow's hierarchy of human needs and part two situates Maslow's hierarchy within Marx's theory of base and superstructure. Part three shows how the Marx-Maslow analytical framework can be used within the field of library science. It is argued that the Marx-Maslow model not only highlights the failings of the traditional public library but also can be used for the revolutionary transformation of public libraries by supporting the development of the community led and needs based public library. Part four outlines the three principal components of the Marxist dialectical method, which provides an account of how public libraries can and must develop if they are to fulfil human needs.

https://doi.org/10.1515/ 9783110533323-005

Part 1: Maslow's Hierarchy of Needs

Abraham Maslow (1943) situated human needs in a hierarchy, whereby lower level needs must be mostly satisfied first, before higher level needs can be pursued. At the bottom of the hierarchy are physiological needs of the human being: food, water, shelter and clothing, which are required for human survival. Physiological needs are the most fundamental needs and must first be met before other needs can be effectively pursued. Once physiological needs are met, safety needs are next in precedence. These include physical and economic safety, good health and well-being and guarding against accidents and illness. After physiological and safety needs are fulfilled, the third level of human needs is love and belonging, which are psychological needs, and include the development of friendship, intimacy and familial relations. Humans need to love and be loved by others. Many people become susceptible to loneliness, social anxiety and depression in the absence of love or a belonging element. The fourth level is achieved when individuals feel comfortable with what they have accomplished and is designated the esteem level, the need to be competent and recognized.

At the top of the needs pyramid, self-actualisation occurs when individuals reach a state of harmony and understanding because they are engaged in achieving their full potential. Once people have attained self-actualisation, they can focus on themselves and build their own images. They may look at this in terms of a feeling of self-confidence, or by accomplishing a set goal. Maslow believed that to understand this level of need, the individual must not only achieve the previous levels of needs, but master them.

Part 2: Maslow and Marx

Marx and Maslow are complementary thinkers because they were both, above all, concerned with fulfilling human needs. In agreement with Maslow, Marx believes that people have to meet lower level physical needs before they can go about meeting higher level needs. Maslow's conception of self-actualisation is synonymous with Marx's conception of human freedom under communism. Both thinkers recognise that feelings of self-determination, community and creativity are essential to human flourishing. Marx contributes to Maslow's hierarchy of needs by situating Maslow's hierarchy within the context of historical economic development, which is his theory of historical materialism.

Historical Materialism: Base and Superstructure

Marx views the history of society as the growth of human productive power. Forms of society rise and fall according to how they promote or hinder that growth:

> In the social production of their life men enter into relations that are indispensable and independent of their will, relations of production which correspond to a definite stage of development of their material productive forces. The sum total of these relations constitutes the economic structure of society, the real foundation, on which arises a legal and political superstructure (Marx 1977, 20).

This theory has three factors, the productive forces, the relations of production and the superstructure, between which certain explanatory connections are asserted. The productive forces are those facilities and devices used in the production process, the means of production and labour power. The means of production are physical productive resources such as tools and machinery, whilst labour power includes the strength and skills the producers apply when working.

The relations of production are economic power, the power that people possess or lack over labour power and the means of production. In a capitalist society, the relations of production include the economic power capitalists have over the means of production, the limited power that workers have over their labour power and their lack of power over the means of production. The sum total of product relations constitutes the economic structure of society, which is also called the base. The superstructure includes legal and state institutions of society, as well as its ruling ideology and culture.

A fundamental proposition of historical materialism is that the economic base determines the political superstructure. The relationship between base and superstructure is an instance of functional explanation. What this means is that the nature of the superstructure is determined by its function, which is to sustain and legitimise the economic base. The existence and shape of the superstructure are explained by this function (Cohen 1978, 278). In contemporary capitalist society, the liberal democratic superstructure and its ideology function to sustain and legitimise the economic base, which comprises private property relations and the productive forces.

Base and Superstructure in Public Libraries

It now remains to elucidate the following question. What do these features mean within the context of library science? The Marx-Maslow analytical framework directly draws upon the base/superstructure model to analyse public libraries.

The productive forces of the public library include the library itself, its architecture and design, its technology, the management structure, the staff and their knowledge, financial resources and guiding strategy. The relations of production of the public library include the relations among the workers, between workers and management and between the workers and patrons. The productive forces and relations of production constitute the economic base of the public library.

The superstructure of the public library includes its prevailing culture, its way of doing things, in addition to the behaviour, personal beliefs and attitudes of its staff and patrons. Just as the economic base of society determines its ideological and political superstructure, so too does the economic base of the public library determine its ideological and cultural superstructure. It means that the culture of a public library, the mentality that governs the people who run and organise it, cannot be explained by the nature of the culture itself, but by something more fundamental, the organisation structure of the public library.

Part 3: The Marx-Maslow Analytical Framework and the Public Library

According to Marx's theory of historical materialism, it is the mode of production of society that determines what level of human needs can be fulfilled. Throughout history, each new mode of production has facilitated a higher degree of political freedom. Connected to this freedom is the attainment of higher-level human needs. The economic base of society determines the shape of the political and ideological superstructure, which in turn determines which needs are prioritised and fulfilled, as well as for whom. The ability of the superstructure to facilitate self-actualisation therefore depends upon the nature of the economic base. Marx's theory of historical materialism contributes to Maslow's hierarchy of human needs by showing that the path to self-actualisation should be sought in the economic base of society and in the economic base of the public library.

According to Marx, society passes through six modes of production. The modes are primitive communism, slavery, feudalism, capitalism, socialism and communism. Whilst Marx studied each of these modes, he devoted most of his study to the last three, and capitalism in particular. In the Marx-Maslow analytical framework, capitalism, socialism and communism directly correspond to three types of public library, traditional, community-led and needs-based.

The traditional public library has many of the features of capitalism, most notably a relatively narrow and homogeneous user base. The people who use the traditional library the most are often those who need it the least, because their lower level needs have already been met. The community-led library has many aspects that are relevant to socialism, such as a focus on the wider community and engagement with those who have lower level needs. The needs-based library is closer to communism in the sense of Marx's (1971, 18) maxim of "from each according to their ability, to each according to their needs". It is therefore worth elucidating the three modes of production to show their characteristics and differences.

Table 1 outlines an analytical framework for defining the characteristics of each mode of production along the traditional, community-led and needs-based continuum. The key features in the framework have been derived from a combination of the UK research project *Open to All? The Public Library and Social Exclusion* (Muddiman et al. 2000) and the *Working Together project* (2008) which piloted the community-led model in four Canadian public library settings in Vancouver, Regina, Halifax and Toronto between 2004 and 2008.

Table 1: Analytical framework.

Marx – Superstructure			
Model	Traditional	Community-led	Needs-based
Strategy	Active users	Potential users	Non-users
	Soon to be non- patrons	Refusing non-patrons	Unexplored non-patrons
	Assumed needs	Assessed needs	Greatest needs
Structure	Hierarchy	Matrix	Holacracy
Staff	Silos	Teams	Circles
Structure	Passive, reactive	Participative, empowerment	Leadership
Services	Buildings, desks	Roving, outreach	Partnerships, community development
Systems	Disabling	Enabling	Empowering
	Rules	Framework	Constitution
Performance	Quantitative statistics	Qualitative evaluation	Outcomes and impacts
Marx – Base			
Model	Traditional	Community-led	Needs-based
Culture	Social control	Social inclusion	Social change
	Status quo	Evolution	Transformation
Maslow – Needs			
Model	Traditional	Community-led	Needs-based
Level	Cognitive, Aesthetic, Self-actualisation	Belonging, Esteem, Cognitive, Aesthetic	Physiological, Safety, Belonging, Esteem

The Traditional Public Library

"Bad libraries build collections" (Lankes 2012). In his day, Marx viewed emergent capitalism to be the most progressive mode of production. Its economic base facilitated an unprecedented amount of political freedom and it was capable of fulfilling basic needs more successfully than all previous modes. However, Marx also identified inherent flaws in capitalism that placed a ceiling on the fulfilment of human needs. Under capitalism, society is divided into two classes. The capitalist class owns the means of production, whilst the working class owns only its labour power. The working class is forced, under threat of starvation, to sell its labour power to capitalists, which is exploited for profit. Due to the fact that the relations of production under capitalism are fundamentally exploitative, the political and ideological superstructure functions in order to sustain and legitimise this exploitation. Capitalist democracy is democracy for the rich and excludes the poor from politics (Lenin 1977, 465). The ruling ideology segments and weakens the working class by fostering racism and political apathy.

According to the Marx-Maslow analytical framework, the traditional public library exhibits many features that are characteristic of capitalism. It is progressive in the sense that it was the first type of public library, whereas all libraries previously were either private or required hefty membership fees. The traditional library is in theory open to all people regardless of wealth or class and is undeniably a step above all previous forms of library.

However, the traditional library is also capitalist in the sense that it is separated into two groups of people. The manager owns and controls the library, whilst the workers own nothing but their labour power and must sell their labour power to the manager. Just as under capitalism, the relations of production are based upon exploitation and domination.

Library workers have no say or control over their work, as they are told what to do by their managers. The same relation of dominance applies to the interaction between the library and its patrons. Patrons have no control over the library and must conform to the rules set by management. The ideological and cultural superstructure of the traditional public library perpetuates exploitation by functioning as an institution for social control. Through a variety of systems, rules and regulations, the traditional public library purposefully excludes and alienates the working class, whilst catering to the middle class, who provides a safety buffer between the workers and capitalists. By frequently preventing working class patrons from enjoying the safety, warmth and shelter of the library, the traditional public library fails to fulfil even the lowest level human needs on Maslow's hierarchy.

The strategy of the traditional library is focused on the needs of existing active library users. Most of the capacity of the organisation is put into meeting the higher-level needs of this group which tends to be homogenous in its makeup. Active library users tend to be mostly white, middle class, female, over the age of fifty-five and educated. The needs of the group can be assumed because they reflect those of the library administration, who share similar attitudes and values. Some capacity is also directed towards soon to be non-patrons, people on the edge of the active user group, waiting to jump ship. Patrons are retained by reinforcing or reinventing the status quo.

The staff structure is a rigid bureaucratic hierarchy with vertical lines of command and communication. Power is determined by position in the hierarchy with control and resources clustered at the top of the pyramid. A small group of administrators is distanced and buffered from front line staff by an intermediate tier of professional librarians. The middle managers interpret and filter power from the top and communication from the bottom of the hierarchy. Staff have little or no autonomy over task, team or time. Roles are closely prescribed and it is not always clear how work performed adds value to the organisation, which can lead to apathy and alienation. Staff reorganisations rarely happen and position descriptions become out of date and bear little resemblance to real work undertaken.

The service structure consists of isolated silos grouped around traditional service departments such as reference services, adult lending and children and young people. The fiefdoms are jealously guarded and maintained with little opportunity for interaction. The structure is reflected in building design with, typically, the reference department, the gods, located at the top of the library, adult lending on the main floor and the children's section in the basement. Service delivery tends to be passive and reactive and there is a strong focus on buildings, collections and desks.

The systems, policies and procedures are disabling, designed to exclude what the founders of Victorian public libraries called the undeserving poor and constitute barriers to use. The systems range from library layouts, signs and classification schemes which make no sense to patrons to arbitrary rules regarding loan periods, loan limits and fines. Overdue fines are one of the biggest barriers, particularly to those on low incomes. Fines are expensive to collect, cause friction with patrons and do not achieve the prime aim of encouraging good behaviour. They are divisive, humiliating and off-putting and effectively exclude those with the greatest needs.

Performance is measured by quantitative statistics such as visitor and circulation counts. With the advent of virtual use of the library, these numbers have been boosted with every click on a library website counted as an active use. But the

numbers mask a long-term steady decline in personal visits and physical circulation as people vote with their feet in rejecting the traditional library model which
cannot meet the full range of needs. In the UK, this has led to widespread public
library closures as low physical usage figures make the libraries low hanging fruit
for neo-liberal ideologues who want to roll back the public sector under the cover
of an austerity agenda.

Public libraries have always been agencies of social control (Corrigan and
Gillespie 1978). They were designed as such, along with museums and public
parks, to control the idle time and reading habits of the working class in the
mid-nineteenth century when the spectre of revolution and communism was
haunting Europe. Public libraries have endured for over 150 years and have seen
significant modernisation with the introduction of computer systems but their
underlying culture has not changed. They are a part of the ideological superstructure which exists to maintain the economic base of capitalist society. As such, traditional public libraries are vested in the status quo and in replicating social relations, means of production and forces of production. The organisational culture
at the base of the traditional public library shapes and determines its strategy,
structures and systems. The base and superstructure of the traditional library are
consistent with many of the defining characteristics of capitalism as described by
Marx. The focus is on meeting higher level cognitive, aesthetic and self-actualisation needs as defined by Maslow.

The Community-Led Library

"Good libraries build services" (Lankes 2012). Under socialism, the means of production come under social ownership. The workers themselves exercise collective
control over the productive process. The political superstructure is more equal,
in the sense that the working class exercises a class dictatorship, the dictatorship of the proletariat over the capitalist class (Lenin 1977, 465). According to the
Marx-Maslow analytical framework, the community-led public library has many
of the characteristics associated with socialism and spreads power more evenly
throughout the organisation. Management and workers are no longer in strictly
hierarchical relations but interact as equals in a cooperative manner. The workers
have more say in how things are managed and so too do the patrons. Working
class patrons are no longer excluded but are instead welcomed and prioritised.
The community-led library facilitates the fulfilment of both higher and lower
level human needs on Maslow's hierarchy, the feeling of community, self-determination and belonging. The community-led public library rejects the tradition-
alist belief that public libraries are institutions of social control and adopts the

position that public libraries are agencies for radical social change. As such, the base and superstructure of the community-led public library are oriented towards the pursuit of this goal.

The strategy of the community-led library encompasses both active users and a wider group of potential users. The latter group includes lapsed users who have used the library in the past but stopped doing so when it could no longer meet their needs or when another provider could better meet their needs. It includes passive users, people who may have used the library for a specific purpose, for example to study for an examination, but who did not take out membership or use the full range of services available. Potential users include those with high, intermediate and lower level needs. Rather than assuming needs, the community-led library assesses needs using various tools such as community profiling and community asset mapping.

The staff structure is a matrix which spreads power and control more widely and equitably than a traditional hierarchy. Position power is not important with resources pushed down closer to the front line. Staff members are encouraged to take an interest in the whole organisation and not just their immediate service areas. There are opportunities to join teams which include staff from other areas and different levels of the library, including members of the administration, professional librarians and front-line workers, thereby helping to break down divisions between the categories. Teams are project-based and involve staff in the planning, design, delivery and evaluation of library services. Team members feel invested in their work and can see the final project and how it adds value to the organisation. This tends to build esprit de corps and morale within the workforce.

The teams cut across traditional departments and silos and enable a participative model of service delivery, in which staff and patrons can be engaged and involved. Staff and patrons feel empowered through an environment created to enable them to step into power and have a say in what services are provided and how they are delivered. The active approach means that staff are not confined to buildings or trapped behind desks. Instead they are free to rove around the library and seek out patrons who require support and assistance. There is also an emphasis on taking library services out of the library through outreach programs and delivering them in a range of community settings.

The systems which support this more active approach are enabling and encourage the use of discretion when rules and regulations are being applied. Fines may still be levied, for example, but staff members have the ability to waive fines for those who cannot afford to pay them. Instead of having a long list of sanctions which must be applied equally to everyone in the name of fairness, there is a loose regulatory framework enabling individual circumstances to be taken into account. The focus is on equity rather than equality. Performance is assessed using qualitative evaluation methods such as patron surveys and focus groups. The emphasis is not on how much the service is used but how and why it is used and by whom. The aim is to gather community intelligence about the quality of library services with a view to constant improvement.

The organisational culture seeks to widen the franchise of the public library to be as socially inclusive as possible. Instead of energy being spent on the core group of active users, some capacity is redirected towards non-patrons, those who have consciously chosen not to use the library because they do not think that it can meet their needs. The group includes affluent young professionals, for example, who can afford to buy their books and pay for high speed internet access at home. Potential patrons can be appealed to via targeted marketing campaigns which reflect specific lifestyles and higher level needs. The culture constantly evolves and changes to keep up with the times and remain relevant to community needs. The base and superstructure of the community-led library are consistent with many of the defining characteristics of socialism as described by Marx. The focus is on meeting a mixture of higher level and basic needs, belonging, esteem, cognitive and aesthetic, as defined by Maslow.

The Needs-Based Library

"Great libraries build communities" (Lankes 2012). Under communism, social classes disappear altogether and society is collectively managed by all people on a truly democratic basis. Domination and exploitation are replaced by mutual cooperation. The productive forces have developed to the extent where there are no shortages of essential human requirements. Universal abundance facilitates the implementation of Marx's (1971, 18) famous maxim, "from each according to their ability, to each according to their needs". People contribute to society what their abilities allow them to give and they receive back from society precisely what they need to live a fulfilling human existence. Communism facilitates Maslow's conception of self-actualisation.

According to the Marx-Maslow analytical framework, the needs-based public library has many of the characteristics associated with communism. It is a democratic holacracy in which workers at the lowest level of the organisation can impact decisions made at the highest level and all patrons can actively participate in the governance of the library. The universal abundance supplied by the library means that there are no longer financial or resource limitations on service delivery. Everyone's needs can be fulfilled and self-actualisation becomes a real possibility. Marx saw communism as an ideal to strive towards, rather than a system that could be achieved in its finality. He argued that as people attained lower-level needs, they would then want to achieve higher level needs, and once those needs were obtained, they would then want to achieve even higher-level needs. In a similar manner, the needs-based library is an ideal social system to aim towards, though it is something that can never be fully obtained. The needs-based library continually looks for ways to improve its services and fulfil the needs of its patrons.

The strategy of the needs-based library encompasses the whole community and seeks to meet the needs of active users, potential users and non-users. Priority is given to those with the greatest need. While the traditional library might meet the needs of 20–40% of the community and a community-led library the needs of 40–60% of the community, the needs-based library aims to meet the needs of 60–80% of the community. These high levels of usage can be found in Cuba and Scandinavia where a needs-based model is more typical. There are many reasons why people with the greatest needs do not use the public library. It can be a generational issue; non-users were not taken to the library as children and so, in turn, they do not take their own children to the library. The rules and regulations of the public library and historical origins and purpose as agencies of social control are other factors. But probably the biggest reason for non-use is that the public library is not relevant and cannot meet everyday needs. The needs-based library is particularly interested in the unexplored non-patrons who have never thought of the library as an option for meeting their needs.

The staff structure of the needs-based library is also a holacracy in which power and resources are diffused throughout the organisation. As stuff comes in to the library, it is processed by working groups or circles, drawn from across the organisation according to their strengths including skills, experience and knowledge. The working groups might be short, medium or long term, depending on the task at hand. Staff members can belong to as many groups as capacity allows. They can choose which group(s) they want to join. Within each working group, each and every worker has the same voice and power. Any tensions between working groups are seen as challenges or opportunities. Tactical meetings include members from each working group and are used to sync and triage next actions. The role of administration shifts from command and control to governance, to clarify and improve the role structure. In this model, staff members have a clear sense of purpose both in terms of their own positions and what the working groups and library are aiming to achieve. Staff have a great deal of autonomy over tasks, teams or working groups and time. Staff develop mastery and flow by building on their strengths.

The service structure of the needs-based library is a leadership model in which the community determines the services required to meet the needs of local people. Required services are then co-produced, planned, designed, delivered and evaluated by library staff and community members working in partnership. This model formed the basis of the project Working Together (2008) in Canada. Community Development Librarian positions were created to carry out this work. By combining the strengths, experience, skills and knowledge of library staff with the strengths of the community, the capacity of the library to meet needs was vastly increased. The needs-based library is able to take from each according to their ability by utilising staff and community strengths and give to each according to their needs by using the increased capacity to provide all library patrons with exactly what they need.

The systems of the need-based library are empowering in the sense that they give staff members the power to identify, prioritise and meet community needs. The power is defined in a written document, the constitution, which replaces the usual plethora of policies, processes and procedures. Everyone in the organisation is bound by the same constitution, even the Chief Executive Officer. The transparency of the constitution replaces the dependence on office politics to get things done. The constitution is made accessible to everyone so there are no hidden agendas or unwritten rules. Anyone in the library can quickly determine the decisions s/he can make and who is held accountable.

The performance of the needs-based library is evaluated in terms of impact and outcomes. The focus is on how the library can make a difference to people's lives in terms of equality, happiness and well-being. The challenge is to identify and measure how the library is making a contribution to these outcomes. Levels of equality, happiness and well-being can be measured over time. Library services, collections and programmes can be evaluated to see what impact they are having on these levels. There is already a high correlation between equality and library visits. Finland, Sweden and Denmark are in the top five countries for income equality (Wilkinson and Pickett 2010). They are also in the top four countries for library visits (Fuegi and Jennings 2004). There is also a high correlation between happiness and circulation. Denmark, Finland and Canada are among the top six happiest countries (World Happiness Report 2015). They are also in the top four countries for library circulation (Fuegi and Jennings, 2004). There is also a clear link between library membership and well-being. Denmark, Sweden and Finland are among the top nine countries in terms of well-being (OECD 2013). They are also in the top nine countries for library membership (Fuegi and Jennings 2004).

The organisational culture of the needs-based library is one of continual transformation. The library is on a never-ending journey of constant improvement as it reaches out towards the ideal of completely meeting community needs. Disruptive innovation is used to avoid a culture of comfort, banishes old habits and stops the library from settling down or becoming complacent. The underpinning philosophy and values of the needs-based library have social justice at their core and the library becomes an agency of social change. The base and super-structure of the needs-based library is consistent with many of the defining characteristics of communism as described by Marx. The focus is on meeting basic needs relating to physiology, safety, belonging and esteem as defined by Maslow.

The Relative Autonomy of Ideology

It is important to understand the relative autonomy of ideology and to dispel a common objection to historical materialism. The base/superstructure model is often accused of economic reductionism, which supposedly places all power in objective economic factors, whilst reducing the influence of ideas to mere echoes or reflections of the economic base. This view could not be further from the truth.

The primacy of the economic base over the political and ideological super-structure does not mean that ideas have no significance or impact on the development of a given social system. On the contrary, historical materialism stresses the important role of ideas in the development of society. There are firstly old ideas which outlive their day and serve the interests of the moribund forces of society. Their significance lies in the fact that they hamper the development and the progress of society (Stalin 1953, 726). For instance, it is inevitable that socialism will retain aspects of capitalist ideology, and that communism will retain aspects of socialist ideology. In a similar manner, it is inevitable that the community-led library will retain vestiges of the old traditional library culture, and that the needs-based public library will retain aspects of both the traditional and the community-led public library culture. These ideological vestiges are moribund, which means that they will eventually dissipate in accordance with the development of the material structure of the social system.

The second kind of ideas is new ideas, which arise only after the development of the material life of society has set new tasks before society. However, once these ideas have been formed, they then become a potent force that can carry out the tasks and goals that have been set by the new material conditions of society. These new ideas therefore actively support, guide and facilitate the progress of society (Stalin 1953, 726).

Whilst it is inevitable that material changes cause old moribund ideas to eventually give way to new, progressive ideas, this does not mean that the old ideas will vanish overnight, and that no active efforts should be made to eradicate them. On the contrary, old ideas can continue to have a strong influence long after there has been qualitative transformation in the material structure. It is therefore necessary to devise all-embracing strategies that can actively diminish the strength of the old ideas. For instance, whilst the Great Leap Forward successfully catapulted China from the feudal mode of production to the socialist mode of production, the old ideas of its feudal past remained intact and lagged behind the material changes. The old ideas had the negative effect of hindering the political, cultural and economic development of China and slowed its attempts to fulfil human needs. Although Mao Zedong acknowledged that the Great Leap Forward was successful in destroying the material obstacles to the attainment of communism, he recognised that only a Cultural Revolution could destroy the ideological obstacles. The Cultural Revolution successfully achieved this objective by mobilising the whole nation in an effort to replace the old ideas with the new. It was in effect an ideological struggle that was waged between the moribund and the progressive, between the past and the future.

The effects of ideology constitute one of the most powerful barriers to progressive political, economic and cultural development for society as a whole and the public library in particular. Traditional public library managers and workers are naturally conservative. They are therefore predisposed to maintaining the status quo rather than revolutionising it. It therefore goes without saying that all progressive librarians should analyse the strategies and achievements of the Chinese Cultural Revolution. If the community-led and needs-based public libraries are to eradicate the old ideas of the traditional public library, then a cultural revolution will certainly be necessary. This will require a new kind of library worker with a different skill set and a new mind set. One of the key skills will be the ability to identify, prioritise and meet community needs. Another will be the ability to engage all sections of the community, active users, potential users and non-users, in the planning, design, delivery and evaluation of library services. The new mind set will be that of critical librarianship, which seeks to be transformative, disruptive, innovative and empowering, and a direct challenge to power and privilege. Librarians that practice critical librarianship strive to communicate the ways in which libraries consciously and unconsciously support systems of oppression.

Part 4: Dialectics and Public Libraries

This chapter has so far outlined the principle categories of the Marx-Maslow analytical framework and its application to public libraries. However, the framework is still static, in the sense that although it can describe the individual components, it cannot explain how or why it is that the traditional public library must become a community-led library, or why the community-led library must become a needs-based library. In other words, the model still lacks an account of social change. This shortcoming can be solved by drawing upon the insights of Marxist dialectics, and by contrasting them against the metaphysical outlook of the traditional public library.

Metaphysics begins with the assumption that the world is composed of immutable substances that do not develop, and which are not subject to change. It believes that nature and society has always been the way it is, and that it will and must remain that way indefinitely. Metaphysics therefore believes that there are no contradictions in nature or society. Capitalism, it argues, is a harmonious social system in which private individuals voluntarily enter into exchange relationships, and trade equal for equal. Metaphysics therefore obscures the contradictions in society, and functions in order to perpetuate the status quo. It is therefore unsurprising that the metaphysical method informs the traditional public library. Its proponents believe that public libraries cannot and should not develop, and that they should remain the same for all time, as static, timeless entities. Underlying this position is the belief that the public library is an institution for social control, which functions in order to perpetuate the conditions of capital accumulation. Traditional public libraries have thereby failed to develop in line with the development of society, and the growing contradictions of capitalism. More fundamentally, they are failing in their ability to fulfil human needs. Metaphysics fails to accept any kind of development in public libraries, and as such, its proponents focus upon preserving the aspects of the traditional public library that are swiftly being made obsolete by the development of society. Focusing on preserving the old is a futile battle, one that will end only in the extinction of traditional public libraries.

In contrast to metaphysics, dialectics recognises that nature and society are in a constant state of motion and development. "For dialectical philosophy nothing is final, absolute, sacred. It reveals the transitory character of everything and in everything; nothing can endure before it except the uninterrupted process of becoming and of passing away, of endless ascendancy from the lower to the higher" (Engels 1949, 328). Unlike metaphysics, dialectics acknowledges the necessity of change in nature. As a result, dialectics does not focus on developing the aspects of the public library that are passing away, but instead, the characteristics which are arising and developing. This mantra forms the basis of the community-led and needs-based library. The dialectical method ensures that the public library remains a fundamental cornerstone of progressive radical change.

The Marx-Maslow analytical framework recognises that society is in a constant state of change and development and that the public library should reflect the material conditions of the community which it exists to serve. The framework can be used as a tool to assess where a public library is currently positioned on the traditional, community-led, needs-based continuum, and what changes are required to the base (culture) and superstructure (strategy, structures, systems) to move from one model to another. What then, is the relationship between the framework and the three principle aspects of dialectics?

The Law of the Passage of Quantitative Changes into Qualitative Changes

In contrast to metaphysics, dialectics argues that nature develops according to the law of the passage of quantitative changes into qualitative changes. Quantitative changes are incremental changes that gradually develop the given object whilst preserving its form. Qualitative changes are sudden leaps that transform the object into something new. The transformation of quantity into quality is not a linear process, in the sense that there is no progressive development. Nor is it a cyclical process, which simply repeats what has already taken place. It should instead be understood as "an onward and upward movement, as a transition from an old qualitative state to a new qualitative state, as a development from the simple to the complex, from the lower to the higher" (Stalin 1953, 716). Describing this process, Engels states that:

> In physics...every change is a transformation of quantity into quality, a consequence of the quantitative change of the quantity of motion of one form or another that is inherent in the body or communicated to it. Thus, for instance, the temperature of water is first of all indifferent in relation to its state as a liquid; but by increasing or decreasing the temperature of liquid water a point is reached at which this state of cohesion alters and the water becomes transformed on the one side into steam and on the other into ice...Similarly, a definite minimum current strength is required to cause the platinum wire of an electric incandescent lamp to glow; and every metal has its temperature of incandescence and fusion, every liquid its definite freezing and boiling point at a given pressure – in so far as our means allow us to produce the temperature required; finally also every gas has its critical point at which it can be liquefied by pressure and cooling. In short, the so-called physical constants are for the most part nothing but designations of the nodal points at which quantitative addition or subtraction of motion produces qualitative alteration in the state of the body concerned, at which, therefore, quantity is transformed into quality (Engels 1954, 87).

The law of the transformation of quantity into quality governs the development of both nature and society. In Engels' example, when water is heated the temperature gradually increases via a series of quantitative changes. A qualitative change occurs when the water reaches 100 degrees and transforms into a gas, an entirely new element. The law characterises the stages of development of human society, which proceeds from primitive communism, through to slavery, feudalism, capitalism, socialism, and finally, communism. The law can be applied to the development of public libraries. It shows that the traditional public library undertakes a series of quantitative changes until it eventually undergoes a qualitative change, by transforming into a community-led public library. The same dialectical process then occurs in the transition between the community-led and needs-based public library. The notion that quantitative change leads to qualitative change shows that the development of public libraries is both evolutionary and revolutionary. Incremental quantitative changes in the governance and policies of the library gradually accumulate over time until they eventually bring about a qualitative transformation in the library culture.

The law of the passage of quantity into quality shows that natural and social phenomena do not transform into new phenomena instantly. They must instead undertake a series of quantitative changes before the qualitative transformation can take place. During the transitional period of quantitative changes, the phenomena in question will gain the characteristics of different phenomena long before undergoing qualitative transformation. For instance, when water is heated, the molecular structure gradually assumes the molecular characteristics of steam. In a similar manner, moribund capitalism develops the characteristics of socialist production as it matures, for instance, by increasing the size of the working class and by creating large-scale factories that bring labourers together. Likewise, the traditional library will gradually take on characteristics of the community-based public library before it undergoes a qualitative transformation. This shows that the traditional, community- and needs- based public libraries should not be conceptualised as distinct categories, as no such distinct categories exist. They should instead be conceptualised as different points on a continuum.

Thunder Bay Public Library

The Marx-Maslow analytical framework places the traditional, community-led, needs-based library in a continuum and recognises that at any given time a library can exhibit characteristics of one or more models. A real-life example illustrates the point. Thunder Bay Public Library (TBPL) had a needs-based strategy, a traditional staff structure, a community-led service structure and traditional systems, reflecting a traditional organisational culture.

The strategy of TBPL was developed using an inclusive process which engaged all major stakeholder groups including the board, staff and partners and every section of the community including active users, passive users and non-users. An outcome of the strategy development process was a Community Action Panel (CAP), a permanent but ever-changing group of local citizens, which ensures that the voice and needs of the community continue to be reflected in library service planning, design, delivery and evaluation.

TBPL had a rigid, fixed, hierarchical bureaucracy in which position power was highly valued. Services were delivered via departments and branches which operated as independent silos with their own power structures and hierarchies. Information and power were transmitted via fixed hard lines which enabled stability, consistency and clarity. The structure was judged on its ability to create and maintain the conditions as they in turn enabled a comfortable working environment. Power and authority were determined by position in the hierarchy. TBPL is taking a community-led approach to service delivery by working with a wide range of agencies and community groups. For example, TBPL formed a partnership with Ohmbase, a local maker group, to develop a makerspace at the Waverley branch library. The service is co-produced by library staff working with volunteers to meet community needs.

TBPL systems are traditional because they are still based on rules and regulations which are designed to be disabling. TBPL continues to charge fines, even though there is evidence to suggest that they can be a significant barrier to access. TBPL also continue to operate other arbitrary rules such as fixed loan periods and other restrictions which tend to disable and limit access.

Quantitative changes have been made at TBPL which have led to qualitative changes in the staff structure and systems. A major staff restructuring has assigned new job titles and position descriptions describing purpose, autonomy and mastery to every member of staff. The new structure is a flexible, agile and nimble matrix in which power is shared both vertically and horizontally via a complex web of hard and dotted lines and overlapping circles. Power and authority are derived from staff strengths, knowledge, skills and talents, and their understanding of community needs. The structure is messy, confusing and sometimes even a little chaotic. These are inevitable, intentional and desirable outcomes of the new way of working. The model requires high levels of planning, co-ordination and communication. It creates a healthy level of discomfort and innovative disruption which will prevent reversion to the status quo or the settling down into new fixed working patterns. No one knows her/his place because there are no fixed places, just ever-changing and overlapping services, projects and programmes. Generalists and all-rounders are able to add as much value as experts and specialists. The outcome of the quantitative changes has led to a qualitative change so that TBPL has progressed from a traditional to a community-led staff structure.

TBPL has also changed its systems from a traditional transactional operating model to a community-led participative model through the implementation of RFID self-check technology, shifting power from the library staff to patrons who can now control most of their interactions with the library. As well as giving patrons the opportunity to step into their own power, RFID has released staff

capacity for interaction with library users and the development of outreach programmes to engage potential users. The outcome of quantitative changes has led
to a qualitative change so that TBPL has progressed from traditional to community-led systems. Over time the changes in the superstructure, staff structure and
systems, will have a quantitative and qualitative impact on the base culture at
TBPL which will shift from traditional to community-led.

The Law of the Unity and Conflict of Opposites

In contrast to metaphysics, dialectics holds that contradictions are inherent in
all natural phenomena, and that development takes place through the unity and
struggle of opposites. "Life consists precisely and primarily in this — that a being
is at each moment itself and yet something else. Life is therefore also a contradiction which is present in things and processes themselves, and which constantly
originates and resolves itself; and as soon as the contradiction ceases, life, too,
comes to an end, and death steps in" (Engels 1962, 167). In capitalist society, these
opposites are the social character of production and the private means of appropriation. Whilst production under capitalism is inherently social, in the sense
that it requires the cooperation of numerous workers, the surplus value created
by the workers is appropriated and controlled by private individuals, the capitalist class. Internal contradiction drives the class struggle under capitalism and its
eventual transformation into socialism.

In the public library, the contradictory opposites are the needs-based and
traditional approaches to service delivery. On the one hand, the needs-based
approach attempts to develop human needs by targeting those who need the
library the most, the working class. On the other hand, the traditional approach
to public libraries hinders the development of human needs by enforcing policies
that alienate the working class from the library and society at large. The needs-
based and traditional approaches to public libraries are in eternal opposition
and it is this internal contradiction that constitutes the source of development
in public libraries. It explains why the traditional public library can and must
develop into the community-led library and why the community-led library can
and must develop into a needs-based library.

According to dialectics, development through the struggle of opposites operates in all times and places. Accordingly, whilst communism is superior to socialism in terms of its ability to develop human needs, there will always be human
needs that cannot be satisfied. In a similar manner, whilst the needs-based library
is better at achieving human needs than both the traditional and community-led
libraries, it will never fully achieve its objective of developing everyone's needs.

The law of the unity and conflict of opposites highlights the eternal struggle that public libraries face in overcoming the obstacles to self-actualisation.

In the Marx-Maslow analytical framework, the contradictions and tensions can be seen between the different elements which make up the superstructure of the library. For example, many traditional public libraries have strategies which include statements about the need to make the organisation more socially inclusive. There is often a focus on diversity, both in terms of meeting the needs of a diverse community and developing a diverse workforce which reflects the community it serves. The strategies feature many of the characteristics of a needs-based library as defined by the Marx-Maslow analytical framework. However, just because a library has a needs-based strategy does not mean that it is a needs-based library. In the example given, Thunder Bay Public Library had a needs-based strategy but it also had a traditional staff structure and systems. This exemplifies the Marxist concept of the unity and struggle of opposites. The internal contradictions led to quantitative and qualitative changes in the staffing structure and systems at TBPL and were the source of its development from a traditional to a community-led library.

The Law of the Negation of the Negation

In contrast to metaphysics, dialectics holds that natural and social phenomena progress in a generally progressive manner via a process called the negation of the negation. According to this law, natural and social phenomena develop through internal contradictions. When one side of the contradiction eventually overcomes the other, the phenomenon negates itself and the negation of the negation occurs. Whilst new phenomena are qualitatively different from the old, they still retain characteristics of their old form. Engels gives the following example to describe the law:

> Let us take a grain of barley...if it falls on suitable soil, then under the influence of heat and moisture it undergoes a specific change, it germinates; the grain as such ceases to exist, it is negated, and in its place appears the plant which has arisen from it, the negation of the grain. But what is the normal life-process of this plant? It grows, flowers, is fertilised and finally once more produces grains of barley, and as soon as these have ripened the stalk dies, is in its turn negated. As a result of this negation of the negation we have once again the original grain of barley, but not as a single unit, but ten-, twenty- or thirtyfold (Engels 1962, 186–87).

When capitalism undertakes a qualitative transformation into socialism, capitalism negates itself and the negation of the negation occurs. Whilst socialism is a qualitatively new form of society, it still retains the progressive characteristics of capitalism, such as the developed productive forces. In a similar manner, when the traditional public library undertakes a qualitative transformation into the community-led public library, it retains the progressive characteristics of the traditional public library. In short, the negation of the negation shows that new phenomena are simultaneously something new yet also something old. The community-led and needs-based libraries do not arise on their own foundations. They instead emerge from the fully developed conditions of the old library form.

In the context of public libraries, any shift from one model to another creates a combination of old and new. For example, the community-led library strategy focuses on active users and potential users. It is a combination of the old in which the traditional library focused only on the active users and the new in which the community-led library focuses on potential users. The same process occurs when the community-led library becomes a needs-based library. The needs-based library continues to focus on the old in terms of the community-led emphasis on active and potential users, while providing a new focus on non-users and those with greatest needs. Such is the Marxist dialectical method when applied to social life, to public libraries. This method can be applied to public libraries by using the Marx-Maslow analytical framework.

One of Marx's greatest discoveries was that all of philosophy is political. It is impossible to take a philosophical position without also taking a political position. Philosophy can be divided into two great camps. The first adopts a metaphysical idealist conception of the world, whilst the latter takes a dialectical materialist conception of it. Whether they recognise it or not, metaphysical idealists support capitalism and the exploitation of the working class. They view the public library as an institution for social control, one that is designed to maintain the rigid class system and false consciousness of the masses. Dialectical materialists support socialism and the emancipation of humanity. They view the public library as a tool for increasing working class consciousness and fulfilling human needs. The fate of the public library depends upon which side prevails.

Conclusion

The public library has all the elements required to meet community needs but lacks the political will to do so. If the public library had never been invented, it is unlikely that it would have got off the ground in today's world which is governed by market forces, neoliberal politics and economic austerity. The public library is a publicly-funded resource which is free at the point of need and can be shared with the whole community. The fact that the library is often used by so few is a tragic waste of a vast potential. For that potential to be realised, strategies which have social justice as their core value are needed. Staff structures must give employees purpose, autonomy and mastery. Services must meet community needs and be provided by people with the right skills in the right places at the right times. And we need an organisational culture imbued with the guiding principle of enabling each according to their ability, to each according to their needs, leading all towards the ideal of a needs-based library. Marx and Maslow have provided the analytical tools. What is needed is the political will to put ideas into action.

References

Cohen, G. *Karl Marx's Theory of History: A Defence*. Oxford: Clarendon Press, 1978.

Corrigan, P.R.D., and V. Gillespie. *Class struggle, Social Literacy and Idle Time: The Provision of Public Libraries in England*. Brighton: Noyce, 1978.

Engels, F. "Ludwig Feuerbach and the End of Classical German Philosophy". In K. Marx and F. Engels, *Selected Works*, 324–368. London: Lawrence & Wishart, 1949.

Engels, F. *Dialectics of Nature*. Moscow: Foreign Languages Publishing House, 1954.

Engels, F. *Anti-Duhring*. Moscow: Foreign Languages Publishing House, 1962.

Fuegi, D., and M. Jennings. *International Library Statistics: Trends and Commentary Based on the LIBECON Data*. 2004. www.libecon.org/pdf/InternationalLibraryStatistic.pdf.

Lankes, D. "Beyond the Bullet Points: Bad Libraries Build Collections, Good Libraries Build Services, Great Libraries Build Communities". 2012. Accessed April 15, 2020. https://davidlankes.org/beyond-the-bullet-points-bad-libraries-build-collections-good-libraries-build-services-great-libraries-build-communities/.

Lenin, V. *Collected Works Vol. 25*. Moscow Progress Publishers, 1977.

Maslow, A. "A Theory of Human Motivation". *Psychological Review* 50 (1943): 370–396.

Marx, K. *Critique of the Gotha Programme*. Moscow: Progress Publishers, 1971.

Marx, K. *A Contribution to a Critique of Political Economy*. Moscow: Progress Publishers, 1977.

Muddiman, D., S. Durrani, M. Dutch, R. Linley, J. Pateman, and J. Vincent. *Open to All? The Public Library and Social Exclusion*. Library and Information Council Research Report 84. London: Resource: The Council for Museums, Archives and Libraries, 2000.

Organisation for Economic Co-operation and Development. *Your Better Life Index*. 2013. Accessed April 15, 2020. http://stats.oecd.org/Index.aspx?DataSetCode=BLI.

Stalin, J. *Problems of Leninism*. Moscow: Foreign Languages Publishing House, 1953.

The World Happiness Report, 2015. The World Happiness Report is a publication of the Sustainable Development Solutions Network, powered by data from the Gallup World Poll. 2015. https://worldhappiness.report/ed/2015/

Wilkinson, R., and K. Pickett. *The Spirit Level: Why Equality is Better for Everyone*. New York: Bloomsbury Press, 2010.

Working Together. *Community-Led Libraries Toolkit*. 2008. Accessed April 15, 2020. www.librariesincommunities.ca. https://www.vpl.ca/sites/vpl/public/Community-Led-Libraries-Toolkit.pdf.

David McMenemy

3 Governance of Public Library Services: How Philosophical Approaches to Service Delivery Impact on Practice

Abstract: This chapter[1] explores how public libraries have been viewed historically in view of the political philosophy of the day, how this has impacted on governance and how an understanding of this can contribute to more effective advocacy on behalf of the profession. Potential ethical stances on free public libraries are discussed, contrasting a utilitarian view with rights-based theory. It is argued that the philosophies of community and virtue when applied to social justice pose both potentially progressive and regressive dimensions. The focus of the chapter is the United Kingdom, but international readers should be able to recognise the theoretical influences discussed and how they might apply within their own countries.

Keywords: Public libraries; Libraries and society; Library science – Philosophy

Introduction

Challenges faced by public libraries since the turn of the millennium have seen the period dubbed a volatile time for their history (Goulding 2006, 3). One of the key challenges faced by public services is how they are viewed from the point of view of prevailing political philosophy by the governance regimes under which they must work. While this might seem a rather esoteric issue to consider in the daily grind of service provision, the political philosophy of any prevailing government will have a significant bearing on how the government approaches the delivery and purpose of public services during its tenure. There is a significant knock-on effect for the professions charged with delivering services with re-interpretations of potentially changing missions and outcomes for their services.

Views on public libraries and their governance are presented from the perspective of the prevailing political philosophy over time. After defining the philosophical terms of reference, the discussion is brought up to date with an analysis

---

1 This chapter is a significantly revised and expanded version of a paper presented at *Ethical Dilemmas in the Information Society: Codes of Ethics for Librarians and Archivists* (IFLA/FAIFE Satellite Meeting, Geneva, 2014): https://www.ifla.org/files/assets/faife/publications/misc/ethical-dilemmas-in-the-information-society.pdf.

https://doi.org/10.1515/9783110533323-006

of how current political thinking challenges the traditional public library ethos which might have been regarded as eternal.

Political Philosophy – the Theoretical Dimension

Political philosophy is largely informed by ethical frameworks. The three main ethical theories that have most informed political philosophy are:
- Consequentialist ethics
- Deontological, or duty-based ethics, and
- Virtue ethics.

Each is summarised below.

Consequentialist Ethics

Consequentialism relates to the potential outcomes of an action and the ethical ramifications of said action. What is important for the consequentialist is that the outcome is satisfactory, not necessarily how that outcome has been achieved. The main consequentialist ethical theory is utilitarianism. The father of utilitarianism was Jeremy Bentham, whose theories were developed further by John Stuart Mill. The basic formula for utilitarianism is the greatest happiness for the greatest number; not individual happiness, but happiness for the largest number of people.

Utilitarianism had a significant effect on political philosophy through the Victorian era and well into the late twentieth century before it was arguably supplanted by philosophies more focussed around individual freedoms. The emergence of major public services, welfare systems, and institutions like public libraries and museums can be attributed to the emerging utilitarian thinkers of the Victorian era. From a purely public libraries stance, then, utilitarianism has had a significant effect on the development of information services to the public, and to this date it remains a political philosophy that curries great favour with many public sector professionals who believe the services they provide give maximum value for the public, and as such can be justified because of the positive results provided for wider society. For instance, with activities like encouragement of reading, helping educational outcomes and providing a neutral space within a community, there are potential utilitarian justifications for library services, since they highlight the wider societal benefits that arise from providing them.

Utilitarianism relates to the happiness and well-being of the majority and in a utilitarian world it is acceptable for some in society to lose out if the happiness of the majority is the overriding consequence. This concept is important, since taken to its extreme, it could advocate harm being allowed to a small number of people to benefit the majority. Clearly this raises significant issues of natural justice that have to be addressed by any ethical thinker. An argument against libraries relates to the requirement of citizens to pay taxes to provide libraries whether they want to or not. This critique, from a liberal standpoint, centres on the argument that the individual's rights should not be subsumed for a greater societal good. The fairness of welfare services, that is a consideration of the balance between those who benefit and those who do not, has been a key feature of the critique of utilitarianism by rights-based philosophers, and an example of it from a public library perspective that occurred, in a blaze of publicity, is provided later in the chapter.

Deontological Ethics

Deontological ethics relate to the concept that there are certain values or actions that are inherently good or bad. Deontological, or duty-based, ethics are primarily based on the theories of Immanuel Kant, a German eighteenth century philosopher. Kant was not convinced by the concept of utilitarianism, believing that it ignored a fundamental point in ethics that some actions were by their very nature good or bad and that this, not the consequences of the actions, were what was important. Taken to its extreme, utilitarianism could arguably support murder or theft or torture, if as a result of these acts the happiness of the majority was guaranteed. The deontologist would instead see the act itself as being right or wrong, regardless of the consequences.

In essence, Kant provided four axioms related to his ethical world view that have been argued to provide basic guidance (Hauptman 1988, 2). Firstly, Kant's concept of goodwill related to the desire on the part of the human being "to act correctly, fairly, or ethically" (Hauptman 1988, 2). The second is duty, which as Hauptman observes could be regarded outside of a strict government role such as military, or security, to be rather an old-fashioned concept from Kant's time. It can, however, be considered to apply to professional ethics (Hauptman 1988, 2).

Kant's categorical imperative is arguably the most important of his theories related to ethics. In his *Groundwork of the Metaphysics of Morals*, published in 1785, he stated two further important maxims that underpin his theories. The first of these maxims states that "I ought never to act except in such a way that I could also will that my maxim should become a universal law". Within this oft-quoted line lies the basis of an ethical theory that has been interpreted and re-interpreted to this day. The basis of the imperative is that any action should be morally justifiable by virtue of being measured against a potential universal law of nature.

Kant's final maxim relates to the morality of how people use other human beings. He states "Act in such a way that you treat humanity, whether in your own person or in the person of any other, never merely as a means to an end, but always at the same time as an end". Using human beings as a means relates to using them to further one's own interests, and not thinking of their interests. Treating them as an end, on the other hand, means considering their interests in any dealings you may have. This essentially means respecting the freedoms of others to make decisions and to act in their own interests. This part of the categorical imperative is the basis of many of the rights-based philosophies that currently exist.

The rights each citizen should expect to be afforded are what forms the main concern of rights-based philosophers. They are considered from myriad standpoints, such as the right of individuals not to have their interests interfered with by society or organisations, as well as the right to maximise one's own happiness first and foremost. As may be obvious, rights-based approaches can clash somewhat with consequentialism in some of their manifestations. Indeed, the rights of individuals versus the rights of the largest number could be seen to be one of the most persistent philosophical debates of the past 40 or so years, since political philosophy from the 1970s onwards has been heavily influenced by rights-based notions of individual freedom, especially related to free markets.

An important aspect of such rights-based theories relates to the concepts of negative and positive rights. Positive rights consider the notion that citizens have a set of expectations as to the services they should receive from the state. Often referred to as welfare rights, they incorporate issues such as education, health, unemployment benefits and the like. In opposition to positive rights, negative rights are based around the notion that people should not be unjustly interfered with, and that the overriding maxim should be one of freedom to pursue one's own interests first and foremost: "negative and positive liberty are not merely two distinct kinds of liberty; they can be seen as rival, incompatible interpretations of a single political ideal" (Carter 2018).

A key theorist around the notion of positive and negative liberty was Isiah Berlin, who believed that proponents of positive liberty could steer into coercion or authoritarianism in trying to achieve the goals perceived as just. Berlin argued that:

> Once I take this view, I am in a position to ignore the actual wishes of men or societies, to bully, oppress, torture in the name, and on behalf, of their 'real' selves, in the secure knowledge that whatever is the true goal of man... must be identical with his freedom. (Berlin 1969, 132–33).

Negative rights inform the thinking of many who label their beliefs as libertarian in origin, and can often mean mistrust of state intervention, publicly-funded services and taxation. Indeed, one of the key thinkers in the area, Robert Nozick, has labelled taxation as tantamount to making the taxpayer a slave of the state (Nozick 1974). He argues that if an individual has worked to earn money, then the state taking part of that money without permission means that a portion of the time spent working was worked on behalf of the state.

For negative rights philosophers, the concept of self-ownership is of paramount importance and the freedom for people to choose how their interests are advanced should be theirs and theirs alone. Another philosopher beloved of negative rights proponents is Ayn Rand, who famously stated that, "Individual rights are not subject to a public vote; a majority has no right to vote away the rights of a minority; the political function of rights is precisely to protect minorities from oppression by majorities (and the smallest minority on earth is the individual)" (Rand 1964).

Clearly there is a direct challenge to the philosophical approach that justifies spending on a public library service with this mindset. Indeed, in the mid-1980s, a right-leaning think tank, the Adam Smith Institute (ASI), argued against public library services on several points that were informed from a negative rights perspective (ASI 1986): the potential coercion of the taxpayer; the cost to authors and publishers; and lastly the funding of leisure, a private pursuit, by the public purse. The report advocated charging for library services rather than paying for them through general taxation.

Virtue Ethics

Virtue ethics have their origins in the classical philosophy of Aristotle. A major consideration in classical mythology was what the virtuous life would actually be and this informed the concept of living the good life and being a good person. At the heart of the concept was eudaimonia or happiness, the point of the virtuous life being to maximise happiness (Crisp 1998; 2011). As Benn has observed, "In contrast to Kantian and utilitarian approaches, Aristotle is not concerned to discover a supreme practical principle telling us what to do, or to derive any secondary moral rules from such a principle" (Benn 1998, 161). In Aristotle's ethical approach, virtue was about individuals developing specific dispositions to act in virtuous ways. The issue is not a simple binary one, since Aristotle saw dispositions on a scale between excess and deficiency, with the ideal disposition being a mean for each category. For instance, in considering the disposition of courage, Aristotle argued that it was the mean on a scale that had fear on one side and boldness on the other. The mean for the virtue of self-control lay between pleasure and pain. The virtuous disposition, then, lay between two other dispositions, both believed by Aristotle to be vices: one of excess and one of deficiency. Importantly, Aristotle saw that the mean might adapt to specific situations. For example, anger in some situations is warranted, when perhaps one witnesses injustice. The virtuous person can respond to circumstances appropriately in various ways, demonstrating the appropriate disposition to meet the situation.

Another key idea relates to the promotion of civic values, that is, the values related to "people's beliefs, commitments, capabilities, and actions as members or prospective members of communities" (Crittenden and Levine 2016). The alignment of the cultivation of virtue with the concept of being a good citizen is an important one to consider not only from classical philosophy but also when considering contemporary policy issues. For instance, in virtue ethics, dispositions such as being charitable are an important aspect of being a virtuous person and can be applied to libraries not only when it comes to the issue of volunteering, but also in terms of how many libraries are governed under new structures related to charitable bodies, along with the broader movement towards seeking donations for public services from philanthropists. While this is a significant departure for UK library governance, it is a direct outcome of the influence of elements of virtue ethics returning to the political consciousness with a consequent impact on public service provision. The impact on library governance is yet to be fully understood.

Communitarianism

An examination of virtue ethics leads to the topic of community with the key debates in political philosophy from the 80s onwards being related to community. Philosophers such as Michael Sandel, Alasdair MacIntyre and Michael Walzer dubbed with the label of communitarians argued that a societal focus on individual autonomy meant that citizens were viewed as atomised individuals, all involved in maximising their own positions in opposition to others. The communitarians believed that this was a reductive way of looking at human beings and it ignored major influences such as family, community and country that were a major part of identity. Importantly for communitarian philosophers, the Aristotelian concept of virtue was inherent in a more community-focussed approach to social justice. The idea was that viewing the good citizen as part of a strong and functioning community was a vital component of social justice.

Macintyre's key "critique of liberalism derives from a judgement that the best type of human life, that in which the tradition of the virtues is most adequately embodied, is lived by those engaged in constructing and sustaining forms of community directed towards the shared achievement of those common goods without which the ultimate human good cannot be achieved" (Macintyre 2013, xv). This is a clear clash with a rights-based approach that advocates no one conception of the common good or morality that should predominate in society. Sandel similarly questioned whether a just society could emerge as a result of a focus on a neutral society that privileged the goals and aspirations of individuals over those of the community values that have emerged through a shared culture, narrative and history:

> At issue is not whether individual or communal claims should carry greater weight but whether the principles of justice that govern the basic structure of society can be neutral with respect to the competing moral and religious convictions its citizens espouse. The fundamental question, in other words, is whether the right is prior to the good (Sandel 1981, x).

The communitarian approach began to have influence in the mid to late 90s in the UK, firstly with some elements of Blairism, but in the most recent past communitarian philosophy has become a major influence in both Conservative and Labour politics through the movements around The Big Society and Blue Labour. For instance, in a speech delivered in 2009, a year before he took power, David Cameron stated that, "because of its effect on personal and social responsibility, the recent growth of the state has promoted not social solidarity but selfishness and individualism" (Norman 2010, 1). How has the approach influenced public library governance?

Applying Theories of Political Philosophy to the Real-World Delivery of Public Library Services

What has been the impact of the theories discussed above on public library governance? The era of utilitarianism was a good one for public libraries. It saw a rapid expansion of their growth and was an easy advocacy opportunity for the profession. The notion that public libraries are a good thing for society is a straightforward proposition in a political climate that advocates the targeted public expenditure to benefit the largest number.

However, the focus on individual rights as the prevailing organiser theme for society saw the expansion of the free market society into all aspects of life in the last forty years. This in turn impacted on professions such as librarianship as they sought relevance in a market society. Space does not permit exploration of the wider impact on librarianship, though readers wishing to do so can find treatments of various aspects in the work of Anderson (2006), Buschman (2003), Budd (1997), D'Angelo (2006) and Usherwood (1996, 2007) among others, and an excellent critique of the impact on society more generally can be found in Sandel (2012). Budd considers the use of the word customers to refer to library patrons and its potential impact on the relationship between the library and patrons.

Notwithstanding individual viewpoints on the importance of changed perspectives, there was a clear attempt from the 1980s onwards to appear more business-like in terms of library provision, even going as far as providing services that mirrored corporate environments such as shops (McMenemy 2009, 189). Concern with the approach has been evident, with issues related to how such a consumerist approach might impact on the mission of the library service or even corrupt it. D'Angelo has stated that library users expect their public library spaces to represent "[...] democracy, civil education and the public good" (D'Angelo 2006, 4). It is difficult to reconcile a commercial imperative with this mission and if the library is positioned to treat the user as a customer in a marketplace as opposed to a citizen receiving services, the change in emphasis and ethos is likely to challenge traditional professional values. Seeing the commercial imperative leading to public libraries becoming populist and dumbing down their collections, Usherwood addressed the issue directly when he stated: "The profession must decide if it wants to maintain public libraries as social institutions serving the public good or as quasi retail outlets that simply seek to maximise their popularity by responding to populist demands" (Usherwood 2007, 29).

Applying the theoretical ideas discussed above to libraries more fully, however, allows further discussion of both past governance issues as well as future trends. The concept of the civically-funded, free public library is one that dates from the middle of the nineteenth century in the UK, US and Europe and across the developed and increasingly the developing world. The campaigns that led to the first public libraries in the UK and US were linked to the growing utilitarian policies that were prevalent among thinkers in the period. The expansion of public libraries, museums and public parks was designed to offer maximum utility for the majority of people, utilising public funds to create a positive shared experience. The idea was that society as a whole would benefit if more people were able to make more productive use of their leisure time. People would be able to educate themselves and contribute more positively to society, benefitting others. As highlighted above, however, this mindset is not one that informs many of the political class of the recent era who believed in a market-driven individualistic world view akin to that of some of the rights-based philosophies, a view increasingly shared by many citizens.

For a rights-based philosopher, public libraries can be criticised from a philosophical perspective on at least two fronts. Firstly, by providing free access to books and other materials they deprive the creators of those resources, and those who publish them and sell them, from income. Simply put, if people are borrowing materials then there is no need to purchase them; this crucial issue is discussed below in terms of the ethical arguments for and against. A second rights-based critique of public libraries is that public taxation is being used to provide services that should be provided by the market, rather than the taxpayer. The issue of public libraries depriving authors and publishers of income is one that has recently been prominently highlighted in the UK. The issue is not a new one; it has been used as a critique of public libraries for a long time and indeed legislation has been adopted in several countries, including the UK and Germany, to ensure public libraries lending their material, a concept known as Public Lending Right (PLR). PLR sees authors given money from a state fund to compensate for books lent by libraries. This was a key argument utilised against public libraries in *Ex Libris* (ASI 1986), where it was argued that libraries account for a fraction of books sold, and the free access provided to the public was a significant cost to authors and publishers who bear the financial burden. The introduction of PLR placed an increased burden on the taxpayer, since the PLR monies distributed to authors came from the public purse.

The reason the debate became media-worthy in the UK in recent years was not necessarily the message, but the messenger. The best-selling author of the *Horrible Histories* series, Terry Deary, raised the issue by suggesting that public libraries deprive authors, publishers and booksellers of income and that the concept of the free public library was one that belonged in a bygone age: "Because it's been 150 years, we've got this idea that we've got an entitlement to read books for free, at the expense of authors, publishers and council tax payers. This is not the Victorian age, when we wanted to allow the impoverished access to literature. We pay for compulsory schooling to do that" (Flood 2013). He went on to argue that "Books aren't public property, and writers aren't Enid Blyton, middle-class women indulging in a pleasant little hobby. They've got to make a living. Authors, booksellers and publishers need to eat" (Flood 2013).

For many in the library and information world, and even in the wider publishing world, these views were disagreeable, but they represent a logical, viable viewpoint shared by many who have a rights-based approach to ethical thinking that informs their world view. Deary's viewpoint is not necessarily wrong; it is merely another way of looking at an issue of rights which needs to be debated appropriately without being perceived as unreasonable. Responses to Deary's stance ranged from reasoned argument advocating the benefits of public libraries to society to hate mail and an initial online petition to remove his books from public libraries.

The key issue at stake in the Deary debate was the right of the author and publisher to maximise income from their outputs. Public libraries as sources of a free supply of books to all citizens potentially limit sales of books and impact on the potential income of both author and publisher. Even in a country where a public lending right exists, like the UK, the income derived from the loan of a book in no way would equate to the income derived from the sale of a book. In addition, in the public lending right scheme used in the UK, it is only the author of the book who receives a contribution when a book is lent by a library and the publisher's income from a library is limited to copies sold for loan. The existence of public lending right as a concept is an acknowledgement that the author deserves recompense for books lent and not sold. Arguably, then, the premise from Deary is one that has already been accepted, or else public lending right would not exist.

On the other hand, the concept of a public library is one that attempts to maximise the benefits for the largest number of people. While it impacts on the income of authors, publishers and booksellers, it provides access to resources for millions of people who may not otherwise be able to afford them. One could also take a rights-based stance to advocate for public libraries as a positive right, from the point of view of empowering people through access to knowledge.

The essential issue of whose benefit takes priority is one that is very much coloured by the political winds of the time. As highlighted above, what is important from an ethical perspective is understanding the arguments of critics like Deary, reacting appropriately to them and being aware of the equally valid counter-arguments that can be presented. The table below gives an indication of where the ethical debate highlighted could be placed from the point of view of the ethical theories discussed:

Table 1: Potential ethical stances on free public libraries – utility and rights-based.

Pro free libraries	Against free libraries
Utilitarian view (Consequentialism):	Rights-based theory (Deontological):
Provision of free public libraries benefits the majority of the population	The author and publisher of a work have the negative right to not have their financial interests damaged through lending of their materials
Rights-based theory (Deontological):	
Citizens have the positive right to access to education and knowledge. Public libraries help support this right	

Some arguments both for and against can come from the same ethical theory as opposing subsets. For instance, it is quite logical to hold a deontological belief that a public library is a positive right, i.e. the right for a citizen to receive a state-funded service, or to believe that a negative right not to have to pay for a library service, i.e. funding libraries for everyone, is an unwelcome and unnecessary interference in people's private interests. Kant's belief that it is wrong to use other human beings to advance one's own interests allows for such a dichotomy in interpretation to exist. A basic understanding of such a dichotomy is vital for any professional who seeks to argue against either stance. As stated above, neither is necessarily incorrect, and any view needs to be argued and understood on its ethical merits cognisant of opposing views.

The Governance Challenges of a Communitarian Focus – the Big Society and Beyond

The election of the David Cameron coalition government in 2010, followed by a majority Cameron government in 2015, placed his Big Society policy at the heart of public services. The concept behind Big Society was a renewal of community narrative, promoting an ideal of a community that had a collective set of values and goals, and was working towards them. The political interpretation led to an emphasis on localism and the establishment of more resourceful communities. Another key goal of the Big Society was to enhance and empower a third sector, neither public nor private, relying on third sector organisations to be able to take on the running of state services. One of the key architects of the big society was Jesse Norman, who reacted to criticism of the expansion of the third sector in the following way:

> It would be absurd to pretend that they are the whole of what is intended by it. The idea that public services could ever simply be transferred wholesale into the third sector is a hopeless canard, given the relatively small size of the latter. But it is equally clear that the third sector is the home of vast innovation and social energy, as is the private sector, and that these resources need to be more widely and intelligently deployed (Norman 2010, 201).

Localism was and remains a key theme, with the *Localism Act 2011* introducing significant new powers for local communities to manage services for themselves if faced with closure. Previously when a library was closed by a local authority, there was no mechanism for the community to take on the running itself. The *Localism Act* allowed communities to take on the responsibility themselves if their library was threatened with closure. The ability to do so was framed by the proposers of the legislation as an issue of empowerment, while the library profession more generally might not see it in such a positive light. Nevertheless, the legislation has greatly empowered local communities to take on the governance of their own community assets, and fits in with the growing trend around community building through Asset Based Community Development (ABCD) which is a trend that emerged in the US in the early 1990s and is growing in the UK. Jesse Norman summarised the benefits of this approach from a Big Society standpoint: "Greater involvement of people in their local communities would reduce isolation, strengthen social ties and increase self-reliance. It would build the capabilities of both individuals and institutions, and bring forward a new generation of citizen leaders. The result would be both a stronger society and better government" (Norman 2010, 197). While the David Cameron era of government is over, the shadow of localism and Big Society remains over public library governance. It is the claims of community that loom large over public libraries and their governance in the current political climate.

Public library managers must seek to understand how this new era differs from the preceding one that focused on individual freedom if they are to be effective in managing opportunities and threats. Arguably the profession got much of the former period of history largely wrong, focussing too much on being more business-like and transforming citizen and societal needs into customer wants, thereby weakening the profession by limiting the social mission. The criticisms applied by authors such as Buschman, D'Angelo and Usherwood highlight where they saw the damage done to public library services through a more commercial, individualistic focus. There was damage to purpose, ethos and potential impact of services in society. In a study of public library policy documents produced under the last Labour government in the UK between 1997 and 2010, Greene and McMenemy identified "a move away from a welfarist approach to a consumerist approach which emphasises individual consumer choice, where choice has been used as a rhetorical tool to introduce public sector reforms" (Greene and McMenemy 2012, 34). More recently, research applying Rhodes' theory of hollowing out of public library services (Rhodes 1994) has identified private sector approaches to service delivery as a key factor in the reduction of library services. Applied to public libraries, hollowing out was defined as "a process of efficiencies and restructuring in which library buildings stay open but the actual services, and the value of those services, is eroded through government and local government policy, cuts, and 'deprofessionalisation'" (Robertson and McMenemy 2018, 13).

In the realpolitik of the twenty-first century, communitarian-inspired politics has seen policies that seek to reduce state solutions and make communities the ultimate arbiters of what services they seek to provide locally. Even the handing over of public libraries to be managed by communities can be seen in this context if the process is to be understood and managed. While some might argue it is simply a right-wing, market-oriented government shrinking the state, the communitarian angle means that there is a prima facie link to social justice also driving it. Both elements need to be addressed to successfully advocate for the importance of both libraries and librarians.

It is difficult for a profession that is aimed at building community resilience to be against a policy that is claiming to do just that. Nevertheless, the highlighting of the issues that community-run libraries present for the longevity and integrity of the service is an important consideration for the profession. The governance challenge faced by the profession is novel. On the face of it, the profession adopting a stance against the use of library volunteers looks like a concern with self-preservation and protecting the status quo. Equally, an acceptance of volunteers in libraries can be argued to be against protecting the library workforce. Policy developers have therefore taken an open-minded but cautious approach, as represented by the Scottish Library and Information Council report, *Evidence on the Use of Volunteers in Libraries and on Volunteer-run Libraries* (2015, 1): "there can be challenges in using volunteers but also highlights the fact that there can be benefits for the volunteer, the library and the wider community in having volunteers undertake tasks that are additional to those of professional staff." Being opposed to community empowerment looks regressive, but blanket acceptance of a volunteer model looks negligent. The dichotomy will remain a significant challenge for the foreseeable future across the UK.

Conclusion

For librarians, words and the meanings of words, matter. This is more the case of the word community than for many others. As Shaw has observed, community

> ...continues to be appropriated to legitimate or justify a wide range of political positions, which might otherwise be regarded as incompatible (Shaw 2007, 24).

It is an important observation, then, that when politicians or other managers use the word community, it may not be what a public librarian has historically considered the term to mean. Public librarians usually take the term to mean provision of services to a community. The needs-based focus is evident in the volume devoted to community librarianship published by Pateman and Williment (2013). However, communitarian philosophy, at least in its Big Society guise practised in parts of the UK, has increasingly focussed on a perceived empowerment of the community through local decision-making. The hypothesis has not yet been fully tested to see if it is progressive or regressive from a governance point of view. Like the other ethical approaches discussed earlier, the philosophies of community and virtue when applied to social justice pose both potentially progressive and regressive dimensions.

There is no doubt that the era now emerging related to public library services in the UK raises significant issues for the longevity of the service. The long-term viability of community-run libraries is a completely new development in public library governance in the UK. The inspiration may come from a communitarian philosophy, but it is a new philosophy with untested maxims, and while the experiment may prove to be a success, the fact that many communities are taking on the governance of library services through the threat of closure, and not through any progressive choice, should be of concern to all.

On a positive note, the era of community arguably calls even more for a profession that can navigate ideas and public discourse and help citizens become informed. As Sandel has argued, "the hollowing out of the public realm makes it difficult to cultivate the solidarity and sense of community on which democratic citizenship depends" (Sandel 2009, 267). No profession is better placed to help this culture develop, and it is public libraries and community librarianship that can help it do so. The profession as a whole needs to battle with all of its collective might to ensure that the governance models that emerge in the era of communitarianism allow the service to move forward into the future with confidence.

References

Adam Smith Institute (ASI). *Ex Libris*. London: Adam Smith Institute, 1986.

Anderson, C.A. *Ethical Decision Making for Digital Libraries*. Oxford: Chandos, 2006.

Benn, P. *Ethics* London: Taylor and Francis, 1998.

Berlin, I. "Two Concepts of Liberty". In *Four Essays on Liberty* by I. Berlin. London: Oxford University Press, 1969. New ed. 2002.

Budd, J.M. "A Critique of Customer and Commodity". *College & Research Libraries* 58, no. 4 (1997): 309–320.

Buschman, J. *Dismantling the Public Sphere: Situating and Sustaining Librarianship in the Age of the New Public Philosophy*. Westport, Conn.: Libraries Unlimited, 2003.

Carter, I. "Positive and Negative Liberty". In *The Stanford Encyclopedia of Philosophy*. (Summer 2018 Edition), edited by Edward N. Zalta, 2018. Accessed April 15, 2020. https://plato.stanford.edu/archives/sum2018/entries/liberty-positive-negative/.

Crisp, R. "Virtue Ethics." In *Routledge Encyclopedia of Philosophy,* edited by E. Craig. London: Routledge, 1998, 2011. Accessed January 25, 2018. http://www.rep.routledge.com/article/L111.

Crittenden, J., and P. Levine. "Civic Education". In The Stanford Encyclopedia of Philosophy (Winter 2016 Edition), edited by Edward N. Zalta. Accessed April 15, 2020. https://plato.stanford.edu/archives/win2016/entries/civic-education/.

D'Angelo, E. *Barbarians at the Gates: How Postmodern Consumer Capitalism Threatens Democracy, Civil Education and the Public Good.* Duluth, Minn.: Library Juice Press, 2006.

Flood, A. "Libraries 'Have Had Their Day', Says Horrible Histories Author". *Guardian.* February 13, 2013. Accessed January 24, 2018. http://www.guardian.co.uk/books/2013/feb/13/libraries-horrible-histories-terry-deary.

Goulding, A. *Public Libraries in the 21st Century: Defining Services and Debating the Future.* Farnham: Ashgate, 2006.

Greene, M. and McMenemy, D. "The Emergence and Impact of Neoliberal Ideology on UK Public Library Policy, 1997–2010". In Spink, A. and Heinström, J. (Ed.) *Library and Information Science Trends and Research: Europe (Library and Information Science,* Vol. 6), 13–41. Bingley: Emerald Group Publishing Limited, 2012. https://doi.org/10.1108/S1876-0562(2012)0000006005

Hauptman, R. *Ethical Challenges in Librarianship.* Phoenix: Oryx Press, 1988.

MacIntyre, A. *After Virtue: A Study in Moral Theory.* Reprint edition. London: Bloomsbury Publishing, 2013.

McMenemy, D. *The Public Library.* London: Facet Publishing, 2009.

Norman, Jesse. *The Big Society: The Anatomy of the New Politics.* London: University of Buckingham Press, 2010.

Nozick, R. *Anarchy State and Utopia.* Oxford: Blackwell, 1975.

Pateman, J., and K. Williment. *Developing Community-led Public Libraries: Evidence from the UK and Canada.* Farnham: Ashgate Publishing Limited, 2013.

Rand, Ayn. *The Virtue of Selfishness: A New Concept of Egoism.* New York: New American Library/Signet, 1964.

Rhodes, R.A.W. "The Hollowing Out of the State: The Changing Nature of the Public Service in Britain". *Political Quarterly,* 65, no. 2 (1994): 138–151.

Robertson, C., and D. McMenemy. "The Hollowing Out of Children's Public Library Services in England from 2010–2016." *Journal of Librarianship and Information Science,* 52, no.1 (2020): 91–105. DOI: 10.1108/S1876-0562(2012)0000006005

Sandel, M.J. *Liberalism and the Limits of Justice.* Cambridge: Cambridge University Press, 1981.

Sandel, M.J. *Justice: What's the Right Thing to Do?* London: Allen Lane, 2009.

Sandel, M.J. *What Money Can't Buy: The Moral Limits of Markets.* London: Allen Lane, 2012.

Scottish Library and Information Council. *Evidence on the Use of Volunteers in Libraries and on Volunteer-run Libraries.* Edinburgh: Blake Stevenson Ltd., 2015. Accessed January 24, 2018. https://scottishlibraries.org/media/1215/volunteers-libraries-report.pdf.

Shaw, M. "Community Development and the Politics of Community". *Community Development Journal* 43, no. 1 (2008): 24–36.

Usherwood, B. *Rediscovering Public Library Management.* London: Library Association Publishing, 1996.

Usherwood, B. *Equity and Excellence in the Public Library: Why Ignorance Is Not Our Heritage.* Farnham: Ashgate Publishing, 2007.

Simon Robinson
4 Corporate Governance and Public Libraries

Abstract: This chapter offers reflections on corporate governance hopefully of use to the public library sector. It notes the reactive nature of the concern for governance across all sectors and critically examines the major theories of corporate governance, noting the lack of substantive engagement with values and purpose. Major codified responses to the issue of governance in business and beyond are addressed. It is argued that corporate governance thinking in its development has focused on the nature of responsibility. In particular, the approach taken in the four King[1] Reports, groundbreaking guidelines for the governance structures and operation of companies in South Africa, is explored. The Institute of Directors in Southern Africa (IoDSA) formally introduced the King Code of Governance Principles and the King Report on Governance in various iterations from 2009 to 2016 (https://www.iodsa.co.za/page/kingIII) The core values at the heart of Mervyn King's work are outlined and suggestions made about how they might be applied to the public library sector. Governance is less about detail and more about direction and continued reflection. Ideas of shared and trans-institutional governance, overlapping autonomy, self-governance, organizational autonomy and sector and profession governance are outlined. The focus is not simply on regulatory codes but on the practice of responsibility; the importance of virtues in the practice of governance; and the importance of dialogue and narrative across institutions.

Keywords: Public libraries; Corporate governance; Corporate governance – South Africa; Corporate governance – United Kingdom

This Must Never Be Allowed to Happen Again

The focus on governance in the last four decades has emerged because of a series of crises in business and the public sector. The crises have occurred in organizations ranging from individual corporations such as Enron and Arthur Andersen to entire industries, not least the finance industry in the financial crisis of 2007/8, as well as religious institutions such as the Roman Catholic Church in relation to child abuse, public bodies such as the BBC post Saville or the Mid Staffordshire

---

1 The chair of the reports was Mervyn King, South African judge.

https://doi.org/10.1515/ 9783110533323-007

Hospital Trust, corrupt activities of members of the UK Parliament, and global bodies such as Fédération Internationale de Football Association (FIFA) and the International Olympic Committee (IOC). In all instances, the same litany has wailed across the press, professions and public: this must never be allowed to happen again. From that firm intention has emerged a series of developments, theories and practices, which have aimed at ensuring the implementation of this worthy intent.

One should be uneasy however about the new age of responsible governance (Randerson 2009). Questions must be addressed. First, what was going on before the crises occurred and what did people think was going on? While finding answers calls for systematic research, it can be hypothesized that systems of governance and leadership which were applied in and maintained organizations were simply accepted. Centuries of tradition led members of the Roman Catholic Church to accept what the clergy said and did, undergirded by a theology of priesthood, which made questioning intention or practice unthinkable (Browne 2012). Centuries of tradition led all to assume that the medical and healthcare professions had patients' best interests at heart. Politicians and business leaders and financiers did not have the same trust credit (Park et al. 2013). It is striking that the outcry against members of parliament and their expense claims presumed a residual belief in the ethics of public service. The outcry was about the abuse of trust. All this offers a picture of unaccountable governance, naïve trust in leadership and wilful blindness, with financial, sexual, relational, professional and therapeutic abuse going on in plain sight. The stunning conclusion suggests that governance is about the nature and behaviour of individuals as members of boards, organizations and society at large and about owning and taking responsibility for identity in different operational contexts.

The second question concerns the dichotomy at the heart of governance, purpose versus practice. Some argue that the essential thing about governance is to have one's heart in the right place; to be clear about purpose and its relationship to the social and physical environment. Clearly this was not enough. However well-intentioned, the leaders of the public bodies were blind to the effects of their actions and held uncritical views of purpose. Others argue that central to good governance is practical capacity, with clarity about aims and objectives and how these might be best achieved. The stress is on management capacity and the development of systems that will be as full-proof as possible. This too was not enough. The finance industry had a great deal of management capacity but little sense of purpose and was blind to its social and physical environment. At the centre was a lack of awareness, both of the organization and the wider social and physical environment. What was going was not what leaders, board members or the wider public thought was going on. It is suggested below that this is more than a lack of transparency.

None of these crises focused on the governance of discrete institutions. Successful governance demanded that different institutions, including professional bodies and industry sectors, each with individual views of governance, should work together. Banks in the financial crisis operated as if they had no relation to other bodies. The Mid Staffordshire Hospital Trust in the UK involved many stakeholders including several care professions, all of whom had professional bodies with clearly articulated purposes; different regulatory bodies whose task was to monitor purpose and practice; the UK Department of Health & Social Care; and the wider government of the UK who set the objectives of governance and were accountable to the people. The people included patients and families who became victims, with over two hundred avoidable patient deaths (Report of the Mid Staffordshire NHS Foundation Trust Public Inquiry 2013). The different bodies involved were focused in discrete areas, with no sense of shared responsibility for the overarching purpose of care and did not follow through on concerns about practice. The focus of governance cannot be solely the discrete institution. The relationship of each institution to the complex social context, including business (Norman 2015), suggests that governance has to be trans-institutional. Other narratives must be given voice to challenge any dominant management narrative (Report of the Mid Staffordshire NHS Foundation Trust Public Inquiry 2013).

What is governance actually about? How does one make sense of it? Is governance about putting regulatory mechanisms in place and securing appropriate directions and practices? Is governance essentially about value and purpose? If so, how is this communicated? Is governance about relationships? Is governance about the character of the organization and of its members? There is general agreement that governance is an aspect of leadership, with the board taking responsibility for setting direction, involving vision and purpose, and ensuring that this is managed.[2] However, different views of corporate governance have offered different approaches to the task.

---

2 The term governance comes from the French *gouvernance* where it was used in the fourteenth century to refer to royal officers rather than to the process of governing or steering (Katsamunska 2016). The Greek etymology is κυβερνάω (*kubernáo*), to steer, direct.

Theories of Corporate Governance

The three most popular theories of corporate governance are agency, stewardship and stakeholder.

Agency Theory

The term agency in this context is used very differently from the concept of rational agency. The agent, the Chief Executive Office (CEO) or Managing Director (MD), is seen as a self-interested operator hired by the principals of the corporation who are the owners and/or shareholders to fulfil the objectives of increasing shareholder value. Purpose is thus assumed and focused on economic value. Governance involves finding ways of controlling the agent through reward or regulation (Jensen and Mecklin 1976; Ekanayake 2004). Key to this theory is the assertion of an underlying world view which asserts a single purpose and seeks to defend the freedom of the executive to maximize shareholder value (Freidman 1983).

The idea that compensation controls the agent is problematic. The board tends to aim for a tight link between performance and compensation which is less acceptable and considered high risk to an agent purely concerned for her/his own ends. Such a CEO would tend to pursue personal short term benefits rather than long term benefits for the shareholders (Bucholtz, Young, and Powell 1998). It is problematic to assume that CEOs are like other shareholders. Arguing that remuneration through shares is based on a coincidence of interests of the shareholders and leaders is flawed. Leaders have inside information enabling them to buy or sell shares at optimal times to maximize compensation, pursuing short term outcomes not necessarily in the best interests of the shareholders.

Agency theory presents the agency problem, which, broadly put, is that the CEO has the technical skills of management and knowledge about the organization and the financial environment which the board does not have. It is difficult for the board to control the CEO. However, the evidence from governance crises seems to indicate the contrary. Some CEOs argue that they could not know about decisions made at different levels in a huge organization (for instance, the CEO of VW: http://www.theguardian.com/business/2015/sep/25/volkswagen-appoints-matthias-muller-chief-executive-porsche-vw). Others in the financial crisis, such as Fred Goodwin, CEO of the Royal Bank of Scotland (Martin 2013), actively avoided gathering data about certain areas of the business, partly to avoid being caught out. In other words the ascription of knowledge asymmetrically in the relationship between board and CEO in agency theory is misleading.

The CEO inevitably has knowledge limitations just as the board has knowledge limitations. This is increasingly the case in the super-complexity of social media and the Internet. How mutual limitations are addressed becomes critical. In other words, the board and CEO must work together to ensure joint/full awareness of what is going on in the organization and beyond through reflective and critical dialogue rather than myths about omniscient charismatic leaders (Robinson and Smith 2014).

The other myth in the agency theory is the view that the CEO is essentially focused on financial reward. Solomon (1992, 118) sums this up as the "impoverished idea of *Homo economicus* who has no attachments or affections other than crude self-interest". In practice, there is often no attempt to critically question such assertions or to refer to research, summed up in Pink (2011) who concludes that financial rewards have a limited motivational efficacy. Beyond a certain level, significant purpose and the practice of professional mastery are more powerful motivators.

There are three things surprising about agency theory. First, it has had an inordinate effect on the development of thinking about corporate governance, due largely to US business schools attempting to develop a non-normative base to business studies and governance. Second, the so-called non-normative theory is clearly based on normative values, not least negative freedom, that is, freedom from regulation or coercion. There has been no attempt to critically establish the basis to the theory. Third, it is astonishing that the agency theory has maintained traction for so long, given its assumptions about leadership. The principal assumption about the CEO, for instance, is that the s/he is essentially untrustworthy, and therefore has to be controlled by the board. This goes directly against much leadership research (Caldwell et al. 2008; Robinson and Smith 2014) which concludes that the development of trust is critical to successful leadership. Moreover, since the financial crisis, the Institute of Chartered Accountants in England and Wales (ICAEW) (2009) has argued that trust in a wider focus of leadership, in this case the finance industry, is essential to the maintenance of social and economic well-being.

In the library world, Bundt (2000) examined professional accountability systems as a potential source of conflict in the relationships between librarians and their overseers. Research on conflict in relationships often uses agency theory to analyse relations between two parties when one party delegates work to another. Under agency theory, each player's behaviour is predicted on the basis of self-interested motivation. Bundt argues that these assumptions are inaccurate when applied to librarians and to many other public servants. Librarians' goals are likely to be the products of professional training, with strong convictions about what libraries should be, how they should be managed and whom they ought to serve. Socialised into the values of the profession, librarians have a professional relationship with patrons based on expertise and service orientation. This relationship contrasts with that of elected officials with differing educational and occupational backgrounds and roles with political relationships based on responsiveness to constituent concerns.

Stewardship Theory

A very different view of trust and governance emerges through stewardship theory (Davis et al. 1997). Bundt (2000) argues that that stewardship theory corresponds to characteristics of librarians and their relationships with boards of trustees and with city officials. Stewardship theory focuses on shared responsibility and value. Board members act as good stewards on behalf of a corporation, in whose values and purpose the members believe. In this theory there is no need to separate the CEO and the chairperson precisely because his or her commitment to the purpose of the organization renders him or her trustworthy. There is no doubt that shared values positively support trust. However, as the case of the Coop Bank (https://www.theguardian.com/business/2013/nov/23/coop-scandal-paul-flowers-mutual-societies) shows, trust demands more than shared values. Competence and testing of authenticity are also required (Boffey 2013). In that case, the chair of the Bank was appointed because as a Methodist minister, it was considered there would be a shared appreciation of cooperative values. However, he knew nothing about banking and was found to have a drug habit. Stewardship theory, like servant leadership, can lack realism. It does not consider the possibility that there might be different purposes of the business, how different views will be handled or how its own dominant narrative is challenged.

Stakeholder Theory

The stakeholder theory of governance (Freeman 1984) lies between the two above. It maintains that stakeholders should be involved in some way. Stakeholders are in effect part of the social context in which the firm operates and may include groups with an interest in the particular product or purpose of the organization in question, workers, consumers, clients and related professional bodies. They may also involve groups which have an interest in the organization as a social agent, sharing values which transcend narrow interests, such as non-governmental organizations (NGOs). Stakeholders may have overlapping involvements, such as supply chain companies who both contribute to the product but also are focused in wider purposes, as in the fight against modern slavery (Forrest and O'Rourke 2015).

The stakeholder theory is more realistic. If it is accepted that governance is about setting direction and monitoring the progress of an organization, it is difficult to do so effectively without some idea of the waters in which the ship sails. Heath and Norman (2004) suggest that there are different forms of stakeholder theory: instrumental, working with stakeholders for the success of the organization; descriptive; and normative. However, examples such as the Nestlé baby milk substitute case (Robinson 2002) show that all three are involved. Taking all three forms into account provides for institutional sustainability, greater clarity of the social context, clarity about core values and the means of developing dialogue around meaning, value and practice. In some European governance models, there are two-tier boards which enable direct representation of and dialogue with stakeholders. Nonetheless, there are major questions about how good governance can best be developed. Should governance be regulated or encouraged?

The Regulation of Governance

In the US, governance post Enron was focused on legal regulation and can be summed up as comply or else. In 2002, the United States Congress passed the Sarbanes-Oxley Act (SOX) to protect shareholders and the general public from accounting errors and fraudulent practices in enterprises and to improve the accuracy of corporate disclosures. It included:

- Penalties for corporate fraud and prison terms up to 20 years for destroying or altering documents in federal investigations
- Penalties for CEOs who certify false accounts of up to 20 years in prison and fines of up to $5 million
- New five-member board to oversee the accounting profession, with disciplinary and subpoena powers
- Restriction of consulting and non-audit services from accounting firms
- Imposition of rules on financial analysts to prevent conflicts of interest.

There are several arguments against this approach, summarised in King III (2009, 6). First, it is not clear that with the great variety of business that one size of governance can fit all. Second, the cost of compliance is burdensome both for the business and for the law, with the danger that the focus on the enterprise might be lost. Third, the legalistic approach has the danger of taking away from individual responsibility and the practice of good governance.

Hence, many countries, including the UK with its Corporate Governance Code (UK Financial Reporting Council 2012a), focus on voluntary codes in listed companies but in addition offer exemplars for other organizations. The emphasis is on self-regulation, with the tag-line comply or explain. This is not a one size fits all mode, and each institution should take responsibility for explaining how any alternative approach fulfils core values, such as fairness and transparency. The framework for good governance includes:

- The board should be effective and is collectively responsible
- The chairman/MD roles and responsibilities should be divided, enabling mutual challenge
- There should be a balance of executives and non-executive directors on the board, enabling critical dialogue
- Appointment of directors should involve formal, rigorous and transparent procedures
- There should be a formal board performance review annually, with planned training, board refreshment and regular elections
- Levels of directors' pay should be sufficient, but not more than necessary
- Significant proportions of executive directors' pay should be linked to corporate and individual performance
- There should be formal procedures for determining remuneration and no director should determine his or her own pay
- Companies should be ready to enter into dialogue with major shareholders based on a mutual understanding of objectives.

The board becomes the transparent environment in which leadership is framed, tested, supported and developed. It has a strong responsibility for shared leadership, and for critical discourse that would make sure that there was no element of leadership that could hide from external gaze. In effect, all this is designed to enable dispersed leadership, a sense of shared responsibility and clear negotiation of responsibility. The board would then begin to reflect wider discourse amongst stakeholders and in the wider community. In addition to transparent practice it requires the development of a board culture that encourages critical dialogue, testing values and practice.

The code provides guidance, and there is some legal support. However, it stresses the practice of corporate and individual responsibility. The problems with the approach include firstly lack of clarity about what explaining might involve which has led to an attempt to develop an understanding (UK Financial Reporting Council 2012b) of how to articulate the explanation. However, the explanation does not begin to address the issues of governance failure. The phrase comply or explain demands a justification of an alternative approach which would require attention to underlying principles, statements of purpose and some indication of how the governance of a particular institution relates to wider society. As O'Neill (2002) notes, to talk in general terms about transparency is not sufficient. An effective relationship demands dialogue (Robinson 2016) which interrogates meaning and purpose as well as practice. Secondly, the UK Code does not begin to address questions about the nature of the organization or how trans-institutional governance can be practised. Increasingly, the nature of business is being viewed as social, not simply private (Rawls 1971; Norman 2015), which in turns raises questions about how institutions relate to different professional, sector and industrial bodies, all of which involve regulatory bodies with differing views of governance.

The South African and the Ethics-Centred Approach

Alongside, and partly influenced by, the developing UK Code is the third King Report (King III 2009, and the more recent King IV 2016), based in South Africa. Some writers suggest that King IV is a hybrid of the comply or else and comply or explain approaches (Andreasson 2009). Between the King II and King III reports, the South African Companies Act (https://www.gov.za/documents/companies-act) established a legal framework to protect stakeholders. King III in some sense is a response to the change, recognising the importance of balancing a legal approach and a principled or self-regulating approach. Both King II and III also move beyond the focus of the UK Code, stressing the importance of ethics and core philosophies.

In King III and IV, ethics is very much at the centre of governance. A six-stage process of governing ethical performance is suggested:

- Identifying through stakeholder engagement the perceptions and expectations that stakeholders have of the ethical performance of a company
- Determining the ethical values and standards of the company and codifying it in a code of ethics
- Institutionalising the values and code of ethics of a company on both the strategic and systems levels
- Monitoring and evaluating compliance to the code of ethics
- Accounting and auditing ethical performance according to emerging global standards on ethical accounting and auditing. At the heart is integrated critical thinking and integrated reporting (https://integratedreporting.org/the-iirc-2/).
- Disclosing ethical performance to relevant stakeholders.

The core principle of *ubuntu*, a pan-African communitarian worldview stressing the interdependent nature of humanity, underpins the process – I am because you are. It stresses empathy, understanding, reciprocity, harmony and cooperation. Moreover, as Andreasson (2009, 14) notes, "it provides a guiding principle for determining how to organise African societies and measure well-being". None of this is fanciful given the UK government's relatively recent attempts to develop shared ideas of happiness that go beyond measuring wealth (BBC 2010). For the South African situation, the philosophy provides an important bridge between business and society.

South Africa has a history of civil strife, poverty and capitalism, seen by many as an extension of colonial power (Mbeki 2007). Consequently, business must take account of its social environment, with a stakeholder inclusive approach, including awareness of developing issues and the continuing culture of reconciliation post-apartheid. Business is viewed as a proactive part of society, contributing to the healing of the nation, and has led King III to stress the use of alternative dispute resolution not only as an action of mediation, but also as part of ongoing governance. The use of *ubuntu* implies that despite the explicit embracing of a stakeholder inclusive view of governance, King III contains elements of stewardship theory, with a strong sense of shared responsibility. One might think of such a principle as being too general to inform practice. However, it addresses perceptions of others, akin to the Western concept of respect (Cranor 1983), involving seeing others as ends in themselves with a direct application to governance.

One of the striking effects of narrow governance practice is that it leads to negative and exclusionary perceptions of others. In the Mid Staffordshire Hospital Trust breakdown (Report of the Mid Staffordshire NHS Foundation Trust Public Inquiry 2013) referred to earlier, the stress on narrow institutional objectives, and in particular on how institutional status could be achieved, led to key practitioners being unable to perceive the actual needs of the patients in the hospital. Family members who complained about patient treatment were perceived as nuisances who were impeding core objectives. *Ubuntu* establishes a shared sense of meaning and context which is backed up by a series of principles: leadership, sustainability and corporate citizenship. Leadership is characterised in terms of the core ethical values of responsibility, accountability, fairness and transparency. The concepts are not analysed in depth by the report. There is an emphasis on taking responsibility for meaning and practice, for a shared understanding of purpose and worth and for the development of awareness of the social and physical environment.

Accountability is framed for all stakeholders emphasising giving a justifiable account of organizational directions and implying mutual dialogue. Fairness is a key element of governance. As Rawls (1971) notes, fairness is, in effect, justice.

Taking responsibility for fairness demands attention to articulating both the principle of justice and the procedural implementation of justice in an institution. It is striking that the UK Governance Code does not begin to address fairness, for instance, in terms of the key area of CEO remuneration (Kolb 2006). Simply to set up a remuneration committee has none of this level of accountability. Hence, increasingly shareholders have held boards to account (Macalister 2016), underlining the need for dialogue beyond boards, and the role of stakeholders in governance (UK Financial Reporting Council 2012c). However, given the fact that any account of justice includes how CEO remuneration relates to wider staff rewards, wide dialogue is required to establish the meaning of justice across the institution and possibly across the sector.

Sustainability is seen by King III as the primary ethical and economic imperative of the twenty-first century. It is at the heart of opportunities and risks for businesses. Sustainability requires attention to and awareness and appreciation of the complex and inter-dependent physical environment, and demands governance that genuinely integrates all aspects both in practice, in reporting (https://integratedreporting.org/) and in development. Inclusivity of stakeholders must also be taken into account in decision-making and strategy. Values such as innovation, fairness, and collaboration are key aspects of transition to sustainability. The integration of sustainability and social transformation in a strategic and coherent manner will, argues King III (13), lead to "greater opportunities, efficiencies, and benefits, for both the company and society".

The sustainability principle is based on a view of responsibility as universal (Jonas 1984), which is problematic and could be interpreted as taking responsibility for everything. However, the core meaning involves first an acceptance that sustainability of the social and physical environment transcends narrow institutional interests and, second, a focus on shared responsibility is needed to develop dialogue on how that can be negotiated. The principles of innovation, fairness, and collaboration are at the centre of shared responsibility. It is striking that a board needs to focus not only on the enterprise but also on justice in the organization and in the surrounding social and physical environment involving integrated thinking and the relationship of justice to well-being and to enterprise.

Corporate citizenship emerges from fairness and sustainability. Business is part of society and responsible for the flourishing of that society. At the heart of this concept is the identity of business and its worth to society and beyond (Norman 2015). Business is not only about making profit and organizational sustainability but about citizenship and leadership in a civilised society. The King Reports are comfortable about the application of these ideas to public bodies partly because they show a way of seeing business as public (Norman 2015).

Governance and Public Libraries

In *The Atlas of New Librarianship*, Lankes (2016a) asserts that although public libraries come in a variety of shapes and sizes, their unifying function is to be the intellectual glue of a community. In one sense the importance of the library service goes without saying and many celebrities, public figures and citizens at large powerfully attest to the importance and value of libraries in their lives. Nonetheless, a detailed consideration of governance of public libraries is required to confirm their worth and value.

First, good governance recognises the wider value which libraries add across both the public sector and the wider community and questions whether the purpose of the library is to provide data of information for those who want or need it; essentially a service provider. Gorman (2000) states that what is happening to libraries is the result of what is happening to social life, social organization and global economic trends. The IFLA/UNESCO Public Library Manifesto 1994 (https://www.ifla.org/publications/iflaunesco-public-library-manifesto-1994) provides a universal framework which expresses the general aims that public libraries should follow and the services that must be developed to provide universal access to global information. A wider view of the purpose and value of public libraries would be about their contribution to lifelong learning, critical education and the development of what Dearing (1997) chose to call a civilised society, both in the context of surrounding educational institutions and wider society, as well as individual requirements. The deep philosophical base of the role of public libraries in a civilised society is summed up by Rowan Williams (2005), with his focus on the nature of the person as essentially a learning being. Such a view takes governance away from the narrow or exclusive end of seeing service as the prime purpose, and accounting for that service, to a more expansive vision. The content of the vision emerges over time through critical reflection and in relation to the social environment in which the library and related institutions operate. A narrow statement of the vision or end must be resisted.

Second, the make-up of the library governing body must enable critical thinking and reflection to occur. The core value of public libraries must be understood and developed. The board or equivalent governing body must focus on variety in its composition and operation, representing diversity, different perspectives and wide-ranging views. Plurality, as Bauman (1989) argues, is precisely what works against totalising. The presence of difference demands that board members examine critically their own views and any combined statement about values and purpose. Such critical difference is key to avoiding the groupthink and the wilful blindness (Heffernan 2011) evident in the corporate governance practice leading to the financial crisis. Fawkes (2014) helpfully puts this in a Jungian perspective.

Jung argued that all individuals have a shadow side which is less a dark or sinister side and more an avoidance of reflection on particular aspects of life. Fawkes argues corporations and professions likewise avoid reflection on particular issues in the boardroom and beyond. The presence of others with differing views and opinions can aid such reflection (Robinson 2016). The assertion of different perspectives challenges perceptions of vision and values. Governance is focused in learning and for libraries ties in directly to a wider vision.

Third, talking about core value is of little use without awareness and appreciation of the social environment and active engagement with it. Whilst values are general, they are not abstract and can be understood only in terms of actual embodiment. What does integrated and critical thinking look like? What does it look like in a specific area? How do public libraries contribute to wider value? How can library professionals meet the demands of policymakers to open up the public library system without destroying its values? Usherwood (2007) advocates that the library profession must argue what is necessary and valuable. The embodiment of purpose and value is key to good governance because it moves away from narrow views of improving service. A good example is Yorkshire Cancer Research.[3] Originally the charity raised money for research on cancer undertaken in universities and health institutions in the Yorkshire region. With a new and more diverse board, the focus began to change to questioning the provenance and practice of cancer care in the Yorkshire region which led to research developing awareness of both excellence in care and inequalities in care and reasons for the differences. Better targeting of funding resulted. The organization moved from general cancer research to a specific focus on the region. It moved from responding to general needs to responding to specific needs, working with others to identify just what that meant. It moved from viewing cancer and cancer care as essentially a technical development to including justice in its meaning and practice.

Similar behaviour for the public library would mean working with others to access data which mapped the centres and absence of centres of integrated thinking and lifelong learning in the region, and exploring ways of developing a culture of integrated thinking in the region. It might mean linking with schools, as is common with libraries. It might mean linking with groups developing debate and dialogue about regional needs and plans, raising questions, for instance, about the nature of cities and about responsibilities for the future, including national dimensions exemplified by recent UK government research on the future of cities (https://www.gov.uk/government/collections/future-of-cities). There are many dimensions: historical, telling the story of how a city has

---

3 I am obliged to Charles Rowett, former CEO, for this narrative.

developed; local, focusing on the nature of a city, what is valued and how the value is appreciated and embodied; and future, addressing the challenges to be faced by all stakeholders. Government research suggested there would be many problems emerging in cities, from technological changes to an increasing wealth gap. The changes identified relate directly to public libraries, in terms of service, data and technology, but also in terms of justice. How far do areas of deprivation in one's region affect lifelong learning? How can the library contribute to that exploration? Lankes (2016b) advocates that the mission of librarians is to improve society through facilitating knowledge creation in their communities. Goulding's (2006) research in the UK found that discourses around partnerships were very strong, recognising that libraries are operating in a cross-cutting policy environment and that partnerships assist in connecting with important political priorities, placing libraries at the heart of local, regional and national activities.

It is not clear how challenges will be addressed without integrated thinking across city regions giving voice to all stakeholders. Any public library can collaborate with educational institutions and the local authority and connect to many stakeholders, linking to established networks who enable conversations about various issues either in library buildings or in the community at large. Awareness and appreciation of the local community would then demand a consciousness of and engagement with at least three kinds of stakeholders: those who have need for the data kept by libraries and relate as individuals; those who begin to establish the need for such data based on shared dialogue around local issues; and those who share responsibility for establishing dialogue and answering need. A good example of the first is schools. Examples of the second are universities, local authorities and others who seek to establish dialogue across all sectors about the well-being of the community. In 2016 the Institute of Directors (IOD) and Leeds Beckett University sponsored a series of dialogues entitled *The Public Square.* Libraries were able to act as hubs for connecting, hosting and advertising events. An example of the third type of stakeholder is networks which focus on opportunities for citizenship action, for example, Citizens UK (http://www.citizensuk. org) which seeks to return power to the people and focuses on specific actions for change.

There remains the caveat that governance is about setting directions, not determining the details of action. The latter is the task of the executive. Implementing appropriate governance requires working though the core values of King III, not least institutional or corporate citizenship, leadership shared with other players in the community, and sustainability of the social and physical environment. A consideration of the nature, purpose and worth of the library places libraries as service providers into a broader context and resists managerialist approaches which focus primarily on service provision. Focusing purely on service provision runs the danger of avoiding wider purposes and putting libraries at risk in a time when the primary goal is cutting back on service provision costs (Chia and Holt 2009; Thompson and Bevan 2013). A broader view of the role of the library demands wide dialogue with the politicians who set targets. The public library in the broader context becomes part of a collaborative project to engage the wider society and its networks, dealing with interconnected problems in society including ignorance, poverty and conflict.

As already noted, the Mid Staffordshire Hospital Trust (Report of the Mid Staffordshire NHS Foundation Trust Public Inquiry 2013) governance failure exemplified how a focus on narrow institutional and professional targets and objectives can lead to a lack of focus on the wider shared purpose, in that case healthcare. The Francis Report (Report of the Mid Staffordshire NHS Foundation Trust Public Inquiry 2013) was highly critical of professions such as nursing for being blind to the core purpose of the profession, the heart of professional identity. In the light of these factors, public libraries become co-responsible for well-being and civil society, contributing and responding to a culture based on dialogue. Dialogue enables the practice of responsibility through testing ideas, values and feelings, developing capacity to account for and accept challenges and increasing possibilities for creative enterprise (Robinson 2016). Developing critical agency or imputability is about owning ideas and making connections to value, meaning and practice. Accountability is mutual and plural and mediated by dialogue. King III argues that governance regulation should be based not simply on codes but on stakeholder dialogue. Stakeholders become not simply people or groups affected by the organization but rather groups who like the organization itself have a stake in wider society and its well-being.

The third mode of responsibility that good governance engages, and which interacts with the first two, is positive responsibility (Ricoeur 2000) and focuses on the idea that responsibility cannot fully be expressed without action. Ricoeur contrasts positive responsibility with negative responsibility where the focus is on avoiding blame and action. The Mid Staffordshire case was dominated by negative responsibility and what Francis (Report of the Mid Staffordshire NHS Foundation Trust Public Inquiry 2013) called a culture of fear. In such a culture, the demands of hierarchy dominate, partly explaining why poor governance leads to wilful blindness. Positive responsibility picks up the theme of universal responsibility and focuses on creative and moral imagination (Lederach 2005). With multiple responsibility for particular tasks, wider purpose, ideas, values and practices emerge with negotiation of how responsibility will be achieved. The values of innovation and collaboration are critical to this mode of responsibility. The negotiation of how responsibility is put into practice further develops the identity of the individual and the organization (Finch and Mason 1993).

The development of active dialogue inside and outside the public library is vital. Macnamara (2015) argues that an effective architecture of listening is needed, such that the virtues are embodied and attention given to the requirements of listening. However, his research indicates even the perception of what constitutes dialogue in organizations needs to be addressed. Many organizations equate dialogue with surveys or the use of consultants. The problem with the first of these is that there is no mutuality or critical challenge involved. The problem with the second is that it often involves dialogue which is on the sidelines and not between workers, other stakeholders and leaders. Leaders avoid responsibility for authentic engagement and understanding of challenges. Macnamara (2015) notes that most of the leaders of the major organizations he studied believed their communication was dialogic. In fact, over 80% of communication was transmissional and one way. There may be many reasons for this, from a lack of clarity about what is required to enable listening to a reluctance of leaders to hold themselves accountable on a regular basis, or to let go of perceived power. Increasingly, dialogic governance is argued for at every level of the organization.

The boardroom has historically been a place which avoided dialogic decision-making but is precisely where dialogue should first be embodied. Part of the problem has been the inability of boards to stand against the power, perceived and real, of the CEO (Martin 2013; Sonnenfeld 2002). Effective dialogue demands different perspectives from board members to test the CEO narrative. Board members in turn tend not to open themselves to dialogue outside the boardroom, which could, properly developed, demonstrate to the workforce how to develop asymmetrically mutual dialogue: dialogue which recognizes power differences but enables mutual listening and challenge. Developing whistleblowing as part of the culture is important (Borrie and Denn 2002). However, reliance on whistleblowing to raise questions can take away from a culture of dialogue, where questions are asked at the time to create a culture of challenge.

The principles of governance in institutions overlap the principles of governance in local and national government. Governance becomes shared and trans-institutional, and involves overlapping autonomy, self-governance, organizational autonomy and sector and profession governance. The focus is not only on regulatory codes but on the practice of responsibility and the importance of dialogue and narrative across institutions. For public libraries, dialogue in the boardroom and dialogue beyond the library are required with the broader purpose of developing critical thinking and lifelong learning. The more that dialogue is developed across a region, the more the services provided by public libraries are recognized and needed.

Governance, Dialogue and the Virtues

Moore (2012) develops the theme of culture to argue that a culture of good governance involves the practice of the virtues, at individual and organizational level. Moore argues (2012; Osterloh and Frey 2004) that reliance on governance systems and regulation can crowd out virtues, with compliance more important than taking responsibility for judgment. The most obvious virtue is practical wisdom, often focused on Aristotle's *phronesis*.[4] Practical wisdom involves the capacity to reflect on purpose and how it is embodied in practice. It is central to the first mode of responsibility and to good judgement in the boardroom and beyond (Osterloh and Frey 2004, 206–7; Chia and Holt 2009; Thompson and Bevan 2013). Critical to effective governance is attention to power and authority.

The power imbalance within a board can be striking, with psychological and intellectual power being asserted through dominant CEOs. Hence, part of any board code of practice needs to address the issue of power to ensure that the views and desires of particular constituencies are not privileged (Sonnenfeld 2002). Attention is required in appointing members to the board to the virtues they would bring to enabling dialogue. Carefully-designed systems of participation and self-governance are required (Norman 2015). Other key virtues are courage, patience, temperance, justice and empathy. Courage is critical to giving an account and to challenging dominant narratives, absent for example in the Mid Staffordshire case. Patience demands pushing back on unrealistic deadlines and developing a level of trust in the workplace. Temperance involves a balanced disposition and is critical for good judgement. The idea of justice as a virtue emphasises that justice involves establishing procedures together with the capacity for justice through giving and receiving equal respect and attention (Robinson 2016). Empathy focuses on the capacity to identity with others, which is critical for hearing and understanding their narratives.

Moore's argument is that good governance does not rely solely on setting up a system of control. It requires the practice of autonomy within the organization and an appropriate culture. Autonomy is defined as self-governance in relation to the different narratives of the individual person, the organization and wider society. The importance of such autonomy is critical to governance in at least four ways, enabling:
- Members of the organization to push back against narrow dominant narratives which obscure purpose
- The workforce to take greater responsibility for purpose. Autonomy and the practice of *phronesis* enable a critical appreciation of the core purpose. The

---

4 There are many other views of wisdom, for example Thompson and Bevan 2013.

purpose is not simply assumed but is rather referenced and tested at every level of practice and decision-making. Is this really what we are about? Inevitably this leads to authentic not rote learning around terms such as vision and mission

- Greater consciousness of complexity and the integration of different narratives inside and outside the organization, reinforcing genuine identity and clarifying how the organization can relate, individually and in collaboration, to the social and physical environment
- Holistic integration including cognitive, affective and practical aspects in planning, with the King Reports and governance crises such as the Mid Staffordshire Hospital Trust suggesting several elements that might be applied to libraries.

The library can be conceived not solely as a place but as an environment in which time and space can be found to reflect on and develop virtues. Indeed, it might be argued that the library could contribute to leadership and citizenship through enabling institutionally and more widely the development of philosophies and approaches to critical thinking and related virtues.

Conclusion

The developments of governance around responsibility, dialogue, narrative and virtues show that governance has come a long way since the early governance crises. Many aspects apply across public and corporate governance and cannot be set in place without a focus on the continued practice of responsibility. The integrity of governance requires an ongoing critical dialogue with national and regional governments. The developments in corporate governance have mirrored the developing debate around public governance theories (Katsamunska 2016), ranging from hierarchical control to contractual arrangements involving markets, developing networks and a communitarian focus, requiring involvement in, from and for the community.

The general developments in governance impact directly on governance and public libraries and demand a recognition of, and dialogue about, library services and their value to society. A consideration of value engages the purpose of the library and the complex context of services. Dealing with the complexity demands ongoing dialogue which addresses the different stakeholders, including professional bodies associated with the sector, and the voluntary sector, pointing to a democratic view of governance. Different views are represented with an active dialogue which critically engages the value of libraries, their complex context, including digital possibilities, and challenges dominant managerialist narratives.

The questions raised are critical. How far are key stakeholders such as children, educational institutions and teaching professions involved in the dialogue? Gorman (2000) notes that the heaviest users of public libraries are the young and poorer senior citizens, the least powerful groups in society. How far is the culture of learning addressed, rather than simply access to data? Are libraries addressing human needs or rights, or both? Libraries are involved in trans-institutional governance and wider debates about core purpose which radically affects how libraries report, demanding integrated reporting with links to purpose and wider views of well-being in society. The dialogue inevitably moves into the nature of public service and about shared responsibilities for service provision, raising questions about co-regulation. If library services reflecting core value and purpose are not regulated nationally, professionally and locally, enabling different levels of autonomy, the danger is that the services will not be equitable and the core purpose will be lost. At the heart of effective governance is the development of genuine dialogue, significant narrative, and the involvement of all stakeholders in articulating and negotiating responsibility.

References

Andreasson, S. "Understanding Corporate Governance Reform in South Africa Anglo-American Divergence, the King Reports, and Hybridization". *Business and Society* 50, no.4 (2011): 647–673.

Bauman, Z. *Modernity and the Holocaust*. London: Polity, 1989.

BBC News. "Plan to Measure Happiness 'Not Woolly' – Cameron". Accessed April 15, 2020. http://www.bbc.co.uk/news/uk-11833241.

Boffey, D., and J. Treanor "The Co-op Scandal: Drugs, Sex, Religion … and the Humiliation of a Movement". *The Guardian*. 24 November 2013. Accessed April 15, 2020. https://www.theguardian.com/business/2013/nov/23/coop-scandal-paul-flowers-mutual-societies.

Borrie, G., and G. Dehn. "Whistle Blowing: the New Perspective." In *Case Histories in Business Ethics*, edited by C. Megone and S.J. Robinson, 96–105. London: Routledge, 2002.

Browne, V. "Theology of Priesthood Behind Sex Abuse Crisis." *The Irish Times*. 21 March 2012. https://www.irishtimes.com/opinion/theology-of-priesthood-behind-sex-abuse-crisis-1.485981.

Bucholtz, A., M. Young, and G. Powell. "Are Board Members Pawns or Watchdogs?" *Group and Organization Management* 23, no. 1 (1998): 6–21.

Bundt, J. "Strategic Stewards: Managing Accountability, Building Trust." *Journal of Public Administration Research and Theory* 10, no. 4 (2000): 757–778. https://doi.org/10.1093/oxfordjournals.jpart.a024290.

Caldwell, C., L. Hayes, P. Bernal, and R. Karri. "Ethical Stewardship – Implications for Leadership and Trust." *Journal of Business Ethics* 78, no. 1–2 (2008): 153–164.
Chia, R., and R. Holt. *Strategy without Design: The Silent Efficacy of Indirect Action.* Cambridge: Cambridge University Press, 2009.
Cranor, C.F. "On Respecting Human Beings as Persons." *Journal of Value Inquiry* 17 (1983): 103–117.
Curzer, H. *Aristotle and the Virtues.* Oxford: Oxford University Press, 2014.
Davis, J.H., F.D. Schoorman, and L. Donaldson. "Toward a Stewardship Theory of Management." *Academy of Management Journal* 31 (1997): 488–511.
Dearing, R. *Higher Education in the Learning Society.* London: Her Majesty's Stationery Office, 1997.
Ekanayake, S. "Agency Theory, National Culture and Management Control Systems." *Journal of American Academy of Business* 4, no. 1–2 (2004): 49–54.
Fawkes, J. *Public Relations Ethics and Professionalism.* London: Palgrave, 2014.
Finch, J., and J. Mason. *Negotiating Family Responsibilities.* London: Routledge, 1993.
Forrest, A., and R. O'Rourke. "The Modern Slavery Bill: A Step in the Right Direction". *Huffington Post, The Blog* 04/06/2015, updated June 6, 2015. Accessed April 15, 2020. https://www.huffpost.com/entry/the-modern-slavery-bill-a_b_7010494.
Freeman, E. *Strategic Management: A Stakeholder Approach.* Boston: Pitman, 1984.
Freidman, M. "The Social Responsibility of Business is to Increase its Profits". In *Ethical Issues in Business*, edited by T. Donaldson and P. Werhane, 239–43. New York: Prentice-Hall, 1983.
Gorman, M. *Our Enduring Values: Librarianship in the 21st Century.* Chicago: ALA Editions, 2000.
Goulding, A. *Public Libraries in the 21st Century: Defining Services and Debating the Future.* London: Routledge, 2016.
Heath, J., and W. Norman. "Stakeholder Theory, Corporate Governance and Public Management." *Journal of Business Ethics* 53, no. 3 (2004): 247–265.
Heffernan, M. *Wilful Blindness.* London: Simon and Schuster, 2011.
ICAEW. *Reporting with Integrity.* London: ICAEW, 2007. Accessed April 15, 2020. https://www.icaew.com/-/media/corporate/files/technical/ethics/reporting-with-integrity-report.ashx?la=en.
Jensen, M., and W. Mecklin. "Theory of the Firm: Managerial Behavior, Agency Costs and Ownership Structure." *Journal of Financial Economics* 3, no. 4 (1976): 305–360.
Jonas. H. *The Imperative of Responsibility.* Chicago: Chicago University Press, 1984.
Katsamunska, P. "The Concept of Governance and Public Governance Theories." *Economic Alternatives*, Issue 2 (2016): 133–141.
King III Report on Governance for South Africa. King Code of Governance Principles for South Africa 2009; Companies Act 71 of 2008. Johannesburg: Institute of Directors in Southern Africa. http://www.library.up.ac.za/law/docs/king111report.pdf
King IV Report on Corporate Governance for South Africa. King Committee on Corporate Governance. Sandton, South Africa: Institute of Directors in Southern Africa, 2016. https://cdn.ymaws.com/www.iodsa.co.za/resource/collection/684B68A7-B768-465C-8214-E3A007F15A5A/IoDSA_King_IV_Report_-_WebVersion.pdf
Kolb, R.W., ed. *The Ethics of Executive Compensation.* Oxford: Blackwell, 2006.
Lankes, R.D. *The Atlas of New Librarianship.* Rev. ed. Cambridge, Mass.: MIT Press, 2016a.
Lankes, R.D. *The New Librarianship Field Guide.* Cambridge, Mass.: MIT Press, 2016b.

Lederach, J.P. *The Moral Imagination*. Oxford: Oxford University Press, 2005.

Macalister, T., J. Treanor, and S. Farrell "BP Shareholders Revolt Against CEO's £14m Pay Package". *The Guardian*. 15 April 2016. Accessed April 15, 2020. https://www.theguardian. com/business/2016/apr/14/bp-pledge-shareholder-anger-ceo-bob-dudleypay-deal.

Macnamara, J. *Creating an 'Architecture of Listening' in Organizations: The Basis of Engagement, Trust, Healthy Democracy, Social Equity, and Business Sustainability*. Sydney: University of Technology Sydney, 2015. Accessed April 15, 2020. https://www.uts. edu.au/sites/default/files/fass-organizational-listening-report.pdf.

Martin, I. *Making It Happen: Fred Goodwin, RBS and the Men who Blew up the British Economy*. London: Simon and Schuster, 2013.

Mbeki, T. *Steve Biko Memorial Lecture delivered by the President of South Africa, Thabo Mbeki, on the occasion of the 30th Anniversary of the death of Stephen Bantu Biko, Cape Town 12 September 2007*. Cape Town: South African Government. Accessed April 15, 2020. https:// www.gov.za/t-mbeki-steve-biko-memorial-lecture.

Moore, G. "The Virtue of Governance, the Governance of Virtue." *Business Ethics Quarterly* 22, no. 2 (2012): 293–318.

Norman, W. "Rawls and Corporate Governance." *Business Ethics Quarterly*, 25, no. 1 (2015): 29–64.

O'Neill, O. *A Question of Trust*. Cambridge: Cambridge University Press, 2002.

Osterloh, M., and B. Frey. "Corporate Governance for Crooks? The Case for Corporate Virtue." In *Corporate Governance and Firm Organization: Microfoundations and Structural Forms*, Edited by A. Grandori, 191–211. Oxford: Oxford University Press, 2004.

Park, A., C. Bryson, E. Clery, J. Curtice, and M. Phillips, eds. *British Social Attitudes: The 30th Report*. London: NatCen Social Research, 2013. Accessed April 15, 2020. http://www.bsa. natcen.ac.uk/latest-report/british-social-attitudes-30/key-findings/trust-politics-and-institutions.aspx.

Pink, D. *Drive*. London: Canongate, 2011.

Randerson, J. "President Obama Hails New Age of Responsibility". *The Guardian*. 21 January 2009. Accessed April 15, 2020. https://www.theguardian.com/environment/blog/2009/ jan/20/obama-inauguration-climatechange

Rawls, J. *A Theory of Justice*. Oxford: Clarendon Press, 1971.

Report of the Mid Staffordshire NHS Foundation Trust Public Inquiry. The Francis Report. 2013. Accessed April 15, 2020. https://www.gov.uk/government/publications/report-of-the-mid-staffordshire-nhs-foundation-trust-public-inquiry.

Riceour, P. "The Concept of Responsibility: An Essay in Semantic Analysis". In *The Just*, translated by D. Pellauer. Chicago: The University of Chicago Press, 2000.

Robinson S. "Nestle and International Marketing". In *Case Histories in Business Ethics*, edited by C. Megone and S. Robinson, 141–158. London: Routledge, 2002.

Robinson, S., and J. Smith. *Co-charismatic Leadership*. Oxford: Peter Lang, 2014.

Robinson. S. *The Practice of Integrity in Business*. London: Palgrave, 2016.

Solomon, R. *Ethics and Excellence*. Oxford: Oxford University Press, 1992.

Sonnenfeld, J. "What Makes Great Boards Great." *Harvard Business Review* 80 no.9 (2002): 106–113. Accessed April 15, 2020. https://hbr.org/2002/09/what-makes-great-boards-great.

Thompson, M., and D. Bevan, eds. *Wise Management in Organisational Complexity*. London: Palgrave, 2013.

UK Financial Reporting Council. *UK Corporate Governance Code*. 2012a. Accessed April 15, 2020. https://www.frc.org.uk/getattachment/e322c20a-1181-4ac8-a3d3-1fcfbcea7914/UK-Corporate-Governance-Code-(September-2012).pdf.

UK Financial Reporting Council. *What Constitutes an Explanation under 'Comply or Explain'? Report of Discussions between Companies and Investors*. 2012b. Accessed April 15, 2020. https://www.frc.org.uk/getattachment/a39aa822-ae3c-4ddf-b869-db8f2ffe1b61/what-constitutes-an-explanation-under-comply-or-exlpain.pdf2004.

UK Financial Reporting Council. *UK Stewardship Code*. 2012c. Accessed April 15, 2020. https://www.frc.org.uk/getattachment/d67933f9-ca38-4233-b603-3d24b2f62c5f/UK-Stewardship-Code-(September-2012).pdf.

Usherwood, B. *Equity and Excellence in the Public Library: Why Ignorance Is Not Our Heritage*. Aldershot: Ashgate, 2007.

Williams, R. "Faith in the University". In *Values in Higher Education*, edited by S. Robinson and C. Katulushi, 25–37. Leeds: Leeds University Press, 2005.

Part 2: **Practitioner Views and Public Policy**

John Dolan
5 The Dilemmas of Governance

Abstract: An overview of the contemporary public library situation in the UK with a focus on England is provided from a personal perspective based on the experience of someone who is not a researcher but a serendipitous recollector, the ideal audience for a public library. Reflections, opinions and observations on the changing face of public libraries consider developments over time, using the city of Manchester as an example. An unashamedly biased view is presented. Public library strategies adopted in various parts of the world are outlined and common themes identified. The role of volunteers is discussed and the part played by the UK professional library and information association, CILIP, and other peak organizations is explored. CILIP has led a high profile, constructive advocacy campaign for public libraries in the UK. On a positive note, many new libraries and library services around England are flourishing but the key question about who leads England's public libraries is posed.

The chapter was written in 2017 since when changes have further informed this individual take on public library governance. Arts Council England (ACE) has assumed responsibility for national strategy and libraries feature in its ten-year strategy *Let's Create* (https://www.artscouncil.org.uk/letscreate). From 2019 it has taken a more deliberate approach to libraries' development, seeing libraries as rooted in the community, supporting aspirations for the arts to reach diverse and excluded communities; Libraries Connected (https://www.librariesconnected. org.uk/) has become a National Portfolio Organisation (https://www.artscouncil. org.uk/our-investment/national-portfolio-2018-22) receiving direct funding from ACE to create a leadership team with a stronger message and a set of development plans; the conservative government elected in December 2019 with its levelling up policy to counter industrial decline in the regions might have seen libraries as a useful vehicle to deliver that policy.

More broadly, the Covid-19 pandemic of 2020 will have a profound impact. It has exposed new levels of poverty, vulnerability and exclusion in British society; it will have so weakened the economy that public services, other than the NHS, social care and infrastructure, are likely to experience significant further funding reductions for some years with the concomitant options to either invest in community-based and digital library services – the single national portal would have proved invaluable in this crisis for access to information, learning, culture and leisure – or to regard them as secondary to more urgent priorities.

Keywords: Public libraries – Great Britain; Public libraries – England; CILIP; Manchester; Corporate governance; Birmingham

https://doi.org/10.1515/ 9783110533323-008

Where to Start?

Governance is more than structures and regulations. In addition, it refers to leadership, vision, strategy and implementation with observable outcomes and ongoing periodic reiterations. Where does this view come from? Manchester in the 1980s and 90s was a city of growth and aspiration. Always a reforming city, the prevailing culture was one of experiment. Innovation was not the overworked word it has become but there was a liberating culture that permitted trial and error. Politicians were forceful but out in the community the librarian was distant, in all but principle, from the machinations of the local authority, although alert to engaging councillors and members of parliament in the activities and events of an increasingly dynamic library service.

With funds for inner-city regeneration, many libraries were built or refurbished; Manchester librarians were the first to try out community information in inner city areas where the traditional reference library had little relevance for people with low educational attainment, poor housing and inadequate incomes. Community librarianship became the professional name for public library work and the term community library replaced branch library denoting the library that was rooted in the life of the local community. As communities became more diverse, Manchester librarians were among the first in the UK to seek out books in community languages; to provide information, as opposed to textbooks, on personal finance, housing, children, health and education; to work in partnership with the law centre, the Citizens Advice Bureau and the refuge; and to stage multicultural programmes of music and literature. All activities were backed up with more diverse and wide-ranging collections for children, teenagers and adults in the many media and formats available.

Ironically, the technique of presenting community information by subject was already successful in Manchester's Commercial Library where, learning from Malcolm Campbell at London's City Business Library (Humphreys 2013), Lesley Smyth organised the stock around industries, products and markets and not in the given structure of the Dewey system. This gave legitimacy to what some saw as the rebelliousness of new librarians who matured, or not, after the 60s cultural revolution, shaking off the inhibitions of post-war austerity and the restraints of interwar and Victorian life. Similar approaches were adopted in many cities, counties and London boroughs.

The developments took place without the tangible formality of governance although of course the structures and the legal and technical aspects of governance were fully subscribed to. Regulations were followed and due diligence exercised over financial, human and physical resources. However, the driver was a new user-facing culture. Governance is not merely regulation. Governance is leadership, vision, direction, a care for the demands, expectations and needs of audiences, both stated and uncovered by research and an empathy with communities.

The Libraries Taskforce in England (https://www.gov.uk/government/groups/libraries-taskforce) has released toolkits through the Department for Digital, Culture, Media and Sport, formerly Department for Culture, Media and Sport, (DCMS), for planning and governance, working with various levels of government such as the Local Government Association (LGA) (including UK DCMS 2017a, c, d; Local Government Association 2014). However, there is no compunction to use them; and there is no external assessment or validation of the results. They are for self-starters and do not represent governance so much as good practice and, perhaps, risk avoidance.

But It Is Not the Same...

There have been many changes which can be viewed from a variety of perspectives including economic, political and digital perspectives.

Economic Times

Austerity policy is defined by ideology as much as driven by economics. The 2008 financial crisis polarised political movements with corporate capitalists pitted against progressive adherents to the welfare state. Recovery could be gained by public service investment through the creation of jobs and more tax income, or austerity, emphasising cuts, outsourcing, private sector adoption of public service roles and volunteering. Social consequences were attached to any action taken.

Austerity won out and, in western economies, exacerbated the exclusion and disaffection of a disadvantaged working class. The subsequent rise of populism, lurking since WWII in the ranks of right-wing groups meeting in the upper rooms of pubs, normalised on living room screens and social media and in the formation of political parties like the UK Independence Party (UKIP), populist movements in continental Europe, US Republicans and the proclamations of Donald Trump.

While British resentment showed itself in the vote to leave the European Union, government in the UK accelerated the release of public services and property into the ownership of private enterprise or close alternatives. The obligation to organise, manage and deliver public libraries shifted away from the traditional council provider to commissioner, dealing in a market of private companies alongside trusts, mutuals, and volunteer-led charities or not-for-profits. Alternative governance models have not only emerged but are actively encouraged and enabled by government as illustrated by the work of the Libraries Taskforce (UK DCMS 2017b).

Political Times

There is an ongoing shift from democratic power to corporate control with the ensuing tussle between the two sectors as seen in debates about responsibility for aggressive, antisocial behaviour on social media or between states and global digital companies about the root causes of radicalisation and terrorism. The consequences of austerity have led to the bigger or smaller, richer or poorer divides, cuts in public services, outsourcing, privatisation and private finance initiatives, low wages and insecure employment and delivered public expenditure into the profits of the private sector. The consequences have been captured by neoliberals to underpin an argument for populist politics (Shuster 2015).

The public library sits in the middle of this maelstrom of change as a place for communal meeting, an access point to global communications, a provider of freedom of access to information and freedom of expression as outlined in Article 19 of the Universal Declaration of Human Rights if, that is, such declarations survive the onslaught on international cooperation.

Digital Times

The current era is digital. No. It is *the* digital era. Library commentators have moved on from concerns about the impact of change to accepting permanent and continuing exponential change as the norm. Government goes digital by default and digital commerce displaces conventional retail, which shifts to the shopping experience. The nineteenth century drive to educate people for production and selling is finally superseded by the recognition of digital skill as essential to ideas, design, education, manufacturing, employment, trading, profit and tax revenues. Society and government may not have wholly acknowledged the underpinning creativity needed to innovate or the necessity of lifelong learning for continuous and irreversible digital change but the need is understood and driven by the self-starter, the entrepreneur and others beyond the education system.

The UK still has a print literacy deficit: "16.4% of adults in England, or 7.1 million people, can be described as having very poor literacy skills" (National Literacy Trust 2017). It is only now being widely acknowledged that there are multiple literacy skills regarded as critical to the total literacy needed for a successfully functioning society including the interrelated skills of reading and writing, numeracy, oracy and the ability to seek, find, interpret and evaluate information in order to uncover the fake, to design, to create and to produce.

Yet it is more than that. In the House of Lords, Martha Lane-Fox's still remarkable speech warned of the need not only for digital skills but for digital understanding:

> But we also need to move beyond skills to understanding. Nearly all UK internet users have the digital skills to use a search engine, but only half know how to distinguish between search results and adverts. Around two-thirds of our digitally skilled population can shop and bank online – but a third don't make any checks before entering their personal or financial information online ... Becoming a nation of people with digital understanding will be different and more complicated than becoming a nation of people with digital skills ... in a world where we spend more time online than we do asleep and where everything from our televisions to our kettles can connect to the internet, digital is something we are. Understanding is not a race to be run and won. It is a lifelong process of learning, one unique to each of us (Lane-Fox 2018).

Internet use and social media participation continue to rise; the preference for mobile devices over personal computers and laptops grows and will grow further. Understanding, however, remains a challenge among lower social economic groups, certain age groups and the vulnerable who lack experience and may be fearful as shown in a study from the Carnegie UK Trust (Wilson and Grant 2017). With demographic shift and upcoming generations, digital use will grow, accompanied by further innovation and a wider range of uses of digital technologies and content (Ofcom 2016).

Meanwhile, the UK government sought to introduce a communications bill which became known as the Snoopers' Charter which would initiate new controls to monitor and/or restrict access to free expression on the web, controlling what people say, lead, cause and organise. The ideal of Internet freedom becomes the digital equivalent of the tussle between state control and liberal society. The overriding case is characterised by the war on terror and its many interpretations by different regimes which serve governments as the reason to take control of Internet communications and rein in the global technology industry to assist. The progressives' fear of the all-powerful Orwellian state is illustrated in the potential of artificial intelligence that can read minds and motives, for example assessing sexual orientation from facial images (Yang and Kosinski 2017; Levin 2017), allowing governments to digitally invade personal space.

Legally, understanding and dealing with such governmental phenomena will surely be beyond the capability of most citizens. Will the public library, or the academic or any other library for that matter, be permitted and enabled to perform the role of helping citizens understand and cope with such intrusions?

Governance or Leadership?

In the context of public libraries in England, governance is undertaken through the legislative requirements, policies and operational work of local government sanctioned by national government. In an ostensibly anomalous combination, the Department for Communities and Local Government provides the funding, but policy responsibility is held by DCMS. Significantly, DCMS is responsible for the British Library, including funding, the Arts Council England (ACE) and for policy and supervision of the performance of public libraries in England. ACE is also the development agency for public libraries in England. The responsibilities are devolved for Scotland, Wales and Northern Ireland.

The Labour government in 2001 introduced the Public Library Service Standards (PLSS) and the Annual Library Plan required of each local authority. The annual plan had to be passed for approval by full council. In many instances, it led to public debate that required of councillors an understanding of libraries and library services, the needs of communities, local and national development strategies and the observation of performance information. The outcomes of the PLSS were recorded, submitted and assessed; marks were eagerly awaited; and success was promoted across council and in the media. The use of the PLSS is the closest that government in England has come to clear and firm governance of the aims, planning, quality and performance monitoring of library authorities and constitutes the most direct and stringent approach taken to the governance of library services. Variations are maintained in the other UK jurisdictions.

The Library is a Growing Organism: Nineteenth to Twenty-first Century Shifts in Library Culture

Commentators revisit Ranganthan's reassuringly eternal vision to fit today's library (Connaway and Faniel 2014). Ranganthan wrote the what; everything since has been about the how. From a personal perspective, the most aggressive determining driver is technological change. It impacts irreversibly on politics, the economy, employment, communications, research and innovation, education and learning and public service delivery. In all areas there is a role for libraries.

A library is not a standalone service but intrinsic to and connected with other aspects of family and community life and economic activity.

From the nineteenth and early twentieth centuries, public libraries were places of resource, originally legislated for in support of education and a populace skilled for the industry and economy of the day. However, access to resources was heavily controlled; protecting the collection was as much a priority as accessibility. By the late twentieth century, the focus had shifted to dissemination, focussed on book lending and using librarian expertise to help find answers to complex questions from unaffordable reference sources. Reading per se was encouraged as an aspirational activity that would both civilise and equip citizens for employment. Many working-class people embraced the library; their immediate successors, alive today, recall in warm wonder their childhood library experiences.

Library performance was measured in the number of books borrowed and the number of enquiries taken. By the twenty-first century, communication had become fluid and fleeting on the Internet. Education could be remote, taken up in any place and on the move. Rapid change today requires lifelong learning to be the norm. Experts and educators compete with common knowledge and the opinions and learning of enthusiasts on *Wikipedia* and social media, discovered by search engines like Google. The once-maligned tweet, of itself minimal, instantly disseminates links to news, reports and research and has become the preferred tool of political and religious leaders, commentators, activists and trolls. Print and broadcast media have moved from the 24-hour timeframe to the live web and podcast, ideal for everything from election results to sport.

The concept of making adds another layer to learning. The appetite for shared experience and co-creation is manifest in new expectations of libraries. The public library could join other knowledge institutions acting as agents for knowledge dissemination and evaluation. The magnitude of web content offers public libraries a new opportunity to help people engage and evade alienation. There is a widespread need to find, analyse, evaluate and exploit knowledge among populations without direct access and, more importantly, without the information and knowledge management skills to benefit from the web. Libraries help people avoid the fake and exploit the valid.

Martha Lane-Fox's speech referenced institutions and initiatives and "other pioneers making digital understanding a reality":

> I call on government to support and amplify the good things that are happening and to bring these people together in a more structured way. How about we create a network of public organisations that can more tangibly build our nation's digital understanding – much of their work is admirable but it is coordination and focus which will embed digital understanding in the fabric of our lives. Perhaps too this network could have a more formal role as a resource for elected and public officials needing support (Lane-Fox 2017).

Lane-Fox did not mention libraries even though they should be making digital understanding central to their mission just as reading skills drove the nineteenth century model, followed by creative reading in the late twentieth century. A government exercising good and deliberate leadership, governance, over libraries might step forward with "Here's one I prepared earlier!" At this time, however, in England, the governance of public libraries has become passive and reluctant.

> By the mid-2000s, government was already pulling back and eventually, through the Museums Libraries and Archives Council (MLA), cancelled the requirement for an annual plan and disposed of the PLSS ostensibly to reduce the burdens on local authorities. Government withdrew from any such level of governance leaving library authorities to go it alone and library leaders struggling to build a single national message for libraries.

> The Sieghart Review in December 2014 (UK DCMS 2014) led to the formation of the Libraries Taskforce. In turn the publication, after two years, of *Libraries Deliver* (UK DCMS 2016) set the sector on course for an action plan. The initiative avoided, however, becoming a national strategy, placing burdens on local authorities but promoting partnership, development and innovation. In the interim, cuts to local government budgets more than strategic planning determined decisions to close libraries, cut resources, make staff redundant and hollow out services. In Birmingham, at the elaborate Library of Birmingham, opened in 2013 as the biggest public library in Europe, hours were reduced to the least respectable level. Scores of staff were made redundant; book funds cut to nothing; outreach curtailed; web services reduced to the perfunctory; and the city's reputation dented.

However, one of the outputs from the endeavour was a good practice guide for Councillors (UK DCMS 2017c). Section 2 of the toolkit describes alternative delivery models (UK DCMS 2017d) and, in explaining the governance implications of each, legitimised them, effectively guaranteeing national government support for the disaggregation of the governance and management of public libraries. The disaggregation creates limitations if not a barrier to the potential for national direction from Whitehall as different governing bodies will wish to exercise their independence in strategy and direction. It does not remove the duty of the Secretary of State to superintend and promote the improvement of the public library service; it does not prevent library organisations from working within the national family; nor does it oblige them to do so. Sharing the direction of public library provision and subscribing to national programmes and initiatives then become matters of local choice.

While community interests are touched upon in the outline of alternative delivery models, for example, the public service mutual, the implications for the public are not referenced in detail. Community engagement with involvement at decision-making level is implicit in some models but the implication that disparity and inconsistency in levels and quality of service would, as now, continue.

What Is Happening Internationally?

Several countries have published national strategies or action plans for public libraries that include a vision, mission or high-level statement of purpose for libraries. A common aim is to deliver against identified national priorities and enable libraries to play a productive part in national prosperity and well-being in cross-government partnership and with other key national or regional agencies. While libraries remain a universal service, most strategies are linked to key national needs and aimed at priority audiences or target groups in the population.

It is notable that some strategies are weighted towards the user and the community, as in Ireland's *Opportunities for All* (Ireland. Department of the Environment, Community and Local Government 2013). Others are about the library service and how it will change, as in England's *Libraries Deliver: Ambition for Public Libraries* (UK DCMS 2016). The distinction between the two approaches is important in the psychology of creating a successful strategy. Examples of national strategies are provided for the United Kingdom, Ireland, New Zealand, Denmark, Sweden, Singapore, India and Bangladesh. Recurring themes in the national strategies are then drawn together.

United Kingdom

Policy strategies vary across England, Northern Ireland, Scotland and Wales.

England

Libraries Deliver: Ambition for Public Libraries in England 2016–2021 (https://www.gov.uk/government/publications/libraries-deliver-ambition-for-public-libraries-in-england-2016-to-2021) sets out a focus for joint action and a combination of aspirations for libraries, highlighting purposive themes.

Northern Ireland

Libraries NI Corporate Plan 2016–2020 (https://www.librariesni.org.uk/AboutUs/OurOrg/Business%20Plans/Libraries%20NI%20Corporate%20Plan%20 2016%2020%20and%20Business%20Plan%202016%2017%20approved%20 by%20DfC%20July%202016.pdf) represents a comprehensive and efficient forward plan that is in all but name a strategy for the whole province delivering a single province-wide library service since 2008.

Scotland

Ambition & Opportunity: A Strategy for Public Libraries in Scotland 2015–2020 (https://scottishlibraries.org/media/1133/ambition-opportunity-scotlands-national-public-library-strategy.pdf) sets out six strategic aims and eighteen recommendations to deliver the aims. Each aim is clearly linked to national outcomes and indicators outlined in the Scottish Government's National Performance Framework (http://www.gov.scot/About/Performance/scotPerforms/pdfNPF).

Wales

Libraries Inspire: The Strategic Development Framework for Welsh Libraries 2012–16 (https://libraries.wales/wp-content/uploads/2016/02/LibrariesInspireE.pdf) is accompanied by several ensuing strategic documents reviewing progress and evaluating impact.

Republic of Ireland

Opportunities for All: The Public Library as a Catalyst for Economic, Social and Cultural Development (https://www.lgma.ie/en/about-us/libraries-development/public-libraries-strategy-2013-2017.pdf) is a five-year plan for public libraries, 2013 to 2017. The plan led to a single nation-wide library management system for over 300 libraries, including a universal membership scheme, national programmes and a growing web presence and digital offer. There is increasing cross-government support to invest in library innovation. A follow-on plan has been made available: *Our Public Libraries 2022: Inspiring, Connecting and Empowering Communities* (https://www.lgma.ie/en/about-us/libraries-development/our-public-libraries-2022.pdf).

New Zealand

Public Libraries of New Zealand: A Strategic Framework 2012 – 2017 (http://www.publiclibraries.org.nz/Portals/150/Resources/NZ_Public_Libraries_Strategic_

Framework.pdf?ver=2015-11-20-202119-673) published jointly by Local Government New Zealand and the Association of Public Library Managers. It is a refresh of the earlier strategy to create a shared understanding of the benefits libraries deliver to communities.

Denmark

The Public Libraries in the Knowledge Society: Summary from the Committee on Public Libraries in the Knowledge (https://slks.dk/fileadmin/publikationer/publikationer_engelske/Reports/The_public_libraries_in_the_knowledge_society._Summary.pdf) has been issued by the Danish Agency for Libraries and Media from a Committee appointed by the Ministry of Culture to focus on the continuous development of public libraries in Denmark. There is a political initiative to promote a revision of the Danish library act. A national discussion on the future of public libraries resulted in a new library strategy. Work continues on policy developments (https://english.kum.dk/policy-areas/libraries/).

Sweden

A national strategy published in September 2017 is accompanied by a government grant for libraries through the Swedish Arts Council of SEK 250 million (23,104,958 euros; 25,475,000US$) over three years to strengthen public libraries and increase accessibility. It emphasizes the crucial role of libraries in ensuring that children and adults have equal opportunities to become readers.

Singapore

The National Library Board within the Ministry of Communications and Information clearly articulates the role, functions and future activities of public libraries in Singapore (https://www.mci.gov.sg/portfolios/libraries/overview). As a website rather than a published document, the approach is novel and flexible as one can discover content under all manner of headings. In strikingly plain language it moves easily between strategic objectives and programmes. Unlike other national strategies there is little preamble about the reasons for or justification of the programme. It is a given to work in this way.

India

The Indian Public Library Movement (IPLM) (Basu 2016) "seeks to transform Indian Public Libraries into information and knowledge centres to address the community needs". The IPLM was the supported by the Global Libraries initiative of the Bill and Melinda Gates Foundation and hosted by the NASSCOM Foundation. Key objectives include:

- Repositioning public libraries re-emphasising their role as information and knowledge catalysts
- Addressing emerging knowledge and information needs of the community through relevant technologies and innovative content and services
- Capacity building of staff
- Policy advocacy, state and local level workshops to improve their functioning and finances; advocacy for integrating public libraries with appropriate mission mode programmes of the Government of India.

Bangladesh

Linked to the Bangladesh government's Access to Information strategy, *Libraries Unlimited* (British Council Bangladesh 2016), co-funded by the government and the Bill and Melinda Gates Foundation, aims to make libraries and library services fit for the twenty-first century needs of a modern society with a focus on women, young people not in education, employment or training and micro entrepreneurs.

Recurring Themes in National Strategies

Many common themes emerge from the national strategies. They focus on either inputs, including buildings and technologies, or outcomes, including information, learning and economic development. Some of the themes are:

- Reading and literacy; children and families; young people not in employment, education or training; and socially excluded communities
- The place of the library in or at the heart of the community; sense of identity and place
- Digital technologies; change and unfamiliar expectations; responding to skills deficits; supported access to online public services; economies of converging access in one familiar venue

- Learning: supplementing formal programmes and continuing education; lifelong learning to adapt to changing expectations of employment
- Information and access to public services: collocation of service delivery; economies of scale; the library as an accessible venue for essential but unattractive services
- Culture: places for performance, exhibition and promotion of the arts and creative expression in literature, poetry, theatre, music
- Participation and citizenship: library as a place of meeting, access and the exchange of ideas; libraries as engine rooms of community life
- New library developments: design for better access; modern approaches to learning and study and social space; the case for a new library is commonly economic; the library as a physical identifier which people adopt as an emblem of community or municipal image and local pride.

In the Scandinavian models, more is achieved through participation with the local community given the initiative in planning and design, supported by a skilled, networked and proactive library leader.

Who Leads England's Public Libraries?

In contrast to the national strategies in many nations, England has a national taskforce, several publications, blogs and guidelines but lacks a single national story that relates to all public libraries. Many authorities have decimated their services and introduced new structures for governance and management, leading to a nationwide public library service characterised by disaggregation and inconsistency. Library voices comprise campaigners whose mostly justifiable laments relate to lack of direction, cohesion, investment and the refusal of government to intervene when ostensibly serious cuts are announced. The outcries focus mainly on building closures, regrettable in themselves, but sometimes seem to protect the status quo, resisting desirable change. Celebrity author support is welcome though often based on nostalgia "for the library I knew as a child". The highly regarded *Public Libraries News* (http://www.publiclibrariesnews.com/) has moved from a campaigning tool to a valued resource source of both bad and good news, in the UK and overseas.

Volunteers make a valiant effort to maintain library services with success in some areas, for example Warwickshire, but with financial and material support from the relevant library authority. In contrast, an anonymous account published on *Leon's Library Blog*, another valued source of informed opinion, is the agonising tale of a library with a volunteer force of 102 people who seem to create more work, be less productive, bring little innovation and are the source of exhaustion for the remaining staff (Leon's Library Blog 2017). The diaspora of provision militates against a coherent and consistent service nationally.

The LGA contributes to the work of the Libraries Taskforce, yet faces insurmountable challenges in social care for the growing population of vulnerable children and older people. Meanwhile individual library authorities go it alone. Library operations are outsourced to private sector companies and volunteer groups. GLL (https://www.gll.org/b2b), a not-for-profit trust, purposefully moves across the country taking library services under its wing. In Dudley, GLL won the contract in competition against a proposed staff mutual, possibly giving the lie to the philosophy of local choice. Not-for-profit enterprises tell of success in York, Suffolk and Devon, though sometimes still impacted by budget cuts. Library staff are unable to speak publicly. Operational staff are afraid of retribution if they make public criticism of their employer's policy decisions. Service heads share the fear or, more likely, are in politically restricted posts which, by prior and conditional acceptance, prohibit them from criticising council policy.

Councillors, of which there are over 18,000 in England, are unable to plan as one. Party and intra-party differences ensure inconsistency. In August 2016, the Lancashire Labour Council resolved to reduce its static libraries from 73 to 44 and the results have been well publicised in *Public Libraries News* (http://www.pub liclibrariesnews.com/about-public-libraries-news/information/flintshire-to-oldham/lancashire-to-medway). Following representations, the responsible Minister was minded to order an enquiry, a unique instance in recent times of his fulfilling his statutory duty to superintend and ensure compliance with legal requirements. After the 2017 elections, the new conservative-led Council announced it was going to re-open eleven libraries at a cost of £850,000 (Finch 2017). How the council reached and funded the policy is not clear, except to demonstrate that national government cuts need not always harm local services. Decline is not always the direct result of budget cuts. Rather, insight into how councils choose to spend available funds in the face of multiple needs and demands which it has to meet, can be the outcome.

In the 1990s, Birmingham City Council began an experiment with localism. By the early 2000s, community-based services transferred into the control of local councillors in the city's dozen electoral constituencies; each constituency had two or three wards each with three councillors; in each constituency there would be between two and four community libraries. Some held the view that professionals, in all services, put their profession first above the community and local choice. This was to change. Library and other services' budgets were disaggregated by geography and reassembled as a pooled constituency budget, with some exceptions such as the library management system. Shortly after, the financial crisis of 2008 led to huge austerity cuts by the new Government of 2010. The locally devolved budgets were reduced to even less effective levels, especially book funds. There ceased to be any citywide plan or strategy for libraries. Local decision-making, intended to enable local choice, was made by councillors and generic managers. Needs analysis might have translated into library provision where low education attainment, lifelong learning, poverty, wellbeing, and demographic characteristics such as children/families; older people, and BAME[1] communities, would inform localised policy. However, many in control saw libraries in terms of traditional transactional services and were not open to library developments and innovations evolving elsewhere.

Library Managers, formerly Community Librarians, detached from a library structure and thereby from national networks were reduced in number and had little power; whatever advocacy skills they had were stretched. Most library-specific training ceased; staff might be interchangeable between services; libraries would house other services while many buildings declined without an adequate maintenance budget. Good quality service emerged sporadically at local level, when driven by the commitment of library managers and staff who understood need and potential but who lacked the resources of a corporate lead organisation. The combination of fragmentation and budget cuts makes it impossible to discern any tangible cohesion in the direction of the city's library service. This illustrates how the absence of a vision and continuous and consistent planning creates a perfunctory service and inhibits innovation and change. This version of localism might deliver success on paper but permits service delivery failure. Ironically, the approach to local choice provided neither library strategy nor local ownership. Legally, the City Council, as the Library authority, is the accountable body but, in the absence of a discernible plan, becomes in governance terms, unaccountable to any national oversight.

In some instances, councils have been challenged on proposed cuts and closures. The subsequent judicial reviews have not necessarily focused on what constitutes the requirements of the 1964 legislation. Judicial reviews rejecting proposals more frequently resulted from a technical failure like inadequate consultation or failure to take account of needs (Anstice 2014). Such shortcomings in the technicalities of governance have not taken into account the social, economic and technological changes that place new expectations on libraries, or point them in a new direction. This aspect of governance rarely arises when judgement is made of the library performance of local authorities.

---

1 UK demographic for Black, Asian and Minority Ethnic.

In contrast, many new libraries and library services around England are flourishing. Among many others, there are high quality new and refurbished libraries in Hemel Hempstead and Watford, Hertfordshire, with makerspaces no less, Southam, Alcester and Stratford, Warwickshire. New libraries in London include Southwark, Camden, Barking and Dagenham. Significantly the new libraries have good events programmes, partnerships and outreach activities. In Manchester, the refurbished Central Library is now both beautiful and vibrant; some local libraries are managed within the Council network while others are remodelled, for example, as a Library, Activity and Information Hub in Burnage, run by volunteers who formed a registered charity or as partners in an outsourced leisure complex; the Arcadia Centre in Levenshulme is a GLL operation. In the wonderful Chester Storyhouse the library is fully integrated in a tremendous new development with theatre, cinema and social spaces.

The Profession Takes the Lead

The inconsistency suggests that the growth and development of public libraries in England will not be the future legacy of national government or local authorities. Instead the profession is taking the lead. The Society of Chief Librarians (SCL) in 2017 was awarded Non-Profit Organization (NPO) status by Arts Council England. With substantial funding for four years, this one-time affiliation of service heads has become a national agency and appointed officers to lead it as a future body of resource as well as influence. SCL has rebadged itself as Libraries Connected (https://www.librariesconnected.org.uk/).

SCL developed Universal Offers (https://www.librariesconnected.org.uk/page/universal-library-offers), a single, clear and shared iteration of what libraries do and what users and communities most respond to. The offers set out the core business around Reading, Information, Digital, Health and Learning plus the Children's Promise and the Six Steps for Blind and Partially Sighted people. The offers are not static and develop over time. SCL launched the Cultural Offer, in October 2017, cementing the relationship with the arts but also reaffirming SCL's role as a national agency for the vision and strategic direction of public libraries in England.

2030 is the horizon for the investigation into the future skills needed in the public library sector. CILIP and SCL/Libraries Connected together will build on the first stages of the Public Library Skills Strategy (CILIP 2017) with funding from ACE. The first iteration of the strategy set out the headline skills needed. Leadership skills at every level are acknowledged as essential which has implications for recruitment and retention as a large portion of the workforce will have retired early in the planning period. The wider library, archives, records, information and knowledge management domains have an ageing pool of workers, with 45% of the workforce due to retire by 2030 (CILIP 2017, 4). Leadership in the community is only mentioned by implication in the skills strategy, yet in the age of predominantly digital communications, public engagement will be key to information sharing, learning and co-creation.

The skills required will have to be developed. The recent stripping away of funds for staff training implies a different approach with library workers themselves learning remotely, online and through sharing and co-creation, moreover doing so on a continuous basis. The 'necessity for self-leadership will be accounted for in any programme taking workforce development into the digital era. The old episodic approach of intermittent workshops and online resources will be insufficient.

Libraries excel at local initiatives linking newly discovered needs to new approaches and potentially longer-term service realignment. The longstanding CILIP *Libraries Change Lives Award* (https://www.cilip.org.uk/page/Libraries ChangeLiv) is a national award for excellence and innovation in UK libraries. It is organised by CILIP and the Community, Diversity and Equality Group. Projects and programmes work with groups in excluded and disadvantaged communities on innovative approaches to learning, communications and community activity. In December 2016, DCMS and the Libraries Taskforce launched Libraries Opportunities for Everyone, a four-million-pound fund to support projects that develop innovative library service activity again aimed at excluded and disadvantaged groups (https://www.artscouncil.org.uk/funding/libraries-opportunities-everyone-innovation-fund). Projects include digital skills development or use digital innovation for better health and wellbeing, learning and creativity.

With Engaging Libraries funding from Carnegie UK Trust and the Wellcome Foundation, libraries help communities explore major health and well-being issues including stress, obesity, body image and even death in new ways. Activities include the development of graphic novels; teddy bear picnics; theatre performances; vlogs and podcasts; and a travelling happiness bar that will visit local communities delivering a series of pop up events (Carnegie Trust UK 2017). Such programmes target small numbers in excluded and disadvantaged groups. They might have a short-term impact but deep effect on the participants. They do not represent a strategy except for that of the funding body. Libraries seek such project funding when their own financial capacity to experiment is removed or reduced. The programmes are sporadic and short term and rarely replicated in other places. Funders will very likely research and promote the outcomes, seek to embed the findings with normal library practice and promote them as advocacy for the social and economic value of public libraries. As projects grow in number, momentum and visibility, their cumulative effect may help change the image of libraries, demonstrate impact and value and evolve the internal culture. Such programmes combine a national focus with local relevance in ways that ought to be transferable.

Core investment in digital resources has been static for some years; library web content is rarely dynamic; some library authorities still restrict staff use of social media in fear of damaging the Council's reputation; filtering policies and acceptable use policies are frequently determined outside of the library management structure (Spaicey and Cooke 2014); in 2015 it took special DCMS funds to install Wi-Fi in those libraries yet to catch up with obvious expectations (UK Department for Digital, Culture, Media & Sport 2015).

Library websites offer access to services but these are largely transactional emphasising use of the catalogue, stock holdings, reservations and what's on. Dynamic, interactive content or topical information and news rarely feature, or are the output of specific projects. A single digital platform (SDP) for public libraries has long been an aspiration with a single public-facing presence on the web. Detail is yet to come but a platform for creativity and collaboration is being researched. A round table was hosted by Carnegie UK Trust and ACE at which the vision was formed and a report produced including comments on governance:

> Governance. Developing and maintaining a SDP would be a considerable undertaking and ensuring its continued success and viability requires accountability, transparency, monitoring, responsiveness and broad-based participation. We have explored two potential models for governance. The first is SDP as government owned and led – as a large state intervention. The second is governance by an independent or arms-length body. (The British Library and BBC being examples of national services one step removed from Government.) There is a third possible option: a SDP could provide an opportunity to develop a different governance model from either government or arm's length body. In this scenario a SDP provides the opportunity to redefine the relationship between state and service. (Peachey and Ashley 2017)

The British Library undertook an 18-month scoping project to establish the demand for and possible shape of a single digital presence for UK public libraries (https://www.bl.uk/press-releases/2019/june/new-research-proposes-five-options-for-a-digital-presence-in-public-libraries#). This could be transformational for services but shifts the question of public library governance in England decidedly into the digital arena and another step away from the increasingly dated model envisaged in the 1964 Act.

CILIP has led a high profile, constructive advocacy campaign for public libraries. While very active with the Libraries Taskforce, CILIP also conceived the

My Library by Right campaign (https://www.cilip.org.uk/page/MyLibraryByRight), and re-established the dormant All-Party Parliamentary Group for Libraries (https://www.cilip.org.uk/page/APPGLibraries) campaigned for school libraries, in particular, librarians in schools. The *#Facts Matter* campaign (https://www.cilip.org.uk/page/FactsMatter) reaches all areas of the profession but has particular resonance with public libraries as the citizen's primary supported access point to digital and print information. CILIP is extending its reach to many information workers and knowledge managers who are in the market for a supportive and representative professional body. A new membership regime, strategy, marketing and branding reaches out to potential new members.

The public library agenda remains however as the highest profile politically and so must continue to be prominent in CILIP's work programme. Furthermore, aspects of the information and knowledge management spectrum are part of the public library agenda; what will seem like a change of priorities should be seen as a change in the weighting of priorities. CILIP's wider reach to information and knowledge managers should raise awareness and motivation among public library workers while for other sectors it should be a reminder that information and digital literacy are as fundamental to the whole profession as they are to society. The citizen's right to access information and knowledge is central to democracy. The rise of the populist movement highlights a lack of access to fact, the creation of fake, deliberately misleading news, confusion between propaganda and insight and the inability to create and articulate informed views.

The library as a feature of civic society is often cited for its open and free access to information but the library's role in supporting democratic dialogue and debate does not feature in national, strategic initiatives. Are library and information professionals innately conservative? Without the library performing its democratic role there is no such place in most communities. Public library advocates highlight the reach of libraries into disadvantaged communities. Digitally disadvantaged describes a new excluded community. It is geographically indiscriminate and exists in all areas of society. It is imperative for libraries that they are realigned to lead communities into the digital age. Libraries Connected's Universal Offers, including the Digital Offer, the Skills Strategy and CILIP's campaigns could help set public libraries firmly in the digital age. Without fully grasping the digital opportunity, libraries will not be in the mainstream of social and economic activity and will be out of the sights of politicians and other stakeholders.

Returning to Manchester

Manchester is a city library of striking presence and opportunity, an active web presence, a combination of council-run libraries, partnerships, volunteer-managed and outsourced libraries, proactive outreach and an inclusive diverse programme of inclusion and engagement. Manchester libraries receive significant Council support because the library visibly responds to the Council's policies as a major regional centre and a cluster of distinct communities. A mixed economy informs the future direction of public library provision in England. Without the national strategic approach backed by government seen in countries like Ireland, it will be up to library leaders to define and direct the public libraries network, co-working through the Libraries Connected and CILIP structures with shared values, aims and demonstrable outcomes. Governance as leadership is the governance of the future.

References

Anstice, Ian. "Judicial Re...phew; Editorial". *Public Libraries News*. 2014. Accessed April 15, 2020. http://www.publiclibrariesnews.com/2014/10/judicial-re-phew.html.

Basu, Sreeradha. "NASSCOM Foundation Launches Indian Public Library Movement; Partners with Bill and Melinda Gates Foundation". *The Economic Times*, March 7, 2016. Accessed April 15, 2020. https://economictimes.indiatimes.com/industry/services/education/nasscom-foundation-launches-indian-public-library-movement-partners-with-bill-and-melinda-gates-foundation/articleshow/51288055.cms?from=mdr.

British Council Bangladesh. *Libraries Unlimited: a Nationwide Library Development Project*. 2016. Accessed April 15, 2020. http://www.britishcouncil.org.bd/en/about/press/libraries-unlimiteda-nationwide-library-development-project.

Carnegie UK Trust. "UK Libraries to Engage Public on Major Health Issues". October 11, 2017. Accessed April 15, 2020. https://www.carnegieuktrust.org.uk/news/uk-libraries-engage-public-major-health-issues/ .

CILIP. *Public Libraries Skills Strategy*. London: Society of Chief Librarians (SCL) and the Chartered Institute of Library and Information Professionals (CILIP), 2017. Accessed April 15, 2020. https://cdn.ymaws.com/www.cilip.org.uk/resource/resmgr/cilip_new_website/plss/plss_july_2017_final.pdf.

Connaway, Lynn Silipigni, and Ixchel Faniel. *Reordering Ranganathan: Shifting User Behaviors, Shifting Priorities: an OCLC Research Report*. Dublin, Ohio: OCLC, 2014. Accessed April 15, 2020. http://www.oclc.org/research/publications/library/2014/oclcresearch-reordering-ranganathan-2014-overview.html.

Finch, Fiona. "Bill To Reopen Axed Lancashire Libraries Nears £1m". *Lancashire Post*, September 14, 2017. Accessed April 15, 2020. http://www.lep.co.uk/news/bill-to-reopen-axed-lancashire-libraries-nears-1m-1-8754752.

Humphreys, Garry. "Malcolm Campbell: Pioneer in the Provision of Business Information". Obituaries. *Independent*, April 8, 2013. Accessed April 15, 2020. https://www. independent.co.uk/news/obituaries/malcolm-campbell-pioneer-in-the-provision-of-business-information-8563532.html.

Ireland. Department of the Environment, Community and Local Government. *Opportunities for All: The Public Library as a Catalyst for Economic, Social and Cultural Development, a Strategy for Public Libraries 2013–2017*. Dublin: Department of the Environment, Community and Local Government, 2013. Accessed April 15, 2020. https://www.lgma.ie/ en/about-us/libraries-development/public-libraries-strategy-2013-2017.pdf.

Lane-Fox, Martha. *Digital Understanding*. Posted by Martha Lane-Fox. September 7, 2017. Accessed April 15, 2020. https://marthalanefoxblog.wordpress.com/2017/09/07/digital-understanding/ .

Lane-Fox, Martha. "Full Text of Martha Lane Fox's Speech on Digital Understanding; Speech Given in House of Lords September 7, 2017". *Doteveryone*. April 4, 2018. Accessed April 15, 2020. https://medium.com/@doteveryoneuk/full-text-of-martha-lane-foxs-speech-on-digital-understanding-1163afd19b0f.

Leon's Library Blog. "One Hundred and Two". 2017. Accessed April 15, 2020. https:// leonslibraryblog.com/2017/09/27/one-hundred-and-two/.

Levin, Sam. "New AI can Guess Whether You're Gay or Straight from a Photograph". *The Guardian*, September 8, 2017. Accessed April 15, 2020. https://www.theguardian.com/ technology/2017/sep/07/new-artificial-intelligence-can-tell-whether-youre-gay-or-straight-from-a-photograph.

Local Government Association. *Rethinking Governance: Practical Steps for Councils Considering Changes to their Governance Arrangements*. London: Local Government Association and Centre for Public Scrutiny, 2014. Accessed April 15, 2020. http://www.cfps.org.uk/ wp-content/uploads/Rethinking-Governance.pdf.

National Literacy Trust. *Adult Literacy: Information on Adult Literacy in the UK and Our Books Unlocked Programme*. 2017. Accessed April 15, 2020. https://literacytrust.org.uk/parents-and-families/adult-literacy/.

Ofcom. *Adults' Media Use and Attitudes*. 2016. Accessed April 15, 2020. https://www.ofcom. org.uk/__data/assets/pdf_file/0026/80828/2016-adults-media-use-and-attitudes.pdf.

Peachey, Jenny, and Brian Ashley. *Building a Single Digital Presence for Public Libraries*. Dunfermline: Carnegie Trust UK, 2017. Accessed April 15, 2020. https://www. carnegieuktrust.org.uk/publications/building-single-digital-presence-public-libraries/.

Shuster, Simon. "The Populists" *Time*. 2015. Accessed April 15, 2020. http://time.com/ time-person-of-the-year-populism/.

Spacey, Rachel and Louise Cooke, with Adrienne Muir and Claire Creaser. *Managing Access to the Internet in Public Libraries [MAIPLE}*. Loughborough: Arts and Humanities Research Council and Loughborough University, 2014. Accessed April 15, 2020. https://www.lboro. ac.uk/microsites/infosci/lisu/maiple/downloads/maiple-report.pdf.

UK Department for Culture, Media and Sport (DCMS). *Independent Library Report for England*. Presented by William Sieghart and an expert panel. 2014. Accessed April 15, 2020. https:// www.gov.uk/government/publications/independent-library-report-for-england.

UK Department for Digital, Culture, Media and Sport (DCMS). "Libraries Taskforce Secures Further Funding to Roll out Free Wifi in Public Libraries across England." *Gov.UK News*. 2015. Accessed April 15, 2020. https://www.gov.uk/government/news/libraries-taskforce-secures-further-funding-to-roll-out-free-wifi-in-public-libraries-across-england.

UK Department for Digital, Culture, Media and Sport (DCMS). *Libraries Deliver: Ambition for Public Libraries in England 2016 to 2021; Corporate Report.* 2016. Accessed April 15, 2020. https://www.gov.uk/government/publications/libraries-deliver-ambition-for-public-libraries-in-england-2016-to-2021.

UK Department for Digital, Culture, Media and Sport (DCMS). *Strategic Planning of Library Services: Longer-term, Evidence-based Sustainable Planning Toolkit.* 2017a. Accessed April 15, 2020. https://www.gov.uk/government/publications/longer-term-evidence-based-sustainable-planning-toolkit/longer-term-evidence-based-sustainable-planning-toolkit.

UK Department for Digital, Culture, Media and Sport (DCMS). "Community managed libraries research – what we'll do next". *DCMS Libraries blog.* 2017b. Accessed April 15, 2020. https://dcmslibraries.blog.gov.uk/2017/09/05/community-managed-libraries-research-what-well-do-next/.

UK Department for Digital, Culture, Media and Sport (DCMS). *Libraries Shaping the Future: Good Practice Toolkit.* 2017c. Accessed April 15, 2020. https://www.gov.uk/government/publications/libraries-shaping-the-future-good-practice-toolkit/libraries-shaping-the-future-good-practice-toolkit.

UK Department for Digital, Culture, Media and Sport (DCMS). *Alternative Delivery Models Explained.* 2017d. Accessed April 15, 2020. https://www.gov.uk/government/publications/libraries-alternative-delivery-models-toolkit/alternative-delivery-models-explained.

Wang, Yilun, and Michal Kosinski. "Deep Neural Networks Are More Accurate than Humans at Detecting Sexual Orientation from Facial Images." Open Science Framework. October 23, 2018. Accessed April 15, 2020. https://osf.io/zn79k/.

Wilson, Gina, and Anna Grant. *#Not Without Me: a Digital World for All? Findings from a Programme of Digital Inclusion for Vulnerable Young People Across the UK.* Carnegie Trust UK Publications, 2017. Accessed April 15, 2020. https://www.carnegieuktrust.org.uk/publications/digitalworld/.

Jenny Bossaller and Jenna Kammer

6 The Power of Public Space: Equal Access in an Era of Fear and Austerity

Abstract: The wicked problem tackled in this chapter is the dissonance between neoliberal conceptions of public space and the ideology of the common good, especially in relation to public libraries. It is posited that public libraries are built to foster community health and that they are built around the notion of empathetic development. However, the very notion of a public library marks the wicked problem at the heart of this chapter. Public space itself is contested. A case study on public libraries and public spending in the US focuses on the *America First* budget blueprint of the Trump administration and was purposefully selected because of the strong reactions from both the library community and the media to proposed cuts. An analysis of media reports identified frames for understanding reactions and suggested ways forward in ensuring that public space remains public and that leaders operate with empathy. A way forward is suggested, emphasizing the involvement of stakeholders, telling stories to demonstrate value, embedding the library in the city, and adopting lean techniques to identify inefficiencies and improved uses of technology.

Keywords: Public interest; Public spaces; Neoliberalism; Public libraries – United States; Trump, Donald – Administration

Introduction

"All power... can be understood in terms of space. Physical places, as well as economies, conversations, politics – all can be conceived of as areas unequally occupied. A map of these territories would constitute a map of power and status: who has more, who has less." (Solnit 2017). The editors of the book propose that libraries are facing wicked problems, problems that are so intertwined in the social, economic, and cultural fabric of society that they are unsolvable.

Wicked problems cannot be solved through strategic planning and data-gathering. A wicked problem "has innumerable causes, is tough to describe, and doesn't have a right answer" (Camillus 2008). Camillus lists ten properties of wicked problems which were originally described by Rittel and Webber (1973). Several apply to the situation libraries and other public services face in today's political culture:

- There is no definitive formulation of a wicked problem
- Wicked problems have no stopping rule

https://doi.org/10.1515/ 9783110533323-009

- Solutions to wicked problems are not true or false, but good or bad
- There is no immediate and no ultimate test of a solution to a wicked problem
- Every solution to a wicked problem is a one-shot operation because there is no opportunity to try to learn by trial and error; every attempt counts significantly
- Wicked problems do not have an exhaustively describable set of potential solutions, nor is there a well-described set of permissible operations that may be incorporated into the plan
- Every wicked problem is essentially unique
- Every wicked problem can be considered to be a symptom of another problem
- The existence of a discrepancy representing a wicked problem can be explained in numerous ways
- The planner has no right to be wrong.

Camillus looks at the uncertain futures of businesses, focusing on Wal-Mart as a case study. A business has many stakeholders; there is discord among the stakeholders; intense competition is faced; and solutions to problems, for example using cheap labor to keep outlays low, often come with unacceptable costs. Technologies, such as Amazon's Fulfillment Technologies (Amazon 2015), have changed business practices and physical stores like Wal-Mart are suffering.

Public libraries do not share a great deal with Wal-Mart in spirit, but Camillus' solutions, especially the use of lean management techniques, are applicable and even proven in the library context (Huber and Potter 2015). Libraries face wicked problems and the main one is that they are public and supported by the people for the people. Public support is however the library's biggest asset. Public funding and public space have been under attack for years. Current economic and political trends strongly favor private development. Libraries are founded on a belief in the common good. They rely on public funding because they are beholden to the public. This is key. Stopgap measures for financial solvency must avoid private influence. Locating and eliminating inefficiencies in internal processes can provide more freedom to meet the library's mission (Huber and Potter 2015).

Background

The wicked problem tackled here is dissonance between neoliberal conceptions of public space and the ideology of the common good, especially in relation to public libraries. The primary focus in considering space is on the physical space of the library: its footprint on the city or town, its meeting rooms and the floor space occupied by books and computers. Also under discussion is what happens within the library, the ideas that are exchanged and cultivated and the websites that are developed to support what goes on in the library. One of biggest assets of the library is that it is public. It is a space reserved for community use and is one of the few spaces still truly public. Dissonance about spatial allocation, though, is demonstrable in rhetoric that states how space is envisioned as a political and social space, for whom it is intended, and how it should be allocated, or who is allowed to occupy space.

Civilized places rely on pooling of funds collected as taxes to support common goals, such as protection from invaders and safety, sanitation and education. Democracies elect people who decide how to allocate income from taxes. However, the people do not always trust that their taxes are being allocated wisely and a tactic politicians use to be elected is by promising to cut taxes. Politicians say that former administrations were wasteful and that new alternatives can provide more and better, for less. The neoliberal era has brought with it a rhetoric of extreme cost-cutting, especially for social services. One experiment in the United States demonstrates the limits of extreme tax-cutting. The state of Kansas drastically cut taxes under the familiar promise that cutting taxes promotes economic growth. Today, the state is facing financial collapse and legislators have revolted against the governor by passing tax increases and overriding the governor's veto. Legislators have faced the fact that there are certain services, for example schools and roads, that must be funded with taxes or civilization will collapse (Lefler and Lowry 2017). Before the 1980s, conservatives "recognized the principle that public purposes sometimes justified the raising of additional revenue. They might have balked at the specific number the Democrats proposed, but they accepted that taxes were negotiable" (Tomasky 2016).

Librarians, as beneficiaries of taxes, know that their budgets are under intense scrutiny. The idea of a public library is still widely embraced. Campaigning against public libraries would generally be considered barbaric. However, libraries have been closing for years in both the United States and the United Kingdom (Sullivan 2003; McMenemy 2009; Goulding 2013). Library systems are cutting positions (Kelly 2011). Libraries are struggling to communicate their value, even as library use remains steady or is rising (Gutsche 2011).

A rhetorical analysis of the proposed budget of the newly elected US President, Donald Trump, aside from criticism of the proposed budget itself, highlights the dissonance between neoliberalism and supporters of public libraries. The proposed budget all but eliminated funding for libraries and the arts, though cuts to library and arts funding constituted only the tip of the iceberg. The language used in the discussion around the budget demonstrated very different views of the relationships between public spending, people, space and governance. Publicly supported entities such as schools and libraries are grounded in a belief that public policy should support human potential and growth as much as growth of capital. Supporters ultimately face a rhetorical roadblock because the world views represented by the two sides are simply so different.

This chapter is predicated on the belief that librarians need to be careful to preserve and promote the library as a public space. Public space itself is a gift to the people, writ large. It is an offer, asks for nothing in return and is equally available to the rich and the poor. Libraries are designed spaces built to nurture interactions of people with books and ideas, to foster the exchange of ideas with other people in meetings and forums and to build a sense of community. Public libraries are built to foster community health and they are built around the notion of empathetic development. Book discussions and reading, for instance, increase interactions between dissimilar people and the world of ideas, which can lead to empathetic growth and healthier communities. Unfortunately, the social and psychological effects of literature are much harder to measure than capital growth. Librarians should be prepared to present efforts that will appeal to the public and to lawmakers to maintain their support.

The public good, empathy and empathetic spaces, and the role of government in relation to public space provide a framework for analysis. We focus on public libraries as a public good that supports personal, prosocial and community development and empathetic growth. While libraries have often framed their worth in terms of access to books and the Internet, discussed below because it is a debated point in public funding, many critics have countered that information is much more easily obtainable because of the Internet. What the Internet fails to provide is space for real-life encounters with people who are unlike oneself. The Internet is worse at bridging social divides than it is at reinforcing existing divisions (Pariser 2011). The space in libraries and other cultural centers can be used to break down the divides. It is argued that bridging cultures contributes to empathetic growth, but requires space and funding. Some of the activities that support empathetic growth and connection are:

- Supporting reading groups and reading, especially fiction (Djikic, Oatley, and Moldoveau 2013)
- Encouraging shared community vision and civic action (Goulding 2008)
- Providing space and opportunities for cross-cultural interactions (Smallwood and Becnel 2013)
- Offering comfortable space for the poor and/or socially excluded (Muddiman et al. 2001; McCook and Phenix 2007)
- Delivering support for design work and engineering in makerspaces and coding camps (Hamilton 2012)

– Sponsoring human library events, in which a person, often someone with a stigma, for example a person who is obese, deaf or of a particular religion or culture, is checked out so that s/he can share her/his story with others (Stewart and Richardson 2011)

The current situation in the United States is described but much literature is drawn from the United Kingdom. Public libraries around the world will be able to see reflections of their own nation's shortcomings in terms of support for the public good.

Public Good and Public Space

A public good, or common good, can be defined as something that is equally beneficial for the entire populace. When more people use a common good it is not diminished; the populace is enhanced. Waste removal and public health are practical examples. Everyone benefits from clean streets, sanitation and reduced communicable disease rates. Another example might be city parks, which are spaces that are set aside so that everyone who lives in or visits the city, regardless of age, social status, or ability to pay, can visit and enjoy the benefits of being outdoors and experiencing nature. The common good is non-competitive. Places like public libraries and public parks are spaces that are not owned by individuals or corporations and people are free to do whatever they want within the boundaries of acceptable behavior. People can gather together or be alone and as long as they do not infringe on others' rights, they can act as they please.

One of the hallmarks of a democratic government in a civilized nation is the appropriate allocation of funding to ensure that everyone has decent living conditions and access to life's necessities, for example affordable housing and education. There are some things that government supports because they hold little market value or because corruption would be fatal. The Federal Drug Administration (FDA) and the military, for instance, work best with governmental oversight because corporate investors do not provide the same level of oversight for the public's good. Corporations are beholden to shareholders' profits and Barley (2007, 201) warns about a shift from a representative democracy to corporate society as it "has placed representative democracy as outlined in the Constitution of the United States in jeopardy". He claims that the founders of the US wanted to exclude corporate monopolies from interfering with governance, which is why the founders enumerated the rights of citizens in the Bill of Rights. A government founded in the public good rigorously preserves the priority of public interest, while the corporate state ensures that businesses will not be impeded from making a profit. Public good is not the prime focus of the corporation and little empathy is felt for people who are unable to compete. A bone might be thrown to the poor to keep them quiet, but no share of the pie is offered.

The shift away from public funding for service provision encompasses a wide array of tactics, such as deregulation of utilities and gentrification. Low and Smith (2006) list ways that privatization has occurred in cities with "closing, redesign, and policing of public parks and plazas and the development of business improvement districts", with the disposal of air rights "for the building of corporate plazas ostensibly open to the public" (82) and with suburban activities extending private commercial developments and gated communities. Conversions of public space to private space happen with the blessing of local government through rules and rezoning, often under the guise of improved safety or economic development. Private developers might be granted permits to charge higher sales taxes in order to develop the land in so-called Transportation Development Districts or promise to let the public use the land in exchange for developing the land, or for tax reductions. Trump Tower in New York is a prime example of a Privately Owned Public Space (POPS). Rosenberger (2016) explains: "the atrium of Trump Tower is what's called a privately-owned public space, the product of an agreement in which a developer receives special permissions from the city in exchange for the inclusion and upkeep of spaces open to the general public." Unfortunately, such deals often result in reduced access to the spaces by the general public with "denial of access, the takeover of public spaces by private ones such as the sales counters, the removal of some of the tables, chairs, or other amenities, occurs sadly in too many POPS" (Rosenberger 2016). Such deals made between public entities and private companies limit public space. Who is allowed to use the space and under what terms? Who holds the power, the people or the corporation?

The placemaking movement offers an alternative vision for allocating and nurturing public space. Erin Toolis (2017) said that privatization is a social problem that contributes to the entrenchment of social, economic, and racial inequality. She presents a theory of critical placemaking that builds more inclusive, participatory, and democratic communities and explains that "the role of public places in shaping life chances and the ability to be an active member of society cannot be understated" (185). Placemaking "refers to a collaborative process by which we can shape our public realm in order to maximize shared value." (Project for Public Spaces, 2009). Placemaking is essentially the opposite of gentrification and gives all citizens a chance to shape their community, rather than giving the power to private and often non-local development corporations. Placemaking helps communities envision better civic spaces and mixed-use development that nurtures small and local businesses. Civic spaces, including public libraries, are anchors of community placemaking. As Eric Stackhouse said, "librarians have to think about our spaces differently. Before we managed book collections, and today we're doing much more management of community spaces" (Nikitin and Jackson 2009).

Public libraries were born from a belief in the public good, as "a means to provide people with access to the cultural record and to provide the resources to support an enlightened population for participation in the democratic process" (McCook 2006 ix). Cities began to create public libraries when citizens realized that it was better to pool their money to give everyone, both rich and poor, access to reading materials. They recognized that libraries benefit society as a whole because when more people are educated, society is improved. Consider that the United States Constitution says that all men are created equal. Over the years, this phrase has been interpreted differently; for instance, the pre-civil war slave states said that slaves were three fifths of a person and women were not included in the concept of all men. Regardless, all can agree that today people are not born into equal opportunity. Some legislation and safety net programs, admittedly contested, are designed to help socially or economically disadvantaged people. Libraries can bridge the gap between people who were born or have fallen into a disadvantaged state. Libraries are equalizers.

Public libraries present a problem to conservatives because they are associated with disadvantaged people and represent a kind of redistributive power. Today's conservatives are often described as neoliberal. In its purest form, neoliberal economic thinking encourages greater efficiencies and progress. However, it has become more of a "rhetorical support for privatization and deregulation that favored business, because the [economy is] not by any stretch of the imagination a free or competitive market" (D'Angelo 2006, 62). Conservatives object to collective goods, or "state commitments to egalitarianism and interventions in the economy (income redistributions, social inclusion and justice)" because they might act as a disincentive to work (Buschman 2016, 5). Libraries help people find help, for free, rather than as a paid service. Many libraries partner with social agencies, such as the AARP (https://www.aarp.org/), for free tax help and for help navigating the Affordable Care Act (Bossaller 2016). If one is more sympathetic or responsive to business outcomes than to equality, free services are problematic because they occupy space where profit could be made and constitute part of the wicked problem. Appeals to empathy can serve as an antidote to a neoliberal ideology and described below is some of the research on empathy that might guide such appeals.

Empathy and Empathetic Space

Empathy can be defined as one's ability to identify with another's situation (Preece and Ghozati 2001). There is some debate about whether empathy can be learned, or if it is simply a natural response. Zanetti (2011) explains that maybe it is not simple. Perhaps empathy is cultivated. Humans tend to empathize with people like themselves: "empathy for those we perceive as unlike ourselves must be actively cultivated and sustained" (Zanettie 2011, 79). In some cases empathy comes naturally. In other cases, experiences need to be created so that empathy can be cultivated within a society. For example, seeing how others live, or interacting with people outside of one's normal social circles, can help one see inequalities.

Segal (2011) describes this as social empathy, which is a combination of empathy and social responsibility. Social empathy occurs when one gains an understanding of the social and economic contexts of oppression. It can provide a "framework for more effective social policies that address disparities and support social and economic justice for all people" (266). The framework provides a means to envision just living conditions for minorities. The "effective way to change structural inequalities and disparities is to provide people with opportunities to gain deep contextual knowledge and have experiences that create empathic insights into the lives of people who are oppressed" (268). Deep knowledge of others reduces scapegoating. Individuals are able to envision the world through the eyes of the oppressed, although willingness and imagination are required.

Funding public spaces requires policymakers to have some degree of empathy so that decisions are made in the public's interest. Huzar (2014) proposed that libraries are "radically inclusive" spaces that specifically aim to reach socially excluded people, or people of all situations and backgrounds. In public policy, empathy involves consideration of the feelings, experiences and passions of the people who will be affected by particular legislation. As Barley (2007) articulates, the shift to a corporate society has led to the exclusion of empathy from the public policy process. Contemporary public policy appears to favor corporations or the artificial person over the average citizen, treating corporations as if they have rights and needs just as a human being would. Because of this, Barley proposes that an ordinary citizen becomes more disconnected from the political process as organizations and corporations have greater influence on legislation.

One problem with favoring the corporation over the individual is that corporations lack feelings, emotions and passions. In effect, the corporation becomes a barrier between government and the people, making it easy to ignore empathy, or the deliberative process altogether. Corporations have a need to make a profit

and are accountable to their shareholders. When governments increase privatization, or give tax breaks to the corporation, the corporation grows in power. As the
power of corporations grows, they receive more space and resource allocation,
with less available for funding public services. Perhaps there is a way that policy
can account for the corporation, while also including the needs of the people.
Morrell (2010) writes about how public space can act as a deliberative forum that
enables the empathy process. Deliberation and sharing of ideas, passions and
needs in public spaces is vital for the process of empathy to occur. In deliberative spaces, people can address misconceptions, share experiences and consider
the perspectives of others. Morrell also proposes that equal consideration can
be given to both the artificial person and the feeling and thinking person when
empathy is included in the deliberative process.

Regulation of Public Spaces

Government maintains a variety of public spaces, including libraries, schools,
parks, and offices. The concept of public space has been a subject of discussion
for years, with theorists challenging what makes a space truly public and what
should be allowed in public spaces. There are limitations on how public spaces,
including libraries, can be used and what behaviors are allowed. Anyone can go
to a public space, but they cannot break the law or cause disturbances. Public
space, though, has experienced the double threat of neoliberal economic policies
and excessive policing, especially since the 9/11 attacks (Low and Smith 2006).

Hayden (2006) describes how public space in urban planning has radically
changed during the twentieth century, explaining that through the 1920s, city
planning focused on town squares, parks, and other public spaces. However,
later in the twentieth century, priority shifted to private space. Consider the differences between the town squares and the malls of the twentieth century and
those of preceding times. There was a shift in focus from citizen to citizen-con-
sumer. Radical changes like this do not happen naturally, but because of a shift
in policies. For example, the real estate lobby spoke against "any alternatives to
the single-family tract house purchased on a long mortgage" (Hayden, 37). Title
1 of the 1949 housing legislation "opened the way to land clearance in big cities
for the benefit of private developers, later called 'urban renewal'" (Hayden, 38).

The Reagan era marked the turn towards the neoliberal political era, in which
production and the economy became the measurement of goodness. State support
for egalitarianism "and interventions in the economy" (Buschman 2016, 5) were
cancelled in favor of programs that would promote economic growth. Brown

delves into the marriage of neoliberalism and neoconservatism as an American phenomenon in which unbridled self-interest in the form of capitalism is justified with evangelical zeal: "more than simply facilitating the economy, the state itself must construct and construe itself in market terms, as well as develop policies and promulgate a political culture that figures citizens as rational economic actors..." (Brown 2006, 694); privatization is one result, as is the expectation that people should take care of their own needs, rather than having a state-supported safety net for vulnerable populations.

David Harvey says that our society is undergoing a transformation in spatial distribution, made possible by Information and Communication Technologies (ICT). ICT has liberated "all sorts of activities from formal spatial constraints, permitting rapid adjustments in locations of production, consumption, populations, and the like" (Harvey 2000, 63). Effective transformation depends on financial deregulation and technology transfer. ICT crosses spatial boundaries. If left unregulated it will allow capitalism to take over every corner of the world, transforming its geography into a homogeneous reflection of the ruling class with no possibility of a government that is empathetic to the poor.

Policy, Public Space and Libraries

In the United States, public libraries were first supported by the federal government under the National Plan for public library service in the late 1930s. They experienced a period of growth and expanded services under the Library Services and Construction Act (LSCA) during the 1960s and 1970s (McCook 2002), under the premise that state and national planning for libraries granted equal access to reading and educational materials. Welbourne discusses the havoc that shifting funding priorities wreaked on the profession and library services in the 1980s, following a long era of support:

> The Reagan 80s... found a library profession ill-prepared for a federal government disdainful of any educational or cultural institution dependent upon federal support... Because these institutions had ignored the opportunity to restructure themselves to survive during hard times, the administrators of these urban libraries used the only response familiar to them: closing down branch libraries in black and poor neighborhoods; eliminating programs for the needy and illiterate... (Welbourne 1994, 126).

Libraries receive the bulk of their funding from local taxes, but the federal budget, through the Institute of Museum and Library Services (IMLS) Grants to States program (https://www.imls.gov/grants/grant-programs/grants-states), funnels over US$150 million to improve library services, such as programs that "expand services for learning and access to information and educational resources in a variety of formats in order to support... education, lifelong learning, workforce development, and digital literacy skills", programs that "target library services to individuals of diverse geographic, cultural, and socioeconomic backgrounds, and to individuals with limited functional literacy..." and "from families with incomes below the poverty line..." (Institute of Museum and Library Services 2017a). The funding priorities target vulnerable populations and are an overt display of the empathetic side of public policy. To deviate from the approach and eliminate or reduce support for public libraries and other social services shows not only a lack of empathy, but active destruction of spaces where free flow of communication can occur and where people can meet in public. Changes in government policy reshape public spaces in favor of private spaces and shift money from public to private hands.

There are at least two ways that shifts in government priorities affect libraries. First, public libraries are inherently public spaces, funded by public money in the form of taxes that cities pass on themselves. Libraries are a living embodiment and testament of a city's will to support what a library represents: opportunity, lifelong learning and public space. They are an important part of the public sphere, which is a "hotly debated topic" and one where "the control of the public domain has been appropriated by corporate, state, ideological, and other interests, leading to the corollary idea that public spaces, as part of the public sphere, are no longer spaces of public engagement and diversity; rather they are spaces of fear and/or surveillance..." (Buschman and Leckie 2006, 13).

As an aside, libraries strive to maintain ideologically neutral spaces, and in content they might succeed (Jaeger, Gorham, Bertot, and Sarin 2013). However, the very notion of a public library marks the wicked problem at the heart of this chapter. Public space is contested. Public libraries offer space for personal enrichment for all, the "deserving and non-deserving" (Birdi et al. 2009, 581). They offer public meeting spaces, unfiltered Internet, and books that span the political spectrum (Bossaller and Budd 2015). Public libraries are also a bastion of the free flow of communication in the form of printed books and debatably unfiltered Internet services. Under the current administration, the newly appointed chairman of the Federal Communications Commission (FCC), Ajit Pai, is currently trying to dismantle net neutrality, which will in effect stop the free flow of communication. Pai's most recent job was legal work for one of the largest Internet and phone companies, Verizon, where he fought the net neutrality protections enacted under the Obama administration. Deregulation of the telecommunication industry has resulted in its current anticompetitive state, which will result in higher prices for Internet services in poor and rural areas, as well as preferential treatment and higher speeds for certain subscription services. Steinbaum and Hwang explain why deregulation of the telecommunications industry has not worked in favor of disadvantaged people:

> As the deregulatory regime was being implemented in the telecoms sector, companies therein were increasingly operating to the benefit of shareholders. Thus, even when mergers realized economies of scale and new technologies unlocked the value of the market, the returns did not accrue to customers in the form of lower costs or better service. Instead, they were captured by shareholders as higher profits and thus higher corporate payouts in the form of dividends and stock buybacks (Steinbaum and Hwang 2017, 8).

Regulation is needed to ensure equal, open access to everyone, regardless of where people live, in either poor inner cities or rural areas. Public libraries are ideally like the Internet under net neutrality rules. They are open and free for all. Free access for all is one of the aspects of libraries that justify taxation. Libraries are public places. It is worth noting that Low and Smith (2006) include the Internet as public space.

As much as libraries support Internet access, they also supply space: space for all people, regardless of their ability to pay. Barclay (2017) points out that while reference use is going down, library visits are going up. The space of the library holds appeal, but it is very difficult to measure such value, and critics of library expenditures can easily point to reductions in reference services as an example of why less funding is needed. It is true. Many people can Google facts. However, as Barclay says, "Comparing library visits to Google searches is simple (and simplistic), while demonstrating to the average person that these two things are different—and that their difference is meaningful—is hard... the idea that public library space—in and of itself—is a key social value of public libraries" (Barclay 2017, 4). He notes that it is the actual space of the library that is special, presenting the possibility for "people to learn, socialize, escape, and connect in ways that no other present-day space – private, governmental, or commercial – can." (5).

Libraries, Librarians and Empathy

Lankes observes that "the mission of librarians is to improve society through facilitating knowledge creation in their communities" (Lankes 2016, 15). The mission is activated by creating spaces where people can commune with ideas and attend events, from book discussions to coding camps. Both solitary reading and community events can cultivate empathy and the type of deep understanding described by Segal (2011). Buschman (2017) states that the very definition of public assumes that the public engages with the library by communicating its interests, needs and wants to the library. In turn, libraries provide services that others have identified as necessary. Many of these services are capable of cultivating empathy, like providing access to literature. Kidd and Constano (2013) found that people who read fiction will score higher on affective and cognitive empathy inventories. Keen (2007), Nussbaum (1997) and Nafisi (2014) have all written about the ability of the novel to allow people to see another's perspective. Fiction can help people to connect to the characters who may or may not be like themselves, thus cultivating empathy by sparking the imagination. The library space serves an important role in developing empathy within the community through both exposure to real people of different social backgrounds and through the provision of reading materials that deepen historical understanding and spark the imagination.

The importance of empathy has been noted. Librarians work with the public in public spaces and must be able to relate to the different types of people in the community. Miller and Wallis (2011) describe empathy as an interpersonal skill necessary in any library service, like the reference interview or research consultation. VanScoy (2013) reiterates the point. Reference librarians' practice is grounded in empathy with their patrons. Even though empathy may be natural for many librarians, Birdi, Wilson and Tso (2009) found that librarians were more empathetic when serving people who were more familiar to them. The writers concluded that empathy should be developed among library staff through proper training to enable them to be more effective at communicating with people from various backgrounds. While empathy skills are important for all librarians, empathy is especially important for librarians who work with the public. Public libraries have an important but tempestuous role in alleviating social exclusion in society because of the association of libraries with the welfare state (Birdi, Wilson and Crocker 2008, 581). When England's Library Act was passed in 1850, "the public library role in social betterment was attributed to the 'deserving' and 'non-deserving, working classes, based on visible and discernible potential for self-improvement." The binary thinking has persisted, as is evident in conversations in the United States and Britain, around homeless people's use of the library (Muddiman, Durrani, Pateman, Dutch, Linley, and Vincent 2001; Gehner 2010).

Case Study: Public Libraries and Public Spending

Examining political rhetoric is a way to feel the pulse of an administration. The way that leaders talk about minority groups, poverty and funding for social services reveals their perceptions on the purpose of governance. Some leaders directly speak of empathy or closely related ideas. For instance, Obama directly called for empathy in terms of perspective-taking for social change (Pedwell 2012), following his predecessor's calls for compassion, such as Clinton's proclamation to feel your pain (Pedwell 2012, 284). Pedwell explains that expressions of empathy might simply be a way to garner support or to call for individuals and faith-based organizations to pick up governmental slack, but the language of empathy is present. The budget is another tangible piece of evidence that expresses values (US Senate 2007, 7206). As an example, a federal or state budget that emphasizes expenditures and equal access to healthcare, quality education, and social services demonstrates empathy for people living in poverty.

In the spring of 2017, the Trump administration published a blueprint of the budget proposed for 2018, *America First: A Budget Blueprint to Make America Great Again* (US Office of Management and Budget 2017). In the budget blueprint, funding for security and defense was increased. Funding for social services, the arts and humanities, including libraries and museums, was completely eliminated (Soffen and Yu 2017). Trump specifically states that the blueprint was framed around "the rebuilding of our nation's military without adding to our federal deficit." This plays into the politics of fear and isolation, as if the United States is a culturally homogenous, gated community. Reactions to the budget from the media provide a window into the thinking of the public, rather than from within the library community, which might be more likely to frame the argument in self-protection. This case study examines the proposed budget blueprint and its rhetoric in terms of its impact on libraries. It includes reflections on determining the value of the library and the analytic process and framings.

Determining the Value of the Library

This chapter explores the belief that libraries should promote themselves as public spaces that need funding. Trump's proposed budget blueprint was an example of a manifestly public threat to funding. How did the media respond? Rhetorical analysis of news articles demonstrates that there is significant public interest in the funding of local public libraries. Saraisky (2015) says that the media can define public problems in two ways, by acting as a gatekeeper for comments on public problems or as a means of finding solutions and framing different ideas around a public policy issue.

The media, in theory, discuss public policy in local terms by outlining how policy affects local communities and the people who live there. Journalists use frames to focus stories to attract audiences. Journalistic framing is a "thriving approach to analyze media content and effects" (Brüggemann 2014, 61). Frames drive interest in the story. For example, a story that describes libraries as feeling the sting of a budget cut sets up the reader to understand that the policy will hurt the library. Frames can help examine how problems and solutions are understood by the people involved by assigning meaning to events, places or other phenomena (Fischer 2003; Goffman 1974; Rein and Schön 1996). One caveat of this method is that many newspapers are no longer locally owned (McChesney 2015) and the media reveal less about local sentiment than in the past.

To learn more about how journalists shaped frames in the aftermath of the publication of the blueprint, the media reaction to proposed cuts for libraries was examined. The *America First* budget blueprint was selected because of strong reaction from the library community which drew attention to the reliance of libraries on government funding and that without it, libraries could fall into crisis. Using the blueprint as an "event of newsworthiness" (Brüggemann 2014), the way that libraries were portrayed in local dailies within the first three months of the budget's release was examined. A search of the EBSCO *Newspaper Source* database was undertaken using the validation of search terms for content analysis as proposed by Stryker, and others (2006). The search string included *Trump* and *budget* and *libraries*, with date limits between January and June, 2017. Of the 25 results retrieved, 92% or 23 were deemed relevant for the purposes of the study with relevance determined by the following criteria:

- Does the article contain an explanation of how libraries are used by the public?
- Does the article reference the proposed budget?
- Does the article suggest that libraries solve problems of society?

To compare local newspaper articles with the reaction from online media, a search was completed using the same search string on Google. The first three pages of results were examined using the same relevancy criteria. The results yielded .33 relevancy with 10 out of 30 articles considered relevant. The comment sections of the articles were also used in the analysis.

The analysis was conducted by first examining the *America First* budget blueprint for complexity and representation of policy issues. Second, media documents were contextualized by identifying author, publication, publication date, type of source and title of article. The resulting extracts were qualitatively coded using categories based on the core values of librarianship (American Library Association 2019[1]) developed before the coding process began, as recommended by Neuendorf (2002). Variables were captured after a preliminary reading of the

---

1 The current version of the *Values* varies slightly from the one used in the study.

texts, and used to deepen the analysis of each article and create a classification of major services provided by the library that the media deemed as essential and in crisis should federal funding be eliminated.

The analysis leverages a political statement to assess the news and media coverage on the value and purpose of libraries to the community. The following questions were developed to examine the articles published about the budget cuts affecting libraries:

- How is public library use framed in the media?
- How is the role of the public library framed in the media?
- How does the media suspect that reduced funding to libraries affect the community?

The Proposed Budget *America First* was shared on the Whitehouse.gov website by the Office of Management and Budget on March 16, 2017. The purpose of the budget blueprint was to present a plan for how the Trump Administration would prioritize government spending. Specifically, the imperative of the budget blueprint was to outline how redistribution of funding would increase the safety of Americans and lead to economic growth: "A budget that puts America first must make the safety of our people its number one priority – because without safety there can be no prosperity" (US Office of Management and Budget 2017, 1). The budget was framed as a plan that would restore safety and security to the United States, in a dangerous time where defense spending is listed as a priority.

Of particular interest in the budget blueprint were the proposed cuts for the IMLS which were explained as necessary in order to enable increased defense spending. The cuts are of considerable significance to the library community because the IMLS is a primary source of funding for museums and libraries in the United States (https://www.imls.gov/). The specific role of the IMLS in libraries has been to support innovation, advancement and development of libraries and museums across the country (https://www.imls.gov/about/mission). The impact of the cuts was noted by the IMLS (Institute of Museum and Library Services 2017b).

The budget blueprint prioritizes defense spending, immigration and border enforcement, law enforcement funding and reducing foreign aid. Agencies that benefit the poor, refugees or the knowledge economy, including scientific research, public broadcasting, libraries and museums, are cut or eliminated, which is concerning given that many of the agencies are aimed at eradicating problems or improving quality of life for those in poverty, or facing inequalities. The budget blueprint's authoritative tone explains that only in this way can national security be improved.

The Analytical Process and Framings

The analysis focused on perceptions of the budget's effect on libraries. Three frame domains emerged from the analysis. The domains characterize the understanding of libraries and their role within the community as described in the media articles following the budget's release:
- Frame 1. Libraries provide for others
- Frame 2. Libraries have a social responsibility
- Frame 3. Libraries improve quality of life.

With Frame 1, Libraries provide for others, reporters presented libraries as places which provide resources for the community. Libraries are presented as a source for resources like books, articles, databases and computers. The articles describe libraries specifically as places for low-income people to access materials they might otherwise not be able to use. One reporter quoted a librarian who said, "There are still people who don't have computers and Internet access, and they rely on us for that. There are people who rely on us to help them search for jobs" (Emerson, 2017). Many articles describe the benefits of checking out books or using computers, but only in the context that it benefits those that do not have money to pay for their own materials. Adversely, the comments sections in web articles presented a different view from the readers, that library materials were used by people from all economic levels who enjoy the variety of materials offered in the library, without having to pay to use them. One commenter from an online news and fashion publication for women described libraries as places that have things to borrow, particularly within the context of saving money for families.

In relation to Frame 2, Libraries have a social responsibility, one of the core values of librarianship is that libraries have a social responsibility to consider economic and human rights, and to participate in solving social problems related to poverty, homelessness, and especially a lack of access to informational and educational resources (http://www.ala.org/rt/srrt). The media analysis found that journalists recognize that libraries do this. Specifically, journalists used direct quotes from librarians in their articles and showed that the library benefits the poor, unemployed and illiterate. In addition, libraries provide access to resources that some people cannot afford and provide services that may not be available anywhere else, such as access to databases, research resources, and programming.

Some journalists framed their entire articles around how the budget cuts would affect the poor. For example, Ferguson (2017) described how the library provided books and magazines for poor children on the south side of Tucson, citing the experience of Raul Grijalva. He writes, "As a boy growing up on the south side of Tucson, Raul Grijalva was constantly inside the school library reading novels, magazines and newspapers." Later in the article, Grijalva is quoted as saying, "It's time we recognize this for what it is – an assault on the poor, plain and simple. Republicans have a choice – they can be complicit in Trump's attack, or they can join us in safeguarding libraries as a vital resource to communities all across this country."

Media coverage highlighted how the unemployed use libraries to search for jobs on library computers or to self-educate by reading, researching or attending library programming. One editorial from the Philadelphia Inquirer (Inquirer Editorial 2017) says that without library funding, "the unemployed looking for a library computer to tap out a job application may have to wait in line because the President wants to terminate the Institute of Museum and Library Sciences." Numerous articles described the library as a haven for the poor, visually impaired, or disabled. However, not all reporters discuss the physical space of the library. For example, Mester (2017) writes how some of the library resources meet a social need for the community: "For Ohio, that would mean a loss of $5 million that goes toward programs like the Ohio Digital Library, research databases, the Talking Book Program for the visually impaired and numerous grants."

As far as Frame 3, Libraries improve quality of life, is concerned, the reporters emphasized that by providing access to resources and programming, libraries also improve the quality of life for the community. Libraries serve as meeting-places, community centers and gathering places, in addition to providing opportunities for lifelong learning and equal access to information and knowledge. Ferguson (2017) quoted a librarian as saying, "The public library is America's great equalizer, providing everyone the same access to information and opportunities for success."

Results and Discussion

The search results yielded eight articles that framed libraries as part of the arts and humanities sector. The articles discussed libraries as cultural centers and gathering places for people of all incomes, races, religions, genders and abilities or highlighted the archival work that many public libraries engage in to preserve local history. Hatmaker (2017) reported the comments of Laura Horrz Stanton, Executive Director at the Conservation Center for Arts and Historic Artifacts in Philadelphia: "We're working with institutions to preserve our nation's shared cultural heritage; things that honestly might be lost if there wasn't the funding to support it." Reporters conveyed the urgency of providing funding to libraries and museums as cultural institutions who bring communities together by promoting literacy. One reporter linked the library to arts institutions when he used the example of a sociologist speaking at the library about his book on equitable housing. Another reported statements from Proctor, Executive Director of Portland's Literary Arts, "Arts organizations across this country are phenomenal at bringing communities together" (Wang 2017).

As shown in the other frames, libraries support the needs of the community and such support can enhance people's quality of life. Wehrman (2017) quotes a Democratic representative: "President Trump has talked a lot about being the 'People's President,' yet his budget request literally rips food, housing, environmental protections, jobs and opportunity from countless American families, seniors, people with disabilities and our most vulnerable citizens" said Rep. Joyce Beatty, D-Jefferson Township.

The three frames identified in the media in the months following the release of the budget blueprint demonstrate that the public has interest in the value of libraries and believe they are institutions that support the common good, fill a gap in social programs and improve the quality of life. Other articles pointed out, echoing Audenson (2016), that libraries enhance lives by promoting fellowship and democracy.

It is interesting to note that while searching for news stories about the proposed budget cuts for libraries, not a single article was found that supported cutting library and museum funding. Every article was supportive of libraries' need for federal funding, though the journalists emphasize different reasons, either to support the poor or to support arts and culture. While one article may have framed the cuts as bad for the arts, culture and humanities, another framed it as an attack on the poor.

Comments from readers were not available for all articles, but when they were available, they provided additional information to add weight to the journalist's viewpoint. For instance, one article said that the budget cuts were bad for the poor or unemployed and that comments tended to focus on the economic value of the library. When another article discussed the cultural aspects of libraries, the comments reiterated the educational aspects of libraries, consistent with the effect of frame setting on public responses (Bruggemann 2014).

The analysis provided insight into how the media, local communities and the library community viewed the proposed elimination of funding for libraries. The reaction indicated that proposing the elimination of funding to public libraries was not a popular sentiment. Analyzing media responses to budget cuts provides an understanding of what may interest the public about the value of libraries. For further exploration, interviews with the general public and librarians may provide additional perspectives on how the library is valued as a place within the community. More research could help promote the value of libraries to the community and provide results to be used in communicating value to legislators who hold power over the federal budget.

Returning to the wicked problem, based on President Trump's past actions, there is little regard in the current administration for public space or public control of the Internet, or the two spaces, real and virtual, in which public libraries operate. Libraries operate under the premise that they are stewards of public funds, ensuring that everyone has equal access to information, regardless of ability to pay. Trump is a real estate developer who has profited from privatizing public spaces. The previous administration ruled that the Internet should be regulated as a public utility, but the protections against private development are being dismantled at the expense of the public good. Because the Internet is the main conduit for information flow, the developments might lead to privatization of the information superhighway, increasing corporate profit and consolidation under the premise of increased services and innovation (Shields 2017).

While focusing in this discussion on responses to library funding during an uncertain economic period, the real point is that the public sees that libraries are a public space where people can talk about community issues that cut across political lines. An analysis of thirteen public forums focused on broadband availability in a rural area of the Midwestern United States and found that the purpose of the forums was to inform citizens about digital inclusion and especially "extending last-mile broadband to low density markets" (Schenck-Hamlin, Han, and Schenck-Hamlin 2014, 291). Access to libraries is crucial for rural communities' well-being. The "cost of digital exclusion is great. Without access, full participation in nearly every aspect of American society—from economic success and educational achievement, to positive health outcomes and civic engagement—is compromised" (Institute of Museum and Library Services 2012). Access to public space and an unmediated, free Internet is crucial for democracy. Studying who has access to both is a study in policy and power. Retaining the library as a space for free, unimpeded access to a free Internet and public space is an act of empathy for people without means to pay for private access. When policy favors the occupation of informational spaces by corporations, it is apparent who holds power over democracy.

Conclusion

The case study analysis found that public libraries are shown in a positive light in the media. Hopefully the media reflects the public's viewpoint and the public sees the library as a space that provides for people who have less and will be there when needed. The Library Services and Technology Act (LSTA) funding prioritizes the poor but libraries benefit the entire society. Everyone benefits from equal access to educational opportunities and higher literacy. Public libraries provide help to citizens to access government information and connect them to services, providing tax help, navigating insurance options and connecting people to social services. Why would the government stop funding libraries? Perhaps that is wrapped up in the debate over the role of government.

Camillus presented ten qualities, listed at the beginning of this chapter, that distinguish wicked problems. He used these to frame solutions in the commercial sector. He states, "It's impossible to find solutions to wicked strategy problems, but companies can learn to cope with them. In accordance with Occam's razor, the simplest techniques are often the best" (Camillus 2008, 4). He said that it is best to recognize the wicked problems, accept them, and use unconventional strategies to solve the problems. In revisiting his recommended approach and adapting it to public libraries, perhaps there is an ironic twist in an admittedly anti-corporate stance. Successful solutions to wicked problems in public libraries can be found through the following actions.

Involve Stakeholders, Document Opinions and Communicate

Libraries must collect not only statistics, but also stories. Statistics help with internal planning and justify expenses, but stories demonstrate value. Communication about the library should focus on the community and the good that the library does for citizens, regardless of their social status. Focus on how the library enhances quality of life for everyone and brings people together, and on the importance of the space of the library in achieving outcomes. The stories should invoke empathy.

Define the Corporate Identity

The library should be embedded as a crucial part of the city or region. Use placemaking techniques to define the civic spaces of the city or region and use the spaces to nurture small businesses. Demonstrate that the library is a space that helps develop local infrastructure. Rather than outsource library services, look to the community for partners in service delivery when feasible. Think about ways to personalize any national slogans and promotional materials to emphasize the local value of the library.

Focus on Action and the Future

Adopt a feed-forward orientation through focusing on the environment, predicting and anticipating the future rather than providing feedback. Host city planning and placemaking meetings at the library where city leaders can interact with citizens with whom they might not otherwise meet. Find out what leaders and citizens want from the city, including the library. Ask questions and seek partnerships between the library and other groups to help improve the local standard of living.

Ultimately, Camillus's article was about lean management techniques. As previously mentioned, Huber and Potter (2015) found that lean management is not only applicable in corporate settings. In public libraries, lean management can enable libraries to implement their missions. Activities include identifying processing inefficiencies and making better use of technology and changing outdated methods used in tasks like getting books on the shelf. The goal of a library is not to support the library and its employees; it is to support the community. Figure out what the community needs from the library, focus on services to meet identified needs and cut old services no longer needed. Looking for ways to save money does not only mean cutting employees and services, though it might eliminate services no longer needed.

While there is optimism about the future, public libraries face an uncertain future. With reductions in funding, the library is a great equalizer and requires continued funding for services, staff, materials, and space. Today's political climate is tough for librarians as public employees and libraries as public spaces. It is more important than ever to embed the library within the fabric of the city.

References

Amazon Fulfillment Technology. 2015. Accessed April 15, 2020. https://www.youtube.com/watch?v=3bdRKaodLK8.

American Library Association. *Core Values of Librarianship.* 2019. Accessed April 15, 2020. http://www.ala.org/advocacy/intfreedom/corevalues.

Audunson, R.A. "The Library and Quality of Life". *Scandinavian Public Library Quarterly* 49, no. 1–2 (2016): 28–29. http://slq.nu/index1173.html?article=volume-49-no-1-2-2016-13

Barclay, D. "Space and the Social Worth of Public Libraries". *Public Library Quarterly* 36, no.4 (2017):267–273. DOI: http://dx.doi.org/10.1080/01616846.2017.1327767.

Barley, S.R. "Corporations, Democracy, and the Public Good." *Journal of Management Inquiry* 16, no. 3 (2007): 201–215.

Birdi, B., K. Wilson, and J. Cocker. "The Public Library, Exclusion and Empathy: A Literature Review". *Library Review* 57, no. 8 (2008): 576–592. DOI: http://dx.doi.org/10.1108/00242530810899568.
Birdi, B., K. Wilson, and H.M. Tso. "The Nature and Role of Empathy in Public Librarianship". *Journal of Librarianship and Information Science* 4, no. 2 (2009): 81–89.
Bossaller, J.S. "Access to Affordable Care through Public Libraries". *Library Quarterly* 86, no. 2 (2016): 193–212.
Bossaller, J.S., and J.M. Budd. "What We Talk About When We Talk About Free Speech". *The Library Quarterly* 85, no. 1 (2015): 26–44.
Brown, W. "American Nightmare: Neoliberalism, Neoconservatism, and De-Democratization." *Political Theory* 34, no. 6 (2006): 690–714. DOI: 10.1177/0090591706293016.
Brüggemann, M. "Between Frame Setting and Frame Sending: How Journalists Contribute to News Frames". *Communication Theory* 24, no. 1 (2014): 61–82.
Buschman, J. "The Library in the Life of the Public: Implications of a Neoliberal Age." *The Library Quarterly* 87, no. 1 (2017): 55–70.
Buschman, J. "Librarianship and the Arc of Crisis: The Road to Institutionalized Cultural Neoliberalism." *Mediatropes* 5, no. 2 (2016): 1–18. Accessed April 15, 2020. http://www.mediatropes.com/index.php/Mediatropes/article/view/26001/19596.
Buschman, J., and G. Leckie. *The Library as Place: History, Community and Culture*. Westport, Conn.: Libraries Unlimited, 2006.
Camillus, J.C. "Strategy as a Wicked Problem". *Harvard Business Review* 86, no. 5 (2008): 98–101.
D'Angelo, E. *Barbarians at the Gates of the Public Library: How Postmodern Consumer Capitalism Threatens Democracy, Civil Education and The Public Good*. Duluth, Minn.: Library Juice Press, 2006.
Djikic, M., K. Oatley, and M. Moldoveanu. "Reading Other Minds: Effects of Literature on Empathy". *Scientific Study of Literature* 3, no. 1 (2013): 28–47.
Emerson, J. "Elimination of Federal Agencies Could Dim The Lights on Music and Arts Scene, Museum and Library Programs". *Leader-Telegram* (Eau Claire, WI).March 26, 2017. Accessed April 15, 2020. https://www.leadertelegram.com/news/front-page/elimination-of-federal-agencies-could-dim-the-lights-on-music/article_8065c908-e756-505e-8894-8bde6862bf96.html.
Ferguson, J. "Proposed Library Cuts an Assault on the Poor, US Rep. Grijalva Says". *Arizona Daily Star*. April 18, 2017. Accessed April 15, 2020. https://thisistucson.com/news/local/proposed-library-cuts-an-assault-on-the-poor-us-rep/article_04755e3f-0d29-50fe-8d4d-9c35b75bc65c.html.
Fischer, F. *Reframing Public Policy: Discursive Politics and Deliberative Practices*. Oxford: Oxford University Press, 2003.
Gehner, J. "Libraries, Low-Income People, and Social Exclusion". *Public Library Quarterly* 29, no. 1 (2010): 39–47.
Goffman, E. *Frame Analysis: An Essay on the Organization of Experience*. Boston, Mass.: Harvard University Press, 1974.
Goulding, A. "Engaging with Community Engagement: Public Libraries and Citizen Involvement". *New Library World* 11, no. 1–2 (2008): 37–51.
Goulding, A. "The Big Society and English Public Libraries: Where Are We Now?". *New Library World* 11, no. 11–12 (2013): 478–493.
Gutsche, B. "A Boon to the Workforce". *Library Journal* 136, no. 14 (2011): 28–31.

Hamilton, B. "Makerspaces, Participatory Learning, and Libraries." [Weblog]. *The Unquiet Librarian*. June 28, 2012. Accessed April 15, 2020. https://theunquietlibrarian.wordpress. com/2012/06/28/makerspaces-participatory-learning-and-libraries/.

Harvey, D. *Spaces of Hope*. Berkeley: University of California Press, 2000.

Hatmaker, J. "Trump's Proposed Budget Cuts for Humanities Would Deal 'Huge Blow' to Philadelphia and Beyond". *Pennlive*. March 16, 2017. Accessed April 15, 2020. https:// www.pennlive.com/life/2017/03/philadelphia_budget_cuts_impac.html.

Hayden, D. "Building the American Way: Public Subsidy, Private Space". In *The Politics of Public Space*, edited by Setha Low and Neil Smith, 35–48. New York: Routledge, 2006.

Huber, J., and S. Potter. *The Purpose-Based Library: Finding Your Path to Survival, Success, and Growth*. Chicago: Neal-Schuman, 2015.

Huzar, T. "Neoliberalism, Democracy and the Library as a Radically Inclusive Space". Paper presented at: IFLA WLIC 2014 - Lyon - Libraries, Citizens, Societies: Confluence for Knowledge in Session 200 – Library Theory and Research. In IFLA WLIC 2014, August 16–22, 2014. Lyon, France. Accessed April 15, 2020. http://library.ifla.org/835/.

"Inquirer Editorial: Trump's Proposed Budget Would Hurt Philadelphia". *The Philadelphia Inquiry*. March 26, 2017. Accessed April 15, 2020. https:// www.inquirer.com/philly/ opinion/20170326_Inquirer_Editorial__Trump_s_proposed_budget_would_hurt_ Philadelphia.html.

Institute of Museum and Library Services, University of Washington Technology & Social Change Group, International City/County Management Association. *Building Digital Communities*. Washington, DC: Institute of Museum and Library Services, 2012. https:// digital.lib.washington.edu/researchworks/bitstream/handle/1773/33274/TASCHA_ Building_Digital_Communities_2012.pdf?sequence=1&isAllowed=y

Institute of Museum and Library Services. *Purposes and Priorities of the Library Services and Technology Act*. 2017a. Accessed April 15, 2020. https://www.imls.gov/grants/ grants-state/purposes-and-priorities-lsta.

Institute of Museum and Library Services. *Institute of Museum and Library Services Issues Statement on the President's Proposed FY 18 Budget*. 2017b. Accessed April 15, 2020. https://www.imls.gov/news-events/news-releases/institute-museum-and-library-services-issues-statement-presidents-proposed.

Jaeger, P.T., U. Gorham, J.C. Bertot, and L.C. Sarin. "Democracy, Neutrality, and Value Demonstration in the Age of Austerity." *Library Quarterly* 83, no. 368 (2013): 4–382.

Keen, S. *Empathy and the Novel*. Oxford: Oxford University Press, 2007.

Kelly, M. "Bottoming Out?" *Library Journal* 136, no. 1 (2011): 28–31.

Kidd, D.C., and E. Castano. "Reading Literary Fiction Improves Theory of Mind." *Science* 342, no. 6156 (2013): 377–380.

Lankes, R.D. *The Atlas of New Librarianship*. Cambridge, Mass.: MIT Press, 2016.

Lefler, D., and B. Lowry. "Brownback's Plan to Sweep More Highway Money Faces Pushback." *The Wichita Eagle*, January 14, 2017. Accessed April 15, 2020. http://www.kansas.com/ news/politics-government/article126644799.html.

Low, S., and N. Smith. *The Politics of Public Space*. New York: Routledge, 2006.

McChesney, R.W. *Rich Media, Poor Democracy: Communication Politics in Dubious Times*. New York: The New Press, 2015.

McCook, K.de la P. "Preface". In *Barbarians at the Gates of the Public Library: How Postmodern Consumer Capitalism Threatens Democracy Civil Education and the Public Good*, by E. D'Angelo. Duluth, Minn.: Library Juice Press, 2006.

McCook, K.de la P. "Rocks in the Whirlpool". *University of Southern Florida School of Information Faculty Publications* 117 (2002). http://scholarcommons.usf.edu/si_facpub/117.

McCook, K.de la P., and K.J. Phenix. "Public Libraries and Human Rights." *Public Library Quarterly* 25, no. 1–2 (2007): 57–73.

McMenemy, D. "Public Library Closures in England: The Need to Act?" Editorial. *Library Review* 58, no. 8 (2009): 557–560.

Mester, A. "U.S., State Budget Proposals Could Cut Funding to Libraries". *The Blade*. March 30, 2017. Accessed April 15, 2020. https://www.toledoblade.com/local/politics/2017/03/29/Proposals-could-cut-fundingto-libraries/stories/20170329141.

Miller, F., and J. Wallis. "Social Interaction and the Role of Empathy in Information and Knowledge Management: A Literature Review". *Journal of Education for Library and Information Science* 52, no. 2 (2011): 122–132.

Morrell, M.E. *Empathy and Democracy: Feeling, Thinking, and Deliberation*. University Park, Penn.: Pennsylvania State University Press, 2010.

Muddiman, D., S. Durrani, J. Pateman, M. Dutch, R. Linley, and J. Vincent. "Open to All? The Public Library and Social Exclusion: Executive Summary". *New Library World* 102, no. 4–5 (2001): 154–158. https://doi.org/10.1108/03074800110390626.

Nafisi, A. *Azar Nafisi on Empathy* [video]. American Library Association [Annual conference]. 2014. Accessed April 15, 2020. https://www.youtube.com/watch?v=R2LV9uZSDms.

Neuendorf, K. *The Content Analysis Guidebook*. Los Angeles, Calif.: Sage Publications, 2002.

Nikitin, C., and J. Johnson. *Libraries that Matter*. Project for Public Spaces. 2009. Accessed April 15, 2020. https://www.pps.org/article/librariesthatmatter-2.

Nussbaum, M.C. *Cultivating Humanity: A Classical Defense of Reform in Liberal Education*. Cambridge, Mass.: Harvard University Press, 1997.

Pariser, E. *The Filter Bubble: What the Internet is Hiding From You*. London: Penguin, 2011.

Pedwell, C. "Economies of Empathy: Obama, Neoliberalism, and Social Justice". *Environment and Planning D: Society and Space* 30, no. 2 (2012): 280–297.

Preece, J., and K. Ghozati. "Experiencing Empathy Online." In *The Internet and Health Communication: Experiences and Expectations*, edited by Ronald E. Rice and James E. Katz, 147–166. London: Sage Publications, 2001. DOI: http://dx.doi.org/10.4135/9781452233277.n11.

Project for Public Spaces. *What is Placemaking?* 2007. Accessed April 15, 2020. https://www.pps.org/reference/what_is_placemaking/.

Rein, M., and D. Schön. "Frame-Critical Policy Analysis and Frame-Reflective Policy Practice". *Knowledge and Policy* 9, no. 85 (1996): 1–104.

Rittel, H., and M. Webber. "Dilemmas in a General Theory of Planning". *Policy Sciences* 42 (1973): 155–169.

Rosenberger, R. "Trump Tower and the Question of 'Public' Space". *The Atlantic*. August 25, 2016. Accessed April 15, 2020. https://www.theatlantic.com/business/archive/2016/08/trump-tower-and-the-question-of-public-space/494027/.

Saraisky, N.G. "Analyzing Public Discourse: Using Media Content Analysis to Understand the Policy Process". *Current Issues in Comparative Education* 18, no. 1 (2015): 26–41.

Schenck-Hamlin, D., S.H. Han, and B. Schenck-Hamlin. "Library-Led Forums on Broadband: An Inquiry into Public Deliberation". *The Library Quarterly* 84, no. 3 (2014): 278–293.

Segal, E.A. "Social Empathy: A Model Built on Empathy, Contextual Understanding, and Social Responsibility That Promotes Social Justice". *Journal of Social Service Research* 37, no. 3 (2011): 266–277.

Shields, T. "FCC Mulls Broadband Deregulation That Would Have AT&T Popping 'Champagne Corks.'" *Bloomberg Politics*, March 30, 2017. Accessed April 15, 2020. https://www.bloomberg.com/news/articles/2017-03-30/in-turnabout-fcc-mulls-broadband-deregulation-sought-by-at-t.

Smallwood, C., and K. Becnel. *Library Services for Multicultural Patrons: Strategies to Encourage Library Use.* Lanham, Md: Scarecrow Press, 2013.

Snow, D., E. Rochford, S. Worden, and R. Benford. "Frame Alignment Processes, Micromobilization, and Movement Participation". *American Sociological Review* 5, no. 4 (1986): 464–481.

Soffen, K., and D. Lu. "What Trump Cut in His Budget." *The Washington Post.* May 23, 2017. Accessed April 15, 2020. https://www.washingtonpost.com/graphics/politics/trump-presidential-budget-2018-proposal/?utm_term=.1f8943a8fee8.

Solnit, R. 2017. "Occupied Territory". *Harper's Magazine* 335 (2006): 5–7. Accessed April 15, 2020. https://harpers.org/archive/2017/07/occupied-territory/.

Steinbaum, M., and A. Hwang. *Crossed Lines: Why the AT&T – Time Warner Merger Demands a New Approach to Antitrust.* Roosevelt Institute, 2017. Accessed April 15, 2020. https://muninetworks.org/sites/www.muninetworks.org/files/2017-03-Crossed-Lines-ATT-TimeWarner-AntiTrut-Roosevelt-Inst.pdf.

Stewart, K.N., and B.E. Richardson. "Libraries by the People, for the People: Living Libraries and their Potential to Enhance Social Justice". *Information, Society and Justice Journal* 4, no. 2 (2011): 83–92.

Stryker, J.E., R. Wray, R. Hornik, and I. Yanovitzky. "Validation of Database Search Terms for Content Analysis: The Case of Cancer News Coverage". *Journalism & Mass Communication Quarterly* 83, no. 2 (2006): 413–430.

Sullivan, M. "The Fragile Future of Public Libraries". *Public Libraries* 42, no. 5 (2003): 303–308.

Tomasky, T. "Finally, Something isn't the Matter with Kansas". *New York Times.* June 12, 2017. Accessed April 15, 2020. https://www.nytimes.com/2017/06/12/opinion/finally-something-isnt-the-matter-with-kansas.html.

Toolis, E.E. "Theorizing Critical Placemaking as a Tool for Reclaiming Public Space." *American Journal of Community Psychology* 59, no. 1–2 (2017): 184–199. DOI:10.1002/ajcp.12118

US Office of Management and Budget. *America First: a Blueprint to Make America Great Again.* 2017. Accessed April 15, 2020. https://www.whitehouse.gov/sites/whitehouse.gov/files/omb/budget/fy2018/2018_blueprint.pdf.

US Senate. March 22, 2007. Congressional Record vol. 153 pt. 5.

VanScoy, A. "Fully Engaged Practice and Emotional Connection: Aspects of the Practitioner Perspective of Reference and Information Service". *Library & Information Science Research* 35, no. 4 (2013): 272–278.

Wang, A. "Oregon Arts Groups Say Trump's Budget Plan Would Cost State in Many Ways". *The Oregonian.* March 16, 2017, updated January 9, 2019. Accessed April 15, 2020. https://www.oregonlive.com/art/2017/03/nea_neh_cuts_oregon.html

Wehrman, J. "Ohio Would Lose Funding for Heating Aid, Arts, Lake Erie Clean-Up Under Trump Budget". *The Columbus Dispatch*, March 16, 2017. Accessed April 15, 2020.

Welbourne, J.C. "Achieving Black Economic Self-Reliance: The Urban Public Library Strengthens the Economic Base of its Community." In *The Black Librarian in America Revisited*, edited by E.J. Josey. Metuchen, N.J.: Scarecrow Press, 1994.

Zanetti, L.A. "Cultivating and Sustaining Empathy as a Normative Value in Public Administration". In *Government is Us 2.0*, edited by C.S. King. Armonk, NY: M.E. Sharpe, 2011.

Zickuhr, K., H. Rainie, K. Purcell and M. Duggan. *How Americans Value Public Libraries in Their Communities*. Pew Research Internet Project, 2013. Accessed April 15, 2020. https://www.pewinternet.org/2013/12/11/how-americans-value-public-libraries-in-their-communities-2/.

Bill Irwin

7 Public Library Board Trustees: Policy Makers, Policy Takers, or Policy Fakers?

Abstract: Who sets the policy direction for the public library? The library board is the institutional decision maker. How does the board develop policy and how is the community involved? This chapter defines good policy practice which is guided by a set of publicly-oriented, outward facing values and principles, exposing the current state of public library governance in the process. Of significant relevance is the interplay between public policy and community and between board members and the community. Are board members policy makers, takers, or fakers? How do values held by board members affect decisions made? Neoliberalism values are addressed and a Canadian personal perspective emphasising issues in Alberta is presented on the topic.

Keywords: Public libraries; Nonprofit organizations – Management; Corporate governance; Boards of directors; Neoliberalism; Alberta.

Introduction

The tactic that public bodies, and in particular public libraries, take in the development and delivery of policy is central in determining the authenticity of their approach to governance. How institutions view the public in the process, and accordingly how the public is acknowledged in the policy enterprise through the initial policy aims, intents and/or purposes adopted at the onset, maps the extent of authenticity. Colebatch (1986) notes that the way a policy is mapped shapes the way the process is understood and how appropriate forms of policy action are identified. Mapping in this context is a way of describing the approach taken in developing the policy. Young (2013, 30), in his review of the purpose of library boards, contends that many communities' public libraries form a vital part of their respective communities' social fabric. The commitment to building social fabric provides an outward focus that enables libraries to generate public service information that engages communities as true policy participants. Community participation in policy development can be seen as an authentic version of policy mapping.

I have observed in the past (Irwin 2012) that public library boards, in their ideal form as identified by Young (2013), serve as representatives of the community's interests. Pal (2006) states that policy and decision making is the creation

https://doi.org/10.1515/ 9783110533323-010

of, or is created by, values, which in turn establishes a set of normative standards. The primary focus of this chapter is to further the understanding of the impact of decision makers' values on the design of public policy. What is of significant relevance is the interplay between public policy and community, particularly the values of the central players; how do they see themselves, as policy makers, takers, or fakers? How do self-perceptions influence and shape the agenda and its delivery? The values displayed form a set of normative processes that influence the responses of local community members.

To build a definition of the term value, I like to draw upon the work of Pal (1987, 2006, 2009). He describes public policies as artefacts that have to be deliberately constructed, and argues that the forces that drive the formation process reside in the creators' interests, values and casual assumptions (Pal 1987, 109). He further describes policies as responses to problems. How the character and nature of the problem is understood will deeply affect the character of the response. Values, in this sense, describe how one sees, or does not see, an issue. If the purpose of a public library board is to represent the community's interest (Irwin 2012), then the board as an entity does not in itself possess an absolute power; rather, it acts in trust for the community, demonstrating and responding to the broader community welfare. As true policy makers, library board trustees are charged with representing the diverse interests and natures of their respective communities. By understanding what their constituents want from the library, they can guide the library in such a way as to match services to identified priorities (Henricks and Henricks-Lepp 2014, 662).

Mapping Policy

The process of mapping policy by the institutional decision makers, the library board trustees, provides an important lens in constructing a deeper understanding of the issue. To better grasp this concept, the set of normative beliefs that lie behind the policy mapping, what Margaret Weir (Clark 2002, 777) has termed a decision maker's "public philosophy" requires unpacking, in a bid to more precisely drill down to the broad perceptions that are tied to values and moral principles. As stated, Pal (2006), in his analysis of policy impacts and their relationship to the broader society, has observed that policy decision making is created by the values of the decision makers. I contend that these normative standards have far-reaching consequences (Irwin 2012). They lay the foundation for a model of civic engagement, what Simmons and Oliver (2013, 24) describe as a choice for trustees to become involved in community life and action which "affords the institution of the public library and public library trustees the opportunity to help shape their community's future". Through acknowledgement of this interpretation of the trustee's role, the trustee can then act as community engager, utilizing public input as a navigational tool in policy development.

Theoretically public libraries are accountable to multiple constituents. Because each constituent can influence decisions about the library, either directly or indirectly, an effective library must understand varying perceptions of priorities (Henricks and Henricks-Lepp 2014, 646). Balancing, and at times favouring, a particular set of priorities to advance the role of the library requires community-focused institutional policy makers to display a fully aware public cognition, demonstrating a type of communitarian sense of purpose or compass. Otherwise the policy makers may end up willingly, and blindly, taking instruction from a type of disembodied global positioning system (GPS) policy approach, arriving at a destination without any real awareness of how they have done so. When library trustees know how constituents conceptualize policy purpose, they can use the information to assist in the decision making process about which services to offer in addition to educating stakeholders about how decisions about the allocation of funds were made (Van House and Childers 1993; Henricks and Henricks-Lepp 2014, 646).

Currently, neoliberal policy approaches such as value for money and outcomes dominate the policy landscape and present their own sets of challenges (Boughey and Cooper 2009, 178). Stein (2001) has labelled neoliberal policy preference as a product of the cult of efficiency, in which no other course of action can be contemplated given the neoliberal emphasis on a performance culture. Decision making is limited to the very narrow range of bottom-line options, creating an underlying paradigm that constrains the cognitive range of solutions available to policy makers. The approach is also known as the neoliberal audit culture.

Case-in-point, prior to the recent global readjustment to oil prices, Alberta was the wealthiest province in Canada. During the apex of its economic prosperity it was also the only jurisdiction in North America where the majority of local library boards charged patrons to use their public libraries. The practice came into being in the 1980s for a variety of reasons; in the main, like the introduction of user fees for other public services, charging for library cards was viewed as a ready source of funds for financially struggling libraries. In addition, having the public paying for access was seen as a positive reflection of demonstrating the public's regard for the service. The fees existed long after the province achieved significant fiscal prosperity. The continuance of the practice rested in the unique form of conservatism espoused by the then popular Alberta premier Ralph Klein, who favoured big business, lower taxes and privatization of public services while leading the province from 1992 to 2006 (Hammond 2007, 1). Klein's policies included a focus on user-pay models for all manner of services. Paying for library cards was something that Alberta's citizens have accepted for the most part. It was infused into their culture as acceptable practice, as the only common-sense option, to the point that any other approach appeared as both alien and abhorrent. The issue of payment for library cards will be further addressed later in the chapter.

Bounded Rationality

Alberta's example of cultural infusion is akin to a type of bounded rationality within the policy making process. Exploration of how the concept of bounded rationality can influence the current public library policy process, through understanding the extent of the bounds, is an essential part of the policy journey. To what degree are public library boards being bounded; by what and for whom? Addressing these questions resides at the essence of the comprehension of a policy's aims and purpose. The concept of bounded rationality is especially valuable when considering the overall policy enterprise in terms of public libraries, as public libraries are arguably one of the few public bodies that currently adhere to the values of traditional embedded liberalism. Libraries give the appearance of remaining relatively free from being driven by a specific ideological imperative, preserving the commons in terms of both place and service, and of also ensuring that the purity of adhering to a public mission remains intact. But is this in reality fact or fiction?

In his research on library fees in Alberta, Hammond (2007, 5) noted the extreme difficulty he had in getting librarians to comment on the record regarding the practice. He noted that a number of librarians requested anonymity as a condition of use of their comments citing how hard it was to speak out publicly against the majority viewpoint. Hammond postulated that there was at that time a dominant cultural acceptance of user fees, and holding an opposing view was tantamount to being seen as an institutional pariah.

Gates (2005, 159), in his recounting of the Buddhist metaphor of the monkey box, illustrates the undesirable consequences of the practice of rigid observance to a set of principles. In the metaphor, one entraps a monkey by placing a piece of fruit inside a box with a hole large enough for the monkey to put its hand inside and grasp the fruit. Gates alludes to this as the intractability of a particular policy mindset. Once the fruit is grasped, the monkey cannot free itself from the box without letting go of the fruit. The monkey refuses to let go and remains trapped with its hand in the box. The fruit can be seen as analogous to blind adherence to marketization principles. Gates proposes that for policy makers to take action equivalent to letting go of the fruit and setting themselves free, they would need to engage and interact with the whole community. Those that successfully do so will be acknowledged as policy makers. Policy takers are bounded by the concept of keeping a firm grip on the fruit itself regardless of the consequence of remaining trapped in the box. Their visualization of any alternative is limited to the existence of the single piece of fruit.

I have suggested (Irwin 2012) that neoliberalism at times dominates the architecture of public library policy development. Contemporary public sector administrative practice writ large can be seen to be guided by a neoliberal hegemony, which has been described (Giroux 2004) as an ideology and as politics buoyed by the spirit of a market fundamentalism that in turn subordinates the art of democratic politics. It favours, and subsequently grasps, market values over all else. A neoliberal preference in public library board governance can be seen as both undemocratic and detrimental to the community for which the board is purported to act in trust. It reduces all decisions to the simple formula of being "business decisions," and, as such, irrevocable, beyond question and irreversible (Irwin 2012, 3), given that business decisions are seen as the idealized norm.

Policy fakers seek, and are bounded by, the easy, and seemingly popular, as opposed to genuine and deep, action. A common policy challenged faced by libraries is the issue of what is appropriate public material. For example, the readily agreeable practice of imposing censorship, banning or limiting access to information, either in print or on the Internet, with the latter sometimes given the rather innocent and ubiquitous term of filtering as opposed to censorship, is an issue. It is an issue easy to grasp, think of the children, and seemingly popular in the media. The trustee is standing up for community decency. Challenging a library's censorship or filtering policies can tend to be a dangerous act. It can at times bring into question the challenger's own moral turpitude. With any quick move to impose censorship, the policy-decider is engaged in a facsimile of action, as opposed to addressing the deeper policy questions of public access, the erosion of civil liberty, the role of information freedom and guarding against the slippery slope of public censorship by the state.

Values

In identifying policy action, it is necessary to distinguish between popularism and communitarianism. The distinction can be seen as the relationship between means and ends. Communitarianism speaks to shared values and moral decision making. Harvey (2006, 206) identifies shared values as "those of an open democracy dedicated to the achievement of social equity coupled with economic, political, and cultural justice," which create an environment for ensuring equitable public institutions. It is the library board that sets the institutional tenor that infuses the organizational culture with a set of values. Setting the culture is a key responsibility of the board in its role as cultural landscaper for the institution. The board's influence filters throughout the organization, setting both the mood and the context of the professional environment. A board fixated on the efficiency agenda can seriously counter the very core of professional librarianship (Irwin 2012, 9), while a board fixated on popularism provides only a shallow reflection of the community it deems to serve.

Returning to the Alberta library fees example, a 2001 provincial survey (Hammond 2007, 12) showed that 92% of library administrators were opposed to the fee model for library service. Many at the time did not actively lobby for removal of the charge. Conversely, the survey of library trustees, ultimately responsible for setting the policy, showed a slight majority was in favour of keeping the fees. Follow-up survey questions to the trustee group found that fees were seen as an easy, direct source of income for the library system rather than the difficult, time-consuming efforts of concerted lobbying, especially in an environment hostile to public funding. Fees were seen as easy and popular and were therefore the chosen option.

Neoliberalism

No discussion of policy takers can occur without exploration of the influence of neoliberal hegemony on the policy enterprise, Stein's (2001) "cult of efficiency". Giroux's (2004, 124) description of a new kind of public pedagogy, the neoliberal metanarrative, as a hegemonic discourse of marketization and efficiency, is important to note when attempting to contemplate why decision makers place considerations of market above all else. Giroux further describes the phenomenon as a pervasive activity whose language shapes and restricts all other approaches. Many policy deciders have adopted the neoliberal approach as instinctive, accepting capital and market relations. The efficiency cult is viewed as the natural order of being. The old natural order, one defined by the democratic social contract and focused on public empathy, institutional ethics and community integrity, is no longer given any real thought. When defining neoliberalism, it is useful to chart its historical development. Theobald and Dinkleman (1995, 14) contend that the emergence of the modern Western state brought into being a new perspective of liberal liberty that failed to recognize that "in its staunch advocacy of individual rights and liberties, [it] does not adequately take into account the social costs of decisions made by individuals, nor does it promote decision making that affords a high value to long-term consequences."

Public Relationship

Finally, policy makers need to consider how they situate the relationship of public library boards with their public. In her review of sensemaking and public policy development, Cavanagh (2004) recounts her story as a manager with the Ottawa Public Library in the early 2000s when systemwide public Internet access was vigorously being introduced. In her reflection, she cites how an emotionally charged media, an institutionally challenged staff and a vocal minority of the public escalated the issue of Internet censorship within the library system. Her experience was by no means unique. I remember my own experience at the time as a director of a different large Canadian public library system, when Internet services were also being grown significantly. I can affirm there was a real sense at the time from a few patrons and staff that libraries were turning into porn palaces. Cavanagh recounts the sensemaking at the time, describes what she calls "the ambiguous meanings socially constructed by the cacophony of voices" (357) in designing a public policy that serves all, but is designed by a vocal few. I remember protracted senior management team discussions at the time. It was important to remain calm and consider the broader purpose of the library, to preserve intellectual freedom and to stand firm against censorship. There was a discussion on the need for listening and acting without being a policy faker, seeking easy, political safe popularism. Avoiding policy faking is the real challenge.

The Literature

The literature on policy makers, policy fakers and policy takers contains many perspectives, some of which are outlined.

Policy Makers

A variety of lens and a range of explanations and theories abound regarding the state of policy formation and delivery that can be applied to the current state of public library policy. Howlett, Ramesh and Perl (2009) offer the classical theoretical approach that policy making is an exercise of choice between a range of policy options and tools to meet specific issues. Hampton (2009) notes a more practical and prevalent trend where policy framers are shying away from the policy maker approach, given the potential cost of public rejection, social upheaval and political damage for elected officials. Avoidance appears to be the approach preferred by policy fakers.

Simmons and Oliver (2013) state that the library and the community should expect that their trustees are linked to the decision makers and understand in which channels of communication decision makers work. Decision makers may reside within government or outside of it. Currently it seems that classical policy making requires a special kind of public courage. As Simmons and Oliver further note, "civic engagement may mean that a trustee or trustees move to the front of the decision queue and facilitate civic deliberations" (25). That is where courage is required. *Censorship Dateline* (2008, 60) recounts the example of the US public library in Fargo, North Dakota where the library board took the policy stance not to act in loco parentis. Parents and guardians should be responsible for what children read, see and listen to, not the library. A child of twelve or thirteen could check out an R-rated video, something very contentious, and challenged by some members of the community. Upon deliberation, the board stood by its decision and stated it should be up to the parent to decide what a child views.

Simmons and Oliver (2013, 25) offer an important definition of civic engagement as it relates to policy making: "civic engagement means reminding others that we are citizens with responsibilities to make our communities better". The stance favouring direct civic engagement requires a communitarian approach, rejecting both neoliberal efficiency and easy popularism as the driving forces behind decision making. *Success Stories* (2007, 117) recounts the case of the Delta Junction, Alaska, Library Board that voted five to two to retain a painting hanging in the public library. The 1912 painting by Frenchman Paul Chabas titled *September Morn*, features a nude woman up to her ankles in water in front of a natural mountainous setting. The painting was donated by a long-time resident and past library board member. The painting was hung on the wall the night before the dedication of the city hall/library complex in 1988. The painting generated controversy in 2000 and a call for its removal. The library board received comments from several residents concerning its display.

Another example of a policy maker is illustrated in *Success Stories* (2007, 117), as demonstrated by the board of the Marshall Missouri Public Library. The board approved a new policy on materials selection agreeing to put two coming-of-age graphic novels back on the shelves. Trustees established a committee to create a selection policy in the wake of a challenge by a single Marshall resident over the appropriateness of *Fun Home* by Alison Bechdel and *Blankets* by Craig Thompson, which were pulled from circulation until guidelines were established. The fact that a challenge by a single resident caused a policy review is troubling in itself. Both examples cited present the challenge of rejecting easy popularism that arises in determining what is appropriate in a public institution. Questions of censorship remain central to many library policy discussions.

Policy Takers

Stein (2001) charts the emergence of policy takers with the hegemonic concurrence of meso-policy stances bounded by neoliberal views. She describes takers as those who have abdicated agency in favour of the market, the cult of efficiency. Neoliberal policy takers have a tendency towards more directive policy analysis which is identified by a strategic potential whereas it becomes a means of promoting a particular perspective that might otherwise be out-evidenced. Peck and Tickell (2002) describe policy takers as those constrained by neoliberalism, a form of high politics that shapes environments, contexts and frameworks and limits choice and options. The phenomenon is evident in the Alberta library fees example. In the provincial document provided by Alberta on public library service policy in 2006, that listed "borrowing library resources in any format as a service to be provided at no charge", the document also stated that "libraries may charge for the issuing of a library card" (quoted in Hammond 2007). This can be seen as a form of high politics in action. At the time, the position was defended thus:

> Pat McNamee, library consultant at Alberta Community Development [the government department in charge of public libraries], chooses her words carefully when describing the government position on fees. "Libraries are not permitted to charge a membership fee. All members of the public are library members, with free access to the five or six basic services that the Act mandates. But library boards are permitted, at their option, to charge for the issuance of a library card, for use in tracking borrowed materials." (Hammond 2007, 4, citing Mardiros 2001)

Alberta makes available various documents on public library policies and templates for use by library boards in Alberta (https://www.alberta.ca/public-library-tools-and-resources.aspx; https://open.alberta.ca/publications/policies-and-bylaws-a-guide-for-alberta-public-library-boards) with the template for by-laws referring to a fee for the issuance of library cards.

Policy Fakers

Arnstein's (1969) *Ladder of Citizen Participation* eloquently defines policy fakery as the difference between the act of empty public ritual and the authentic possession by the public of real power, the ability or desire to affect policy outcomes. Campbell (2010) denotes substantial research regarding the relative ease of tokenistic engagement of citizens which in turn supports current system legitimacy and elite prerogatives. Campbell and Marshall (2000) state that all too often the policy process focuses on the how of public participation and not the why. They argue that ignorance of why opens up the process for misdirection and/or manipulation.

Arnstein's (1969) ladder of citizen participation re-emerged forty years after its initial introduction and has formed the basis of much of today's thinking on the subject in the public policy arena. Arnstein's research originally focused on the role of the citizen in the urban planning policy process. She employed the image of an eight-rung ladder as a means of identifying a continuum of approaches with respect to citizen participation. Arnstein contended that the continuum could be divided into three main categories: nonparticipation involving manipulation and therapy, tokenism comprising information, consultation, and placation, and citizen power encompassing partnership, delegated power and citizen control. Her typology clearly demonstrated that not all participation is of equal value and that, at the time of her original authorship, tokenism dominated as the method through which the majority of citizens participated (Irwin 2012, 8). Policy fakery is alive and well practised today. The illusion of action, public consultation after a decision has been made, and choosing a safe, populist decision with the possibility of little immediate public backlash, are real and actual aspects of policy fakery.

In Search of Praxis

The underlying purpose of this chapter is to define good policy practice which should be guided by a set of publicly-oriented, outward-facing values and principles and expose the current state of public library governance in the process. The principles can be defined as an alternative to both infused neoliberal hegemony and a growing reliance on unproblematic populism. Library trustees as genuine policy makers ensure that citizens will be seen as co-creators of public work, rather than simply consumers of expert-shaped policies (Campbell 2010). The policy maker approach may very well require a re-democratization of the policy paradigm, perhaps ultimately leading to processes described by urban planners as wicked, messy, costly, lengthy and ultimately democratic.

The Alberta library fee issue caused many individuals to abandon library cards. A $10 to $20 per year fee may not seem much to most people but at the time social assistance paid about $1000 per month and Alberta was one of the most expensive provinces in Canada. If the choice was between rent and food or a library card, the answer was no library card (Hammond 2007, 7). As one Albertan librarian interviewed at the time, who requested anonymity, stated, perhaps a darker purpose was also at play: "I suspect that many thought that the addition of front-end payment instils value in library services [but] some may have thought that such fees keep out the 'riff-raff'" (Hammond 2007, 8).

Cavanagh (2004) demonstrates the policy fakery of the Ottawa Public Library board on the Internet filtering issue. The issue resolved itself through a technical solution. A technical workaround was developed. The introduction of Internet management software enabled filtered access to be selected through a menu option with a default choice of filtered access for all children, leaving the policy language intact. As she noted,

> This adjustment to the standard public desktop configuration combined with changes in use regulations were gratefully approved by all board members in a specially convened meeting in late April 2003. Both at that meeting and afterwards, board members privately expressed their individual residual concerns that they would be wrongly perceived to have changed their minds about the library's overall position on intellectual freedom. (Cavanagh 2004, 356)

Why does it seem that library boards, like many other public bodies, adopt an approach that tends to "eliminate democratic politics by making the notion of the social impossible to imagine beyond the isolated consumer and the logic of the market" (Giroux 2004, 107)? This is especially true when public library users are considered to be consumers and not citizens, a disturbing trend in many public libraries. If users are deemed consumers and not citizens, how a library board arrives at its decisions in terms of democratic transparency is not seen as important as the safety of the decisions made by the board members themselves (Irwin 2012, 7).

The matrix in Table 1 encapsulates the discussion from this chapter and provides readers with a device, a yardstick or tool, to examine current policy processes, directions and goals.

Table 1: Policy Matrix.

Policy Type	Policy Collaboration	Policy Creation	Policy Plan	Policy Substance (Principles, objectives, measures)
Policy Maker	Broad collaborative dialogue	Goals identified and shared by all stakeholders	Organizational strategy and alignment	Values a combination of local and expert knowledge.
	Public is partner in issue identification and design	Starts with community/ needs assessment	Community visioning	Focuses on the policy, why
			Issue response and transparent problem solving	
		All participants have access to the same information		

Table 1: (continued)

Policy Type	Policy Collaboration	Policy Creation	Policy Plan	Policy Substance (Principles, objectives, measures)
Policy Taker	Sees the public as customers, not as collaborators or co-creators Limited by a market orientation Fiscal bounded rationality	Closed, in-house decision making Board sees itself as an executive decision making body Board does not view itself as trustees, but rather as a Board of Directors	Cult of efficiency mindset is prevalent Strategic potentials drive all considerations	Principles of neoliberal marketization define and drive the process Focuses on the policy, how
Policy Faker	Tokenistic Appearance of policy input but no real care about public considerations	Focuses on avoiding negative political consequences Media driven (perception is focus) Stymied managerial approach	Path of least resistance Easy populism	Managerial approach to the process Defined by tokenistic community engagement model Looks for safe policy, path of least resistance

The question remains: who gets to set the policy direction for the public library? Librarians can make ethical principles operational at the local level by adopting practices that affirm professional codes of ethics. But it is board policy that gives the institutional mandate for behaviour. Policies enable the institution to behave in accordance with its mission and philosophy. They establish the code of conduct to be followed in anticipated events that numerous writers have identified where policies are seen as a means to make sure decisions and actions align with the library's principles and mission. For example, Weingand (2001) states that policies "articulate the library's position on matters of philosophy and operations" and help the library fulfil the roles and provide the services it has selected to meet community needs (73). The future of the public library as a relevant civic institution rests on how the question concerning the setting of policy directions is answered.

References

Arnstein, S.R. "A Ladder of Citizen Participation". *Journal of the American Planning Association* 35, no. 4 (1969): 216–224. DOI: 10.1080/01944366908977225
Boughey, A., and M. Cooper. "Public Libraries: Political Vision Versus Public Demand?" *Aslib Proceedings* 62, no. 2 (2010): 175–201. https://doi.org/10.1108/00012531011034982.
Campbell, D. "Democratic Norms to Deliberate Forms: Managing Tools and Tradeoffs in Community-Based Civic Engagement". *Public Administration and Management* 5 (2010): 305–342.
Campbell, H., and C. Marshall. "Public Involvement and Planning: Looking Beyond the One to the Many". *International Planning Studies* 5 (2000): 321–344. DOI: 10.1080/713672862
Cavanagh, M. "Sensemaking a Public Library's Internet Policy Crisis". *Library Management* 26, no. 6/7 (2005): 351–360. https://doi.org/10.1108/01435120410609761 .
"Censorship Dateline: Libraries: Fargo, North Dakota" *American Library Association. Newsletter for Intellectual Freedom.* 57 no.2 (2008): 60–61 https://journals.ala.org/index.php/nif/issue/view/462
Clark, D. "Neoliberalism and Public Service Reform; Canada in Comparative Perspective". *Canadian Journal of Political Science* 35 (2002): 771–793.
Colebatch, H. "What Work Makes Policy?" *Policy Sciences* 39 (1986): 309–321.
Gates, G. "Awakening to School Community: Buddhist Philosophy for Educational Reform". *Journal of Educational Thought* 39 (2005): 149–174.
Giroux, H. *The Terror of Neoliberalism.* Boulder, Co: Paradigm, 2004.
Hampton, G. "Narrative Policy Analysis and the Integration of Public Involvement in Decision Making". *Policy Sciences* 42 (2009): 227–242.
Hammond, J. "Cash Cow: User Fees in Alberta Public Libraries". *Partnership: The Canadian Journal of Library and Information Practice and Research* 2, no. 1 (2007): 1–23.
Harvey, D. *A Brief History of Neoliberalism.* New York: Oxford University Press, 2005.
Henricks, S., and G. Henricks-Lepp. "Multiple Constituencies Model in the Identification of Library Effectiveness". *Library Management* 35, no. 8/9 (2014): 645–665. http://nppl.ir/wp-content/uploads/Multiple-constituencies-model-in-the-identification-of-library-effectiveness.pdf.
Howlett, M., M. Ramesh, and A. Perl. *Studying Public Policy: Policy Cycles and Policy Sub-Cycles.* 3rd ed. Don Mills, Ont.: Oxford University Press, 2009.
Irwin, B. "The Value of a Communitarian Approach to Public Library Governance: Rejecting Neoliberal Practice". *Canadian Journal of Information and Library Science* 36, no. 1–2 (2012): 1–15.
Mardiros, S. "Spreading the Word: Banff's Very Public Library". *Alberta Views* (Jan.–Feb.2001): 37–39. http://www.albertaviews.ab.ca/issues/2001/janfeb01/janfeb01social2.pdf
Pal, L. *Public Policy Analysis: An Introduction.* Toronto, Ont.: Methuen, 1987.

Pal, L. *Beyond Policy Analysis: Public Issue Management in Turbulent Times*. 3rd ed. Toronto, Ont.: Nelson, 2006.

Pal, L. *Beyond Policy Analysis: Public Issue Management in Turbulent Times*. 4th ed. Toronto, Ont.: Nelson, 2010.

Peck, J., and A. Tickell. "Neoliberalizing Space." *Antipode* 34, no. 3 (2002): 380–404.

Simmons, K., and K. Oliver. "Library Trustees as Community Connectors". *National Civic Review* 101 (2013): 24–26. DOI: 101002/ncr:21097.

Stein, J.G. *The Cult of Efficiency*. Toronto, Ont.: Anansi Press, 2001.

"Success Stories: Libraries: Delta Junction, Alaska: Marshall, Missouri" *American Library Association. Newsletter for Intellectual Freedom* 56 no. 3 (2007): 117 https://journals.ala.org/index.php/nif/issue/viewIssue/467/214

Theobald, P., and T. Dinkleman. "The Parameters of the Liberal-Communitarian Debate." *Peabody Journal of Education* 70 (1995): 5–18. DOI: 10.1080/01619569509538845.

Weingand, D. *Administration of the Small Public Library*. 4th ed. Chicago: American Library Association, 2001.

Young, R. "More than Just Books: the Role of Public Libraries in Building Community and Promoting Civic Engagement." *National Civic Review* 101, no. 4 (2012): 30–32. doi.org/10.1002/ncr.21098.

Ian Anstice

8 Trusting in Others: The Experience of Councils Transferring Libraries to Other Organisations Since 2010

Abstract: The last decade has seen considerable change to the governance of English public libraries. This chapter examines how and why the transformation has taken place and its impact on public library service. A wide variety of models of governance is present in the United Kingdom today. The spectrum of library governance ranges from libraries run by volunteers who need to fundraise for their electricity and rely on book donations at one end to well-funded council libraries at the other with numerous variations in between. Examples of public libraries run by non-profit trusts, various kinds of social enterprises, volunteers and partnerships are provided in this chapter, and advantages and disadvantages explored. The tough questions about the causes of the current situation are asked. Innovative thinking is required to find the most appropriate way forward to ensure effective library services meet identified user needs.

Keywords: Corporate governance; Public libraries – United Kingdom; Volunteer libraries

Introduction

There has been more change to the governance of English public libraries in the last decade than in the previous century. Public libraries have long been a facilitator of access to information to those without the ability to otherwise pay. The Victorians were clear that this was to aid in the education of the enlightenment of the working population (Wikipedia 2020). The purpose of the public library has continued to provide equal and equitable access to information and imagination to this day, with an expansion into free computer and internet access being the most obvious modern development. While this mission has never been formally challenged, the way it should be delivered has increasingly changed, or been questioned, in recent years.

The public library service within the United Kingdom is a highly atomised one, with 151 different public library services within England alone, in addition to those present in Scotland, Wales and Northern Ireland. The service is one of the longest established in the world, with public libraries becoming widespread in the Victoria era and receiving periodic boosts since then, with around 3800

https://doi.org/10.1515/ 9783110533323-011

separate buildings in 2017 (CIPFA 2018). The total library spend is around £900 million in 2016/17, falling from a peak of £1 billion in 2009/10 (Kean 2016; CIPFA 2019). The libraries vary from large central libraries to small neighbourhood branches or rooms, and everything in between. The loan of books and membership is, by law, free, with fines and other charges accounting for 8% of expenditure (Locality 2015, 4) with the rest being met by local and central government funding. Library usage amongst the adult population was over one half in 2000 but has since declined to around one third (UK DCMS 2017c)

Faced by pressures to reduce expenditure due both to austerity and diminished faith in the standard council-run model, library decision-makers have tried a variety of experiments. There has been a proliferation in the variety of ways of running libraries and in the overall numbers administered differently. The UK has seen a dramatic increase in the number of authorities that has passed their library services to non-profit trusts of various stripes from almost none in 2010 to over thirty today. In addition, the number of volunteer libraries has increased in the same period from a bare handful to nearly five hundred (Public Libraries News 2019b). How and why has this transformation taken place? What impact has it made on the public library service?

The Movement of Libraries from Local Government Control: Action and Reaction

There are both financial and ideological reasons for moving libraries away from direct local government control. What appears to be the most powerful motivator is the need to seek cheaper ways of running library services following significant reductions in local council budgets. The Association for Public Service Excellence estimates a reduction of £3 billion in money available for neighbourhood services, such as bins and leisure, since 2010 (Butler 2017). The cut would be serious enough if spread equally but, in practice, has been widely variable, with the worst affected authorities facing reductions of 22% and the best off a mere 5%. Faced with such reductions, councils naturally look to any savings they can make, especially in areas where there is little practical statutory protection.

The public library service, delegated to local authorities, technically enjoys protection under the 1964 Public Libraries and Museums Act (UK). The terms of the legislation require the Secretary of State to superintend the sector and ensure all councils operate a "comprehensive and efficient" service. Ed Vaizey, Culture Minister from 2010 to 2016, despite his somewhat bellicose statements before he came to power (Page 2010), failed to intervene in a single council while in office, despite some of the deepest reductions to library services in history. His decision to avoid action in authority after authority effectively led to a green, and ever more beckoning, light to councils who were considering the legality of reducing library services (UK Parliament 2012). His successor, Rob Wilson, in office from 2016 to June 2017, showed a slightly increased willingness to intervene (Kean 2017) but his defeat in the snap election meant he never actually did so.

The public library sector itself has struggled to come up with a sustained or even uniform response to the financial challenge. The Society of Chief Librarians (SCL) consisted as the name suggests of all the heads of library services and was a strongly apolitical organisation whose members saw themselves as council officers unable to criticise council or government policy. Their response has been to work on advocacy, such as the Universal Offers that library services should provide, rather than argue against changes to library budgets per se. SCL has been replaced by Libraries Connected (https://www.librariesconnected.org. uk/), which continues with Universal Offers (https://www.librariesconnected. org.uk/page/universal-library-offers), the provision of training and resources and advocacy. The professional association for librarians, the Chartered Institute of Library and Information Professionals (CILIP), initially took a similarly conciliatory approach, aiming to work with the minister, but membership votes (Farrington 2013) and a change in Chief Executive, has led a more active campaign to promote the need for paid professional staff. CILIP membership is low in public libraries; the organisation itself has little funds; and its impact so far has been limited. Librarians themselves are council employees and unable to openly criticise decisions made in their own authorities.

The trade unions, notably Unison and Unite, have been involved in local actions but have largely had other larger problems with local government cuts in other sectors. The baton has been taken up by local campaign groups, whose support can be co-opted by the council, or by a relatively small number of people in national groups like the Library Campaign (http://www.librarycampaign. com/) or the now defunct Voices for the Library (http://www.voicesforthelibrary. org.uk/2017/10/an-announcement-and-final-blog-post-from-voices-for-the-library/) , who lack resources. Indeed, the whole sector has little or no promotional budget and has thus found itself largely without a significant voice, outside of the occasional quote in a news story.

Following on from the *Independent Library Report for England*, written in December 2014 by William Sieghart, reporting through the Department for Digital, Culture, Media and Sport (formerly Department for Culture, Media and Sport) (DCMS) (UK DCMS 2014), the government formed in 2015 a Libraries Taskforce for England (https://www.artscouncil.org.uk/supporting-libraries/libraries-taskforce). The role of the Taskforce is to implement the Independent Library

Report, provide leadership, and help reinvigorate the public library service. The Taskforce attempts to co-ordinate responses to change and to plan for the future, within its boundaries as an agency funded by the Government. It has produced several reports on various forms of governance which will be examined in the relevant sections below. While library closures were hardly unknown under previous governments, the combination of reduced budgets and ineffective intervention led to a kind of open season on public libraries. The number of library service points went down by 146 in 2010/11 and then by 201 in 2011/12 (Flood 2012). The closure of local service points led to a high level of protest by those who wished to see their local library remain open, including the first national day of action in 2011 (Page 2011). The protests, along with an increased awareness of alternatives to closures, led to a decline in closures after their peak in 2011/12, with the Chartered Institute of Public Finance and Accountancy (CIPFA) counting the total number of libraries in the UK as 3850 in 2015/16, compared to 4023 in 2013/14, 4482 in 2009/10 and 4622 in 2003/4 (CIPFA 2018; CIPFA 2019).

The Big Society and Encouragement of Volunteers

Because the percentage of the library budget spent on staffing has always been high, with salaries accounting for up to one half of the total, the first and most obvious alternative to closing a library is to use volunteers. Moreover, volunteers can be an income-generator, rather than a cost, as they are motivated to raise funding. They are not an entirely untested concept. Volunteer libraries are known historically and internationally, with other countries, such as Germany (Decher 2017), and Australia, sometimes having thousands, but unusual in the UK due to the prevalence of council funding. There appear to have been fewer than ten by the end of the late twentieth century, albeit with some remarkably long-lived examples such as Morrab in Cornwall that has run continuously since 1818 (BBC News 2012).

The change of political climate under prime minister David Cameron led to volunteer schemes becoming more and more politically acceptable. The Big Society concept, although ultimately a failure or at least renamed, gave strong encouragement to those faced with a library that would otherwise have closed. Almost from the start, as far back as July 2010, the sector was specifically mentioned by Cameron (BBC News 2010) as a possibility for community takeover, with the BBC reporting that the "prime minister said groups should be able to run post offices, libraries, transport services and shape housing projects". Indeed, this was a continuing theme with a Prime Minister not otherwise known for his close relationship with libraries, with a further quotation on the subject in July 2014 (BBC News 2014).

While the idea of volunteers replacing paid staff was brought to the fore, it is notable that the Government did not see the approach primarily as a way of reducing costs. Indeed, the Big Society movement, while obviously partially concerned about budgets, was also about communities and volunteers somehow being better custodians for services than local councils. The Community Knowledge Hub (https://libraries.communityknowledgehub.org.uk/content/community-knowledge-hub) identified five reasons for volunteer libraries, only one of which was associated with reduced costs. The others were increased community involvement, increased take-up of services, innovation, diversification and improved access. The idea is that the local community knows best what it wants and is the most motivated to seek improvements, with the corollary that paid staff, perhaps in it only for the money, and jaded after years of service, do not understand needs and are apathetic.

The Libraries Taskforce publication on volunteer libraries, *Community Managed Libraries: Good Practice Toolkit* (UK Libraries Taskforce 2018) sidesteps the question of whether they are a good thing or not by focusing on how they can best be established and maintained. The terminology is also interesting, in that all public libraries are effectively community managed: the council is a directly democratically elected part of the community. The term community library is increasingly a term widely accepted for volunteer libraries. It used to mean a smaller public library. Use of the word community with all its positive connotations, obfuscates what a community library actually is. By publishing the toolkit, the Taskforce not only recognised the current state of play but also endorsed it, giving helpful guidance to others about how to run libraries themselves. There is a little or no criticism of the model in the report, although it does include discussion of some of the practical difficulties involved. The Government commissioned a further report in 2017 which looked at volunteers: *Research and Analysis to Explore the Service Effectiveness and Sustainability of Community Managed Libraries in England* (UK DCMS 2017b). Again avoiding any value judgements, the report analysed how volunteers were performing in several areas such as sustainability and recommended ways to improve.

The Reality of Volunteer Libraries

There is an element of Pandora's Box when it comes to the first introduction of volunteer libraries. For many years, it was considered that paying staff for their work, in public libraries or elsewhere, was the natural order of things. Once it was discovered that volunteers could take over a library and keep it running, the floodgates opened. In Buckinghamshire, those fighting library closures in 2006, such as in Little Chalfont, took the libraries, initially, and perhaps ironically, with some resistance from the council, into their own hands and, vitally importantly, succeeded in keeping them open (Community Knowledge Hub 2012). While the example had little initial impact at a time when budgets were generally healthy on a national scale, the experience was not forgotten when the need later arose. There are two non-monetary advantages, perhaps rarely acknowledged, to encourage volunteer libraries. The first is that the council can legitimately claim that it is not closing a library, for it is clearly still open, albeit now run by people doing it for free. Secondly, as is clear from private correspondence, the new model effectively co-opted those protesting against the withdrawal of council support to the council side to work with the council even while the paid staff were being removed. Indeed, there can be divisions between those campaigning for a local library: those who want a library in some form, no matter what; and those who are willing to countenance paid staff only.

There have been many criticisms of volunteers replacing paid staff in libraries (Public Libraries News 2019c). Professional librarians and their supporters fear that simply having willing members of the public doing the job will lead to the library losing necessary skills such as neutrality and information-seeking. Author Alan Gibbons argued that "A room with books in it is just a room, without a trained librarian, it's not a library" (McIntyre 2016). Quite apart from the demeaning of librarianship as a profession by replacing librarians with anyone wishing to do the job for free, volunteers have been accused of unwittingly assisting libraries in removing paid staff by giving politicians a different course of action than the politically undesirable closing of libraries.

The success or otherwise of volunteer libraries is still up for debate. There has been almost no government research on the subject and other studies on the subject are flawed either via bias, small sample sizes, or both. What is clear is that the first significant volunteer libraries to open, in Buckinghamshire, are surviving more than ten years on from their founding. Little Chalfont Community Library claims that it has "gone from strength to strength" (Yellowley 2019) in that time, with a building extension and the receipt of a Queens Voluntary Service Award. Critics, and even Jim Brooks, former Chairman, pointed out that their success is not easily duplicated (Triskele Books 2011). The most obvious reason is that the successful volunteer libraries are all in highly prosperous areas, run largely by retired professionals who know how to manage a building and how to fundraise.

Such a happy combination cannot be said to exist everywhere and fertile ground may not always be needed. Volunteer libraries in poorer urban areas have some chance of success, such as in the case of New Cross Library. Council funding was withdrawn from the Lewisham branch in 2011. Since then, volunteers have managed to raise the £13,000 per annum needed to keep the building open, although they worry that the council will start charging rent, which would bring charges up to a possibly unsustainable £22,000. The library has survived by transforming itself into a community hub[1], signified by renaming the building New Cross Learning and offering a substantial range of training and events (https://newxlearning.org/). Another example of a so far successful volunteer library is Frecheville in Sheffield with reports that it is thriving (Dunbar 2019). Nor is this experience unique even in Sheffield, as a similar rosy story was painted in neighbouring Greenhill Library with growing confidence (Greenhill Community Library 2019).

Funding can come from a wide range of sources. Donations of books and free staff time reduce costs, and annual fundraising events are reported to bring in the necessary money to pay unavoidable bills, finding alternative funding through social enterprises and partnerships. Funding is always an issue for volunteer libraries, with a wide variety of fund-raising possibilities being considered, including in one case an application to sell alcohol (BBC News 2017b). Libraries raise funds through financial donations (https://uk.virginmoneygiving. com/charity-web/charity/finalCharityHomepage.action?charityId=1011988) but applications for grants are also common, especially for larger ticket items such as building renovations, which may otherwise be a problem for groups with limited incomes. Rather perversely, funding from the council for volunteers can sometimes exceed the amount reported to have been saved by replacing paid staff. A letter from Sheffield noted that the staff budget was cut by £98,000 at the same time as volunteers were receiving £200,000 per year instead, despite reported reductions in usage when paid staff were lost (Friend 2017). A similar situation in Surrey is reported in *Private Eye* in May 2017 where:

> The annual costs of this centre exceeded £400,000 in the three years from 2012/13 to 2014/15 and fell slightly to £356,525 in 2015/16 – costs remarkably similar to Milton's original savings target for slashing librarians' jobs. Meanwhile, nine out of ten of the volunteer-run libraries have seen borrowing fall since they lost their paid staff. Tattenhams library near Epsom, for example, lent more than 45,000 books in 2009/10 and just over 30,000 in 2015/16 (Reported in Anstice 2017).

Volunteers working in libraries can be just part of a change of governance in a building. Holme Wood Library, in "one of Bradford's most deprived estates", is

---

[1] Quotes and figures taken from email from News Cross People's Library to author, 6th March 2017.

now staffed by volunteers but with a training company having effective control (Wilde 2017). Another, larger example, is that of Eco Communities (http://eco communities.co.uk/) in Lewisham, which runs three libraries which would otherwise have been closed. The non-profit organisation has 25 paid members of staff and provides training, cafes and recycling services as well as libraries.

The number of volunteer libraries that has closed since 2010 is unknown but is likely to be very small (Public Libraries News 2019b). The calculation is made difficult by the fact that councils, and the groups themselves, are understandably more likely to publicise success rather than failure. The number of unsuccessful libraries over the period is likely to be under 20, which is a very high survival rate when one considers there are probably around 500 surviving volunteer libraries in the UK and the success rate of a new business is 50% over five years (Anderson 2014). It is thus possible to see that volunteer libraries are sustainable in the short to medium term, although there are too few examples to confidently say the same for the long term.

There is a confusing statistic that the volunteer proportion of the library workforce was greater than that of paid staff as far back as 2012 (Young 2012). But the proportion cited is simply in terms of overall numbers of people and not total working hours. It also includes those who are complementary to library staff, such as summer reading challenge volunteers. In practice, a volunteer library can have far more staff, perhaps five to fifteen times more, than the number of paid library staff it previously employed. Volunteers may work for only half of one day per week, or even one hour (Rahman 2017), compared with the far greater hours put in by paid staff.

It is worth pointing out that there is no clear model for volunteer libraries. Each of the 151 library authorities in England does things slightly differently with volunteer libraries, with sometimes several different models even in one council area. It is possible at one end of the spectrum to find volunteer libraries which are effectively entirely council run, with almost no or very few paid staff. On the other extreme, there are branches where there is almost no council involvement at all, with no council books, computer catalogue or even advice being offered.

The Move Towards Libraries Being Run By Leisure Trusts

Another solution to reduced funding for public libraries has been to move the direct management of libraries away from a council to an arms-length organisation such as a non-profit trust. There are multiple varieties of trusts, but, in the public library sector, they come in two flavours: the leisure trust, where libraries are in a joint body with leisure centres and other allied council services, and the library trust, where libraries are run largely alone. The statutory responsibility for libraries in both cases remains with the council, which is commissioning another organisation to do work on its behalf.

By far the most numerous of the two is the leisure trust, with over 30 examples in the UK (Public Libraries News 2019a). The reasons for moving services into a trust are numerous but are succinctly listed by the DCMS as "The requirement for councils to reduce the level of funding allocated to services has often been the driving force behind the development of these new models. Other issues such as encouraging increased engagement with staff and communities, promoting innovation and reducing dependence on council funding have also encouraged library services to investigate and establish new models" (UK DCMS 2017d, Section 2 Paragraph 3). It is considered that the library service can sometimes be smothered by council bureaucracy. An example is the case of social media where councils can be highly risk-averse, not allowing library services to have their own dedicated accounts. Another example would be in the case of ICT, where library services need to abide by general council rules, often not designed with use by the public in mind. Similarly, building and maintenance contracts may be managed on a large scale, missing the opportunity for lowering costs through the use of smaller firms. By passing governance into the direct control of trusts, who understand the needs of the service more, it is argued that savings can be made. In addition, the promotional priorities of the council, such as improving waste collection, may override the needs of library services who can become frustrated that their publicity needs are given lower priority or funding, or none at all.

It is possible that economies of scale can be achieved, although seemingly evident in only one case, because a trust is not limited to a geographic area. Unlike a council library service which, normally covers its own territory and nowhere else, with exceptions like Essex which runs the library service for Slough, trusts can look for business elsewhere. A trust could have its own management structure and back office that cover several different library services. The problem with this model is that it depends on the trust keeping the contracts it already runs. Otherwise, it would need to periodically lay off staff as well as gain new employees, causing inefficiencies. There is of course, nothing stopping council library services benefitting from economies of scales themselves by being part of consortia (Public Libraries News 2020), such as in the case of LibrariesWest (https://www.librarieswest.org.uk).

The experience of libraries in leisure trusts has been very mixed. Wigan, which was a frontrunner in the practice, having moved libraries and leisure into a separate trust back in 2003, eventually deemed it a mistake and returned library services in-house in 2014 (Library Shake-Up... 2016). The reason for the original move appears largely to have been cost reduction.

The case of Warrington in 2016 and 2017, administered by the leisure trust LiveWire (https://livewirewarrington.co.uk/), raised concern. The suggestion to close several libraries and replace them with lending lockers led to much discussion and consultation (https://livewirewarrington.co.uk/159-libraries/live wire-modernisation-consultation). The proposed move of the historic Central Library into a unit in the town centre vacated by a shoe shop caused widespread protests and then a reversal by the trust (Skentelbery 2016), which is now working with the Council at keeping its libraries open, albeit likely with the use of volunteers and community groups with active community action continuing (https://www.facebook.com/groups/SaveWarringtonsLibraries/). The lack of senior management with a librarian, along with a subsequent misunderstanding and downplaying of the importance of libraries, may have played a part in what became a public relations problem for the trust. It is important to point out that the ultimate responsibility for the cuts to the LiveWire budget rests with the council. Indeed, the council leader has gone on record as saying "LiveWire have taken a bit of stick lately but they have done what we have asked them to do" (Laversuch 2017). There is now a new working group on libraries being composed of two council officers, three from LiveWire and two independent advisors.

Library services run by a leisure trust can be successful. An example is Greenwich Leisure Limited (GLL), rebranded as Better (https://www.better.org.uk/news) which runs library services in Greenwich, Wandsworth and Lincolnshire as well as, more controversially, three libraries in Lambeth (Slingsby 2016) and other extensive leisure interests nationwide. Greenwich Libraries have been some of the most successful, at least in terms of visits, in the country with 2.5 million visits in 2016/17 (Dempsey 2017), albeit with considerable investment by the council itself. GLL are active in looking for further opportunities for further library contacts outside of their home in London, as their successful bid for Lincolnshire showed (Lincolnite 2015). It is not just one leisure trust looking for such opportunities in other areas. Redbridge Leisure (https://visionrcl.org.uk/about/) was a strong contender to run that county's library services and has been commended by the Libraries Taskforce for its work in libraries (Settle 2017), especially in linking them with museums. Competitive bids for running library services is now an accepted part of the process.

All in all, the experience of leisure trusts running library services has been a somewhat mixed bag. There have been successes but, at the same time, notable failures. Such a record is perhaps inevitable considering the wide and varied number of trusts in operation but shows that the model does not represent automatic success.

Library Trusts in Control

The Libraries Taskforce provides guidance on trusts in its *Libraries: Alternative Delivery Models Toolkit* (UK DCMS 2017a), and approaches the options in a similar way to its report on volunteer libraries by offering helpful hints as to how to do it. The report does not offer a value judgement per se as to whether they are superior or not but rather accepts that what may be right for one library service may not be right for another. The guidance covers only library services wishing to convert to stand-alone library trusts and, curiously, does not address the more common practice of a leisure trust taking over a library service. Judging by the training sessions offered, the Taskforce is notably more keen on library trusts than on leisure ones. Library trusts are far less numerous, with currently only four: Devon, Nottinghamshire, Suffolk and York, in 2017. The obvious advantage of the library trust is that it can focus entirely on library services, with priorities and budgets being set to meet the need of libraries and nothing else. As library budgets are small, typically just 1% of the overall local government budget, it allows for detailed examination of outcomes for value-for-money purposes. Williams, as Chief Executive of Explore York Libraries and Archives, argues that moving to mutual status allowed "greater flexibility and speedier decision making so we can take advantage of opportunities" (Williams 2017).

Trusts are regarded as more able to seek alternative sources of funding. A reliance on council funding is naturally ingrained in council library services, as councils have been the source of the great majority of their resources from the beginning. Councils are legally limited from applying for certain types of grants. Trusts have more opportunities. Another advantage is that Boards can be set up for trusts with local movers and shakers who bring relevant expertise and influence (https://www.librariesunlimited.org.uk/about/our-board/). The human resources and ICT chiefs will get to know libraries very well, rather than seeing them as a small part of a larger entity. It is also argued that a library mutual, with library workers on its board, is more open to ideas from all parts of its workforce. A trust can also have tax advantages, depending on the type used and if it has charitable status (https://www.gov.uk/charities-and-tax/tax-reliefs). Another advantage is that a trust can publicly argue against budget cuts imposed by the council. Such is not the case with a traditional library authority, whose staff would face disciplinary action if seen publicly lobbying against proposals put forward by their employers. For example, Suffolk Libraries publicly discussed the impact of a £250,000 cut to their budget by the Suffolk Council (Mitchell 2017). A library trust creates a situation similar to the US and Canada where library services will often publicly ask for more money and protest at the impact of budgetary cuts.

The library trust model has received much prominence in the last couple of years. DCMS and the Libraries Taskforce for England are providing guides with step by step instructions (UK DCMS 2017a) and workshops on the subject. Existing library trusts have set up a separate mutual in order to best sell their expertise to other authorities. The guidance is clear that such a move will not suit every authority and that the model will not automatically result in savings. It is worth noting that savings may not be ones that the library workforce would necessarily like.

There is no attempt to sell the model as a cure-all which is encouraging as there are, indeed, highly successful library services, such as the Idea Store of Tower Hamlets (https://www.ideastore.co.uk/), which are run by councils. In addition, the move to a different mode of governance can be very expensive in terms of the time and resources required. The process can take two years and cost hundreds of thousands of pounds. Such time and money could have been spent on improving services in-house. The challenge for each authority is, therefore, whether such a change is worth it. The impression should also not be given that trusts are considered only where the Conservative Party is in control. There is little to choose between parties on the issue, with the then Shadow Secretary of State for Culture and Deputy Leader, Tom Watson, praising Nottinghamshire Inspire for doing "incredible" work (Gainsborough Standard 2017) and arguing that the trust had not only protected but enhanced the service.

Privatisation

For-profit companies have not yet made significant footholds into UK public libraries. In the US, private companies, such as Library Systems and Services (https://www.lsslibraries.com/company) compete to run libraries and make money for their shareholders in much the same way as do other business enterprises. The argument for private companies taking over public libraries is that it removes all inefficiencies. The alleged "slacks and trainers mentality" of British staff would, it was argued, be swept away by a "rigorous service culture" (Dutta 2011). While Library Systems and Services failed to make any impact in UK libraries, John Laing Integrated Services (JLIS) operated Hounslow Libraries for several years after the failure of a leisure trust there. Claiming to make big savings (John Laing 2011) was helped by £5 million of council investment (Buckland 2009). John Laing, and its competitor, Carillion, bid for other library services contracts, until John Laing eventually sold its library arm to the latter in 2013 (Carillion 2013). Carillion ended up controlling four London library authorities, Hounslow,

Ealing, Croydon and Harrow, and unsuccessfully bid for Bromley in 2017 (King 2017). Later in the year, faced with financial problems unconnected with libraries, Carillion lost the Hounslow and other contracts (Alderson 2017; Grewal 2017). Carillion was running the library services as part of a non-profit arm called Cultural Community Solutions which has since gone into liquidation (https://beta.companieshouse.gov.uk/company/06607841). It could be said that there are currently no for-profit libraries in the UK.

The intrinsic problem with for-profit control of library services is that a private company possesses no real competitive advantages over the council. There is nothing that a private company can do, such as reducing staff or pay, that a council public library service cannot do, or indeed has done. The suggested economies of scale can also be countered with the example of library consortia. Indeed, private companies possess an intrinsic disadvantage when it comes to value for money. To be successful, they need to make a profit. Money is taken from the budget and paid as dividends into the pockets of shareholders, who often have no connection to the location of the service provided. Private companies are undoubtedly good at the construction of tender documents but not necessarily any better than other providers at delivering a service. There is no real loyalty to a location, as demonstrated in the case of Croydon, when John Laing won the contract to run the libraries and, within a month, sold it to Carillion. The ultimate lack of accountability does not sit well with the local democracies funding the majority of such services, regardless of other income generation the company can introduce.

Partnerships

A type of governance that provides direct council control but has the advantage of economies of scale is where more than one library service merges any or all of its features with another service. The most obvious example is the Tri-Borough involving Hammersmith and Fulham, Kensington and Chelsea and Westminster, which attempted to combine their library services into one. Commencing in 2011, the experiment initially gained stellar reviews, with an estimated £40m a year across the three councils being expected to be saved over four years (Roe 2012). Unfortunately, a flaw was demonstrated when one of the boroughs, initially all Conservative, became Labour-controlled and no longer agreed with the other two, which led to the eventual collapse of the experiment (BBC News 2017a).

The two London boroughs of Bexley and Bromley merged their background library services, with the loss of 70 posts, in 2011. A few years later, they examined the joint outsourcing of the libraries to a third party. The weakness of the partnership came into play when one borough, Bexley, decided to keep services in-house while the other, Bromley, sought a third party to run its service (Allin 2016). Undeterred, two other councils, Bournemouth and Poole merged their library services (Wilson 2017).

Partnerships between libraries appear to have a better chance of surviving when each is less directly involved in the control of the service. The Central Buying Consortium (https://westsussex.moderngov.co.uk/documents/s11216/FRC01_19-20_Central%20Buying%20Consortium%20Library%20Group%20Report.pdf) operates successfully to buy books for several authorities, as does the East Midlands and Mid Anglia (EMMAC) book purchasing consortium (http://www.sourcenottinghamshire.co.uk/contracts/award/id/18105). More obvious to the public are council partnerships for joint lending and catalogue use which are in place in Greater Manchester, with eleven authorities involved, and London, with an impressive seventeen. There are various other examples of joint projects, such as Time To Read (http://time-to-read.co.uk/), with twenty two authorities pooling funds to co-ordinate reading development work in the North West.

Conclusion

There is a wide variety of models of governance of public libraries in the United Kingdom today. One could once expect all public libraries to be staffed by paid staff, whose salaries along with the costs of building maintenance were met by the relevant local council. Now, anything goes. There is a spectrum of library governance, ranging from libraries run by volunteers fundraising for electricity and relying on book donations to well-funded council libraries.

While seeing a hundred flowers bloom is doubtless releasing energy and innovation in the sector, it is also atomising it. Nationwide projects like the book campaign by the Reading Agency (https://readingagency.org.uk/), face the prospects of dealing with hundreds of different library services, with the only entirely unified library service being that of Northern Ireland, including around five hundred volunteer libraries. While organisations such as the Libraries Taskforce are working on sharing best practice, there must be a large amount of waste and much reinvention of the wheel.

Although serious research has sadly not been conducted, one suspects that the library sector could paradoxically squander resources as new management structures are created and voluntary redundancies given. The proponents of such a strategy, if such it can be called, would argue that change allows for the tailoring of the library service as closely as possible to the needs of its population, and this may indeed be so. The postcode lottery of a system, where some taxpayers can expect viable library services while those in less fortunate areas, cannot, is hardly a strategy that will see libraries fit for their vital role in years to come. A national service demands at the least a national strategy. However, what England is faced with is that libraries even one mile away may look like they not only belong to different countries but to different eras. Disparate outcomes are perhaps inevitable in a time of forced evolution in the sector but it is unfair on those who lose in a fight of tooth and claw.

A fundamental change in the sector has been brought about almost entirely by simply financial and local considerations. When a council has been faced with a reduction, it has looked at the easiest way to trim the library service to cope with the cut. Councils have not seriously considered the dangers of passing a service previously under direct democratic control to the cheapest and most similar practical replacement. The lack of effective statutory protection for the library service, along with a public perception, at least amongst decision makers, that the work of public libraries can be done by anyone, has led to dramatic changes. Unless the profession, hamstrung by atomisation and poor resources of all kinds, can more clearly and effectively advocate its case then such change is likely to continue.

What is the current management reality of the UK library service? Why is the state of affairs happening? Can the inherent dangers of embracing hegemonic neo-liberalism be explored? Is there a a disconnect between how policymakers, library professionals and library users see the role of the public library and its role in the 21st century and why is it so? Are UK libraries communicating their real role effectively in today's society? Perhaps the role of the volunteer community hub library is more aptly and appropriately described, conveyed and implemented, and its story more powerfully told than the library picture presented by professional librarians. To what degree are libraries and librarians responsible for the current situation? If libraries are victims of government policy making, how much is their victimhood their own fault?

References

Alderson, Lucy. "Carillion Library Services Contract to End". *CN Construction News*. July 19, 2017. https://www.constructionnews.co.uk/news/contractors-news/carillion-library-services-contract-to-end-19-07-2017/.
Allin, Simon." Council Scraps Library Privatisation Plans". *Bexley Times*. October 3, 2016. https://www.bexleytimes.co.uk/news/council-scraps-library-privatisation-plans-1-4721406.

Anderson, Elizabeth. "Half of UK Start-Ups Fail Within Five Years". *The Telegraph*. October 21, 2014. https://www.telegraph.co.uk/finance/businessclub/11174584/Half-of-UK-start-ups-fail-within-five-years.html.

Anstice, Ian. "Labour Manifesto on Libraries and Questions Over Volunteer Libraries: Editorial" *Public Libraries News*. May 17, 2017. https://www.publiclibrariesnews.com/2017/05/labour-manifesto-on-libraries-and-questions-over-volunteer-libraries.html.

BBC News. "David Cameron Launches Tories' 'Big Society' Plan". July 19, 2010. https://www.bbc.com/news/uk-10680062.

BBC News. "Donation Enables Penzance's Morrab Library Expansion". April 28, 2012. https://www.bbc.com/news/uk-england-cornwall-17881291.

BBC News. "London Councils Walk Away From Share Services Agreement". March 28, 2017a. https://www.bbc.com/news/uk-england-london-39415618.

BBC News. "Police's 'Rare Objection' to Bridgend Hub's Alcohol Plan". March 27, 2017b. https://www.bbc.com/news/uk-wales-south-west-wales-39366949.

BBC News. "'Urgent' Talks to Save Lincolnshire County Council Libraries". July 18, 2014. https://www.bbc.com/news/uk-england-lincolnshire-28361796.

Buckland, Lucy. "£5m Investment to Upgrade Hounslow's Libraries". *Richmond & Twickenham Times* June 28, 2009. https://www.richmondandtwickenhamtimes.co.uk/news/4461905.__5m_investment_to_upgrade_Hounslow_s_libraries/.

Butler, P. "Council Spending on 'Neighbourhood' Services Falls by £3bn Since 2011" *The Guardian*. April 25, 2017. https://www.theguardian.com/society/2017/apr/25/spending-on-council-services-in-england-fell-3bn-in-past-five-years-study-bin-collections-local-government.

"Carillion Snaps Up £65m – Turnover John Laing Arm". *Insider Media Limited*. October 21, 2013. https://www.insidermedia.com/news/midlands/101030-carillion-snaps-john-laing-support-services-arm.

Chartered Institute of Public Finance & Accountancy (CIPFA). "Libraries Lose Branches and Staff as Spending Continues to Drop". *CIPFA Press Releases*. 7 Dec. 2018. https://www.cipfa.org/about-cipfa/press-office/archived-press-releases/2018-press-releases/libraries-lose-branches-and-staff-as-spending-continues-to-drop.

Chartered Institute of Public Finance & Accountancy (CIPFA). "Decade of Austerity Sees 30% Drop in Library Spending". *CIPFA Research Analytics News*. 2019. https://www.cipfastats.net/news/newsstory.asp?content=23214.

Community Knowledge Hub. Libraries. "Little Chalfont Community Library – Case Study". October 3, 2012. https://libraries.communityknowledgehub.org.uk/study/little-chalfont-community-library-case-study.

Cumber, Robert. "The Sheffield Suburb 'No One Wants to Leave' After Discovering Its Understated Charms". *The Star*. February 14, 2019. https://www.thestar.co.uk/news/sheffield-suburb-no-one-wants-leave-after-discovering-its-understated-charms-114644

Decher, Laurel. "A Behind-the-Scenes Tour of Public Libraries in Germany". 2017. https://laureldecher.com/2017/05/03/a-behind-the-scenes-tour-of-public-libraries-in-germany/.

Dempsey, Joe. " Greenwich Bucks National Trend as Libraries Post Highest Annual Visits on Record" *News Shopper*. May 4, 2017. https://www.newsshopper.co.uk/news/15265252.greenwich-bucks-national-trend-as-libraries-post-highest-annual-visits-on-record/.

Dutta, Kunal. "Ssshhh! The Noisy US revolution Coming to British Libraries". *Independent*. March 7, 2011. https://www.independent.co.uk/arts-entertainment/books/news/ssshhh-the-noisy-us-revolution-coming-to-british-libraries-2234236.html.

Farrington, Joshua. "CILIP Rejects Name Change, Votes No Confidence in Vaizey" *The Bookseller*. September 21, 2013. https://www.thebookseller.com/news/cilip-rejects-name-change-votes-no-confidence-vaizey.

Flood, Alison "UK Lost More than 200 Libraries in 2012". *The Guardian*. December 11, 2012. https://www.theguardian.com/books/2012/dec/10/uk-lost-200-libraries-2012.

Forrest, Adam. "This Man is Saving London's Ailing Libraries from Closure". *The Big Issue*. February 15, 2017. https://www.bigissue.com/interviews/library-community-doorstep/

Friend, Dorothy. "YP Letters: Library Policy That's a Real-Life Work of Satire". *Yorkshire Post*. May 13, 2017. https://www.yorkshirepost.co.uk/news/yp-letters-library-policy-thats-real-life-work-satire-1777256.

Gainsborough Standard. "'Incredible' Worksop Library Praised By Deputy Labour Leader Tom Watson". April 5, 2017. https://www.gainsboroughstandard.co.uk/news/incredible-worksop-library-praised-deputy-labour-leader-tom-watson-2098684.

Greenhill Community Library. *Newsletter*. Autumn 2019. https://greenhill-library.org/category/newsletters/.

Grewal, Herpreet Kaur. "Croydon Councillor Criticises Carillion's Service to Borough's Libraries" *Facilitate*. November 3, 2017. https://www.facilitatemagazine.com/news/croydon-councillor-criticises-carillions-service-to-boroughs-libraries/.

John Laing Integrated Services. *Case Study: Outsourcing Library Services to John Laing Integrated Services Delivers Over £1 million of Efficiencies for Hounslow*. London: John Laing, 2011. https://www.laing.com/uploads/assets/JLIS_CaseStudy_Outsourcing-Hounslow.pdf.

Kean, D. "Libraries Minister Promises to Act if Councils Cannot Justify Cuts". *The Guardian*. 2 Feb.2017. https://www.theguardian.com/books/2017/feb/01/libraries-minister-promises-to-act-if-councils-cannot-justify-cuts.

Kean, D. "UK Library Budgets Fall by £25m in a Year". *The Guardian* 8 Dec 2016 https://www.theguardian.com/books/2016/dec/08/uk-library-budgets-fall-by-25m-in-a-year.

King, Emily. "Bromley Labour Leader Angela Wilkins Defends Unite's Campaign to Stop the Privatisation of Bromley's Libraries" *Bromley Times*, March 13, 2017. https://www.bromleytimes.co.uk/news/bromley-labour-leader-angela-wilkins-defends-unite-s-campaign-to-stop-the-privatisation-of-bromley-s-libraries-1-4929800.

Laversuch, Chloe. "Focus Turns to Working Group as Livewire's Library Plans Approved by Councillors". *Warrington Guardian*. February 15, 2017. https://www.warringtonguardian.co.uk/news/15093441.focus-turns-to-working-group-as-livewires-library-plans-approved-by-councillors/.

"Library Shake-up is Next Savings Plan". *Wigan Today*. September 20, 2016. https://www.wigantoday.net/news/library-shake-next-savings-plan-1199131.

The Lincolnite "Lincolnshire Heritage Sites Included In Libraries Outsourcing Contract". April 16, 2015. https://thelincoln ite.co.uk/2015/04/lincolnshire-heritage-sites-included-in-libraries-outsourcing-contract/.

Lindley, Jonathan. "Mutuals and Other Alternative Delivery Models: Workshops". *DCMS Libraries Blog*. February 16, 2017. https://dcmslibraries.blog.gov.uk/2017/02/16/mutuals-and-other-alternative-delivery-models-workshops/.

Locality. *Income Generation For Public Libraries: Learning And Case Studies From A National Pilot Project In England*. Supported by funding from the Arts Council England. May 2015. https://libraries.communityknowledgehub.org.uk/sites/default/files/locality_income_generation_2015.pdf.

McIntyre, Sarah." #Save Libraries: Carnegie Library Protest March". *Jabberworks*. April 9, 2016. https://jabberworks.livejournal.com/742080.html.

Mitchell, Gemma. "Suffolk Libraries Launches Donation Scheme As Budget Is Cut By 33% Since 2010". *Ipswich Star*. April 5, 2017. https://www.ipswichstar.co.uk/news/suffolk-libraries-launches-donation-scheme-as-budget-is-cut-by-33-since-2010-1-4962969.

Page, Benedicte. "Vaizey on Libraries: 'We Can't Go On Like This'". *The Bookseller*. February 7, 2010. https://www.thebookseller.com/news/vaizey-libraries-we-cant-go.

Page, Benedicte. "Library Protesters Declare Day of Action". *The Guardian*. January 25, 2011. https://www.theguardian.com/books/2011/jan/24/library-protest-day-action.

Public Libraries News "32 examples of UK Public Libraries Working Together". 2020. https://www.publiclibrariesnews.com/campaigning/efficiencies-2/efficiencies-sharing-services.

Public Libraries News. "List of Library Trusts and Prospective Library Trusts". 2019a. https://www.publiclibrariesnews.com/about-public-libraries-news/trusts-current-uk-situation.

Public Libraries News. "List of UK Volunteer Libraries". 2019b. http://www.publiclibrariesnews.com/about-public-libraries-news/list-of-uk-volunteer-run-libraries.

Public Libraries News. "Cons: Reasons Against Volunteer 'Community Libraries'" 2019c. https://www.publiclibrariesnews.com/campaigning/volunteer-run-libraries/cons.

Rahman, Miran. "Volunteers Come Forward to Make a Success of Silsden Library Re-Launch". March 27, 2017. *Keighley News*. https://www.keighleynews.co.uk/news/15184170.volunteers-come-forward-to-make-a-success-of-silsden-library-re-launch/.

Roe, Phillipa. "One Year On, Does Sharing Services Work?" *The Guardian. Local Network Blog*. June 18, 2012. https://www.theguardian.com/local-government-network/2012/jun/18/london-boroughs-shared-services-project?CMP.

Settle, Kathy. "Co-Location in Redbridge and Exploring the Prosperity Outcome: 12th Meeting of the Libraries Taskforce". *DCMS Libraries Blog*. February 15, 2017. https://dcmslibraries.blog.gov.uk/2017/02/15/co-location-in-redbridge-and-exploring-the-prosperity-outcome-12th-meeting-of-the-libraries-taskforce/.

Skentelbery, David "Library in a Shoe-Shop Plan Withdrawn". *Warrington Worldwide*. November 10, 2016. https://www.warrington-worldwide.co.uk/2016/11/10/library-in-a-shoe-shop-plan-withdrawn/.

Slingsby, Alan. "Library Campaigners Challenge GLL". *Brixton Blog*. April 6, 2016. https://brixtonblog.com/2016/04/library-campaigners-challenge-gll/36789/.

Triskele Books. "Who Do We Want Running Our Libraries? The Reality of Running a Community Library". *Words with Jam: the Ezine for Writers and Publishers Brought to You by Triskele Books*. January 18, 2011. http://www.wordswithjam.co.uk/2011/01/who-do-we-want-running-our-libraries.html.

UK Department for Culture, Media and Sport (DCMS). *Independent Library Report for England*. Presented by William Sieghart and an expert panel. London: DCMS, 2014. https://www.gov.uk/government/uploads/system/uploads/attachment_data/file/388989/Independent_Library_Report-_18_December.pdf.

UK Department for Digital, Culture, Media and Sport (DCMS). *Libraries: Alternative Delivery Models Toolkit*. London: DCMS, 2017a. https://www.gov.uk/government/publications/libraries-alternative-delivery-models-toolkit.

UK Department for Digital, Culture, Media and Sport (DCMS). *Research and Analysis to Explore the Service Effectiveness and Sustainability of Community Managed Libraries in England*. London: DCMS, 2017b. https://www.gov.uk/government/publications/research-and-analysis-to-explore-the-service-

effectiveness-and-sustainability-of-community-managed-libraries-in-england/
research-and-analysis-to-explore-the-service-effectiveness-and-sustainability-of-
community-managed-libraries-in-england.

UK Department for Digital, Culture, Media and Sport (DCMS). *Taking Part Survey: England Adult
Report, 2016/17.* National Statistics. London: DCMS, 2017c. https://assets.publishing.
service.gov.uk/government/uploads/system/uploads/attachment_data/file/664933/
Adult_stats_release_4.pdf.

UK Department of Digital, Culture, Media and Sport (DCMS). *Why Consider an Alternative
Delivery Model?* London: DCMS, 2017d. https://www.gov.uk/government/publications/
libraries-alternative-delivery-models-toolkit/why-consider-an-alternative-delivery-model.

UK Libraries Taskforce. *Community Managed Libraries: Good Practice Toolkit.* London:
Department for Digital, Culture, Media and Sport (DCMS), 2018. https://www.gov.uk/
government/collections/community-libraries-good-practice-toolkit.

UK Parliament. Publications and Records. Commons Select Committee. *Culture, Media and
Sport Committee: Third Report Library Closures.* www.parliament.uk. 2012. https://
publications.parliament.uk/pa/cm201213/cmselect/cmcumeds/587/58702.htm.

UK *Public Libraries and Museums Act* 1964. http://www.legislation.gov.uk/ukpga/1964/75

Wikipedia. "Public Libraries Act 1850". 2020. https://en.wikipedia.org/wiki/Public_Libraries_
Act_1850.

Wilde, Clare. "New-Look Library Reopens as Community Hub After Dodging Closure
Threat" *Telegraph & Argus.* May 6, 2017. https://www.thetelegraphandargus.
co.uk/news/15268973.new-look-library-reopens-as-community-hub-after-dodging-
closure-threat/.

Williams, Fiona. "Could an Alternative Delivery Model be Right for Your Library Service?" *DCMS
Library Blog.* February 16, 2017. https://dcmslibraries.blog.gov.uk/2017/02/16/could-an-
alternative-delivery-model-be-right-for-your-library-service/.

Wilson, Kate. "Bournemouth and Poole Could Create Joint Tourism and Library Services to Save
£1m". *Daily Echo.* March 8, 2017. https://www.bournemouthecho.co.uk/news/15140726.
bournemouth-and-poole-could-create-joint-tourism-and-library-services-to-save-1m/.

Yellowley, Graham. "Chairman's Introduction". *Little Chalfont Library. News.* October 23, 2019.
https://www.littlechalfontlibrary.org.uk/news.

Young, Niki May. "Number of Volunteers in Libraries Overtakes Number of Staff". *Civil Society
News.* December 13, 2012. https://www.civilsociety.co.uk/news/number-of-volunteers-in-
libraries-overtakes-number-of-staff.html.

Part 3: **International Perspectives**

Marian Koren

9 Library Governance in View of the Rights of the Child: The Sustainable Development Goals as Catalyst

Abstract: In the development of human rights, various UN human rights treatises and other instruments have elaborated the rights for specific groups including women, refugees and persons with a disability, and for specific situations, including war and times of conflict. The focus in this chapter is on the Rights of the Child, its international Convention, and the rights especially relevant for public libraries. The distinction between needs-based and rights-based library governance and practice is discussed, namely newer aspects of human rights development. Child participation and co-creation are elaborated. International examples of implications and applications in libraries give context. The leading question is: in what way do the SDGs help the governance of library services in respect of children and their rights? Several SDGs are analyzed from the perspective of children, with library examples and conclusions drawn for library governance.

Keywords: Convention on the Rights of the Child; Children's rights; Corporate governance; Public libraries

Introduction

Why would library governance be of interest to study in depth and from an international perspective? If one looks up governance in the core publication related to public library service guidelines prepared by IFLA, one finds in both editions not more than a short paragraph (Gill 2001; Koontz and Gubbin 2010). Various elements of governance are mentioned: a properly established governing body made up largely of representatives of the local community; openness in rules of procedures and minutes for library committees and boards; accountability, division of tasks, and relationships between the board or governing body and chief librarian or manager; and involvement of citizens and the local community in policy making and development of services. Nowadays one might need to look at the wider context in which governance takes place, especially to include relevant elements for current and future library service. So the theme of this volume is well-chosen. What contribution will this chapter offer?

Governance might be considered as mainly a case for leaders, managers and decision makers. But citizen involvement brings users closer to governance. What

https://doi.org/10.1515/ 9783110533323-012

would good library governance be like in the views of users? And what would happen if the focus is especially on users under 18 years of age, as they often are the majority of library users? What are their views and do leaders, practitioners, researchers, and decision makers include the views of children, in their governance?

The basis to involving children in governance is the full acknowledgement of children as human beings, and respect for their human dignity and rights. In other words: human rights, as formulated in article 1 of the United Nations Universal Declaration of Human Rights (1948) (Relevant documents are available at http://www.ohchr.org/EN/ProfessionalInterest/Pages/InternationalLaw.aspx): "All human beings are born free and equal in dignity and rights. They are endowed with reason and conscience and should act towards one another in a spirit of brotherhood." And article 2 adds the principle of non-discrimination. Many human rights instruments are based on an elaboration of the Declaration. For those who are in doubt whether children are included in the declaration, the United Nations Convention on the Rights of the Child (United Nations 1989) makes it very clear that children are legal subjects and have human rights, among them for example the right to information, the right to education, to privacy, and the right to express views and to be heard. These rights taken together and especially the latter are considered as forming the right to participation.

It is the combination of human rights which is relevant for new library provision and affects policy making and governance. Human rights are the international fundamental framework for library provision and its governance. But has this been truly acknowledged and realized in the library sector? It might be that the reference to the IFLA/UNESCO Public Library Manifesto in library governance documents is not enough. There is, however, a new opportunity as the United Nations, representating the international community, has launched the UN Agenda 2030 with concrete sustainable development goals (SDGs). In fact, they are a more pragmatic approach to realize human rights by summing up concrete goals and measures, to be monitored by indicators. This chapter would like to build on earlier research on the child's right to information, closely related to the development of the child as an authentic human being (Koren 1996). It will explore the human rights of children, especially their basic rights of access to information in view of library governance, and the relevance of the SDGs for library provision to children worldwide.

Human Rights and Libraries

The concept of human rights is very much related to history and civilization and as such is subject to evolution and change. The first examples of human rights formulations date back to the Enlightenment, but their roots can be traced in older texts on principles of law. The spirit of Enlightenment depicts a human being as rational and autonomous, who should be guaranteed his/her freedom to think for himself/herself, to speak and express himself/herself on various matters. It is the same period in which the basic principles of libraries are rooted: equality, freedom of access to knowledge, and culture for all. Different types of human rights have evolved. Civil rights or liberties seek to secure the freedom, the security, and the physical and spiritual integrity of the human person. The state should refrain from intervening in the private life of citizens, thereby respecting their civil rights or liberties.

Political rights, for example the freedom of assembly, the freedom of the press, of thought, and religion are stressing the societal role and democracy. Since the industrial revolution, the evolving group of social, economic, and cultural rights demands that the state is active in order to support the social and cultural well-being of all citizens, including the right to healthcare, social provisions, education, and participation in culture. The United Nations has elaborated the Universal Declaration and developed human rights treaties and instruments with legal and monitoring mechanisms to maintain human rights standards. Nowadays human rights are regarded as inviolable, even in times of economic crisis, conflict or war; the maintenance of a human rights standard has become a matter of international concern.

Relating human rights to libraries with their mission of giving access to information and knowledge in the widest sense, the right to freedom of expression which includes the right of access to information is the primary one contained in Article 19 in the Universal Declaration of Human Rights. But there are other rights with relevance and implications for library governance, policy and practice. To mention a few, there is the right to privacy, and the right to freedom of thought, conscience and religion contained in Articles 17 and 18 of the International Covenant on Civil and Political Rights, 1966 (https://www.ohchr.org/EN/ProfessionalInterest/Pages/CCPR.aspx), the right to education, and the right to participation in cultural life and the enjoyment of the benefits of scientific progress and its applications in Article 13 and Article 15 of the International Covenant on Economic, Social and Cultural Rights 1966 (https://www.ohchr.org/EN/Profes sionalInterest/Pages/CCPR.aspx).

Libraries have much to offer to citizens, helping to realize their rights, especially for those with special needs and disabilities. As information and knowledge are so important in daily social, cultural, and scientific life, libraries are closely related to a large set of human rights. For example the right to health-care cannot be realized without the right to have access to health information. The right to form an opinion or to participate in democracy cannot be reached without the right to know an impartial overview of facts and approaches (Thomas 2007). In the same way, respecting the rights and protecting them in the library setting means that the governance of the library must be in line with the human rights standard, involving a reference to the IFLA/UNESCO Public Library Mani-festo and an active formulation of how the library is going to respect and protect human rights and de facto to promote the right of access to information.

Some libraries, especially in UK and Australia, have formulated a sepa-rate Library Service Charter so library users know what they may expect from the library regarding library services, customer care, non-discriminative access in case of special needs and cultural diversity and customer consultation. The example of Buckinghamshire County Library given in the Public Library Service Guidelines (Gill 2001; Koontz and Gubbin 2010) seems nowadays to have been replaced by a more general one for the County as a whole, with customer services included in a customer charter and data protection in an information charter with a shorter library charter regarding digital services. The tone seems somewhat dif-ferent, not so much guaranteeing user rights but rather managing expectations especially regarding digital services (www.buckscc.gov.uk).

Looking back at the relationship of human rights to libraries, it seems that, apart from the period of critical activism of the seventies, it was only in the nine-ties of last century that libraries acknowledged clearly that they shared values from the human rights development. The IFLA General Conference confirmed its commitment to article 19 of the Universal Declaration in 1989, followed by the establishment of a Committee to address the issue (Evans 1997), and later estab-lished the Freedom of Access to Information and Freedom of Expression (FAIFE) initiative (https://www.ifla.org/about-faife). However, progress initially did not get much further than cooperation with UNESCO for qualifying the professional library framework which remained the main source of reference.

In the nineties, a number of UN Conferences renewed the international com-munity's commitment to the promotion and protection of human rights. The Vienna Declaration and Programme of Action meant "a new vision for global action for human rights into the next century" (http://www.ohchr.org/EN/AboutUs/Pages/ViennaWC.aspx). It confirmed human rights as basic minimum standards of human life, that they are universal and inalienable, meaning all people are born with the same human rights everywhere and at all times. They cannot be taken away or given up, are indivisible and interdependent and neces-sary for human life and dignity (United Nations 1993).

An important paradigm shift took place. Inspired by the international human rights framework, many organizations in civil society changed their approach and attitude, taking away the charity dimension of development by emphasising rights and responsibilities. Applying a human rights-based approach (HRBA) goes not only further than a charity approach, seeing individuals as victims, but also further than a needs approach where individuals are viewed as objects of interventions. HRBA goes beyond the notion of physical needs and includes a holistic perspective of human beings in terms of their civil, political, social, economic, and cultural roles. Individual entitlement is recognized and supported to empower human beings (Kirkemann Boesen and Martin 2007, 10). HRBA means a totally different structure and dynamic to actions in society.

Apart from applications in the field of social work in relation to poverty and marginalized groups, development, and healthcare (OHCHR/WHO 2012), one of the most remarkable changes took place at UNICEF. Originally an emergency fund for children, later involved in child development, it radically turned to human rights as its base, after a serious debate of traditional developmentalists and human rights advocates (Santos Pais 1999). In 2003, the UN issued a Common Understanding on a Human Rights-based Approach for all their activities (United Nations Development Group 2003). The Child Rights Information Network (CRIN) developed rights-based programming resource pages, with guides for children and practitioners, such as health professionals, journalists, legal professionals, parliamentarians, social workers, teachers and NGOs (https://archive.crin. org/en/guides.html). They are a good source of inspiration, but it would even be better to have one developed on librarians as well.

How Did Developments Affect the Library Sector?

Around the millennium, libraries worldwide became more aware of their political contexts. In 1992, it was impossible to speak with the IFLA Board on human rights as the general framework for libraries but around 2000, IFLA picked up signals from its member library associations that libraries should be more involved in the international agenda setting, and advocate for their place in the global information society. The participation in the World Summit on the Information Society in Geneva and Tunis in 2003 and 2005 (https://en.unesco. org/themes/building-knowledge-societies/wsis) was a first test case, learning the human rights topics, the international advocacy language and the need for increasing awareness in the library sector. It became clear that human rights represented the strongest values on which the library and information profession and the library mission could be based and that human rights instruments provided a mechanism to strengthen the library's advocacy for access to knowledge.

Nevertheless, at that time IFLA and the library associations had little competence or capacity to participate in the UN monitoring mechanisms, such as submitting regular country reports, participating in international dialogue and accountability, and making representations to international committees. HRBA in library services as part of an explicit programme and professional principle and method had not been developed. It was only with the start of the Building Strong Library Associations' Programme (BSLA) that international capacity building came into view, with consequences for the governance of library organizations at various levels. In other words, there is still space for extended implementation of HRBA in library governance and policies, and the further development of international library advocacy work.

Rights of the Child, Relevance and Implications for Libraries

What do developments mean in view of children and their rights? Can children rely on libraries? Can libraries find more support and guidance for their mission in human rights instruments, especially concerning children? The first formulations of human rights of children date from the early twentieth century with inclusions in the Declaration of Geneva and the UN Declarations of 1948 and 1959, but its core internationally binding instrument is the UN Convention on the Rights of the Child 1989[1] (Koren 1996, 161–168). It not only confirms for children below the age of eighteen, civil and political rights, and social, economic and cultural rights, but pays special attention to specific situations of children in such areas as non-separation from parents, adoption, access to information related to full development and right to play, and categories of children, such as refugees, handicapped children, children of minorities and children caught up in armed conflicts. In this way the Convention popularly speaking enshrines protection, provision, prevention and participation.

There are four articles in the Convention that are known as the General Principles and they help interpret all the other articles and play a fundamental role

---

1 The United Nations Convention on the Rights of the Child (UNCRC adopted 20 November 1989) has been signed and ratified by all states with the exception of ratification by the USA. For an analysis of the latter see Todres, Wojcik, and Revaz 2006.

in realizing all the rights in the Convention for all children. They are also relevant for the design of library governance and services. They are: non-discrimination in Article 2; best interests of the child in Article 3; right to life survival and development in Article 6; and the right to be heard in Article 12. Article 12 addresses the principle of participation and says that all children have the right to express their views, feelings and wishes in all matters affecting them, and to have their views considered and taken seriously. This principle recognizes children and young people as actors in their own lives and applies at all times throughout a child's life and is the truly innovative recognition stated in the Convention. It refers to the rights of children to participate in society, to act in certain circumstances, to be involved in decision-making and to take part in decisions affecting their own destiny, by receiving information (Article 17), by forming and expressing an opinion (Article 13), by discussing and being heard on issues which matter to themselves and to their surroundings (Article 12), by freedom of thought and religion (Article 14), and by the right to freedom of association (Article 15). It is clear that information and participation are closely linked. It is in fact essential that children be provided with the necessary information about options that exist and the consequences of such options so that they can make informed and free decisions. Providing information enables children to gain skills, confidence and maturity in expressing views and influencing decisions.

By acknowledging that children have views and their own perspectives on their situations, the Convention is also setting a standard for a child's perspective in all services, procedures and situations regarding the child which would apply to libraries. A child's perspective means that children themselves are involved and make contributions which is different from a child-centred perspective constructed not by the child but by an adult, an advocate of the child with a focus on trying to improve children's living conditions and looking after their best interests (Björklid and Nordström 2012, 44–45). A position paper by Save the Children clarifies:

> Child participation goes beyond opportunities to engage with political decision-making processes at a national level. There are few areas of family, community, region, national or international decision making that do not affect children. Moreover, participation rights stretch far beyond 'children's topics' or areas otherwise mentioned specifically in the UNCRC. This means that there are no areas of traditional parental or adult authority – the home or the school for example – that can ever be considered 'child opinion free zones'. While States Parties have the obligation to ensure that children's participation rights are fulfilled, a great deal of this work can only be realized if States promote and introduce policies which require other actors – such as parents, teachers, social workers, judges – to ensure children's participation. This includes a clear task for States to adopt legislation and

support measures which aim at changing attitudes and practice among adults and professionals (Save the Children 2011a).

Libraries can act to ensure children's participation in society.

Right to Information, Right to Participation

In the Convention, one Article should draw the special attention of libraries, as it has no equivalent in any other human rights treaty or instrument. Article 17 describes explicitly the child's right of access to information. It is formulated in relation to the mass media, and libraries are part of the infrastructure. The Convention speaks of access to information and material from a diversity of national and international sources, especially those aimed at the promotion of the child's social, spiritual, and moral wellbeing and physical and mental health. It relates information to the social and cultural benefit of the child and the child's fullest development. Special attention is paid to the production and dissemination of children's books, and to the diverse linguistic needs of children and indigenous groups (Koren 2000, 277; Lee 2006, 179). Annex 1 to this chapter contains the full text of Article 17.

The international UN Committee surveying the Committee on the Rights of the Child holds open discussions and publishes General Comments to clarify the principles and articles. It gives a useful elaboration of the child's right to participation in General Comment no. 12 (https://www2.ohchr.org/english/bodies/crc/docs/AdvanceVersions/CRC-C-GC-12.pdf). If participation is to be effective and meaningful, it needs to be understood as a process, not as an individual one-off event. Basic requirements for effective, ethical, and meaningful implementation of Article 12 are recommended to the States parties for integration in legislation and other measures. All are relevant to implementation in libraries, especially those related to information, and in this article's context also to governance. Paragraph 134 of the General Comment outlines that processes in which a child or children are heard and participate must be:

1. Transparent and informative – children must be provided with full, accessible, diversity-sensitive and age-appropriate information about their right to express their views freely and how this participation will take place
2. Voluntary
3. Respectful – children's views have to be treated with respect and they should be provided with opportunities to initiate ideas and activities. Adults should build on good examples of children's participation, and be aware of the cul-

tural context of children's lives and also respect children's views with regard to participation in public events

4. Relevant – children must have space to identify issues which they consider as relevant, and give views on what they consider important
5. Child-friendly – children will need differing levels of support and forms of involvement according to their age and evolving capacities; working methods should be adapted to children's capacities. Adequate time and resources should be made available to ensure that children are adequately prepared and have the confidence and opportunity to contribute their views
6. Inclusive – participation must be inclusive. Children are not a homogenous group and equality of opportunity for all, without discrimination, marginalisation or cultural exclusion on any ground should be offered in the programmes
7. Supported by training – adults need training to facilitate children's participation effectively. Children themselves can be involved as trainers and facilitators on how to promote effective participation; and children in turn require capacity-building to strengthen their skills in awareness raising and advocacy
8. Safe and sensitive to risk – as expression of views may involve risks, adults have a responsibility to minimize the risk to children of violence, exploitation or any other negative consequence of their participation
9. Accountable – a commitment to follow-up and evaluation is essential. In any research or consultative process, children must be informed as to how their views have been interpreted and used, are entitled to comment on the analysis of the findings and to be provided with clear feedback and opportunity to participate in follow-up processes or activities. Monitoring and evaluation of children's participation needs to be undertaken, where possible, with children themselves.

These requirements can be used as a checklist for all library regulations, governance and service and programme activities.

There are two more important elements for libraries in the Committee's General Comment on Article 12 as they highlight the child's right to information as essential. Paragraph 25 states:

> The realization of the right of the child to express her or his views requires that the child be informed about the matters, options and possible decisions to be taken and their consequences by those who are responsible for hearing the child, and by the child's parents or guardian. The child must also be informed about the conditions under which she or he will be asked to express her or his views. This right to information is essential, because it is the precondition of the child's clarified decisions.

Paragraph 82 states:

> Fulfilment of the child's right to information, consistent with article 17 is, to a large degree, a prerequisite for the effective realization of the right to express views. Children need access to information in formats appropriate to their age and capacities on all issues of concern to them. This applies to information, for example, relating to their rights, any proceedings affecting them, national legislation, regulations and policies, local services, and appeals and complaints procedures. Consistent with articles 17 and 42, States parties should include children's rights in the school curricula.

The Committee exemplifies the implementation of the right to be heard in different settings and situations in which children grow up, develop and learn. The situations include the family, alternative care, healthcare, education and school. Paragraph 115 indicates that play, recreation, sports and cultural activities should be designed taking into account children's preferences and capacities. Children, including young children and children with disabilities should be consulted. Libraries are explicitly mentioned in Paragraph 128: "In addition, children can contribute their perspectives, for example, on the design of schools, playgrounds, parks, leisure and cultural facilities, public libraries, health facilities and local transport systems in order to ensure more appropriate services. In community development plans that call for public consultation, children's views should be explicitly included", providing a clear indication that a child perspective must be included in library design, services and governance.

The Response of Libraries to the Convention

How have libraries worked with the rights of the child, implementing the Convention in their policies and practices? Has the right to information (Koren 1997) found reception in further recommendations and practices? Have libraries understood the obligation to empower children and young people through their services and activities (Koren 2004)? In a German Handbook, explaining the theoretical foundations and standards on children's libraries, Article 17 of the CRC is quoted as the library's obligation to deliver free access to information and materials, and gives examples of participation (Keller-Loibl 2009).

Overall, explicit references to the rights of the child in the library field have been modest. The *Guidelines for Children's Libraries Services* (IFLA Libraries for Children and Young Adults Section 2003) has a general reference to the Convention, whereas the background paper confirms it as the basis for defining the rights of the child in the context of children's libraries. It stresses the right of every child to the development of his/her full potential, the right to free and open access to information, materials and programmes, under equal conditions for all, irrespective of age, race, sex, religious and national background, language or social status, referring particularly to Articles 1, 2, 4, 13, 14, 17, 23, 28, 29, 30, 31 and 42 but significantly omitting Article 12. Children's libraries promote the rights of the child through different activities designed for children and adults and relate the rights to democracy in a society. "They should empower children for active participation. Through early access to information and books, creative contacts with peers and pursuing interests in the library, the child learns how to live with others, how to protect their own rights while respecting the rights of others" (IFLA 2003b). An explicit elaboration on Articles 13 and 17 is contained in the IFLA statement on Internet and children's library services (https://www.ifla. org/publications/internet-and-children-s-library-services).

The *Guidelines for Library Services to Babies and Toddlers* (IFLA 2007) have a clear reference to the Convention and the examples included show true commitment and support of children's creativity but are not related to children's feedback on the library services and programming itself. The *Guidelines for Library Services For Young Adults* (IFLA 2008) require that the library has established clear policy statements concerning the right to free access by young adults to library resources and information sources and respect for the rights of young adults to select materials. The need for youth participation is expressed but not as a right: "Libraries who wish to offer effective and meaningful programs for young adults must seek out their participation at all stages of the program process. Involving young adults in decision making, planning, and implementing programs for themselves is highly recommended as a best practice that contributes to positive youth development" (IFLA 2008, 5).

A Canadian exploration notes:

> "It is interesting to compare the UN's stance on children's rights with libraries' stance on intellectual freedom. These are excerpts taken from the Canadian Library Association's position on intellectual freedom and we can see how it upholds the UN's position. Theoretically, libraries are following the UN with this intellectual freedom position statement and have created a noble ideal. And, theoretically, by striving for intellectual freedom, we should be supporting the rights of children. But how do you ensure you are upholding this ideal and supporting children's rights while still respecting Federal and Provincial law, parental rights and expectations, community beliefs, and still make sure that everyone gets their coffee break?" (Thomson 2004, 46–47).

The Convention states in Article 3 as a General Principle that the best interests of the child shall be a primary consideration. Is it fully understood that this nowadays more than ever means that a child's perspective on his/her best interests must be included? De Langen (1989, 47) provides a reminder: "The fact that children are not yet grown up is used as an excuse by parents, social workers, teachers, judges and many other adults to follow their own interpretation of the child's interest and to set demands and make decisions that may have far-reaching consequences for children which no one can foresee. (...) Why are adults, who are in a much stronger position in many respects, so afraid to take children seriously and to grant them a large degree of autonomy?"

A few early recommendations give perspective to the role of libraries in protecting and realizing children's rights. It was concluded in 2004:

> It is now up to the international library community, librarians and other professionals to show commitment. Works needs to be done at the international, national and local level: to start partnerships between IFLA and e.g. UNICEF, and vice versa on the local level; to include children's rights in national library policies and statements; to give training to librarians on children's rights and include references in their codes of ethics; to include the right to information and library services in UNICEF-projects; to implement widely protection of children's rights in library practices; to adopt the 20 November as a day of activities in the library on the Rights of the Child; to select children's literature for human rights education projects; to create a reliable and safe environment where children themselves can seek and find information, express their opinions and work with their skills; to discuss with children possibilities for improvements in their daily lives; and first of all, to listen to children and every individual child!" (Koren 2004, 7)

Most of these recommendations are still awaiting fulfilment. Some efforts have been made. One early example is a human rights education project including the role of the school library in supporting developmental rights of the child and helping children with information on rights (Stričević 2001, 37). But it is surprising how little libraries have been involved in the monitoring mechanisms of the Convention, nor in fact in other human rights monitoring of relevant treaties and instruments.

One small exception, in fact a personal action, was made at the special day of the Committee on the Rights of the Child, devoted to the child and the media. On the basis of group discussions, one of the recommendations for thematic debate reads in Paragraph 256: "3. Active child libraries. The experience of dynamic child libraries, or child departments within public libraries, should be documented and disseminated" (https://www.ohchr.org/EN/HRBodies/CRC/Documents/Recommandations/media.pdf). But no further action was taken and page 11 of the report notes: "The Working Group discussed the value of sharing experiences on active child libraries and children's departments within public libraries, while noting that many children, particularly in developing countries, live in societies where libraries and, indeed, books and reading, are not major sources of information. At the close of the discussion, it was agreed to record that the project to compile best practices of child libraries remains unfunded....". Would it have concluded otherwise if a strong international library advocacy had been undertaken? The library sector was not then ready.

Part of the monitoring mechanisms are country reports to be regularly delivered by the States parties to human rights conventions. Governments can seek information from a variety of sources, including their library agencies and national libraries. Quite common are alternative reports published by civil society indicating a more nuanced and sometimes problematic situation with regard to the state of the art of human rights. Library associations could for example express concerns about literacy or access to information, in short, all issues related to the realization of human rights including children's rights, women's rights and rights of persons with disabilities, in such reports which are valued by the monitoring Committees. It also offers the library associations opportunities to partnerships and coalitions with other children's rights related organizations, as has been done by the Dutch NGO Coalition for Children's Rights (Kinderrechten-collectief 1999).

Researching the child's right to information under Articles 13 and 17 of the UN Convention on the Rights of the Child, DeCaen highlights the public librarian's moral obligation to both empower and protect and "concludes that the human rights framework demands a more nuanced approach to children's intellectual freedom and their rights in the public library" (DeCaen 2007, 1). Being aware that more needs to be done, and that children's libraries have shown commitment to children's rights, one may ask, how can the obligations towards children be realized?

A New Era for Library Involvement at the International Level?

Looking at the general state of the art of libraries, one may observe that political awareness in the library sector has grown. The advent of new technologies, the financial crisis, the obvious inequalities regarding access to information, the inadequate balance of the public sector and private copyright regulations, and the local and global nature of these events and trends have awakened and strengthened the search for adequate responses from the library sector. Whereas management and marketing have been buzzwords for some time, nowadays advocacy and lobbying are part of common library speak. Gradually IFLA has changed from a mere professional association to the global voice of the library sector. Two important IFLA committees, FAIFE and Copyright and Other Legal Matters, give

IFLA input for advocacy actions and concrete lobby in the case of the Marrakesh (https://www.wipo.int/marrakesh_treaty/en/) treaty (Bonnet 2017), the World International Property Organization (WIPO) (http://www.wipo.int), the World Trade Organization (WTO) (https://www.wto.org), and the UN Agenda 2030 (https://www.un.org/ga/search/view_doc.asp?symbol=A/RES/70/1&Lang=E). Library associations are involved as national partners to influence national governments and their views, and prepare for international negotiation and decision-making.

Thanks to substantial external funding from the Bill and Melinda Gates Foundation, IFLA can truly take up its role as a global player leading libraries. It does so by seizing the opportunities offered and committing to the UN framework of Agenda 2030. IFLA is making libraries aware of what they can contribute to help in achieving the SDGs. From an international perspective, one may note that most international organizations need about a decade to really change their strategies, becoming aware of and responding to the changing global environment and its challenges. Nevertheless, the obligation to improve the situation of millions of human beings, especially vulnerable ones including children, people with special needs and those living with a handicap, realizing their basic human rights, remains.

The United Nations Millennium Development Goals (MDGs) (https://www.un.org/millenniumgoals/) set in 2000 to give concrete results in a 15 year plan were considered the most prominent initiative on the global development agenda and had a great deal in common with human rights commitments. But neither the human rights nor development communities embraced the linkage with enthusiasm or conviction. Research led to a call upon the human rights community to engage more effectively with the development agenda, to prioritize its concerns rather than assuming that every issue needs to be tackled simultaneously, and to avoid being overly prescriptive (Alston 2005). As it became clear that the challenges for a sustainable future only grew, a new global impetus and a follow-up 15 year plan were deemed necessary.

The new approach, adopted in 2015 by the United Nations under the name of Agenda 2030 formulated 17 sustainable development goals (SDGs) to be achieved by joined effort, not only by all states, all members of United Nations, but also by joining the forces at local and national level of government, the business sector, civil society and people themselves. "We are determined to mobilize the means required to implement this Agenda through a revitalized Global Partnership for Sustainable Development, based on a spirit of strengthened global solidarity, focused in particular on the needs of the poorest and most vulnerable and with the participation of all countries, all stakeholders and all people" states the Preamble to the document *Transforming our World: the 2030 Agenda for Sustainable*

Development (https://sustainabledevelopment.un.org/post2015/transformingour world). In the Declaration one finds a spirited vision articulated, with references to universal literacy and also to children:

> 7. In these Goals and targets, we are setting out a supremely ambitious and transformational vision. We envisage a world free of poverty, hunger, disease and want, where all life can thrive. We envisage a world free of fear and violence. A world with *universal literacy*. A world with equitable and universal access to quality education at all levels, to health care and social protection, where physical, mental and social well-being are assured.

> 8. We envisage a world of universal respect for human rights and human dignity, the rule of law, justice, equality and non-discrimination; of respect for race, ethnicity and cultural diversity; and of equal opportunity permitting the full realization of human potential and contributing to shared prosperity. A world which invests in *its children* and in which *every child* grows up free from violence and exploitation. A world in which every woman and girl enjoys full gender equality and all legal, social and economic barriers to their empowerment have been removed. A just, equitable, tolerant, open and socially inclusive world in which the needs of the most vulnerable are met.

> 9. One in which democracy, good governance and the rule of law as well as an enabling environment at national and international levels, are essential for sustainable development, including sustained and inclusive economic growth, social development, environmental protection and the eradication of poverty and hunger. The call for action includes: 51. What we are announcing today – an Agenda for global action for the next fifteen years – is a charter for people and planet in the twenty-first century. Children and young women and men are critical agents of change and will find in the new Goals a platform to channel their infinite capacities for activism into the creation of a better world (https://sustainabledevelop ment.un.org/post2015/transformingourworld).

It is clear from these paragraphs that children and their human rights and literacy are themes in the global development agenda. The 17 Goals to be achieved both at national and international level cover the world problems of combatting poverty, inequality, unsafe environment and industry and climate change. The initial IFLA suggestions for library responses are contained in Annex 3 to this chapter.

IFLA's Involvement with the UN and the SDGs

As an international player, IFLA was involved at an early stage in the UN processes, and the library field prepared its input, starting with the Lyon Declaration on Access to Information and Development, which states: "Sustainable development must take place in a human rights-based framework, where: (...) Inequality is reduced by the empowerment, education and inclusion of marginalized groups, including women, indigenous peoples, minorities, migrants, refugees, persons with disabilities, older persons, children and youth" (https://www.lyon declaration.org/). Children are clearly included when speaking on human rights and access to information. Examples of the contributions to be made by libraries can be found at https://www.ifla.org/publications/node/9639?og=7409.

In a statement from IFLA's Literacy and Reading Section, an extensive analysis of literacy is given, recognising "that literacy and reading are essential for access to information for personal growth and for the development of communities within society and that libraries have a unique role in the promotion of literacy and reading". Literacy and reading are extremely important elements for sustainable futures. Examples are given of literacy activities of libraries, with communities in Bangladesh and Nepal, incarcerated parents and their children in Western Australia, book buddies and terminally ill children in Malaysia (https://www.ifla.org/files/assets/hq/topics/libraries-development/documents/ literacy-and-reading-brief.pdf).

IFLA's Libraries for Children and Young Adults Section published a statement on supporting development by providing access to information. Relating equal access to information, literacy skills to lifelong learning and participation in the community, and referring to the personal development to the full potential as guaranteed in the Convention, libraries' activities supporting development are listed and examples given. They range from the internationally well-spread Bookstart, bilingual books for babies and digital storytelling in Northern Australia, e-learning tablets for slum school children in Kenya and street libraries in poor areas in France to health and technology information camps in Uganda, the Green Children's Library for Kids in Singapore and teenage workshops on media skills, health information and financial literacy. The examples are encouraging. However, participation of children and young people is seriously missing, likewise a more precise reference to a specific child right (https://www.ifla.org/files/ assets/hq/topics/libraries-development/documents/libraries-for-children-and-young-adults.pdf).

The Public Libraries Section responded by adapting the UNESCO Public Library Manifesto and relating library services to support development and SDG-related aspects, showing examples, some of which are listed here in relation to children:

– Support people to make informed decisions through access to information, skills, media and information literacy and digital literacy, for example in Kenya with the help of the mobile digital librarian bringing the magic of e-books to hospitals, young offenders' institutions, child care centres and schools, reaching hundreds of children who do not have access to books and would otherwise not hear the stories

- Secure cultural heritage for current and future generations, for example by mapping the community such as in Medellin, Columbia, with library support
- Support governments, civil society and local communities to achieve development goals, for example in Kenya and Uganda, where schools are engaging in lively inter-school debates, quizzes and spelling competitions through Kisumu Public Library's smartphone, laptop and video conferencing project
- Support creators and provide a rich foundation for new forms of creativity, demonstrated in Fablabs, the Devon Library, writers workshops, media studios and robotics workshops, especially valued by young disabled people, including the Yes They Can programme and MultiCentre in Olsztyn, Poland (https://www.ifla.org/files/assets/hq/topics/libraries-development/docu ments/public-libraries-brief.pdf).

Another IFLA section, School Libraries, also closely related to children, states its contributions to the UN development goals. Economic and educational inequality continues in many countries. The top 1% or 10% can afford to give their children private education with top quality school libraries. To improve everyone's lives, the benefit of a quality school library needs to be extended to all and the school librarian is a key contributor to development. School libraries help close the achievement gap for poor children, minority children and children with disabilities and in countries with deep gender gaps, for girls. A Canadian example testifies about a teacher-librarian in Edmonton in a school with many immigrant and refugee families, inviting families into the school library and taking them on a school-funded field trip to the local public library and bookstores as part of helping parents to support the literacy development of their children and of the adults themselves.

Other examples can be found in the international study *Global Perspectives on School Libraries: Projects and Practices* (Marquardt and Oberg 2011) which refers to camels, burros, elephants, boats and trucks being used to bring books and literacy to children in remote communities in Azerbaijan, Columbia, Ethiopia, Finland, Kenya, Norway, Thailand and Venezuela. In Zambia, the Lubuto Library Project provides culturally relevant resources and educational experiences to orphans and other vulnerable children and youth. With the annual Readathon, Namibia promotes a reading culture by providing children with stories in their home languages. Namibia has 13 written languages and the library gives the impetus for publishing children's books in the home languages for schools and libraries (https://www.ifla.org/files/assets/hq/topics/libraries-development/docu ments/school-libraries-brief.pdf).

IFLA has worked hard to have access to information included as an item into the global development agenda with its 169 targets (https://www.ifla.org/publi

cations/node/8641?og=7409). Sustainable Development Goal 16 relates to peaceful and inclusive societies, access to justice for all, and effective, accountable and inclusive institutions at all levels. Access to information has been recognized as target 16.10: "Ensure public access to information and protect fundamental freedoms, in accordance with national legislation and international agreements". Other goals and targets impact on libraries with target 11.4 referring to the world's cultural and national heritage and information and communications technology-related goals and targets 5b, 9c and 17.8. "Half of the world's population lacks access to information online. In our knowledge society, libraries provide access and opportunity for all", opines IFLA in how libraries can connect the next four billion (https://www.ifla.org/publications/node/10618). And, as already mentioned, universal literacy is recognized in the vision for the UN 2030 Agenda.

Indicators will be used to measure progress towards meeting the SDGs. To ensure that governments are on track with meeting targets 16.10 concerning access to information, 11.4 safeguarding cultural heritage and 4c universal literacy, IFLA has contributed to consultations on appropriate indicators for access to information, ICT, culture and literacy indicators and continues to do so (https://www.ifla.org/libraries-development). IFLA's consistent position is that access to information is essential in achieving the SDGs, and that libraries are not only key partners for governments but are already contributing to progress towards the achievement of the 17 Goals. The responses from various sections on the Lyon Declaration served as a first proof.

In the IFLA brochure, *Access and Opportunity for All: How Libraries Contribute to the United Nations 2030 Agenda* (https://www.ifla.org/publications/node/10546), one finds two explicitly child-related examples:

Goal 4: Ensure inclusive and equitable quality education and promote lifelong learning opportunities for all... Netherlands: Boekstart works with day care and healthcare centres, public libraries and the first two years of primary school to provide books and literacy training to 75,000 children aged 0–4 per year. The programme is supported by national and local government, and aims to establish long-term collaboration between organizations that support children's literacy.

Goal 15: Protect, restore and promote sustainable use of terrestrial ecosystems, sustainably manage forests, combat desertification, and halt and reverse land degradation and halt biodiversity loss. Libraries are sustainable institutions; they share resources in the community and internationally and ensure everyone has access to information. All libraries play a significant role in providing access to data, research and knowledge that support informed research and public access to information about climate change, and a key role in the preservation of indigenous knowledge, including local decision-making about fundamental aspects of life including hunting, fishing, land use and water management...Singapore. The National Library Board Singapore (NLB) has worked with sponsors to build a

Children's Green Library that provides special collections on environmental conservation and interactive public education programmes, notably aimed at helping children understand climate change. Much of the building is also made of recycled materials, confirming the conservation message.

IFLA and Capacity Building

The SDGs have to be achieved at the national level and IFLA has started a new International Advocacy Programme (IAP) which focuses on capacity building of libraries and their associations for promoting and supporting the role libraries can play in the planning and implementation of the UN 2030 Agenda and the national plans (https://www.ifla.org/libraries-development). The IAP-training programme is at the same time a commitment of libraries at the national level resulting in advocacy to have libraries included in the national Agenda 2030 plans which every UN member is obliged to make. How much awareness is there to relate the libraries' role and children's rights and perspectives to the UN Agenda and the SDG plans? Screening the IAP Newsletters which keep the library community informed on progress, some examples can be found in which children are mentioned. In the German National Plan 2016, *Deutsche Nachhaltigkeitsstrategie* (https://www.bundesregierung.de/breg-de/themen/nachhaltigkeitspolitik/eine-strategie-begleitet-uns/die-deutsche-nachhaltigkeitsstrategie), libraries are not directly mentioned in the different strategies for reaching the goals, but they are mentioned once as an example of how they could contribute to meet the challenges of the demographic changes in rural areas in the Trafo project. A large federal government project for cultural education is included as an example, to which libraries contribute. It has reached about 15,000 educational disadvantaged children and young people in Germany. Regular updates record achievements (https://www.ifla.org/ldp/iap) and contain many examples of programmes for children.

An example of true children's participation is found in Algeria, where a workshop on the UN 2030 Agenda, the SDGs and libraries was organized in the public library of the state of Djelfa in cooperation with the Association of Algerian Libraries and Information. The workshop was supervised by children. Each child presented an SDG and placed it in different spaces in the library, after which the children explained the SDGs to the attendees. In Tunisia, in the context of the National Reading Days, an information workshop was organized, *Libraries, Development and the 2030 Agenda*, to train the nineteen heads of public libraries of Ben Arous Governorate. Discussions took place about the need to update the internal law of public libraries to give children in the preschool age right to access to information and libraries contributing to SDG 4 Quality Education.

The IAP liaison participant discussed with the Jordan Library and Information Association (JLIA) the UN SDGs and the strong link with libraries. Examples were provided particularly of the Abdul Hameed Shoman Public Library, the largest public library in Jordan, whose services for children and researchers greatly contribute to SDG 4.

To start gathering evidence of how libraries support development in Bermuda, IAP participants highlighted the Bermuda Youth Library's Born to Read programme with its packages of information given to new mothers at Bermuda's only hospital and agreed to look into ways to collect data on how many children actually become library members, clearly related to SDG 4. A press conference in Cuba, organized by the libraries, presented the results and winners of the National Read to Martí Contest, one of the main actions of the National Program for Reading, part of the Cuban Librarians Association (ASCUBI)'s IAP advocacy plan. The contest, created in 1998, has contributed to the promotion of reading of the work of the Cuban José Martí, and the development of reading and cognitive skills and values of children, teenagers and youth throughout the country, one of the examples of the contribution of libraries to SDGs 4 and 16.

In Guatamala the first assembly of the Guatemala Library Association (ABG) took place. Partnerships were formed with the Riecken Foundation and Child Aid to discuss plans to involve public and community librarians as much as possible in the IAP activities in Guatemala. Both institutions expressed their interest and support for activities to promote the SDGs and the important role libraries play. In Kenya, reports on youth and women programmes running in public libraries were presented at ministerial level to help the advocacy work in connection to the SDGs. The Zimbabwe Library Association (ZimLA) held discussions with local authorities on the role of libraries. Consultations were done between ZimLA and the United Nations Populations Fund (UNFPA) to develop partnerships to involve libraries in their programmes supporting gender equality, programmes for women and girls on rights and health, and ICT and literacy programmes to support women to build their entrepreneurial skills. Even small islands like Aruba in the Caribbean can take advantage of the IAP programme, and draw attention to the library SDG activities in providing youth with tablet cafés and code hours (Scholing and Britten 2017).

Apart from training and awareness activities in the IAP programme, IFLA has also sought scientific support. The *Development and Access to Information Reports* DA2I (https://da2i.ifla.org/) provide regular details on advocacy initiatives. The reports are produced by IFLA in partnership with the Technology and Social Change Group (TASCHA) at the University of Washington, underlining that for access to information to be meaningful, people need skills and the right conditions; and that libraries can play a unique role in delivering both. The DA2I is a tool for national, regional and global advocacy initiatives related to access to information and libraries. The reports look through the lens of access to information at the SDGs. "Access to information (A2I) is not an end in itself, but rather a driver of progress across the board. It empowers people and communities, laying the foundations for equality, sustainability, and prosperity. It provides a clear illustration of the rights-based, holistic approach to development taken in the 2030 Agenda" (https://da2i.ifla.org/wp-content/uploads/da2i-2017-ex_sum_english.pdf). Are materials related to children to be found in the reports? It is interesting to note that the researchers relate access to information to youth's social and economic participation and discuss this role related to SDG 8 on youth employment. The importance of quality education (SDG 4.4) is also relevant.

Screening the 2017 report (https://da2i.ifla.org/da2i-report-2017/) with other chapters on agriculture, health, gender equality and sustainable infrastructure, on child-relevance, a few examples can be found:

> In Burkina Faso, the Girls' Mobile Health Clubs found in four village libraries expand access to quality health information while also providing support to the participants to increase their information literacy and technology skills. While library staff provide training in information literacy skills, local health clinics ensure that the health information is current and relevant, and the youth build shared information resources for their communities with the assistance of library staff. (...) In Indonesia, public libraries have offered micro-entrepreneurship training to more than 84,000 women and youth over the past six years. Training participants have researched a variety of ideas for small or household-based businesses, including starting or expanding initiatives related to food processing, growing markets for traditional fabric crafts, and improving methods for crop and livestock production (IFLA 2017, 54).

Chapter 2 of the report is devoted to Libraries as Agents for Sustainable Development:

> A library can also be conceived of as a social space, where community members meet, participate in programs together, and learn from each other. From children's story times to cultural events, libraries offer a wide variety of programs that leverage their physical spaces as part of a community's social infrastructure... Libraries promoting civic engagement: Libraries are well-positioned to provide opportunities for public dialogue and civic participation. With strong local roots, they are typically regarded as safe and trusted institutions in their communities, characteristics that can prove valuable when tackling challenging issues. (IFLA 2017, 52–53).

Another example worth noting includes programmes to address youth unemployment in South Africa, where a partnership has emerged between the National

Library of South Africa and private industry aimed at expanding ICT related employment opportunities for youth. The programme includes training in digital skills and a graduate internship programme for youth to gain practical experience. The collaboration contributes to the skills development initiatives of the National Development Agenda.

> The above examples – a small sample of the work of public libraries globally – show how proactive, community-centred public libraries are stepping into areas where there are information gaps and unexplored potential in local communities. It can be as simple as expanding access through improved infrastructure, such as launching free Wi-Fi hotspots and lending laptops, or deploying a mobile library to take access to the point of need. It can also be one of the many training programmes for women, girls, and youth focused on specific domains to ensure improved literacy, equality, health, and economic development. (IFLA 2017, 56).

Related to SDG 5 Gender Equality, chapter 5 describes how access to information empowers women and girls, and refers to public and community libraries: "These libraries offer girls and women information opportunities that can help them improve their lives and those of their families, empower themselves, and advance gender equality... Libraries should follow the principles of serving first those who need the most but now have the least. Their outreach to girls and women should prioritize information initiatives that involve ICT access and training as well as critical thinking." (IFLA 2017, 81).

The report states:

> Access to information can transform lives. It can help lift people out of poverty, promote gender equality, and create countless opportunities for youths. However, its transformative ability is bounded by local, social, political, and economic forces. While ICT infrastructure is key to achieving the Sustainable Development Goals, the tools that provide access to information are not enough. To help create more just and equal societies, the access must be meaningful.(IFLA 2017, 48).

The SDGs and Children: Catalysts for Libraries

How can public libraries help to make access to information meaningful for children? The question remains. Reporting examining the SDGs from a child's rights perspective is still missing. In spite of the many contributions to IFLA advocacy work, an explicit overview and analysis of the SDGs and libraries' roles from the perspective of children is much needed. It is a challenging subject, which could take into account the knowledge and information already provided by some IFLA sections. Are there more resources and ways to focus on what the UN Agenda

2030 means to children and how it would help to realize their rights, especially related to their right to information?

The UN Agenda 2030 gives a new outlook and incentive to human commitment; this applies also to libraries, especially library services for children and young people. But before anything else a true commitment is necessary. Can all library leaders and professionals say and follow after the UN Secretary-General António Guterres, on International Youth Day: "I am committed to the empowerment and inclusion of every young person around the world. In this spirit, I have appointed an impressive new Youth Envoy, Jayathma Wickramanayake. She is the youngest member of my team — and one of the most important. Governments must work with young people to successfully achieve the Sustainable Development Goals. Empowered young men and women can play a critical role in preventing conflicts and ensuring sustainable peace. Join us in mobilizing young people. Together we can create a peaceful world for generations to come." (Guterres 2017).

Good governance is essential for children's well-being. It is about a government being responsible to its citizens in terms of delivering services, being open and transparent about decision-making processes, making information accessible and having established independent mechanisms that can hold it accountable for its actions and inaction. In this way children can and should participate in governance, and report their views. The Save the Children's report to the UN Committee on the Rights of the Child 'It's All About Children includes seven case studies of child participation and ten steps to meaningful children's participation (Save the Children 2011b).

It is important to make use of the comments and research that specific child-oriented organizations have done regarding the SDGs. For example, UNICEF commented on the SDGs and stressed continuing the work on children's rights. Its report, *A Post-2015 World Fit for Children: A Review of the Open Working Group Report on Sustainable Development Goals from a Child Rights Perspective* (https://www.unicef.cn/media/10611/file/A%20Post-2015%20World%20Fit%20for%20Children.pdf), welcomes the proposed goals and targets related to children while stressing the need to maintain progress for children's rights in negotiations on the post-2015 development agenda. The report has the key message that "investments in the rights of all children in every place in the world—regardless of the child's gender, ethnicity, race, economic, disability or other status" is the fundamental building block for achieving the world's shared vision of the future we want (UNICEF 2015, 2). UNICEF Executive Director Anthony Lake commented that the SDGs are the beginning:

Today's welcome decision marks the end of a process – and a beginning. The drive to turn commitments into action. We will measure our progress, yes, through statistics. But the true measure will be in every child lifted out of poverty; through every mother who survives childbirth; every girl who does not lose her childhood to early marriage. By helping the most disadvantaged children today – by giving them a fair chance in life – we can help break the bonds of extreme poverty tomorrow. (https://www.unicef.org/media/media_85630.html).

Both quantitative and qualitative research of libraries' contributions to giving children fair chances through access to information is an SDG commitment.

Regarding libraries' contributions to supporting universal literacy, UN Secretary-General Ban Ki-Moon had a clear message for International Literacy Day: "Literacy stands at the heart of the 2030 Agenda. It is a foundation for human rights, gender equality, and sustainable societies. It is essential to all our efforts to end extreme poverty and promote well-being for all people. That is why the Sustainable Development Goals aim for universal access to quality education and learning opportunities throughout people's lives. One of the targets of Sustainable Development Goal 4 is to ensure that all young people achieve literacy and numeracy and that a substantial proportion of adults who lack these skills are given the opportunity to acquire them" (Ki-Moon 2016).

In relation to SDG 13, Climate Action, Save the Children estimates that for every year of the coming decade, natural disasters will affect 175 million children, increasing the risks to their health, education, protection and lifelong opportunities (Save the Children 2009, 2). Further research has looked at the role of children.

Frequently forgotten in the global discussions and agreements on climate change are children and young people, who both disproportionately suffer the consequences of a rapidly changing climate, yet also offer innovative solutions to reduce greenhouse gas emissions (climate change mitigation) and adapt to climate change. Existing evidence is presented of the disproportionately harmful impact of climate-induced changes in precipitation and extreme weather events on today's children, especially in the Global South. This paper examines the existing global climate change agreements under the UN Framework Convention on Climate Change for evidence of attention to children and intergenerational climate justice, and suggests the almost universally ratified Convention on the Rights of the Child be leveraged to advance intergenerational climate justice. (Gibbons 2016, 19)

Gibbons refers to the work of the Intergovernmental Panel on Climate Change (https://www.ipcc.ch/). When children and young people receive a strong education that develops environmental awareness and resilience from an early age, they become an indispensable resource as:

the potential disaster management experts of the future and [today's] teachers of disaster management within the family. The rapidly changing climate also adds urgency to the realization of children's right to information about what is and will happen. By realizing their right to information, children are empowered to participate meaningfully in risk reduction, community climate adaptation, and policy discussions for addressing climate change at local and national levels. Children have a unique capacity to perceive risks that are particular to their age and circumstances, and to propose child-friendly ways overcome them. Climate change is irrevocably transforming their world; therefore, supporting the agency of children and young people in developing creative solutions is both a right and a necessity (Gibbons 2016, 24–25).

These findings were confirmed in June 2017 when the UN Human Rights Council (UNHRC) held a day-long debate on climate change and the rights of the child. The discussions were based on two studies contributing to the implementation of SDG 13, Climate Action and SDG 10, Reduce Inequality, as children in developing countries are disproportionately affected by climate change. The first study is a summary of the panel discussion on the adverse impact of climate change on States' efforts to realize the rights of the child and related policies, lessons learned and good practices including an interactive discussion on the negative impacts of climate change on a broad array of children's rights. The discussion focused on ways to facilitate effective, rights-based climate action through the exchange of knowledge and good practices among States, international organizations and stakeholders. The second one is an analytical study on the relationship between climate change and the full and effective enjoyment of the rights of the child, and examines climate change impacts on children, related human rights obligations and responsibilities of States and other actors, including elements of a child rights-based approach to climate change policies. The study provides examples of good practices and offers recommendations, including to: ensure children's rights policy coherence; empower children to participate in climate policy making; guarantee children's access to remedies; better understand the impacts of climate change on children; and mobilise adequate resources for child rights-based climate action (http://sdg.iisd.org/news/un-human-rights-council-discusses-child-rights-based-approach-to-climate-action/; https://www.ohchr.org/EN/Issues/HRAndClimateChange/Pages/RightsChild.aspx).

These are just a few of relevant reports, which may help libraries to understand the wider array in which access to information as a right of children is to be understood especially in working on the SDGs. Both UN and research sources give explanatory information on what it means to work on a human rights-based approach, and apply this to the various situations in which access to information and children's participation should play an essential role.

Children's Rights-Based Library Governance

Building on library values and the human rights framework, the rights of the child and the consequences for libraries, and the commitment to the SDGs, it is time to focus on library governance from the perspective of the child, taking advantage of the SDGs as catalyst.

The first observation is that library governance as a professional subject is sparsely treated in library and information science. As already noted, the IFLA Public Library Service Guidelines (Gill 2001; Koontz and Gubbin 2010) contain only a short paragraph. One may also think of IFLA's Manifesto on Transparency, Good Governance and Freedom from Corruption (https://www.ifla.org/publica tions/ifla-manifesto-on-transparency--good-governance-and-freedom-from-cor ruption?og=7409), but close reading reveals that it refers to libraries' contribution to transparency and good governance of the state, supporting citizens by offering access to information, and not so much to transparency and governance of the library itself. Secondly, the subject of library governance related to children is almost if not totally invisible. Only in the case of some innovative libraries, working not only for but also with young adults, a glimpse of governance from a different perspective may appear.

In other words, library governance from a child's perspective still has to be built up with the help of various conditions and sources in order to be meaningful and successful. Some building bricks should be the following:

- Library governance should be based on respect and promotion of human rights; in this case especially the UN Convention on the Rights of the Child (CRC), and other child-relevant human rights treaties and instruments
- The rights of the child most relevant are the rights to information and to participation, as acknowledged in the CRC; they are also most important for developing library governance from a child's perspective
- For implementation of children's rights in the library field, and especially related to library governance, an in-depth study of children's rights is necessary. This applies both to library theory and policy and practice in library and information service institutions. The CRC Committee has time and again required that professionals working with children are aware of and well-trained in respecting and promoting children's rights
- Not only should the text of the Convention, especially articles related to the rights to information and participation, be part of professional knowledge and attitudes, but a number of General Comments by the CRC Committee would help even better to understand and formulate a clear library governance policy.

Several relevant CRC General Comments (http://tbinternet.ohchr.org/_layouts/ treatybodyexternal/TBSearch.aspx?Lang=en&TreatyID=5&DocTypeID=11) are taken as requirements for library governance. The child's right to development is closely related to his/her right to education. General Comment no. 1 clarifies the aims of education in Article 29 to which also Article 17, Access to information, refers, and puts the child's full development at the centre. In relation to the child's right to be heard, General Comment no. 12, participation applies to almost all processes and activities of an organization and its context and role in society. The question is not: would children be given a say in library matters, because they have a right to it, but how the library together with children can come to effective exercise of the right. The requirements for processes of participation are included in Annex 2 to this chapter. The principle of non-discrimination is fundamental in any human rights-based approach. The Committee refers to Articles 2 and 23 in the Convention, addressing the rights of inclusion of children with a disability which was written before the adoption of the UN Convention on the Rights of Persons with Disabilities. General Comment no. 9 elaborates what inclusion means, implementing the rights for children in various fields. In every Comment, and also in discussing the national reports on the state of the art of children's rights, the Committee requires special attention to children with a disability, and to groups of vulnerable children mentioned in the UN Agenda 2030. The outcome of a General Discussion on Digital Media and children's rights (https://www. ohchr.org/Documents/HRBodies/CRC/Discussions/2014/DGD_report.pdf) also refers to their rights and encourages ratification of the Marrakesh Treaty (https:// www.wipo.int/marrakesh_treaty/en/).

Very young children are often forgotten especially when it comes to participation. It is important to shift from a needs-based to a rights-based perspective (Jonsson 1998). Experiences in Early Childhood Development (ECD) demonstrate that young children have their own way of expressing views, which should be taken into account: "Young children use gestures and facial expressions, laughter and tears to express messages about their interests and wishes, to share their joy and excitement and to communicate their fears and worries" (Realising the Rights of Young Children 2009, 3). "You can see that the Committee is aware that the conditions under which children grow up are changing, and that new insights emerging from social science or experience in the field have to be reflected in the Committee's interpretation of child rights (Realising the Rights of Young Children 2009, 7).

General Comment 7 of the Committee on the Rights of the Child (https:// www2.ohchr.org/english/bodies/crc/docs/AdvanceVersions/GeneralCommen t7Rev1.pdf) states in paragraph 33: "The right to express views and feelings should be anchored in the child's daily life at home and in his or her community;

within the full range of early childhood health, care and education facilities, as well as in legal proceedings; and in the development of policies and services, including through research and consultations".

Together with UNICEF and the Bernhard van Leer Foundation, a *Guide to General Comment 7: Implementing Child Rights in Early Childhood* (https://www. unicef.org/earlychildhood/files/Guide_to_GC7.pdf) was published with comments and practices. Among them is a clear example of what libraries can do:

> The Home of Books for Children in Tirana, Albania. Research shows that reading and visiting libraries from an early age on can... clearly benefit children in terms of developing language skills, improving literacy levels and providing a sound basis to future educational achievement, as well as introducing young children to the delights of books and reading... In 2000, SOS Kinderdorf International supported the creation of a children's library in the centre of Tirana... The project was suggested by the Albanian section of International Board on Books for Young People... More than 1,000 children have already registered at the library. In order to reach children in the suburbs, the team uses the system of portable libraries, which consist of large suitcases containing a wide range of books. The library is designed in such a way that it is accessible to younger children. For younger children, a corner was designed based on the tale of Snow White and the Seven Dwarfs in order to create an appropriate environment for story-telling, theatre plays and puppet shows. The library is housed in a big room so that younger children can run around and move freely... An exhibition of children's drawings was organized based on the Convention of the Rights of the Child and according to the following themes: 'I am', 'My family', 'My future', 'I have the right to' (CRC 2006, 85).

Public budgeting is part of children's right to participation as it affects them and makes a big difference in the realization of children's rights when appropriate budgets have been established. The Committee does not only require effectiveness, efficiency, equity, transparency and sustainability of the States parties, but describes what transparency of public budgeting means from a perspective of children's rights:

> Transparency is also a prerequisite for enabling meaningful participation of the executive, legislatures and civil society, including children, in the budget process. The Committee emphasizes the importance of States parties actively promoting access to information about public revenues, allocations and spending related to children and adopting policies to support and encourage continuous engagement with legislatures and civil society, including children. (...) Past and potential impacts of budget decisions on children should be investigated. This can be done by conducting audits, consulting children, their caregivers and those working for their rights, and giving the results serious consideration in budget decisions. Legislation, policies and programmes directly or indirectly affecting children are to be translated into budget lines; hearings regarding the budget proposal with stakeholders within the State, including civil society, child advocates and children themselves. (CRC 2016a, paragraph 62).

In implementing library governance from a child perspective, some other sources may be helpful. A number of child rights organizations, including UNICEF and Save the Children, have invested in good online availability of relevant resources. Very relevant for understanding governance in relation to child rights is the distinction which UNICEF makes between child-led organizations, networks and movements on the one hand, and on the other hand child and youth participation in adult organizations. It might be helpful to apply this also in the library field. Examples from the resource guide include a report from Gaza about adolescents making a difference in their communities. Fifty adolescent-led initiatives supported by UNICEF include: creating a library out of recycled materials; building a waiting area for students from scratch; allowing people who cannot see to pick their dishes in restaurants; and helping students avoid allergies caused by chalk dust at school. UNICEF reports on Mongolia in 2015 detail how it had formalized a partnership with the Mongolian National Broadcaster (MNB) and Mongolia's National Library including 16 local public libraries, resulting in increased equity and child rights advocacy to much larger audiences. Many more examples, including those related to libraries, can be found in various UNICEF publications and resources.

Environmental studies include research on children's involvement. Here one finds examples of integrating children's rights into municipal action, with examples like poor urban children in Mumbai, participatory projects in Johannesburg, participatory budgeting initiatives in Latin America and Brazil, the Youth Planner Initiative in Hampton, Virginia and Bolivia's Children's Parliament (Bartlett 2005). In the field of social sciences one may also find examples of children's participation in budgeting and governance. For example, In the case of city planning, particularly in spaces for children and young people, the involvement of children and their right to participation should not be forgotten:

> Although children and teenagers intensively use public spaces, they are often marginalized in local planning debates. In Belgium, like in other West-European countries, spatial planning policy is managed by an extensive set of judicial procedures and officially established participation moments, from initial planning to budgeting to implementation. One youth organization succeeded in having an effective, although limited, influence on the final Implementation Plan. A former youth leader, who was an expert in spatial planning, obtained information and informed people involved in the planning process about the ways that development decisions could harm the youth organization, including elements of budgetary decisions. In Staden, the municipal youth worker is a member of the environmental council. Children's advocates have to deal with the use of different discourses at the different levels of decision-making, including the budget. When a community can set up a network of people in favour of the interests of children in public space, comprised of individuals who possess influence on decision making and budgeting then opportunities for

children's participation in spatial planning become attainable. (Lauwers and Vanderstede 2005).

Other research focuses on children's views and experiences in the digital age, with their comments on the role of libraries, Internet use, and expectations of their rights of access to information (Third et al. 2014). Not all projects on children's empowerment and application of the rights to participation are immediately positive and have lasting effects. This can be a warning for libraries in starting child participation projects. One study found that children accessed training in child rights, received a variety of information materials to enhance participation and had the opportunity to air their views in the Charitable Children Institutions (CCIs) in Kenya. Despite the scenario, children were not given the opportunity to participate in all decision-making processes affecting their lives. The staff involved thought that children should participate only in decisions in regard to their hygiene, leisure and immediate personal life and have nothing to do with the management of the institutions like budget formulation. Children were only involved in creative activities, such as art and dance (Wainaina 2015).

A similar example was found by Davey (2010) in a survey of organizations on child participation in England where children tended to be involved in decisions which seemed obviously important to their immediate needs such as leisure, recreation and play activities and were unlikely to have input into major decisions such as regeneration of their local area housing environment and transport. The survey showed that children were rarely involved in setting budgets, yet the request to have more of a say on how money for children's resources was allocated emerged as one of the key areas they wanted to have a say in. The finding is further supported by Hari (2007) in a study in Nepal on child participation in school governance and management. The findings were that there was no meaningful involvement of children in decision-making. Children were allowed to participate in extra curriculum activities only, yet the other stakeholders were involved in decision-making including monitoring and evaluation (Wainaina 2015, 61).

The lack of power in governance is also confirmed by active field organizations:

Children remain invisible in the debates about how countries are governed. By ignoring children, the governance community is missing a trick. Involving children in discussions about governance and ensuring that the realization of their rights is a measure of good governance can help improve government performance and build more effective states, especially in challenging environments. The leading agencies in the governance debate, including the UK's Department for International Development (DFID), the United Nations Development Programme (UNDP), the Organization for Economic Co-operation and Development (OECD) and the World Bank, are largely silent about the relevance of children and their rights to improving governance and building effective states. (Save the Children 2010).

The human rights case for governance has been largely accepted, but children's rights all too often fail to be included. But sometimes there is a victory: "Despite the hardship in getting heard, children do manage to influence governance in some of the world's most impoverished and democratically starved countries. In Zimbabwe, the continued demand by children's organizations to participate in issues that affect them has resulted in the budgeting process being reviewed and democratised" (Dina Jensen and Ladegaard 2012, 3).

Although since the early 1990s, participation has grown to become a key notion amongst child-focused international and intergovernmental development organizations, who by means of participatory projects commonly seek to achieve transformation of children's lives, little attention has been paid to the political context in which such transformation is sought. Hart argues that societal change leading to the realization of the rights of impoverished and marginalized children requires greater political will and new forms of alliance amongst international child-focused development organizations (Hart 2008).

Policies and Practices in Children's Participation in Governance

Even if there is political will to actually realize participation of children, differences in understanding children's participation may form an obstacle. A Belgian research study on children's influence and participation in youth work and local policy concluded that participation in the domain of youth policy differs from the concept in the domain of culture. The former understands it as participating in policy making, defending interests, whereas culture takes it as participating in activities. "There is little to no attention for the question: how to involve children and young people in making cultural policy?" (Tubex, De Rynck, and Coussée 2006, 135–136). It seems that the library sector until now has mainly followed the cultural understanding of participation.

Including children's perspectives in library governance, policies and practices is not a matter of taste or part of a library's life cycle. It is first and foremost inherent in taking the library's mission seriously, compliant with the human rights framework and the requirements for its implementation. Without respecting as a daily practice the human dignity of children and their rights, library service is missing the point: supporting a human being to live and develop her or his fullest potential. True human development lies at the heart of the library's mission. The library's governance, policies and practices should demonstrate how the library realizes this basic human right. The UN Agenda 2030 can be a formal and practical impetus for checking the library organization in this respect, especially the right of access to information and participation.

What kind of participation could bring a children's perspective closer to the library? The following provides examples of different kinds of participation which may stimulate further exploration. They include participation in such areas as: library customer panels, library design, programming, service development and potentially the governing board.

Library Customer Panels

Several libraries have innovated their relationships to their audiences, particularly in marketing and customer relations. The library establishes a continuing relationship with a panel comprising a diverse group of users who address various issues. The panel is brought together to discuss questions related to many matters including library services, premises, collections and opening hours. Libraries use the feedback for improvements and tests. As an example, Biebpanel is a collective online customer panel initiated by ProBiblio and working in 91 Dutch public libraries (https://www.probiblio.nl/producten/marketing-communicatie-onder zoek/marktonderzoek/biebpanel). The minimum age of participants is sixteen years. Some libraries have formed separate library groups for children and/or young adults for getting a better view on their wishes. Initiatives have included working with a youth group to learn about their preferences and views on communication and responding to initiatives of school children through media-workshops and literacy events for peers.

Library Design

When a new library was to be built in Heerhugowaard, Netherlands, children were not only consulted but also participated in masterclasses of architecture, design, creativity, journalism and exploration with professionals, including the architect team. From idea to actual functioning of the library, the children of ten schools were involved and continued as *Biebkidz* teams. The multi-way of addressing children in a strong cooperation of child-oriented organizations, including schools, libraries, museums and architects, is based on the working methods of the Library of 100 Talents, an elaboration of the pedagogical and cultural principles of the Reggio Emilia approach. According to Howard Gardner's (1983) theory of multiple intelligences, every child has a unique talent and the methods of revealing it should be carefully chosen. Following this concept, librarians ask children what they would like to learn. Instead of organizing ready-made games, librarians search various methods matching the best with children's wishes. It might be reading books, going on an excursion to learn more about sustainability, or creating artworks in the children's lab. Since many children are attracted by learning by doing, the library has to be a platform for experimenting, for example Coderdojo workshops.

In 2008, Heerhugowaard Library was awarded the Janusz Korczak Award for its dedication to children and children's perspectives in both design and programmes of the library. Similar Dutch examples of the 100 Talents approach can be found in Hoorn, where children also started to run a library branch themselves, and in Beverwijk. The libraries in Horsen and Arhus, Denmark, also practise child participation. In Stockholm, Sweden, in preparation of building an annex, school children followed architect workshops and learned about space and design, interviewing users, building scale-models and demonstrating their views on the library annex. In Dresden, Germany, teenagers and students were involved in the set-up of a new concept of youth library, called medien@age. The themes and presentations and digital settings and devices developed are based on their wishes and views, and follow their suggestions for browsing and searching.

Library Programming

Early examples of young people's involvement were in Alingsås and Eskilstuna, Sweden, and in Rostock and Hamburg, Germany. These libraries involved young people in both design and programming, with the result that they created their own way of accessing and using media, and learning and reading styles, reflected in the programmes. Music and diversity are important aspects for them to feel at home in the library. In Bosnia, librarians saw hundreds of high school children wasting time at the Zavidovici bus station while waiting for buses to take them home to their villages. They consulted youth organizations, the municipality and the children, and the idea of the Youth Corner and Multimedia Centre was born and realized: a safe place with the extras of media workshops, homework support, learning journalism, film and photography, and all subjects of youth interest (EIFL-PLIP 2011).

In Latvia, Valmiera Public Library, concerned that poor reading skills would limit young Latvians' chances in life, engaged young people in creating new services and spaces. The Read and Get Followers project uses digital technology to motivate teenagers to read, with the help of a social reading app. Young readers created their own e-book libraries, built networks of followers to chat with their friends and shared opinions about books online. The project changed the library's approach to working with young people. For the first time, the library involved teenagers in co-creating a library service. Fifteen reading ambassadors were trained and helped to design the app and a new reading space. The reading ambassadors have begun setting up a new group of young volunteers to consult with the library about future youth services and librarians are committed to continue consulting with teenagers (EIFL-PLP 2015).

Service Design

Especially with the advent of digital and online services, libraries have begun to involve their young users in the design of services. Frequent talks and focus groups with young people can give advice on collection development and acquisition for various genres like fantasy or Manga or even games and PlayStations, as young people have considerable technical competence. Younger generations identify more with the library. They may also serve as tutors and help peers in digital matters. Practical services like SMS for reservations and loans, innovations like medien@age in Dresden and digital newsletters or blogs by young people, such as in Solingen, Germany, are other options (Keller-Loibl 2009, 124).

Some libraries in the Netherlands engaged young people in other ways to participate in services. The Party Animals was a concept and the name of a group of young people helping library customers with primary digital skills and the introduction of digital media. Rijeka library in Croatia is known for its creative dialogue with teenage users, making their voices heard and their views seen in new services, labs and international exchange. The Hoeb4U in Hamburg is a youth library totally run by young people, especially apprentices and students of design, media and information. Those who do not yet know what they would like to do after secondary education can also work, do a browsing apprenticeship in a Hamburg branch and implement their knowledge in the Hoeb4U, while continuing in another library or another job, with additional skills and enhanced self-esteem.

Governing Boards

The ultimate step in implementing child rights in libraries would be to have children represented in the library board. The easy way and minimal option is to reserve a place and select an adult with a child rights friendly profile. Another way might be to be more explicit in the board membership profile and require someone under eighteen years of age. Still a better possibility would be to have a group of children attached to the library as perhaps Friends of the Library or a Council of Children and agree with them on a mechanism to formal representation. Symbolic representation is out of the question. Children have a right to be taken seriously. And there are many other additional arguments to include children and young people in governance. One is the educational one. By being part of a board, having to deal with essential questions, children will get chances to learn about governance, communication skills, a feeling for diversity of opinions and cooperation. Although not primarily based on child participation as a right, this method is used by The Missing Chapter Foundation (https://www.missingchap ter.org/) established in 2009 by Princess Laurentien of the Netherlands who was also the UNESCO Special Envoy for Literacy. The Foundation specializes in child inclusion and intergenerational dialogue and works toward a sustainable world to which human beings of all ages contribute taking children's participation in yet another direction.

Children are needed for helping organizations to think out of the box on issues in their businesses and in society. Children are active as councillors to companies and organizations who put forward essential questions, which are considered by the children in their own honest and creative way. Companies should not only have a Board of Trustees but also a Board of Children is the slogan. Around 70 companies, ministries and municipalities now have a Council of Children. Other themes considered by children are sustainability, energy, migration and healthy food (Rijlaarsdam 2017). Would concrete aspects of universal literacy and access to information be subjects to discuss at library leadership or director level with children? Not because of children's creativity, not because of symbolic representation, but because they have a right to it.

Some Recommendations

The human rights children's rights approach in access to information policies needs to be taken further than simple references to the UN Declaration and other Human Rights texts or the UN Agenda 2030. Linking human rights and international law to the discipline of librarianship helps librarians and information professionals to get a better understanding of the wider context of their profession, and role in society, and also provides a stronger political framework to establish a smooth working mechanism for global library advocacy by national and international library associations. The following recommendations at the national and international level, and at the local and regional level, are suggested going forward.

National and International Level

- Base library policies on the human rights framework and strengthen IFLA Guidelines in this respect
- Promote a human rights-based approach in all governance, policies and practices of libraries, and include such in library and information science education and training
- Demonstrate commitment to the UN Agenda 2030 and relate the 17 SDGs and their targets to relevant library governance and services, distinguishing local, national and international levels of advocacy
- Start a series of IFLA in-depth studies, through cooperation of specific target group sections, and library and information science research sections, in cooperation with UN and field organizations on human rights and SDGs in the field of libraries and access to information. Both quantitative and qualitative research of libraries' contribution to giving children fair chances through access to information is an SDG commitment
- Make contributions from IFLA, as the accredited international professional library organization, to the United Nations Economic and Social Council (ECOSOC) and submit library-related reports to the relevant Human Rights Committees, monitoring, the Covenants on Human Rights (OHCHR), the Convention on the Rights of the Child (CRC), the Convention on the Elimination of Discrimination against Women (CEDAW), the Convention on the Rights of Persons with Disabilities (CRPD) and the Marrakesh Treaty to Facilitate Access to Published Works for Persons who are Blind, Visually Impaired, or Otherwise Print Disabled
- Encourage and set examples to the national library associations to give input to national periodic reports on human rights to the UN. Pay special attention to the right of access to information for vulnerable groups including children in all circumstances
- Make contacts and memoranda of understanding/agreements with UN related bodies such as UNICEF, UNESCO, UN High Commissioner for Refugees (UNHCR) and with international partners such as World Health Organization, World Blind Union and Save the Children to mark libraries as global partners for the benefit of children as users.

Local and Regional Level

- Implement children's rights as basic principles in local youth policies and library services and include children in all strategies and work on the SDGs
- Show how libraries are supporting children's access to information
- Present libraries as communication forums for children and connect to children's groups
- Research children's information needs, develop question and answer sessions particularly for schools and develop services provided and the skills of librarians
- Develop special education and training of librarians for services to children and young people, paying special attention to children's rights and child participation and develop a Rights-Based Programming and Action resource for librarians as practitioners
- Discuss professionally at board, staff, children and municipality levels what the impact of new developments such as digitization or reorganization of library services means to children
- Show that libraries respect children's rights and create child participation in library governance, policies and services, fulfilling the requirements for child participation, as noted by the Committee on the Rights of the Child
- Cooperate with schools, with teachers and children in children's rights-based literacy and participation programmes, working particularly on SDG 4, Quality Education
- Cooperate with local and regional organizations in the fields of healthcare, social support and the environment, to demonstrate what access to information means to children and how libraries contribute in joint efforts, providing examples for inclusion in any SDG reports
- Cooperate with child advocacy organizations, such as UNICEF, Save the Children, National Commissioner on the Rights of the Child and children's ombudsmen especially on the position of the child having access to information and library services including children in reporting on these issues
- Encourage, collect and distribute examples of children's true participation and co-creation and their active roles in library governance.

It is a privilege to work in and for libraries. It is a privilege to work for and with children. The highest human values are at stake. Let us not disappoint ourselves.

References

Alston, Philip. "Ships Passing in the Night: The Current State of the Human Rights and Development Debate seen through the Lens of the Millennium Development Goals." *Human Rights Quarterly* 27 no. 3 (2005): 755–829.

Björklid, Pia, and Maria Nordström. "Child-friendly Cities – Sustainable Cities." *Early Childhood Matters* 118 (2012): 44–47.

Bonnet, Vincent. "The Marrakesh Treaty for Visually Impaired People: a Focus on (Public) Libraries in Europe." Paper presented at the IFLA World Library and Information Congress, Wroclaw, Poland, August 19–25, 2017. Accessed September 15, 2017. http://library.ifla.org/1811/1/096-bonnet-en.pdf.

Committee on the Rights of the Child. *General Comment No 7. Implementing Child Rights in Early Childhood.* CRC/C/GC/7/Rev.1. 2005. Accessed September 15, 2017. http://www2.ohchr.org/english/bodies/crc/docs/AdvanceVersions/GeneralComment7Rev1.pdf.

Committee on the Rights of the Child. *General Comment No. 12. The Right of the Child to Be Heard.* CRC/C/GC/12. 2009. Accessed September 15, 2017. http://www2.ohchr.org/english/bodies/crc/docs/AdvanceVersions/CRC-C-GC-12.pdf.

Committee on the Rights of the Child. *General Comment No. 19 (2016) on Public Budgeting for the Realization of Children's Rights (Art. 4).* CRC/C/GC/19. 2016a. Accessed September 15, 2017. http://tbinternet.ohchr.org/_layouts/treatybodyexternal/Download.aspx?symbolno=CRC%2fC%2fGC%2f19&Lang=en.

Committee on the Rights of the Child. *Report of the 2014 Day of General Discussion "Digital Media and Children's Rights".* 2014. Accessed September 15, 2017. http://www.ohchr.org/Documents/HRBodies/CRC/Discussions/2014/DGD_report.pdf.

Committee on the Rights of the Child. *Report of the 2016 Day of General Discussion: Children's Rights and the Environment.* 2016b. Accessed September 15, 2017. http://www.ohchr.org/Documents/HRBodies/CRC/Discussions/2016/DGDoutcomereport-May2017.pdf.

DeCaen, Vincent. *On the Child's Right to Information under Articles 13 and 17 of the UN Convention on the Rights of the Child: the Public Librarian's Moral Obligation to Both Empower and Protect.* Toronto: University of Toronto, 2007. Accessed September 15, 2017. http://homes.chass.utoronto.ca/~decaen/papers/Rights_paper.doc.

De Langen, Miek. "Children's Rights". In *Ombudswork for Children,* edited by Eugene Verhellen and Frans Spiesschaert, 481–493. Leuven/Amersfoort: Acco, 1989.

Dina Jensen, Lisbeth, and Lotte Ladegaard. *Child Right's Governance: Children in Politics. A Collective of 11 Inspiring, Motivating, and Suggestive Case Studies on Children's Engagement in Governance."* Save the Children, 2012. Accessed September 15, 2017. https://resourcecentre.savethechildren.net/library/child-rights-governance-children-politics-collection-11-inspiring-motivating-and-suggestive.

EIFL-PLIP. *Public Library Provides a Safe Space for Youth: Public Library Zavidovici, Bosnia and Herzegovina.* Electronic Information for Libraries. Public Libraries Innovation Programme. Impact Case Study. 2011. Accessed September 15, 2017. https://www.eifl.net/resources/public-library-zavidovici-bosnia-and-herzegovina-safe-space-young-people.

EIFL-PLIP. *E-books App Motivates Teenagers to Read: Valmiera Public Library, Latvia.* Electronic Information for Libraries. Public Libraries Innovation Programme. Impact Case Study. 2015. Accessed September 15, 2017. https://www.eifl.net/resources/how-public-library-latvia-used-social-reading-app-motivate-teenagers-read.

Evans, A.J. *"Committee on Access to Information and Freedom of Expression. A Report prepared for the IFLA Council Meeting in Copenhagen, Denmark."* 1997. Accessed September 15, 2017. https://www.ifla.org/files/assets/faife/publications/policy-documents/caife_e.pdf.
Gibbons, Elizabeth D. "Climate Change, Children's Rights, and the Pursuit of Intergenerational Climate Justice". *Health and Human Rights Journal* 16, no. 1 (2014): 19–31.
Gardner, Howard. Frames of Mind: The Theories of Multiple Intelligences. New York: Basic Books, 1983.
Gill, Philip, ed. *The Public library Service: IFLA/UNESCO Guidelines for Development."* Edited for the IFLA Section of Public Libraries. IFLA publications 97. München: Saur, 2001.
Guterres, António. "Secretary-General Stresses Role of Empowered Young Men, Women in Message for International Youth Day". UN *Meetings Coverage and Press Releases. Press Release* SG/SM/18638-OBV/1735. 2017. Accessed September 17, 2017. https://www.un.org/press/en/2017/sgsm18638.doc.htm.
Hart, Jason. "Children's Participation and International Development: Attending to the Political." *The International Journal of Children's Rights* 16, no. 3 (2008): 407–418.
IFLA. *The Background Text to the Guidelines for Children's Libraries Services: Prepared as a Basic Information During the Process of Developing The Guidelines Published in December 2003.* 2003. Accessed September 15, 2017. https://www.ifla.org/files/assets/libraries-for-children-and-ya/publications/guidelines-for-childrens-libraries-services_background-en.pdf.
IFLA. *Development and Access to Information 2017.* DA2I report. Edited by M. Garrida and S. Wyber. The Hague: IFLA and the Technology and Social Change (TASCHA) Group University of Washington, 2017. Accessed September 15, 2017. https://da2i.ifla.org/da2i-report-2017/.
IFLA. *Guidelines for Library Services to Babies and Toddlers.* IFLA Professional Report 100. The Hague: IFLA, 2007. Accessed September 15, 2017. https://www.ifla.org/files/assets/hq/publications/professional-report/100.pdf.
IFLA. *Guidelines for Library Services For Young Adults*, rev. ed. IFLA Professional report. The Hague: IFLA, 2008. Accessed September 15, 2017. https://www.ifla.org/files/assets/libraries-for-children-and-ya/publications/ya-guidelines2-en.pdf.
Jonsson, Urban. *"A Rights Compared to a Needs Perspective on ECCD."* UNICEF, Regional Office for South Asia. Kathmandu, Nepal, 1998. [ECCD=Early Child Care and Development].
Keller-Loibl, Kerstin. *Handbuch Kinder- und Jugendbibliotheksarbeit.* Bad Honnef: Bock+Herchen, 2009.
Ki-Moon, Ban. "Aim at Universal Literacy to Build Foundation for Sustainable Development Secretary-General Urges Governments, Partners on International Literacy Day". *Meetings Coverage and Press Releases*, SG/SM/18044-OBV/1655. September 8, 2016. Accessed September 15, 2017. https://www.un.org/press/en/2016/sgsm18044.doc.htm.
Kinderrechtencollectief: Dutch NGO Coalition for Children's Rights. *Children's Rights as a Mirror of Dutch Society.* Updated January 1999. Amsterdam: Dutch NGO Coalition for Children's Rights. Accessed September 15, 2017. https://www.kinderrechten.nl/assets/2016/11/NGO1999-SCAN-Report-1.pdf.
Kirkemann Boesen, Jakob, and Tomas Martin. 2007. *"Applying a Rights-based Approach: an Inspirational Guide for Civil Society."* Copenhagen: The Danish Institute for Human Rights, 2007. Accessed July 30, 2020. https://gsdrc.org/document-library/applying-a-rights-based-approach-an-inspirational-guide-for-civil-society/.
Koontz, Christie, and Barbara Gubbin. *IFLA Public Library Service Guidelines.* 2nd ed. IFLA Publications Series 147. New York: De Gruyter Saur, 2010. Accessed September 15, 2017. https://www.degruyter.com/viewbooktoc/product/43971.

Koren, Marian. "*Tell Me! The Right of the Child to Information.*" PhD dissertation, The Hague: University of Amsterdam, 1996. Accessed September 15, 2017. https://pure.uva.nl/ws/files/3663626/1758_06.pdf.

Koren, Marian. "The Right to Information as a Condition for Human Development." Paper presented at the IFLA World Library and Information Congress, Copenhagen, Denmark, August 31–September 5, 1997. Accessed September 15, 2017. http://origin-archive.ifla.org/IV/ifla63/63korm.htm.

Koren, Marian. "The Right of the Child to Information and its Practical Impact on Children's Libraries". *The New Review of Children's Literature and Librarianship* 4 (1998): 1–16.

Koren, Marian. "Children's Rights, Libraries Potential and the Information Society". [FAIFE-special] *IFLA Journal* 26, no. 4 (2000): 273–279.

Koren, Marian. "Empowering Children: Rights-Based Library Services." Paper presented at the IFLA World Library and Information Congress, Buenos Aires, Argentina, August 22–27, 2004. Accessed September 15, 2017. https://archive.ifla.org/IV/ifla70/papers/004e-Koren.pdf.

Lauwers, Hilda, and Wouter Vanderstede. "Spatial Planning and Opportunities for Children's Participation: A Local Governance Network Analysis." *Children, Youth and Environments* 15, no. 2 (2005): 278–289. Special Focus: Children and Governance. Accessed September 15, 2017. https://www.jstor.org/stable/10.7721/chilyoutenvi.15.2.0278?seq=1.

Lee, Syeon. "Children's Right of Access to Information." In *The U.N. Convention on the Rights of the Child: An Analysis of Treaty Provisions and Implications of U.S. Ratification*, edited by Jonathan Todres, Mark Wojcik, and Cris Revaz, Ardsely, 177–188. NY: Transnational Publishers, 2006.

Marquardt, Luisa, and Dianne Oberg. *Global Perspectives on School Libraries; Projects and Practices.* IFLA Publications 148. Berlin/Munich: De Gruyter Saur, 2011.

OHCHR/WHO. *A Human Rights-based approach to health.* 2012. Accessed September 15, 2017. http://www.ohchr.org/Documents/Issues/ESCR/Health/HRBA_HealthInformationSheet.pdf.

"Realising the Rights of Young Children: Progress and Challenges". *Early Childhood Matters* Bernard Van Leer Foundation 113 (2009). Accessed September 15, 2017. https://earlychildhoodmatters.online/wp-content/uploads/2019/06/ECM113-2009_Realising_the_rights_of_young_children_progress_and_challenges.pdf.

Rijlaarsdam, Barbara. "Kinderen zeggen waar het op staat." [Children say what it is about] *NRC*, July 15 & 16 (2017): E6–E7.

Santos Pais, Marta. *A Human Rights Conceptual Framework for UNICEF.* Innocenti Essays, no. 9. Florence: UNICEF, 1999. Accessed September 15, 2017. https://www.unicef-irc.org/publications/2-a-human-rights-conceptual-framework-for-unicef.html.

Save the Children. *Children and Climate Change: Policy Brief.* 2009. Accessed September 15, 2017. https://resourcecentre.savethechildren.net/node/3955/pdf/3955.pdf.

Save the Children. *Children and Good Governance: Policy Brief.* 2010. Accessed September 15, 2017. https://resourcecentre.savethechildren.net/node/3294/pdf/3294.pdf.

Save the Children. "*The European Union and Child Participation.*" 2011a. Accessed September 15, 2017. https://www.savethechildren.net/sites/default/files/libraries/Child-Participation-Position-Paper-FINAL.pdf.

Save the Children. *It's All About Children: Seven Good Examples and Ten Steps to Meaningful Children's Participation in Reporting to the Committee on the Rights of the Child.*" 2011b. Accessed September 15, 2017. https://resourcecentre.savethechildren.net/library/its-all-about-children-seven-good-examples-and-ten-steps-meaningful-childrens-participation.

Scholing, Peter, and Astrid Britten. "Tablet Cafés, Code Hours, Preservation, and Sustainability in Libraries. The Aruba National Library and the UN Agenda 2030. A Small Island Case Study from the Caribbean." Paper presented at the IFLA World Library and Information Congress, Wroclaw, Poland, August 19–25, 2017. Accessed September 15, 2017. http://library.ifla.org/1712/1/139-scholing-en.pdf.

Third, Amanda, Delphine Bellerose, Urszula Dawkins, Emma Keltie, and Kari Pihl. "*Children's Rights in the Digital Age: A Download from Children Around the World.*" Melbourne: Young and Well Cooperative Research Centre, 2014. Accessed September 15, 2017. http://www.uws.edu.au/__data/assets/pdf_file/0003/753447/Childrens-rights-in-the-digital-age.pdf.

Thomas, Nigel. 2007. "Towards a Theory of Children's Participation." *The International Journal of Children's Rights* 15, no. 2 (2007): 199–218.

Thomson, Valerie. "Children's Rights in the Library". *School Libraries in Canada* 24, no. 4 (2004): 38–42. Accessed September 15, 2017. http://accessola2.com/SLIC-Site/slic/244childrensrights.html.

Todres, Jonathan, Mark Wojcik, and Cris Revaz. *The U.N. Convention on the Rights of the Child: An Analysis of Treaty Provisions and Implications of U.S. Ratification.* Ardsely, NY: Transnational Publishers, 2006.

Tubex, Stefaan, Filip De Rynck, and Filip Coussée. *Inspraak en participatie van kinderen, jongeren en het jeugdwerk in en aan het lokale beleid. Een onderzoeksproject in opdracht van het Ministerie van de Vlaamse Gemeenschap Afdeling Jeugd.* Gent: Hogeschool, Universiteit Gent, 2006. Accessed September 15, 2017. http://www.sociaalcultureel.be/jeugd/onderzoek/lokale_beleidsparticipatie_eindrapport.pdf.

UNICEF. *Climate Change and Children: A Human Security Challenge. Policy Review Paper.* Florence: UNICEF Innocenti Research Centre in cooperation with UNICEF Programme Division, 2008. Accessed September 15, 2017. https://www.unicef-irc.org/publications/509-climate-change-and-children-a-human-security-challenge-policy-review-paper.html.

UNICEF. *A Post-2015 World Fit for Children: A Review of the OWG Report on SDGs from a Child Rights Perspective.* 2015.

United Nations. Human Rights Office of the High Commissioner. Convention on the Rights of the Child. 1989. Accessed September 15, 2017. http://www.ohchr.org/EN/ProfessionalInterest/Pages/CRC.aspx.

United Nations Development Group. *The Human Rights Based Approach to Development Cooperation: Towards a Common Understanding Among UN Agencies.* 2003. Accessed September 15, 2017. https://unsdg.un.org/resources/human-rights-based-approach-development-cooperation-towards-common-understanding-among-un.

Wainaina, Rebecca Wambui. *Factors Influencing Application of Child Right to Participation in Decision Making: The Case of Selected Charitable Children Institutions in Juja Constituency, Kiambu County.* Research report submitted for Master of Arts University of Nairobi. Kenya: University of Nairobi, 2015. Accessed September 15, 2017. http://erepository.uonbi.ac.ke/bitstream/handle/11295/90613/Wainaina_Factors%20influencing%20application%20of%20child%20right%20to%20participation%20in%20decision%20making:%20the%20case%20of%20selected%20charitable%20children..pdf?sequence=1.

Annex 1: Relevant Articles in Convention on the Rights of the Child (1989)

(http://www.ohchr.org/EN/ProfessionalInterest/Pages/CRC.aspx)

Article 3

1. In all actions concerning children, whether undertaken by public or private social welfare institutions, courts of law, administrative authorities or legislative bodies, the best interests of the child shall be a primary consideration. (...)

Article 12

1. States Parties shall assure to the child who is capable of forming his or her own views the right to express those views freely in all matters affecting the child, the views of the child being given due weight in accordance with the age and maturity of the child.
2. For this purpose, the child shall in particular be provided the opportunity to be heard in any judicial and administrative proceedings affecting the child, either directly, or through a representative or an appropriate body, in a manner consistent with the procedural rules of national law.

Article 13

1. The child shall have the right to freedom of expression; this right shall include freedom to seek, receive and impart information and ideas of all kinds, regardless of frontiers, either orally, in writing or in print, in the form of art, or through any other media of the child's choice.
2. The exercise of this right may be subject to certain restrictions, but these shall only be such as are provided by law and are necessary:
   (a) For respect of the rights or reputations of others; or
   (b) For the protection of national security or of public order (ordre public), or of public health or morals.

Article 17

States Parties recognize the important function performed by the mass media and shall ensure that the child has access to information and material from a diversity of national and international sources, especially those aimed at the promotion of his or her social, spiritual and moral well-being and physical and mental health.
To this end, States Parties shall:

(a) Encourage the mass media to disseminate information and material of social and cultural benefit to the child and in accordance with the spirit of article 29;

(b) Encourage international co-operation in the production, exchange and dissemination of such information and material from a diversity of cultural, national and international sources;

(c) Encourage the production and dissemination of children's books;

(d) Encourage the mass media to have particular regard to the linguistic needs of the child who belongs to a minority group or who is indigenous;

(e) Encourage the development of appropriate guidelines for the protection of the child from information and material injurious to his or her well-being, bearing in mind the provisions of articles 13 and 18.

Article 18

1. States Parties shall use their best efforts to ensure recognition of the principle that both parents have common responsibilities for the upbringing and development of the child. Parents or, as the case may be, legal guardians, have the primary responsibility for the upbringing and development of the child. The best interests of the child will be their basic concern. (...)

Article 24

1. States Parties recognize the right of the child to the enjoyment of the highest attainable standard of health and to facilities for the treatment of illness and rehabilitation of health. States Parties shall strive to ensure that no child is deprived of his or her right of access to such health care services.

2. States Parties shall pursue full implementation of this right and, in particular, shall take appropriate measures:
(...)

(e) To ensure that all segments of society, in particular parents and children, are informed, have access to education and are supported in the use of basic knowledge of child health and nutrition, the advantages of breast-feeding, hygiene and environmental sanitation and the prevention of accidents; (...)

Article 29

1. States Parties agree that the education of the child shall be directed to:
   (a) The development of the child's personality, talents and mental and physical abilities to their fullest potential;
   (b) The development of respect for human rights and fundamental freedoms, and for the principles enshrined in the Charter of the United Nations;
   (c) The development of respect for the child's parents, his or her own cultural identity, language and values, for the national values of the country in which the child is living, the country from which he or she may originate, and for civilizations different from his or her own;
   (d) The preparation of the child for responsible life in a free society, in the spirit of understanding, peace, tolerance, equality of sexes, and friendship among all peoples, ethnic, national and religious groups and persons of indigenous origin;
   (e) The development of respect for the natural environment.
   (...)

Article 31

1. States Parties recognize the right of the child to rest and leisure, to engage in play and recreational activities appropriate to the age of the child and to participate freely in cultural life and the arts.
2. States Parties shall respect and promote the right of the child to participate fully in cultural and artistic life and shall encourage the provision of appropriate and equal opportunities for cultural, artistic, recreational and leisure activity.

Article 42

States Parties undertake to make the principles and provisions of the Convention widely known, by appropriate and active means, to adults and children alike.

Annex 2: The Committee on the Rights of the Child Comments on the Right of the Child to be Heard, Participation

Basic Requirements for the Implementation of the Right of the Child to be Heard (General Comment no. 12 (2009) (CRC/C/GC/12) pp. 26–27 http://www2. ohchr.org/english/bodies/crc/docs/AdvanceVersions/CRC-C-GC-12.pdf)

132. The Committee urges States parties to avoid tokenistic approaches, which limit children's expression of views, or which allow children to be heard, but fail to give their views due weight. It emphasizes that adult manipulation of children, placing children in situations where they are told what they can say, or exposing children to risk of harm through participation are not ethical practices and cannot be understood as implementing article 12.

133. If participation is to be effective and meaningful, it needs to be understood as a process, not as an individual one-off event. Experience since the Convention on the Rights of the Child was adopted in 1989 has led to a broad consensus on the basic requirements which have to be reached for effective, ethical and meaningful implementation of article 12. The Committee recommends that States parties integrate these requirements into all legislative and other measures for the implementation of article 12.

134. All processes in which a child or children are heard and participate, must be:
    (a) Transparent and informative – children must be provided with full, accessible, diversity-sensitive and age-appropriate information about their right to express their views freely and their views to be given due weight, and how this participation will take place, its scope, purpose and potential impact;
    (b) Voluntary – children should never be coerced into expressing views against their wishes and they should be informed that they can cease involvement at any stage;
    (c) Respectful – children's views have to be treated with respect and they should be provided with opportunities to initiate ideas and activities. Adults working with children should acknowledge, respect and build

on good examples of children's participation, for instance, in their contributions to the family, school, culture and the work environment. They also need an understanding of the socioeconomic, environmental and cultural context of children's lives. Persons and organizations working for and with children should also respect children's views with regard to participation in public events;

(d) Relevant – the issues on which children have the right to express their views must be of real relevance to their lives and enable them to draw on their knowledge, skills and abilities. In addition, space needs to be created to enable children to highlight and address the issues they themselves identify as relevant and important;

(e) Child-friendly – environments and working methods should be adapted to children's capacities. Adequate time and resources should be made available to ensure that children are adequately prepared and have the confidence and opportunity to contribute their views. Consideration needs to be given to the fact that children will need differing levels of support and forms of involvement according to their age and evolving capacities;

(f) Inclusive – participation must be inclusive, avoid existing patterns of discrimination, and encourage opportunities for marginalized children, including both girls and boys, to be involved (see also para. 88 above). Children are not a homogenous group and participation needs to provide for equality of opportunity for all, without discrimination on any grounds. Programmes also need to ensure that they are culturally sensitive to children from all communities;

(g) Supported by training – adults need preparation, skills and support to facilitate children's participation effectively, to provide them, for example, with skills in listening, working jointly with children and engaging children effectively in accordance with their evolving capacities. Children themselves can be involved as trainers and facilitators on how to promote effective participation; they require capacity-building to strengthen their skills in, for example, effective participation awareness of their rights, and training in organizing meetings, raising funds, dealing with the media, public speaking and advocacy;

(h) Safe and sensitive to risk – in certain situations, expression of views may involve risks. Adults have a responsibility towards the children with whom they work and must take every precaution to minimize the risk to children of violence, exploitation or any other negative consequence of their participation. Action necessary to provide appropriate protection will include the development of a clear child protection strategy which recognizes the particular risks faced by some groups of children, and the extra barriers they face in obtaining help. Children must be aware of their right to be protected from harm and know where to go for help if needed. Investment in working with families and communities is important in order to build understanding of the value and implications of participation, and to minimize the risks to which children may otherwise be exposed;

(i)   Accountable – a commitment to follow-up and evaluation is essential. For example, in any research or consultative process, children must be informed as to how their views have been interpreted and used and, where necessary, provided with the opportunity to challenge and influence the analysis of the findings. Children are also entitled to be provided with clear feedback on how their participation has influenced any outcomes. Wherever appropriate, children should be given the opportunity to participate in follow-up processes or activities. Monitoring and evaluation of children's participation needs to be undertaken, where possible, with children themselves.

Annex 3: Sustainable Development Goals in United Nations Agenda 2030 and IFLA Response. Libraries Can Drive Progress Across the Entire UN 2030 Agenda, How Libraries Support the SDGs

(https://www.ifla.org/libraries-development)

Goal 1. End poverty in all its forms everywhere
– Public access to information and resources that give people opportunities to improve their lives
– Training in new skills needed for education and employment
– Information to support decision-making by governments, civil society, and businesses to combat poverty

Goal 2. End hunger, achieve food security and improved nutrition and promote sustainable agriculture
– Agricultural research and data on how to make crops more productive and sustainable

- Public access for farmers to online resources like local market prices, weather reports, and new equipment

Goal 3. Ensure healthy lives and promote well-being for all at all ages
- Research available in medical and hospital libraries that supports education and improves medical practice for health care providers
- Public access to health and wellness information in public libraries that helps individuals and families stay healthy

Goal 4. Ensure inclusive and equitable quality education and promote lifelong learning opportunities for all
- Dedicated staff who support early literacy and lifelong learning
- Access to information and research for students everywhere
- Inclusive spaces where cost is not a barrier to new knowledge and skills

Goal 5. Achieve gender equality and empower all women and girls
- Safe and welcoming meeting spaces
- Programmes and services designed to meet the needs of women and girls, like rights and health
- Access to information and ICT that helps women build business skills

Goal 6. Ensure availability and sustainable management of water and sanitation for all

Goal 7. Ensure access to affordable, reliable, sustainable and modern energy for all
Libraries support these goals 6 and 7 by providing...
- Access to quality information and good practices that support local water management and sanitation projects
- Free and reliable access to electricity and light to read, study, and work

Goal 8. Promote sustained, inclusive and sustainable economic growth, full and productive employment and decent work for all
- Access to information and skills training that people need to find, apply for, and succeed in better jobs

Goal 9. Build resilient infrastructure, promote inclusive and sustainable industrialization and foster innovation
- Widespread existing infrastructure of public and research libraries and skilled library professionals

- Welcoming and inclusive public spaces
- Access to ICT like high-speed Internet that may not be available anywhere else

Goal 10. Reduce inequality within and among countries
- Neutral and welcoming spaces that make learning accessible to all, including marginalized groups like migrants, refugees, minorities, indigenous peoples, and persons with disabilities
- Equitable access to information that supports social, political, and economic inclusion

Goal 11. Make cities and human settlements inclusive, safe, resilient and sustainable
- Trusted institutions devoted to promoting cultural inclusion and understanding
- Documentation and preservation of cultural heritage for future generations

Goal 12. Ensure sustainable consumption and production patterns

Goal 13. Take urgent action to combat climate change and its impacts

Goal 14. Conserve and sustainably use the oceans, seas and marine resources for sustainable development

Goal 15. Protect, restore and promote sustainable use of terrestrial ecosystems, sustainably manage forests, combat desertification, and halt and reverse land degradation and halt biodiversity loss
Libraries support these goals 12–15 by providing...
- Sustainable system of sharing and circulating materials that reduces waste
- Historical records about coastal change and land use
- Research and data needed to inform climate change policy
- Widespread access to information needed to guide decision-making by local and national governments on topics like hunting, fishing, land use, and water management

Goal 16. Promote peaceful and inclusive societies for sustainable development, provide access to justice for all and build effective, accountable and inclusive institutions at all levels
- Public access to information about government, civil society, and other institutions

- Training in the skills needed to understand and use this information
- Inclusive, politically neutral spaces for people to meet and organise

Goal 17. Strengthen the means of implementation and revitalize the Global Partnership for Sustainable Development.
- Global network of community-based institutions, primed to support local development plans.

John Abdul Kargbo
10 The Public Library and Good Governance: Perspectives from Sierra Leone

Abstract: This chapter is a contribution to the ongoing debate on good governance and the role of the public library with especial reference to Sierra Leone. The argument is that the public library is a catalyst for human development and can help promote good governance in society through information provision and knowledge creation in the community. Public librarians know their communities first-hand, and are often the first to recognize pressing local needs, simply because they interact on a daily basis with patrons from different walks of life. This puts the public library and librarians in a best position not only to bring local issues to central governments and social agencies but also to partner with local governments and agencies to address the needs of their communities. This chapter addresses a number of issues. First, it discusses the role of libraries in society, noting the views of various organizations and individuals about the public library. Second, the chapter discusses good governance in general and how it is practised in Sierra Leone. Third, the chapter discusses information in the governance debate. Fourth, the chapter discusses public library services and what the library should do to promote good governance in Sierra Leone. The chapter ends with recommendations for improved performance in promoting good governance in the country.

Keywords: Public libraries – Sierra Leone; Corporate governance; Community development.

Introduction

The twenty first century is widely acclaimed as the age of information availability. Toffler (1980) contended that a revolution swept society into an infosphere where information and communication technologies (ICT) drastically altered our social, political, economic, and work environment. In the infosphere, information is the key resource for effective functioning and participation in society. Brodnig and Mayer-Schönberger (2017) stated that accurate and reliable information is a vital element for sustainable development. For any society to attain economic growth, promote good governance, fight poverty, reduce diseases, eliminate hunger and improve on the lifestyle of its people, information needs must be given enormous attention.

https://doi.org/10.1515/ 9783110533323-013

Libraries are crucial in the provision of information to people. It is through libraries that information from basic life information to entrepreneur information is disseminated to society. Through the knowledge derived from libraries, the world is capable of improving human lives and as a result libraries strengthen world economies. Libraries from public to national are central points for information access through their collections, materials processing, storage, retrieval and dissemination of information, cross-pollination of ideas, supporting skills, lifelong learning and workforce development, provision of access to resources through the use of ICT as well as information provision and support for research (Kargbo 2006). Libraries provide employability and entrepreneurial knowledge by providing knowledge-based services such as skills enhancement, act as magnets for business and enhance the quality of life in communities.

To buttress their roles Debowski (2003) stated that libraries and information services aim at achieving six key outcomes:

– Ensuring the needs of users and accessible information sources suitably matched at all times
– Delivering those information sources to the user in a timely and appropriate fashion
– Ensuring the information provided is high quality, accurate and appropriate
– Assisting the user in interpreting the materials, if necessary
– Promoting user awareness of new services and information sources as they develop
– Providing users with individualized guidance and support as they build their information search and application skills (2627).

At the first World Summit on the Information Society (WSIS) in 2003, representatives, articulating a vision premised on the Universal Declaration on Human Rights, declared their common desire and commitment to build a people-centred, inclusive, and development-oriented information society where everyone can create, access, utilize, and share information and knowledge to enable individual communities and people to achieve their full potential and improve their quality of life. The public library is a logical partner in the attainment of the vision as it provides a broad range of information sources and support for diverse constituencies. It can play an important role in the political life of a community by bringing together community people to talk about issues of freedom, justice, democracy, and good governance for informed political and developmental issues (Mamafha, Ngulubu, and Ndwande 2016).

The Public Library

The public library is an institution set up to provide a comprehensive and efficient service for all persons desiring to make use of it. It is popularly much used all over the world; ordinary citizens, from children to pensioners, may visit the public library confident of receiving a public service, whether they are seeking reference materials on a school project, advice on a planning application or simply to read a novel. The public library is set up and developed on the basis that information is a resource which belongs to everybody rather than being a commodity which might have propriety (Kargbo 2006). Thus public librarians have an obligation to facilitate the flow of information and ideas and to protect and promote the rights of every individual to free and equal access to sources of information without discrimination. Without the public library it is hard to imagine people getting ready access to diverse sources of information across disciplines and information about educational institutions, charitable organizations, and political affairs. Without the public library the informational environment of citizens would be significantly impoverished. The public library is a symbol of a civilized society, one viewed as a public good for promoting literacy, education, and culture (Sturges and Neill 2009).

UNESCO (1972) has proclaimed belief in the public library as a living force for education, culture, and information and as an essential agent for the fostering of peace and understanding between people and between citizens. UNESCO viewed the public library as a product of modern democracy and a practical demonstration of democracy's faith in universal education as a life-long process. As a democratic institution operated by the people and for the people, the public library is established and maintained under clear authority of law supported from public funds and open for free use on equal terms without due regard to occupation, creed, class or race. The objective is to offer not only public information and educate the citizenry to participate in a creative manner in community life but also to stimulate freedom of expression and constructive critical attitudes towards the solution of social problems. IFLA/UNESCO *Guidelines for Public Library Service* (Gill 2001) stated that the primary purpose of the public library is to provide resources and services in a variety of media to meet the needs of individuals and groups for education, information, and personal development including recreation and leisure. The public library has a role in the development and maintenance of a democratic society by giving the individual access to a varied range of knowledge, ideas, and opinions.

The purpose of the public library is to promote the spread of knowledge, education, and culture by making its materials free of charge to the public served. This requirement is fulfilled by quality, comprehensive, and actual choice of materials based on their literary value and not by religious, moral or political viewpoints. In addition, the public library is intended to further any phase of thought and action in which its collection can be of value. Thus its objectives should be to:

- Collect, process, organize, preserve and administer materials in order to promote an enlightened citizenship and enrich personal lives
- Serve the community as a general centre of reliable information
- Provide an opportunity and encouragement for children, young people, men and women to educate themselves continuously.

In view of these objectives, the public library should devote its resources under these headings: research, vocations, information, public affairs, citizenship, aesthetic appreciation, and recreation (Kargbo 2006).

The public library is a dynamic institution. It meets readers and is anxious to know their needs, and to attract readers by offering various ways and means for them to obtain information, cultivate their minds, and find relaxation. Mujudith, Naicker and Zondi (2006) observed that public libraries build communities through a broad range of programs and practices that have reached far beyond the simple lending of books and disseminating information to a selected few in the community. Today public libraries not only offer safe and inclusive meeting places for diverse cross sections of the community but also organize programs for marginalized groups, offer study space, provide Internet access, facilitate ICT training, and act as gateways to community, government, and business institutions. Public libraries facilitate employment and skills development.

The public library has become an agency for change in the community through the functions it carries out:

- Education, supporting both formal and non-formal education and teaching information literacy as well as supporting literacy campaigns
- Information, providing access to a broad range of information and learning resources by collecting materials, organizing them, and assisting users to exploit information
- ICT provision of access to the Internet, tele-centres and information kiosks, helping to bridge the digital gap
- Knowledge, providing access to knowledge and works of the imagination for personal development
- Helping the young, inspiring children and the young to be excited about knowledge and works of the imagination at an early age
- Culture, providing a focus for cultural and artistic development in the community

- Space, providing public spaces for meetings in which contacts can be made and networks forged (Sierra Leone Library Board Annual Report 2008).

Good Governance

Governance is a concept traced from ancient Greece. Aristotle and Plato spoke of governance as distinct from government. It is a generic term which can be applied to all forms of human organizations, economic, cultural, religious, and military. The UNDP (1997) defined governance as the manner in which power is exercised in the management of a country's economic and social development. Governance is both a condition and a practice. As a desirable condition it denotes that those who exercise political, economic, and administrative authority to manage a nation's affairs should be held accountable to the governed through institutionalized legal and administrative instruments and a regulatory framework. In the language of global economic governance, governance is a way power is exercised in managing a country's economic and social resources for development (Obiyo 2010).

Democratic governance denotes that for any government to be legitimate, its authority should derive from periodic and regular free, fairly contested elections through an inclusive participatory process. Democratic governance provides the institutional mechanisms that allow citizens to make judgments about political reforms, the trustworthiness of their leaders, and to signal the type of trust required. Democratic governance provides the necessary overall conditions within which empowerment is potentially achievable through participation, knowledge, skills, new capabilities, freedom of information, and regulatory institution of skills, income, land and other resources. From an institutional point of view, governance involves creating capable political actors who understand how political institutions work and are able to deal effectively with them (Anderson 1990).

Good governance, on the other hand, is conceived from the rule of law, accountability, participation, transparency, and the employment of human and civil rights. It is a normative concept and a subset of governance that refers to the norms of governance. Centred on the people, their concerns and needs, good governance enables citizens to develop the whole of their creative capabilities to improve their conditions and apply them actively in the decisions that affect their lives, preserving the interests of the whole of humanity including future generations (Silver 2011). Good governance goes beyond the dictates of the state. The private and public sectors have their roles to play in the promotion of durable human development. Good governance is under the auspices of the promotion of capacities, cooperation, equity and control policies, making it possible to attain human development at local, national, regional, and global levels.

The UNDP (1997) Workshop on Governance for Sustainable Human Development identified nineteen characteristics among which are participatory, sustainable, legitimate, acceptable to the people, transparent, able to promote equity and equality, able to develop the resources and methods of governance, promote gender balance, operate by rule of law, and are accountable. These characteristics, according to Wiseman (2011) are categorized by the World Bank into four areas: accountability, participation, predictability, and transparency. For Wiseman, in a democratic environment, accountability is given to the electorates by the elected to show how far they have gone to achieve their promises. Through accountability, public officials working for government, who in turn represent the taxpayers, give account of their stewardship. Participation involves bringing everybody on board for national development. Effective participation and respect for the decision of citizens could lead to improved performance and sustainability of policies, programs and projects. It could also enhance the capacity and skills of stakeholders as each regime will endeavour to impress citizens to continue to be in power.

Predictability, on the other hand, relates to the governance element that places the instruments of government in such a way that the rules, regulations, and policies could be consistently applied in similar situations. Predictability means that there must be laws and the laws must be fairly and consistently applied in society. Transparency in good governance is regarded as the possibility of citizens seeing what public office holders are doing and how they are using resources, both material and human, entrusted to them in carrying out government business for the people (Cartwright 2013). In Sierra Leone for instance, the four elements are not only intertwined but also enshrined in the 1991 constitution where public figures can be called upon by Parliament to answer questions or explain certain issues pertaining to their institutions. Accountability is related to participation in the sense that government accountability will allow citizens to participate in its activities, making room for predictability because government's accountability will allow and encourage the rule of law, as well as making policies, rules, and procedures clear. Similarly, accountability means that transparency is observed in the actions of public officials. Transparency needs predictability to function fully because of the very fact that the legal framework to address derivation will ensure accountability in all the actions of public officials. Observing the elements should lead to good governance (Obiyo 2010).

Good Governance in Sierra Leone

Good governance in Sierra Leone has become a crucial issue in the quest for the establishment and sustenance of democracy and growth-oriented institutions. It involves the management of public affairs in a manner that is participatory and responsive to the needs of the people and the impartial, transparent, and effective management of resources for the achievement of goals beneficial to the country. Before 1996, the disparity between the country's potential for social, economic, and political development and the stark reality of the poverty of the vast majority of Sierra Leoneans was blamed on bad governance. There was general deterioration of key institutions, undemocratic political and administrative practices, and widespread disregard for the rule of law.

To compound the situation further, an eleven-year (1991–2002) civil war broke out which tore the country apart and brought untold human suffering and displacement. Matters became worse when the National Provisional Ruling Council (NPRC) took over the reins of government from 1992–1996 (Silver 2011). According to Silver, the Junta's rule was marked by rapid military promotions, transfers, suspensions, and outright dismissals of public officers which completely undermined the confidence of the public service. Besides, past governments failed to tap the enormous economic potential of the country, while Local and District Councils were wrecked. There was a demoralized and discontented public service, extensive institutional and infrastructure decay, widespread poverty, and rapid corruption and mismanagement, leading the country to near paralysis.

However, with the return of democratic governance on March 29, 1996, the Ahmed Tejan Kabba-led government tried to reverse the situation with the implementation of a National Strategy for Good Governance and Public Service Reform (Sierra Leone 1997), which encompassed:

- Measures and instruments for improving the ability of government to formulate and implement national policies
- Reactivation of local government institutions through decentralization of authority and responsibility and devolution of power to district and chiefdom councils
- Awareness raising of the public about their rights, privileges, and obligations as citizens and enhancing their capacity to participate fully in the social, political, and economic life of the country
- Strengthening the capacity and efficiency of the public sector to deliver essential services in a manner that discourages corruption and fosters transparency and accountability
- Reinforcement of judicial instruments for safeguarding the rule of law and human rights.

Other specific reform programs targeted the Executive, Legislative, Judiciary, Military, Police, Prisons (now Correctional Services), the media, electoral system, political parties, and civil society. Institutions such as the Office of National Security (ONS), Open Government Initiative (OGI), the African Peer Review Mechanism (APRM), and Campaign for Good Governance (CGG) were set up to promote good governance. Currently, parliament scrutinizes and calls on the Executive to account for its actions and performance; civil society is empowered to play a large role in the governance process; women's groups are tolerated; non-governmental organizations and civic groups participate in national development issues; local government has been reinstituted; chieftaincy powers are relied upon; press freedom is guaranteed while there has been massive restructuring of the military and police forces for improved performance (Sierra Leone Vision 2025 2003; Sesay 2011; Silver 2011).

A Right to Access Information Act was passed by Parliament on October 29, 2013 (Sierra Leone 2013) for people to have direct access to needed information without hindrance. The Right to Access Information Commission (RAIC) Sierra Leone was established in 2014 to ensure the implementation of the new Act. The Act is consistent with Article 9 of the African Charter on Human Rights which provides for the right to seek, receive, and impart information and ideas, through a variety of channels and regardless of borders, in tandem with Article 19 of the Universal Declaration of Human Rights and the International Covenant on Civil and Political Rights, with the appropriate internationally accepted exemptions to protect individual privacy and safeguard national security, among others. Further in the quest for good governance, Sierra Leone has developed policies based on a written Constitution (Sierra Leone 1991) and a democratic system of governance that protects the rights of individuals. In this regard, the state and civil society have critical roles to play in ensuring the quality of life of the people.

Participatory democracy has laid down acceptable rules for the decision-making process that is inclusive and open. Freedom of association, freedom of the press, and periodic elections of representatives are enshrined in the 1991 Constitution, among others. The government has gone ahead in enacting a national policy on ICT with the objective of developing the country into a true information and knowledge society. The use of radio, television, land telephone, GSM phones, and computers has been on the increase nation-wide. The democratization process and liberalization of the airwaves have led to the setting up of community FM radio stations where national issues are discussed with phone-in facilities which draw the attention of the public to participate (Sierra Leone Vision 2025 2003; Sesay 2011).

The transition from authoritative rule to democratic governance has created demands from citizens for effective participatory governance, structures, and services, of which information is the essence. Further sustained resourcing and maintenance of information service systems and institutions are needed to make relevant and readily usable information available and accessible to decision makers and the general public. Cornwell and Gaventa (2001) argued that an informed citizenry is clearly in a position to participate effectively in national affairs with their capacities built through popular education on rights and responsibilities. The question that begs an answer is what has the government of Sierra Leone done for the citizenry to ensure awareness of good governance practices including the right to information to empower citizens to subject government to scrutiny?

The following are some strategies used by the government to empower the citizenry:

- Constitutional guarantee: the 1991 Constitution makes provision for freedom of information as a fundamental human right
- Public education: constitutional bodies such as the Open Government Initiative, Campaign for Good Governance, Democracy Sierra Leone, and The Right to Access Information Commission have been set up to promote and enhance civic education; the bodies are mandated to inculcate in the citizens' awareness of their civic responsibilities and appreciation of their rights and obligations
- Decentralization: the development and governance agenda of government for accountability, responsiveness, participation, and accessing and incorporation of information on local needs, conditions, and priorities has been featured in local development plans
- Media: the country has over 30 community radio stations, television stations, media centres, and 25 newspaper titles. These are some of the channels for the dissemination of information to the public. The Independent Media Commission (IMC) has been set up to regulate their functions
- Non-formal education. Given the high rate of illiteracy in the country, government since independence in 1961 has adopted non-formal educational programs to educate the masses, especially in the rural areas for people to be able to read and write as well as develop numeracy skills
- Distance learning. Government has made complementary efforts to extend learning opportunities to people who would otherwise be denied good education
- E-governance. Web-based technologies have been adopted to deliver and conduct government services for improved performance, increase transparency of government, and empower citizens to more closely monitor government performance

- Public Libraries. Public libraries have been set up in all district headquarter towns including the western rural area to share knowledge and disseminate information. The central library in Freetown doubles as the national library.

The efforts are however not without challenges. Worthy of note are: lack of political commitment and support on the side of government which results in inadequate budgetary provision for information services and the absence of a national information policy especially related to libraries and information service institutions; lack of openness by government officials and their penchant for adhering to administrative regulations such as strictly confidential, classified information, thereby making it impossible for the citizenry to have access to information; a large scale illiteracy rate which makes information literacy abilities difficult to imbibe; improper documentation and record keeping which results in an inability to retrieve information; and misinformation and disinformation as a result of improper reporting of briefings by government officials such as the presidential spokesmen and information officers in Ministries, Departments and Agencies (MDAs).

Information in the Governance Debate

Information is a powerful and pervading force in the operations and functioning of society: "Relevant information delivered conveniently to the user in a timely manner represents significant value by enabling informed decisions and actions" (Mapflow 2002, 6). The World Bank (1992), writing on governance, stated that the determinants of governance include "freedom of information, ensuring citizens' voice in decision-making process, rule of law... transparency, accountability, maintenance of civil peace and order, curbing corruption and providing competent civil service..." (58). Information, according to Salih (2004) entered the governance debate from different perspectives related to the freedom of speech and the organization and freedom of the media. Curtailment of the freedoms could directly impact on citizens' rights to freedom of opinion, expression, and information. The right to seek and receive information is part and parcel of human rights. Freedom of expression as an essential value in any democratic society is enshrined in international law as exhibited in Article 19 of the Universal Declaration of Human Rights and Article 19 of the International Covenant on Civil Aviation and Political Rights. Article 19 prohibits States from interfering with the enjoyment of rights, requiring States to take practical steps to ensure freedom of expression.

Sierra Leone is gradually moving towards an open society. There are: open mining government policies; open government activities through the formation of the Open Government Initiative (OGI); open data for sustainable socio-economic development, transparency, accountability, and good governance; an open records system; asset declaration by public servants; and a right to freely access information through the formation of the Right to Access Information Commission-Sierra Leone. All the initiatives are geared towards providing relevant information to the public without hindrances (Obiyo 2010; Silver 2011). Information is essential for ensuring better governance practices. Without information it will be difficult to conceive how to obtain reliable knowledge on the performance of government. The right to seek, receive, and impart information for individual and community participation is also important in the promotion of good governance in every society. Information is used to influence the behaviour of citizens, shape public opinion on national issues and inform and support public policy decisions. In Sierra Leone for instance, the Right to Access Information Act, 2013 clearly stipulates in Section 2 (1–3) that:

– Every person has the right to access information held by or under the control of a public authority
– Every person has the right to access information held by or under control of a private body where that information is necessary for the enforcement or protection of any right
– Nothing in this Act limits or otherwise restricts the disclosure of or the right to access information pursuant to any other enactment, policy or practice.

The right to access information is subsumed in Section 25 (1) of The Sierra Leone National 1991 Constitution which states that:

> Except with his own consent no person shall be hindered in the enjoyment of his freedom of expression and for the purpose of this section the said freedom includes the freedom to hold opinions and to receive and impart ideas and information without interference, freedom from interference with his correspondence, freedom to own, establish and operate any medium for the dissemination of information, ideas and opinions and academic freedom in institutions of learning.

The role of information in ensuring good governance in Africa is becoming an issue of critical importance as democracy gains grounds on the continent. For instance, Sy (1999) hypothesized that democracy and participation will not fully develop in Africa without access to information, especially if the Internet, distance learning opportunities, computerized library packages, and strategic databases remain out of reach for isolated and poor African nations unable to integrate their economies and intellects with a powerful and respected community of states. Information is a key public resource. Development partners regard it as a governance transition and consequently have paid considerable attention to the development potential of information creation, dissemination, storage, and retrieval (World Bank 1999). Governments therefore should be concerned with not only the quality of information they hold but also the responsibility to ensure that members of the public have the information they need to fulfil their rights and obligations (Brown 2005).

Information is crucial for good governance. Sy (1999) further argued that the practice of democracy contributes greatly to bringing out information. Through access to information and freedom of expression, citizens are able to gain civic competence, air their views, engage in discussion, and deliberate and learn from one another, all of which provide citizens with enlightenment of government's actions. Access to information also concerns the availability and use of public domain information to strengthen participation in public policy debates. Access to information is crucial to the health of democracy and the governance process because it ensures that citizens make responsible informed choices rather than acting out of ignorance or misinformation.

Information serves as a checking function by ensuring that elected representatives uphold their oaths of office and carry out the wishes of the electorate (Dahl 1998). Without information, good governance may be undermined owing to the inadequacies of the information available to the public and even more if the citizenry is denied or spurns reliable information. When citizens are woefully ignorant, questions must be asked about the calibre of the information sources used. As James Madison, the Fourth President of the United States of America and the architect of that country's constitution observed a "popular government without information is ... but a prologue to a farce or tragedy or perhaps both. Knowledge will forever govern ignorance and a people who mean to be their own governors must arm themselves with the power which knowledge gives" (1953, 337).

Public Library Service in Sierra Leone

The public library In Sierra Leone originated as an outcome of an Act passed in the House of Parliament in June 1959. The setting up of the Sierra Leone Library Board (SLLB) was envisaged in the Government's White Paper on Educational Development in 1958 (Sierra Leone 1958) and its functions outlined as follows:

The provision of a national library service will seek to serve the following main purposes:

(a) Support and reinforce programs of adult education and fundamental education
(b) Provide effective services for children to young people including requisite services for schools
(c) Provide needed information and reference services
(d) Promote and stimulate reading for pleasure and recreation
(e) Provide where needed adequate services for special groups including women and girls and language groups.

In practical terms, the programs outlined in the White Paper called for a national library, a country-wide library service, and the supply of books to primary school children and teachers, and advice and assistance to secondary schools and teacher training college libraries. With modest beginnings of a central library in Freetown, the capital city, there is currently a public library in all twelve districts, supported by regional libraries in the North, East, and Southern Provinces (Sierra Leone Library Board 1961). There is a branch library at Kissy and an outlet at Goderich serving the western rural area. The central library in Freetown serves as a repository for legal deposit. The institutions are heavily depended upon by varied users and more so by school pupils and college students for pertinent information, photocopying, Internet services, holding meetings, and displaying vital public information on their notice boards. With the devolution of functions following decentralization, the libraries are run by Local and District Councils while there is a central administrative board which oversees their activities. To facilitate use, the libraries are open from 9:00 a.m. to 6:00 p.m. Monday through Friday and from 9:00 a.m.to 1:00 p.m. on Saturday. The libraries are closed to the public during public holidays and on Sundays (Sierra Leone Library Board 2015).

Libraries naturally are assessed in public estimation by the services they give. It is regretted that public library services in Sierra Leone face serious criticisms. For instance, the public library is criticized for being too elitist. Its services are geared mainly towards the literate few while the vast majority of the population especially the rural poor are left unserved. Hence the public library has no meaning for the rural people as the services it provides are not relevant to their needs. No nationwide research has been carried out since 1991 to determine user needs. Public librarians, it is observed, are accountable to themselves and they provide what they feel is important for users rather than the reverse. There are reservations about the way and manner the public library is managed. The library stands accused of being short of management talent, of having few inspirational goals, and lacking in capacity to deliver (Kargbo 2006).

In addition the library fails to move with the times and its collection is mainly dependent on donations due to inadequate financial support from the central government through the Local and District Councils. Thus its services are out-dated with custodians fixated on books rather than on the modern forms of electronic delivery. Basic items such as furniture and equipment including chairs, tables, book trolleys, and display racks are desperately needed in all the Board's libraries as most of the existing furniture is dilapidated. There are problems of sitting accommodation especially during peak periods. In spite of the above reservations about the public library, the library is nevertheless a one-stop information access point for its varied clientele with a mission of providing quality service to the community. A vast majority of the people relies on it heavily for the provision of relevant information. If therefore good governance is to be promoted in Sierra Leone there is every need for the public library to be a partner in the governance process.

What to Do

There is much that can be done to improve the current situation with additional activities in information provision, collection development, services for targeted groups including vulnerable communities, staffing, information and communications technology, Internet use, developing the library as a public sphere, information literacy and lifelong learning, reading, targeted programs in areas like health information and shaping governance.

Information Provision

The public library is a reservoir of knowledge and information. Matarasso (2000) stated that the fundamental goal of the public library is to empower the individual to improve his or her social and economic situation through access to information, education, and culture. And it is impossible to speak of any workable democratic governance without access to information, the key medium of the governors and the governed not only to determine public preferences but also to understand how the state and its resources are best managed and distributed. There will be no credible accountability without information and no transparency in government operations if information about the operations is not made accessible to the public through reliable information and information sources. Good governance requires accountability of citizens and the governors. Governors can be held accountable by the governed only when publicity, transparency, and critical scrutiny provide a basis for an informed citizenry (March and Olsen

1995). Cornwell and Gaventa (2001) posited that "where citizens are able to take up and use the spaces that participatory processes can open up, they have been able to use their agency to demand accountability, transparency and responsiveness from government institutions. An informed mobilized citizenry is clearly in a better position to do so effectively" (33). Information is the glue that binds the variety of governance concerns. Without adequate and reliable information there can be little or no room for accountability and there will be complete absence of transparency. To nurture good governance, competing information sources are needed. The public library therefore, by virtue of its location, provisions and services as well as opening hours, is in a unique position to provide a focus on information for good governance.

Collection Development and Targeted Groups

The public library is an institution that should help to sustain an open society, opening the mind of the rational, truth-seeking citizen to a whole range of opinions, giving him or her both sound judgment and tolerance. It should supply literature and information of different kinds to sustain technical innovation and progress in the national and individual interests. The prime function of librarianship is to provide the best and most useful materials people are willing and wishful to use (Maswabi et al 2011). The public library exists to serve, to give without question, fear, favour or limitation. It should be an instrument for promoting the activities of its readers. The role must be catholic. The public library should provide vital materials for ordinary people to broaden their cultural understandings to enrich society (Alemna 2000). To support this end, the public library must be readily accessible to all; its use must be free; it must be non-partisan and provide access to the whole of the literature available within the laws of the land. The focus of the public library is the people who use it so that the assessment of their growing needs and interests is paramount. Therefore the collection should reflect the changing interests of readers and must provide sufficient materials to sustain and intensify growing interests. The materials provided should include material on civil rights, governance, child rights, local and national history, democracy, politics, economic development, health, gender, management and public administration, some of which, especially local history materials, could be digitized for the benefit of the local community (Akparobore 2011).

Library Staff

Consistent with collection development, public library staff must be organized to provide readers with guidance to the map of literature and not merely the map of the library. Staff must seek every opportunity to ensure access for its readers to all the materials and initiate and foster activities which extend the influence of the library within the community. The principle underlying service is that the library exists for the training of citizens. The library aims to provide both print and non-print literature to develop the citizen's intellectual, moral, and spiritual capabilities (Ebiwolate 2010). Public librarians should aim at, among other things, placing at their disposal the information necessary for the duties of the citizen. They should enable rural inhabitants to acquire without difficulty general knowledge which alone can enable them to appreciate in full what they see and hear. Public librarians should impart knowledge of public affairs and of the history of neighbourhoods which a citizen must possess if he or she is to perform with intelligence his or her duties as a member of the community ultimately responsible for government. Partnership with governance agencies, civil society, gender advocacy groups, and human rights organizations to cite but a few examples is needed to provide the best services for the community. Such partnership if well-organized could *inter alia* help the public library in its fundraising activities, lobbying with government and other donor agencies for support, collection development, and promoting its image (Newman 2004).

Vulnerable Communities

Sierra Leone has a very youthful population most of whom though educated are unemployed and found in ghettos, Ataya bases,[1] and small scale business activities. Some are not in school, not working, and not looking for employment. Often youths are grossly misused and abused especially during elections when politicians use them as thugs to gain control over their opponents only to dump them thereafter when they gain victory. There are a few youths who are transitioning from being ex-combatants and victims of civil conflict to becoming productive civilians in a peaceful society. The youths are affected by the social and economic crisis as they migrate from rural to urban areas. Drug abuse, delinquency, and traditional family structures constantly affect them. This does not mean that they do not have a commitment to change (Obiyo 2010; Sesay 2011). They want greater social justice and better opportunities to participate in the running of public

---

1 Ataya bases are centres where people converge to drink a special green tea called ataya.

affairs and therefore constantly advocate for greater respect, justice and equality in society. Similarly there is a nation-wide cry for gender equality, equal represen-tation, appropriate legislation, and equal opportunity for participation in the for-mation of policies and budget appropriation to cite a few examples. The participa-tion of vulnerable groups in good governance requires awareness raising through massive education, information, and training through meetings, seminars, talks, workshops, conferences, and symposia in which the public library should play a leading role by making its premises and services available to institutions and groups advocating the promotion of good governance in society. Public librarians should repackage information on such topics as adolescent pregnancies, drug abuse, behavioural patterns in sexual relations, education opportunities, special information on skills using ICT, and self-employment (Islam and Nazmul 2007; Mahmood 2008), and make the information available to users.

Information and Communication Technology

Use of ICT could promote the governance process. Olowu (2004) suggested four major areas where ICT has contributed to the improvement of governance:
- Transformation of the manner in which governmental agencies do business
- Government-business relations have been greatly improved because of e-gov-ernment. Correct information can be accessed and timely processes achieved through the ability to download forms, apply for licences online, and make contact with the most relevant officers
- Improved governance service delivery with citizens obtaining more prompt and effective delivery of services by online means rather than through tradi-tional or conventional processes
- Feedback from citizens is secured through online service delivery surveys with electronic voting making a great difference in voting patterns.

The public library should actively promote the use of ICT as a fundamental working tool by citizens and local authorities (Drake 2002). The use of new tech-nologies could offer new possibilities for more open communication with the public. Citizens can access public information easily, discuss issues with each other, and communicate directly with authorities. It is an occasion to broaden citizen participation in decision-making by involving marginalized groups such as young people and women who feel under-represented or left out of gover-nance. The use of ICT can support transparency, create a public space for citizens, and offer a readily available consultation mechanism for good governance. The public library should therefore provide training in basic computer literacy, web browsing skills, desktop publishing, use of email, networking, data selection and interpretation, information access, and retrieval to its multifarious users for them to have quick and easy access to materials on the Net (Eve and Brophy 2010). For these ventures to succeed, public librarians themselves need good research online skills in the use of information databases and other electronic resources. The library must also have reliable and fast Internet connectivity and local and wide area networking facilities. The public library is for everyone, educated and uneducated, rich and poor, male or female and old or young. It is a democratic force in availing access to computers, the Internet, information, learning and training, and therefore should play a pivotal role in information sourcing, storage, packaging, dissemination, and utilization by end-users (Bangura 2016).

Internet Provision

The growth of the Internet has led to increased availability of content and there is a great demand for knowledge to be shared freely or cheaply (UNCTAD 2005). The public library must provide an effective Internet service to people who would not ordinarily have access to online information as well as reference services to those looking for in-depth information within a public library collection. The public library should facilitate E-government initiatives by making its facilities available and providing transparent access to government information. The public library should be upgraded as a major resource centre that can develop and maintain databases on governance and document collection via electronic networking. The public library should invest in state-of-the-art ICT with high end hardware and software including high performing workstations and computers and fileservers. It is important for the public library to create its own website which will improve the quality and capacity of Internet connectivity, access, and communication including email services (Haneefa 2007; Max 2007). The investments, coupled with efforts to advance the public library's role as a research and knowledge centre, will enable the institution to harness information and knowledge to meet the development challenges facing Sierra Leone in the twenty-first century.

Public Sphere

A vibrant public sphere is at the heart of any prudent democratic governance. Management of the public library should transform the library to a public sphere where social forces, interest groups, religious organizations, youth and gender groups, civil society, private sector operators, and pressure groups can interact to ensure that the governors are responsive to the concerns and legitimate demands of the governed. Efforts of the afore-mentioned bodies can improve the governance process and increase transparency as well as promote good governance as a basic requirement for peace, security, and sustainable political and socio-economic development. The public library should formulate a framework to facilitate information flow and knowledge through songs in local languages, drama sessions, advertisements, campaigns and demonstrations, and traditional cultural gatherings to cite a few examples (Motumi 2012).

The content, form, and packaging of messages as well as the channels used should be compatible with the customs of the people. User-friendly message channels such as posters, flyers, and billboards can be used by the public library to promote good governance in society. To complement these efforts, the public library should introduce the human element to library service where experienced personalities are invited to tell their stories and experiences in their communities, with the audience drawn from different sectors. Sessions should be interactive. In a similar vein, since there are many community radio stations in the country, public librarians could be the panel members and phone into programs to discuss good governance issues in their communities and educate the masses about what the public library can offer. The main purpose is to create knowledge and spread information on good governance.

Information Literacy and Lifelong Learning

In addition to strengthening capacity of the citizenry, there is a need for the public library to introduce information literacy and lifelong learning activities to help users find relevant materials and information in their areas of interest including good governance. A significant proportion of the Sierra Leone population is illiterate and poverty is common place. Corruption and embezzlement of state funds are widely practised in spite of the formation of the Anti-Corruption Commission to handle the issues (Bangura 2016). Access to modern ICT facilities is rare especially in the rural areas, not considering people's ability to make use of them. Besides, there is no reading culture in the country even with the literate few, nor is there a policy controlling what information is to be given to the population. At times some of the information given out is adulterated and people have to depend on hearsay. In other instances, it is the government that poses difficulties in the sense that some information is twisted to suit its whims and caprices to enable it to hold on to power.

In these circumstances information literacy and lifelong learning are crucial in promoting good governance. Information literacy could empower people in all walks of life to seek, evaluate, and use information effectively to achieve their personal, occupational, and educational goals. It is a human right in a digital world and promotes social and political inclusion; it provides the key to effective access, use, and creation of vital information and goes beyond current technologies to encompass learning, critical thinking, and interpretative skills across professional boundaries, and empowers individuals and communities (Garner 2006). Lifelong learning enables people and communities to attain their goals and take advantage of emerging opportunities, especially in promoting good governance and understanding of human rights. Appropriate services could encourage the private sector, civil society, young people, women's groups and those involved in human rights and promotion of good governance to have access to online resources in strengthening their learning and skills with use of digital tools.

Reading

To address the problem of reading and to enable people to participate in good governance activities, the public library should be moved from district headquarter towns to chiefdom level to cultivate the habit of reading with materials available in local languages. Both teachers and public librarians should be trained to teach literacy in their localities. Mass sensitization should be carried out by the public library for people to be aware of the importance of reading and information in promoting good governance and understanding of their civic, social, and political rights in their different communities. This kind of sensitization should be carried out using the national broadcaster, community radio, and television stations to reach the general populace. To this end, the public library should lobby government, business investors, the private sector, and agencies to increase funding of public library programs (Okolo 2010).

Traditional Governance

The role of traditional governance, the chieftaincy, in relation to the modern state is receiving attention in the country. Chiefs have their own courts where they decide cases in their respective chiefdoms. There is a Council of Paramount Chiefs; chiefs are represented in parliament; there is the Ministry of Local Government that deals with chieftaincy and local government matters, and there is a whole division in that Ministry on chiefs. The incorporation of traditional governance into mainstream governance maximizes utilization of traditional leadership which represents a rich human focus; it brings into focus the broader issues of good governance, culture, and development (Bangura 2016). Records of traditional authorities are available in some quarters but the pace for access is slow. The public library could address the issue through digitization and packaging of records and data of the House of Chiefs and Traditional Councils, increasing access to research resources of local communities. Digitization of records would provide easy access to historical data and help mine current data and observe causal relationships that may not always be apparent.

Health Information

There is a popular assertion that information is power but most importantly good health is a prerequisite for the acquisition of power and wealth. Correct information has the ability to make a u-turn in the life of an individual, family, community, region, and the nation at large if properly exploited. Information and consequently good health are indispensable instruments for the promotion of good governance and national development. Good governance requires a healthy population empowered with the right kind of information and tools (Davies 2012). Diseases such as malaria, Lassa fever, river blindness, Gonorrhea, HIV, and AIDS are endemic in Sierra Leone and in the not too recent past Ebola, not forgetting to mention early childhood pregnancy, infant mortality, and drug abuse among young people. These diseases have succeeded in killing a great many people and are a threat to the existence of the state. A major cause is widespread ignorance and poor health education.

To achieve better health for the greater majority of the population so that they can effectively take part in community affairs including good governance, the right kind of information must be obtained through a variety of channels. The public library should be seen playing a leading role in providing health information as a result of its mission. Through well designed studies, the public library could, concertedly with medical research teams, collect primary health data. Information is needed by the public about the location and distribution of hospitals and clinics in the country, health personnel, availability of free medical care facilities, identification of areas where new facilities can be constructed, information about infant mortality, malnutrition, immunization, and the provision of essential drugs (Fitzgerald and Savage 2011). The public library should maintain databases of all of these. In the communities especially in rural areas, the facilities of the public library could even be used to hold meetings to discuss health issues while its billboards could be used to display posters, handbills and any other vital information on health intended for public consumption. To facilitate ease of access and use, the databases should be user friendly. Once the public know that they can get information befitting their health needs, they will frequently patronize the public library. Public librarians could even use such visits to their advantage by educating people about their civil rights and thereby promoting good governance.

Recommendations

There is much to be done going forward. Effective leadership is required; financial support; education levels must be raised; partnerships must be forged; and a shift in thinking.

Institutional Leadership

Effective and sustainable intervention for promoting good governance requires strong institutional leadership. Public library management must be able to utilize the knowledge and expertise of library staff through capacity building, equipping staff with the necessary knowledge, skills, and attitudes through workshops, seminars, and short and long term formal courses. Management should also be involved in effective sensitization strategies for awareness raising (Ebiwolate 2010). To this end, management must undertake a serious analysis of the situation and design appropriate strategies and actions.

Financial Support

One cannot overemphasize the importance of planning, with measurable and realistic goals, implementation and continuous process of monitoring and evaluation of activities of the public library concerning the promotion of good governance across the country. To this end, adequate budget lines need to be established to demonstrate commitment and sustainability of activities. National and global resources should be mustered for the promotion of good governance. Links and networking with educational institutions, civil society, faith-based organizations, and the private sector should be promoted for sharing resources and knowledge. For wider impact, various options such as use of interactive media could be implemented.

Education

It would be a crime to let people continue to suffer in ignorance without being educated about their rights. Lack of action when information is available is inexcusable. Failure to act when enough is already known is indefensible because there are many reasons to act, immense lessons to draw, and huge potentials to tap particularly in the use of technology. The public library is the real powerhouse in ordinary lives. People should use its uniqueness, reach, and sheer potency as leverage in the cross-cutting government agenda. No one has to use the public library; people choose to do so. There is no other service that the majority of the people can use whether they be rich or poor, young or old, save the public library. The Latin word for library, *liber*, means book and freedom: freedom of access to information and materials and finding places where one can better oneself and explore knowledge, imagination, and learning. Libraries are places for dreaming and thinking for oneself, real powerhouses in ordinary lives (Davies 2012).

Partnerships

It simply does not make sense to leave out the public library as a key player in the governance process. It is the first stop chosen by many to start out and seek information across every sector of society. The public library is a reflector of the community and anticipates and satisfies needs. It should therefore be the catalyst to ensure that none is left behind or left out in understanding the rudiments of the governance process. The public library welcomes people of all ages and stages to read and screen. It can contribute to all the themes of good governance: social inclusion, the learning society, modernizing local government, and decentralization (Bill and Melinda Gates Foundation 2012). Since its inception, the public library in Sierra Leone has been involved in learning for life and has contributed to creating and recording the cultural life of the nation. Local government, under whose auspices the public library is managed, needs to ensure that it is liberated by its place in the Councils' structure to contribute on the widest possible policy framework. Sitting in focus groups run by Local Councils will lead to discovering that people do not know how to access public library services because they do not understand what the public library does, whom to contact or how the structure works. Similarly, people just do not understand what Local Councils do. The public library has to make sense of how things work in Local Councils. It has to be transparent, talk, and share resources. The public library can help; it is adept at forging partnerships and is valued by local contacts. It is on the spot and widely seen as an information broker. It is the first port of call for many people with problems. It is the local authority's shop window, a gateway into the local community. It reaches into every community in the country. If decentralization is to succeed in Sierra Leone the public library must help in keeping people, particularly the rural poor, informed of their rights and the opportunities available to them. While it might not directly improve the basic conditions of life of the rural poor, it will make an indirect contribution towards improving knowledge choice and self-esteem (Ayee 1996).

Paradigm Shift

For many years the public library has regarded itself as undervalued by government with its potential contribution to the wider government agendas, Agenda for Change and Agenda for Prosperity, unrecognized. The Information Age recognizes that the public library can counter the threats of new forms of exclusion created by the digital revolution and bridge the knowledge gap by providing public access to digital resources as it has always provided access to print resources. The public library is a neutral and inclusive place enabling freedom of access to knowledge, information and imagination; offering enrichment through cultural diversity; giving access to learning opportunities; underpinning community development; becoming a local access point for interaction with government; and providing information infrastructure as well as support for good governance, democracy, citizenship, and enterprise.

Delivering outcomes required by government necessitates a paradigm shift for the public library. Public librarians must think outside the box; work with their communities; develop strategic approaches; be accountable for performance against policy interventions; work with new political structures; and face up to the choices of good governance (Clark 2010). That is to say the public library should reinvent itself as a social agency and engage more actively with good governance activities in its locality. It can do this by developing and marketing innovative services to all stakeholders, including the general public, civil society organizations, the government and its agencies, local councils, human rights organizations, and gender groups. The new agenda calls for extensive research into user needs and the role of the public library in promoting good governance in Sierra Leone.

Conclusion

Gradually recovering from the throes of an eleven-year civil war from 1991–2002 and the Ebola epidemic of 2014, the government of Sierra Leone is prioritizing its activities. Libraries are grudgingly tolerated by government and are placed low on the national list of priorities. But all is not lost, for libraries are perceived as potentially monumental, and regarded with civic and institutional pride. Public librarians must exhort each other to convince the decision makers about the importance of the public library in promoting good governance. By playing the roles suggested and taking the actions recommended, the public library will be able to make important contributions to the process of transforming Sierra Leone into a viable democratic society based on a solid foundation which is universal, objective, timely, and drawing from a variety of sources. Access to the right information for all people in society is necessary for reaching government's development goals. That is all the more reason why the government, civil society, private sector and funding agencies must join forces with the public library to improve facilities and contribute to staff capacity building. Government bodies at all levels including Local and District Councils must see the public library as a key public service partner and use it to drive the agenda in promoting good governance. And public librarians should be enterprising enough to play an advocacy and influential role in placing their institutions into Government and Local Council agendas.

References

Akparobore, D.O. *The Role of Public Libraries in Promoting Adult Education*. London: Oxford University Press, 2011.

Alemna, A.A. *Libraries, Information and Society: An Inaugural Lecture Delivered in November, 19, 1998, University of Ghana, Legon*. Accra: Ghana University Press, 2000.

Anderson, C.N. *Pragmatic Liberalism*. Chicago: University of Chicago Press, 1990.

Ayee, J.R.A. "The Measurement of Decentralization and Service Delivery: the Gambian Experience". *African Affairs Journal* 95, no. 378 (1996): 31–50.

Bangura, S.A. "On Paramount Chiefs and the Promotion of Good Governance in Sierra Leone". *The Awareness Times Newspaper* XL, no. 25 (2016): 7–8.

Bill and Melinda Gates Foundation. *Beyond Access: How Public Libraries Contribute Towards Reaching the Millennium Goals*. London: University Press, 2012.

Brodnig, G., and V. Mayer-Schönberger. "Bridging the Gap: the Role of Spatial Information Technologies in the Integration of Traditional Environmental Knowledge and Western Science". *The Electronic Journal on Information Systems in Developing Countries*. 1, no.1 (2017) Accessed March 24, 2020. https://onlinelibrary.wiley.com/doi/full/10.1002/j.1681-4835.2000.tb00001.x.

Brown, D.C. "Electronic Government and Public Administration." *International Review of Administrative Science Journal* 71, no. 2 (2005): 241–254.

Cartwright, J.R. *Political Leadership in Serra Leone.* Toronto: University of Toronto Press, 2013.

Clark, I. *We Need Libraries in the Digital Age.* Oxford: University Press, 2010.

Cornwell, A., and J. Gaventa. "Bridging the Gap: Citizenship, Participation and Accountability." *Participatory Learning and Action Series* 40 (2001): 32–35. Accessed March 24, 2020. https://pubs.iied.org/G01307/.

Dahl, R. *On Democracy.* New Haven: Yale University College, 1998.

Davies, N. *Shifting Roles for Public Libraries: From Supporting Player to Community Engagement Leader.* New York: University Press, 2012.

Debowski, S. 2003. "Services to Remote Library Users". In *Encyclopedia of Library and Information Science.* 2nd ed. vol. 4, 2626–2635. New York: Mercel Dekker, 2003.

Drake, W. *How Can Governments Make the Best Use of ICTs?* Geneva: International Telecommunication Union, 2002.

Ebiwolate, P.B. *Nigerian Public Library Services to Rural Areas: Libraries in Niger Delta State.* Lagos: University Press, 2010.

Eve, J., and P. Brophy. "Vital Issues: the Perception and Use of ICT services in UK Public Libraries". *LIBRES: Library and Information Science Research Electronic Journal* 10, no. 2 (2000). Accessed March 24, 2020. https://cpb-us-e1.wpmucdn.com/blogs.ntu.edu.sg/dist/8/644/files/2014/06/Vol10_I2_Vital.pdf.

Fitzgerald, B., and F. Savage. *Public Libraries in Victoria and Australia: an Overview of Current ICT Development, Challenges and Issues.* New York: Macmillan Publishing Limited, 2011.

Flinders, M. *The Politics of Accountability.* Aldershot: Ashgate, 2001.

Garner, Sarah D. ed. *High-Level Colloquium on Information Literacy and Lifelong Learning, Bibliotheca Alexandrina, Alexandria, Egypt November 6–9, 2005: Report of a Meeting Sponsored by the United Nations Education, Scientific, and Cultural Organisation (UNESCO), National Forum on Information Literacy (NFIL) and the International Federation of Library Associations and Institutions (IFLA).* The Hague: IFLA, 2006. Accessed March 24, 2020. https://www.ifla.org/publications/high-level-colloquium-on-information-literacy-and-lifelong-learning.

Gill, P., ed. *The Public Library Service: IFLA/UNESCO Guidelines for Development.* Edited for the IFLA Section of Public Libraries. IFLA publications 97. München: Saur, 2001.

Haneefa, M. "Application of Information and Communication Technologies in Special Libraries in Kerela (India)." *Library Review* 56, no.7 (2007): 603–20. https://doi.org/10.1108/00242530710775999.

Islam, Md., and Md. Nazmul. "Use of ICT in Libraries: an Empirical Study of Selected Libraries in Bangladesh." *Library Philosophy and Practice* 9, no.2 (2007). Accessed March 24, 2020. https://www.researchgate.net/publication/28184621_Use_of_ICT_in_Libraries_An_Empirical_Study_of_Selected_Libraries_in_Bangladesh.

Kargbo, Abdulai A. *The Establishment of a Modern Public Library System: An Assessment of the Quality of Services Offered by the Sierra Leone Library Board.* MPhil. Thesis. Unpublished. Freetown: University of Sierra Leone, 2006.

Madison, J. *The Complete Madison: His Basic Writings.* New York: Kraus Reprint, 1953.

Mahmood, K. *ICT Based Services in Public Libraries of Pakistan.* Leeds: Leeds University Press, 2008.

Mamafha, Takalani M.M., P. Ngulumbu, and S.C. Ndwande. 2016. "Utilization of Information and Communication Technologies in Public Libraries at Ekurhuleni Metropolitan Municipality in South Africa." *Information Development Journal* 32, no.3 (2016): 313–326.

Mapflow. *LBS and MMS: Enhancing Your Position (White Paper)*. Dublin: Mapflow, 2002.

March, J.G., and J.D. Olsen. *Democratic Governance*. New York: The Free Press, 1995.

Maswabi, T.,T. Sethate, S.E.M. Sebusang, and R. Taolo,. "Public Libraries: Pathways to Making Botswana an Educated, Informed Nation." *Library Review* 60, no. 9 (2011): 409–420. https://doi.org/10.1108/00242531111135272.

Matarasso, F. "The Meaning of Leadership in a Cultural Democracy: Rethinking Public Library Values." *Logo* 11, no.1 (2000): 38–44.

Motumi, M. "Ekurhuleni library services in the community." *Star Africa*, May 2, 2012. Accessed June 18, 2017. https://www.iol.co.za/the-star/ekurhuleni-libraries-serve-the-community-1286884.

Mujudith, S., S. Naicker, and N. Zondi. "Ethekwini Libraries and Communities: a Priceless Synergy." Paper presented at the Ninth Annual Conference of the Library and Information Association of South Africa (LIASA), September 25–29, 2006.

Newman, W. *Public Libraries in the Priorities of Canada: Acting on the Assets and Opportunities: Prepared for the Provincial and Territorial Library Directors Council (PTLDC)*. Ottawa: Libraries and Archives Canada, 2004. Accessed March 24, 2020. https://www. collectionscanada.gc.ca/obj/s7/f2/03-e.pdf.

Obiyo, Hyacinth Uzodinma. *The Nexus Between Governance and Economic Development: A Case Study of the Political Economy of Democratic Governance in Sierra Leone, 1996–2010*. PhD Dissertation. Unpublished. Freetown: University of Sierra Leone, 2010.

Okolo, E.O. *The Use of Library by Students in Tertiary Institutions*. Ibadan: Endtime Publishing, 2010.

Olowu, Dele. "Bridging the Digital Divide In Africa: Making the Governance Discourse Relevant". In *African Networking: Development Information, ICTs and Governance*, edited by Karima Bounemra Ben Soltane, Nino Orlando Fluck, Aida Opoku-Mensah, and M.A. Mohamed Salih, 81–92. Addis Ababa: Economic Commission for Africa, 2004.

Salih, M. A.M. "Governance, Information and the Public Sphere." In *African Networking: Development Information, ICTs and Governance*", edited by Karima Bounemra Ben Soltane, Nino Orlando Fluck, Aida Opoku-Mensah, and M.A. Mohamed Salih, 25–56. Addis Ababa: Economic Commission for Africa, 2004.

Sesay, M.G. *State Construction Collapse and Reconstruction: the Case of Sierra Leone*. PhD dissertation. Unpublished. Freetown: University of Sierra Leone, 2011.

Sierra Leone. *The Constitution of Sierra Leone*. Freetown: Government Printing Department, 1991.

Sierra Leone. *National Strategy for Good Governance and Public Service Reform*. Freetown: Government Printing Department, 1997.

Sierra Leone. *Right to Access Information Act*. Freetown: Government Printing Department. Accessed March 24, 2020. http://www.sierra-leone.org/Laws/2013-02.pdf.

Sierra Leone. Ministry of Education and Welfare. *White Paper on Educational Development*. Sierra Leone, 1958.

Sierra Leone Library Board. *Annual Report 2008*. Freetown: Government Printing Department, 2008.

Sierra Leone Library Board. *First Report, June 1959–March 1961*. Freetown: Government Printing Department, 1961.

Sierra Leone Library Board. *Manual*. Freetown, 2015.

Sierra Leone Vision 2025: "Sweet-Salone": United People Progressive Nation Attractive Country. National Long Term Perspectives Studies (NLTPS) Strategies For National Transformation. August 2003. Accessed April 15, 2020. https://unipsil.unmissions.org/sites/default/files/vision_2025.pdf

Silver, C.J. *Political Parties and Democratic Governance in Sierra Leone*. PhD Dissertation. Unpublished. Freetown: University of Sierra Leone, 2011.

Sturges, P., and R. Neill. *The Quiet Struggle: Libraries and Information in Africa*. London: Mansell, 2009.

Sy, Habib J. "Global Communications for an Equitable World". In *Global Public Goods: International Cooperation in the 21st Century*, edited by I. Kaul, I. Grunberg, and M.A. Stern, 326–343. New York: OUP, 1999.

Toffler, A. *The Third Wave*. New York: Morrow, 1980.

UNCTAD. *E-commerce and Development Report*. New York: UNCTAD, 2005.

UNDP. *Reconceptualising Governance: Discussion Paper 2*. New York: UNDP, 1997.

UNDP. *Human Development Report 1999*. New York: Oxford University Press, 1999. Accessed March 24, 2020. http://hdr.undp.org/sites/default/files/reports/260/hdr_1999_en_nostats.pdf.

UNESCO. "UNESCO Public Library Manifesto." *UNESCO Bulletin for Libraries*, 26 no.3 (1972): 129–131.

Wiseman, J.A. *The New Struggle for Democracy in Africa*. London: Ashgate Publishing, 2011.

World Bank. *Governance and Development*. Washington, DC: World Bank, 1992.

World Bank. *World Development Report: Knowledge for Development*. Washington, DC: World Bank, 1999.

Umut Al and Seda Öz

11 The Role of Municipal Public Libraries in the E-Transformation of Turkey

Abstract: The Libraries for Everyone/Herkes için Kütüphane Project commenced in Turkey in 2016. Funded by the Bill & Melinda Gates Foundation Global Librar- ies Initiative, the main goal of the project was that municipal public libraries become centres to support the lifelong learning of local citizens, particularly those who belong to disadvantaged segments of society. Libraries are invited to join the project which offers collaborative opportunities. There is a key role in the project for the Turkish Library Association/Türk Kütüphaneciler Derneği' (TLA/ TKD) and the sustainability of the project is especially important for the future of librarianship in Turkey. Partnerships created between the local government and the branches of the Turkish Library Association are expected to enhance the e-transformation efforts of Turkey. An overview of public libraries in Turkey is provided and the achievements of the project outlined.

Keywords: Public libraries – Turkey; Continuing education; Information technol- ogy – Study and teaching; E-government; Internet in public administration.

Introduction

Opportunities provided by new information and communication technologies (ICT) open up ways for novel approaches to public administration. Thanks to ICT, there are new communication modes between governments and communities, as well as the potential for faster operations, enhanced activity in policy determina- tion and resolution processes, that bring transparency to the forefront, and ensure the participation of relevant social spheres and subjects in the decision-making processes. To be able to adjust to changes and augment citizens' quality of life and their social welfare, it is necessary to form new organizational structures, to redesign work and service periods, and to achieve public administration reform which is integrated, sustainable, and extensive (Republic of Turkey Ministry of Development 2014). Additionally, the digital divide in Turkey, especially between urban and rural, old and young, man and woman, educated and uneducated, is a well-known fact that may benefit from these efforts.

Through libraries relevant services that may decrease the digital divide can be planned and realized. However, lack of resources causes obstacles and hinders libraries from achieving their full potential. Even though several collaboration

https://doi.org/10.1515/ 9783110533323-014

activities and project supports are brought to the agenda to overcome the problems in question, sustainability of new endeavours has remained as a problem. At this point, the Libraries for Everyone/Herkes için Kütüphane Project, which is funded by the Bill & Melinda Gates Foundation's Global Libraries Initiative, tries to achieve a range of outputs, by being the most comprehensive project about municipal public libraries in Turkey so far. Within the scope of the Project, first an infrastructure enabling computer and Internet access for the citizens is supported. Second, municipal public libraries offered free training programs for the use of Internet-driven services, especially e-government and e-municipal services, and for the acquisition of information and communication skills. This chapter outlines, the general information about the Libraries for Everyone Project, summarizes e-government and e-transformation efforts in Turkey. Project activities in the area of e-government services are analysed in the light of data acquired through research undertaken by the library usage survey, which is conducted by the Project (Al, Öz and Taşkın 2016; Al, Doğan, Soydal and Taşkın 2017).

Municipal Public Libraries in Turkey

There have been important library activities in Turkey since the era of the Seljuqs of Anatolia, the Beglik period, and the Ottoman Empire. In the Ottoman era, libraries were first built as parts of mosques, madrasahs (Moslem educational institutions), and as private foundations. Independent libraries were built by donations to various private foundations. An early example of this kind of library was built in Istanbul in 1678 by Köprülü Fazıl Ahmet Pasha and named the Köprülü Library. In the Ottoman era, in 1884, the *Kütüphane-i Osmaniye*/Osmaniye Library was founded by the government. It is considered to be the first government library and is still open to service today under the name of the *Beyazıt Devlet Kütüphanesi/* Beyazit State Library under the Ministry of Culture and Tourism (KYGM 2016).

In the past, the main goal of the Turkish libraries and librarianship was to preserve and protect the collection and the information sources. In addition to this main goal another role of the libraries was the transfer of information to future generations, and making information available to the public through libraries (Anameriç 2006). Today, goals and practices of the libraries have changed according to their specialty. For example, when the focus is on manuscripts, the traditional approach concentrating on the collections has been maintained. However, for public libraries, with the changing goals and practices, making information publicly available has gained increasing importance in recent years.

Public libraries in Turkey have a centralized structure, represented by the General Directorate of Libraries and Publications in the Ministry of Culture and Tourism (GDLP). GDLP plans the public library services, realizes all the financial, personnel, collection and building requirements, creates new service areas, prepares strategies, does inspections, and decides on standards. Yet, contrary to its responsibility areas, GDLP does not have enough resources for the support of all public libraries in Turkey. For example, in some cities which may have six to seven public libraries, there is only one librarianship graduate employed. (Al and Akıllı 2016, 302). Moreover, in a big country like Turkey, it is problematic to coordinate all the activities from one single place. Thus, various scholars and relevant parties have suggested the transfer of public libraries to local governments and municipalities.

For years in Turkey, municipal public libraries have not received significant attention. They are not even included in the statistics shared by the Turkish Statistical Institute (TÜİK 2016a; TÜİK 2016b). However, during recent years, municipal public libraries have started to make significant achievements. Accordingly, there have been various studies on municipal public libraries in Turkey, and the most important discussion has focused on the transfer of public libraries to local governments. However, there are still objections to the transfer of public GDLP libraries to local governments. It is especially indicated that any change or transfer of public libraries to local governments without first changing the public library regulations may create irreversible harm (Yılmaz 2013, 399). Other studies (Acıkgoz and Yılmaz 2013; Demircioğlu Faydalıgul and Yılmaz 2007; Yılmaz et al. 2010) which focused on different aspects, including librarians and library managers, are also indicating concerns in regards to the issue.

The context and local needs are important factors in delivering library and information services. Theoretically, the most effective planning and implementation of library services depend on taking into consideration the local variables which will result in greater productivity and benefits to users. At this point, the investment made by municipal authorities in their library services should be discussed. One study (Pektaş 2010, 12) pointed out that with the rise of urbanization in Turkey in the 1950s and the increase in the population in the cities, municipal authorities prioritized urban infrastructure services in relation to other social activities. In the same study (Pektaş 2010, 15), while focusing on the poor, disabled, children, the elderly, women, and young people within the understanding of social municipality was mentioned, the importance of opening arts and sports facilities, and extending or integrating library and cultural services was also highlighted. With similar motivations, as a social innovation project that aims to provide improved library services particularly for the disadvantaged in society, the Libraries for Everyone Project commenced its activities in 2016.

Libraries for Everyone/*Herkes için Kütüphane*: Project Overview

The main goal of the Libraries for Everyone Project was to turn municipal public libraries and information centres into centres of attraction for citizens. The official slogan of the Project was Local Transformation, Global Access. The LIFE Project envisioned the stimulation of a process of radical transformation and advancement at selected municipal public libraries representing locales at the province, district and township levels. The Project was funded by the Bill & Melinda Gates Foundation and implemented by the Hacettepe University Technopolis-Technology Transfer Center. It involved collaboration activities with significant other institutions, such as the Turkish Library Association[1]/*Türk Kütüphaneciler Derneği'* (TLA/*TKD)* (http://kutuphaneci.org.tr/), Turkish Informatics Association/*Türkiye Bilişim Derneği* (TIA/TBD), Near Eastern University (NEU), and Turkish small and Medium-sized Enterprises and Independent Business Members and Executives Foundation (TOSYOV). The various institutions together with the working group formed within the TLA ensured the collection of statistical data of municipal public libraries, and were responsible for leading the Project at the municipal public libraries for two years after the Project was finalized. TLA also committed to support the Project activities in locations where its branches and members exist. TIA and NEU supported the Project in terms of distance education, information and communication sciences, and sustainability. NEU also contributed to the sustainability of the Project by allowing libraries to use its corporate data processing unit for three years after the Project was finalized. By preparing learning content for the target audience, especially for the disadvantaged segments of society, and by holding training programs, TOSYÖV will support the Project in terms of training and advocacy.

Project activities started with an invitation letter sent to all municipality authorities. Information on those who intended to join the Project was collected through responses to the letters. Within the scope of the Project, the local libraries would support Project activities as well as providing free Internet access to their users. Computers, Internet access tools, training and advocacy materials, and staff training would be freely provided by the Project. The Project included some specific efforts, such as the provision of 3D printer services for public access in designated libraries to provide examples of what could be achieved. At the end of the Project, in addition to the general library services, it was expected that municipal public libraries would transform into centres of attraction that are capable of supporting

---

1 Sometimes referred to in English as the Turkish Librarians' Association.

lifelong learning efforts of local citizens, especially those belonging to disadvantaged segments of the society (Herkes için Kütüphane 2017).

Activities of the Libraries for Everyone Project were carried out through four different work groups, namely, advocacy, ICT, training, and impact assessment. While the advocacy work group was responsible for the public relations and marketing related activities of the Project, the ICT work group was responsible for planning, implementing, and maintaining ICT related works of the Project. The training work group assessed the training needs and the ICT skills of the library staff and the citizens. It is also the responsibility of the training work group to develop sustainable onsite and online training programs as a result of the assessment. Lastly, the impact assessment group worked on the evaluation of the success of the Project in terms of reaching its goals, and the follow up of all the relevant project outcomes (Herkes için Kütüphane 2017).

As of June 2017, there were 172 municipal public libraries in the Project. The distribution of the libraries is seen in Figure 1. Istanbul had the highest number with 47 Project libraries. Given the population density of Istanbul, the most crowded city of Turkey, this is understandable. Even though every single city did not have a library as a part of the Project, the Project aimed to have at least one library from every single geographical region. Since the Project had a dynamic nature, during the process libraries joined the Project, as well as leaving it. The reasons for leaving the Project or being expelled from it are about unrealized Project requirements, such as an inability to provide free Internet access to the public, having no staff to assist or lack of commitment to the Project. It was expected that there would be an increase in the number of Project libraries and the opening of new municipal public libraries in places where they did not exist, particularly with increased local and national media interest in the Project.

Fig. 1: Distribution of the libraries that are a part of Libraries for Everyone Project.

Internet Usage Statistics and e-Government Services in Turkey

In April 2016, according to the Household Information Technologies Usage Research (TÜİK 2016c), the people within the age range of 16–74 accounted for 55% of computer usage in Turkey and 61% of the Internet usage rate. The rates vary according to gender. For men, the figures were 64% and 71% respectively, and for women they were 46% and 52%. While there have been steady increases over time (Figure 2), Turkey still lags behind many countries (Table 1).

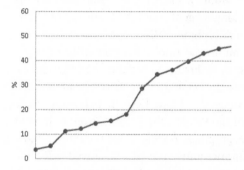

Fig. 2: Percentage of individuals using the Internet (ITU 2016).

Various sources show that the Internet usage ratio of most countries is higher than Turkey (ITU 2016). For example, Denmark has an internet usage ratio around 96% (Table 1). There is much that could and should be done in Turkey to extend Internet usage. A project that can reach wide numbers of people and provide ICT information and skills for everyone is needed. With this kind of a project, the goal should not only be the popularization of internet usage, but also the ability to make effective use of ICT for the enhancement of and individual's life quality. The Libraries for Everyone Project aimed to benefit from the use of relevant ICT while transforming libraries into places to meet the information needs of citizens.

Table 1: Internet usage ratios of various countries as of 2015 (ITU 2016).

Country	%
Argentina	69
Austria	84
Belgium	85
Denmark	96

Table 1: (continued)

Country	%
Italy	66
Japan	91
Malaysia	71
Mexico	57
Portugal	69
Spain	79
Turkey	54

Digital transformation related works in Turkey started on December 18, 2008 through the E-Government Gate. As of June 2017, there are 330 institutions, 2011 services, and 32,844,660 registered users in the E-Government. The tax delinquency check, retirement pension check, and mobile line check are among the most used services. The rapid growth in the number of registered users is worth noting (Figure 3).

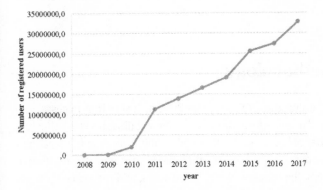

Fig. 3: The annual increase in the total number of registered users at The Turkish e-Government Gateway (e-Devlet Kapısı 2017; Republic of Turkey Ministry of Development 2014).

As the world develops digitally, it is unthinkable for Turkey to remain behind other countries, considering the new generations of young people demanding everything from the digital environment. As a result of pressing demands, various public and private institutions have begun to deliver their services into a digital environment. Bodies that cannot keep pace with the changes and organizations resisting change have no chance of survival. Accompanying the digital developments, concepts like computer literacy, information literacy, and media literacy have come to the fore and been discussed in the literature. However, there is still more to be done. The concepts must be defined, explored, and further developed with new understandings of the skills and knowledge required for competence. To help people to enhance their existing skills and knowledge and gain new proficiencies, various training programs have been prepared and implemented. An important factor for the people who are demanding training is to receive it from reputable people and institutions. At this crucial time, libraries play an important role. Due to the responsible and respected position that they hold in public opinion, libraries can be transformed into institutions in which potential users can augment their information skills and experiences.

One of the main problems in ICT in Turkey is the digital divide. As previously mentioned, women's Internet usage is lower than men's use. Through various statistical indicators, it is also known that there are regional and geographical inequalities. For example, according to research data (EUROSTAT 2016a), the percentages of people who do not use the Internet is as follows: Istanbul 33%, West Marmara 41%, East Marmara 41%, Aegean 43%, Mediterranean 47%, West Anatolia 38%, Central Anatolia 49%, Northeast Anatolia 60%, Central East Anatolia 60%, West Black Sea 50%. East Black Sea 48%, and Southeast Anatolia 57%. The starting point of the Libraries for Everyone Project was the goal of reducing inequality.

The Project Methodology

Within the scope of the Libraries for Everyone Project, it was first necessary to gather analytical data. Various information on the Project libraries was collected, such as the total number of library staff, the number of information management graduate staff, the number of computers used by the library staff, the number of public access computers, the number of registered users, and the areas of usage.

In addition, between August and September 2016, a questionnaire was conducted on municipal public library users. The findings of the questionnaire were presented and the statistics of the related training shared. Sample size was determined according to the number of registered library users, and every library in Turkey had a place in the sample based on the number of registered library users. From the data gathered from the libraries, registered library users of the Project libraries numbered 434,930. Accordingly, a survey on 4,121 people resulted in a 99% confidence level with a possible 0.02 sampling error. As a result, 4,317 people from 140 libraries received the questionnaire.

The questionnaire comprised 32 questions. Most of the questions were related to an extensively used questionnaire designed by the Global Libraries Initiative, entitled Common Impact Measurement System (CIMS), born out of the necessity of analysing outcomes of similar conditions in different countries. Even though the Global Libraries Initiative does not encourage amendments to the data instrument, it allows significant adaptation based on countries' characteristics. Countries receiving grants can adapt the questionnaire to gain more efficiency. To do so, they can delete some questions to avoid potential misunderstanding, change wording of the questions, or add new questions for their own purposes. Within CIMS, in addition to demographic questions, there are seven categories: digital inclusion, education, health, e-government, culture and leisure, economic growth, and communication, under which questions are developed. Besides these questions, optional questions are also listed in CIMS. All of the question-naires were administered face-to-face in the libraries. In this way, questions from users were answered along the way. Data was also compiled on the e-government training provided as part of the Project. The results of the questionnaires, espe-cially the data on the government and governance section, are presented and the e-government training usage statistics shared in the following discussion.

Findings and Discussion

The findings are analysed under three different categories: first, users' ICT usage skills; second, responses concerning e-government and governance; and last, data gathered from the Akademi | HİK platform, the distance education system used for the Project.

Municipal Public Library Users' ICT Skill Levels

People must be computer- and internet-literate for e-transformation to occur. Even if one designs the best system, it would only be a waste of resources if there is no one to use it. For this reason, the Libraries for Everyone Project aimed to help citizens use ICT services through municipal public libraries. To do so, it is important to measure users' ICT skills. The questionnaire used questions and choices prepared by EUROSTAT which are based on conceptual definitions about people's computer and Internet usage skills. EUROSTAT (2016b) collects peo-ple's skills in three groups, low, middle, and high level. When computer and Internet usage abilities of the users are assessed, people who can perform one or two tasks are classified as low, three or four as middle, and five or six as high level. There are also people who are incapable of performing any duty. Table 2 and Table 3 provide raw data on the municipal public library users' computer and Internet usage skills and Figure 4 and Figure 5 give the levels based on EUROSTAT. People who are not capable of performing any duties are represented as inexperienced.

In Table 2, among the first five choices of users, the lowest percentage of computer skills was: Compressing, or zipping, files with 49%. There is a 40% difference between this choice and the lowest one: Writing a computer programme using a specialised programming language. Table 4 translates the findings in Table 2 into EUROSTAT's conceptualization and operationalization logic, with 37.7% of users at a high level of computer usage skills ratio, showing that the Turkish community users surveyed did not constitute a computer literate populace.

Table 2: Municipal public library users' computer usage skills.

Computer usage skills	n	%
Copying or moving a file or folder	3833	88.8
Using copy and paste tools to duplicate or move information within a document	3740	86.6
Using basic arithmetic formulas in a spreadsheet	3096	71.7
Compressing, or zipping, files	2119	49.1
Connecting and installing new devices, e.g. a modem	2636	61.1
Writing a computer program using a specialised programming language	437	10.1
None of them	411	9.5

Figure 4 shows that the percentage of municipal public library users who were inexperienced in computer usage was 10%. The question "Have you ever used a computer?" was answered as "no" by 4%. Given the number of library users who declared that they had never used a computer before, and the ones who had used a computer but picked "None of them" in the EUROSTAT skill level questions, it is clear that computer usage training should start from a basic level for a particular group.

The group of people who picked "None of them" in the EUROSTAT skill level questions was composed of comparably older people. The study clarified that 10% of municipal public library users are 46 years and older. One third of the people who chose "None of them" are also 46 years and older. The results show that it is mostly older people who have low level skills in computer usage. By offering training to this group as a part of the Project, there would be a chance of equality between old and young people.

Table 3, which shows municipal public library users' computer skills and answers to the question "Have you ever used the internet" shows municipal public library users have a higher level of Internet literacy than the rest of the public. People who picked "None of them" for their Internet skills constitute 4%. Other data (EUROSTAT 2016a) show that, even though there are differences in usage across regions, there is still a large number of people who have never used the Internet in their lives. At this point, it was considered that the Libraries for Everyone Project had a huge potential to minimize the digital divide within society. For this reason, project planning included an emphasis on library staff efforts to appeal to non-library users and people inexperienced in computer usage, by offering training and the advocacy of online training materials.

Table 3: Municipal public library users' Internet usage skills.

Internet usage skills	n	%
Using a search engine to find information	4119	95.4
Sending e-mails with attached files (documents, pictures, etc.)	3454	80.0
Posting messages to chatrooms, newsgroups, online discussion forum	3541	82.0
Using the Internet to make telephone calls	3627	84.0
Using peer-to-peer file sharing for exchanging movies, music, etc.	2928	67.8
Creating a web page	1087	25.2
None of them	173	4.0

Municipal public library users' Internet skills appeared to be better than their computer skills. While people deemed high level Internet users, in other words able to perform more than five or six skills, registered at 62% Internet usage (Figure 5), their computer usage registered at 37.7% (Figure 4). Use of mobile devices make it possible for people to benefit from the Internet without using a computer. Digital services, to be offered to the public by municipal public libraries, should be designed for use from mobile devices.

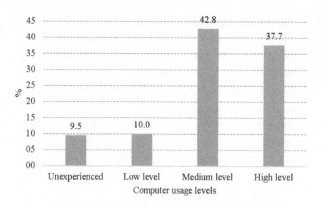

Fig. 4: Municipal public library users' computer skill levels.

As a result of the studies conducted for the Libraries for Everyone Project, it became clear that a varied series of training programs needed to be planned and implemented. It was planned to conduct some training online and to deliver some programs onsite offered both by the Project team and library staff. Curriculum content was developed using the online training platform Akademi | HİK which was extended to support training activities. In the curriculum of Akademi | HİK there are various training packages including e-government applications, safe Internet use, institutional social media use and website design. Productive use of the training modules helps move the inexperienced, low, and middle level users identified in Figures 4 and 5 to higher levels. During the design and development of the training curriculum, users' levels and their demands and choices are taken into consideration.

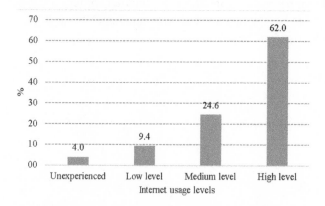

Fig. 5: Municipal public library users' Internet skill levels.

Responses Related to Government and Governance

As noted, CIMS collects data in various areas. Every single impact area within the CIMS contains various metrics. There are two types: optional and required. Within the scope of the municipal public library usage research in Turkey, only the required metrics about government and governance (Table 4) were collected. Metrics about the government and governance impact area can be found in Table 5.

Table 4: CIMS indicators related to government and governance.

Metrics	Required/Optional
# of library visitors who search for government information (e.g. laws or regulations, descriptions of government programs and services, forms, government jobs) using technology at the public library (e.g. Wi-Fi, computer, Internet, Facebook)	Required
# of library visitors who use a government service (e.g. download/fill out/ submit forms, pay taxes, request documents/licenses) through technology at the public library (e.g. Wi-Fi, computer, Internet, Facebook)	Required
# of library visitors who participate in governance processes (e.g. research politicians or citizens' rights, interact with public authorities or elected officials, learn how to volunteer for political events, participate in political movements) using technology at the public library (e.g. WiFi, computer, Internet, Facebook)	Required
# of library visitors who save time by accessing a government service using technology at the public library (e.g. Wi-Fi, computer, Internet)	Required
# of library visitors who receive money/subsidies/support owed to them by the government as a result of their ability to access government services using technology at the public library (e.g. Wi-Fi, computer, Internet)	Required
# of library visitors who share government information that they found using technology at the public library (e.g., Wi-Fi, computer, Internet)	Optional
# of library visitors who save money by accessing a government service using technology at the public library	Optional
# of library visitors who are satisfied with the government services they access using technology at the public library	Optional
# of library visitors who found a job by searching for government information using technology at the public library	Optional
# of library visitors who exercise their citizens' rights as a result of the information they found using technology at the public library	Optional

While the data about the metrics in government and governance impact area in CIMS was analysed, it was seen that important tasks were undertaken by municipal public library users. For example, with the two research questionnaires, it was found that there were 406 library users who used municipal public libraries for technology related government services. This number corresponds to 9.4% of library users (Table 5). However, the percentage was lower during an earlier pilot project named Librar-e Turkey Planning and Pilot Project with 8.5% (Al, Öz and Taşkın 2016, 8). Again, according to Table 5, while the number of library visitors who use a government service, download/fill out/submit forms, pay taxes, and request documents/licenses through technology at the public library using Wi-Fi, computer, Internet or Facebook was almost 8%, the number of library visitors who save time by accessing a government service using technology at the public library, WiFi, computer, and Internet was around 7%.

Table 5: Findings about government and governance indicators.

Metrics	n	%
# of library visitors who search for government information (e.g. laws or regulations, descriptions of government programs and services, forms, government jobs) using technology at the public library (e.g. Wi-Fi, computer, Internet, Facebook)	406	9.4
# of library visitors who use a government service (e.g., download/ fill out/ submit forms, pay taxes, request documents/licenses) through technology at the public library (e.g. Wi-Fi, computer, Internet, Facebook)	341	7.9
# of library visitors who save time by accessing a government service using technology at the public library (e.g. Wi-Fi, computer, Internet)	292	6.8
# of library visitors who participate in governance processes (e.g., research politicians or citizens' rights, interact with public authorities or elected officials, learn how to volunteer for political events, participate in political movements) using technology at the public library (e.g. Wi-Fi, computer, Internet, Facebook)	84	1.9
# of library visitors who receive money/subsidies/support owed to them by the government as a result of their ability to access government services using technology at the public library (e.g. WiFi, computer, Internet)	25	0.6

Few library users were in the category seeking to receive money/subsidies/support owed to them by the government as a result of their ability to access government services using technology at the public library or to participate in governance processes. The questionnaire was conducted during August–September 2016, which was also the planning period of the Project, hence the percentages are acceptable. Furthermore, the questionnaire showed that municipal public library users are willing to attend training to elevate their own information, skills, and experiences. To meet the demands, the Project team prepared various training programs with online options provided on the training platform Akademi | HİK.

Use of the Akademi | HİK e-Government Training Programs

There are various training topics offered through the Akademi | HİK platform, which is open access and licensed by Creative Commons 4.0 BY-NC-SA. Among the programs, there are topics like e-government applications, safe Internet and safe information, institutional social media use, basic computer use, 3D design, CV design, and website design. Moreover, popular cultural training programs, as well as specialty training, are offered through the web. Specialty training specifically related to librarianship is provided with the following courses: Marketing of Library Services, Librarianship Philosophy, Cataloging and Categorizing, and Public Library Management. Since the Project aims to help library staff gain an educator role, there are also courses entitled Class Management and Personal Development and Self-Consciousness. All courses can be found both at http://akademi.herkesicinku tuphane.org/ and the Project's YouTube channel. Seventeen short training videos related to e-government were produced for the Project, while 14 were uploaded to the YouTube channel on April 20, 2016. The total time for the 17 videos is 37 minutes 2 seconds, the longest being about the General Directorate of Security services with a time of 3 minutes 40 seconds. The reason for keeping the videos short is that audiences are unlikely to watch longer ones (Carr and Ly 2009, 417). In addition to the videos, there are also lecture notes and presentations. The usage statistics of the videos related to e-government provided on YouTube can be seen in Table 6.

Table 6: Usage statistics of training videos related to e-government.

Course	Duration	Upload date	Views	Views %
Department of Justice services	2:43	April 20, 2016	113	0.9
Family doctor information query & registration	1:19	April 20, 2016	113	0.9
Military status information	2:20	April 20, 2016	6651	54.6
Presidency communication query	1:48	April 20, 2016	127	1.0
ICT Institution services	1:21	April 20, 2016	140	1.1
e-Pulse personal health system	1:31	April 20, 2016	116	1.0
General Directorate of Security services	3:40	April 20, 2016	176	1.4
Revenue Administration services	1:10	April 20, 2016	71	0.6
İŞKUR services	3:16	April 20, 2016	730	6.0
Centralized doctor appointment system	2:14	April 20, 2016	247	2.0
Citizenship affairs services	1:37	April 20, 2016	204	1.7

Table 6: (continued)

Course	Duration	Upload date	Views	Views %
Social Security registration and services	1:29	April 20, 2016	506	4.2
Other social security services	3:13	April 20, 2016	80	0.7
Higher Education services	1:57	April 20, 2016	86	0.7
e-Government Application General Information	2:22	June 10, 2016	447	3.7
e-Government sign-up process	3:21	June 14, 2016	2302	18.9
Ministry of Education e-School system	1:41	January 18, 2017	73	0.6
Total	**37:02**		**12,182**	**100.0**

Note: Courses are listed according to their upload date.

The most visited course is Military status information, which is related to young people in the community and the user population of municipal public library users. Even though the e-Government sign-up process course was uploaded two months after the rest of the courses, it is the second most visited and accounts for almost one fifth of the entire content (Table 6). According to the feedback received from the libraries, it was learned that most people preferred to come to the library personally to sign up for e-government services, demonstrating the high level of trust accorded to the libraries.

Conclusion

Libraries for Everyone is the most extensive project conducted in Turkey in regards to municipal public libraries. With the efforts of the Project, municipal public libraries, which are not sufficiently visible in Turkey, came to the forefront. The goal of the Project was to transform municipal public libraries into centres of attraction, in which citizens can access and use computer hardware, software, and educational services that enable them to benefit from ICT resources. Accordingly, it also aimed to elevate the life quality of Turkish society, especially people who belong to disadvantaged segments.

Even though the importance of libraries has always been mentioned in the digital transformation of Turkey, concrete steps have never been taken. Since the Libraries for Everyone Project has the most solid applications in this context, it will be a guiding light for possible efforts in the future. The most important outcomes of the Project are in the field of education. It is expected from the educational activities in the Project to create a snowball effect in public libraries. The Project team trained library staff, and those library staff found a chance to apply their learnings in their own local environments. Webinars brought people together. Prepared training materials were shared through social media, and according to feedback new training materials were prepared.

As seen from the results, it cannot be expected that every training program will make the same impact or receive the same amount of attention. But analyses of feedback and the information received from various channels including face to face meetings, statistics on views of courses, and usage statistics of public access library computers, as well as additional training modules, which may have more potential of use, can be created.

Sustainability of the Project is especially important for the future of librarianship in Turkey. Partnerships created between local government and the branches of the Turkish Library Association, which is the biggest non-government organization in the field, are expected to enhance the e-transformation and digital development outcomes in Turkey both during and after the Project.

Acknowledgments

Thanks are given to the Bill & Melinda Gates Foundation for their support.

References

Açıkgöz, Orhan, and Bülent Yılmaz. "Türkiye'de Halk Kütüphanesi Hizmetlerinin Özel İdarelere Devri Konusunda Özel İdare Yöneticilerinin Görüşleri." [Opinions of Special Provincial Administration Directors on the Transferring of Public Library Services to the Special Provincial Administrations in Turkey]. *Türk Kütüphaneciliği* 27 (2013): 136–153.
Al, Umut, and Sinan Akıllı. "Public Libraries in Turkey: A Retrospective Look and the Present State." *Journal of Librarianship and Information Science* 48 (2016): 298–309.
Al, Umut, Güleda Doğan, İrem Soydal, and Zehra Taşkın. "Herkes için Kütüphane Projesi Başlangıç Çalışması." [Baseline Study of Libraries for Everyone]. *Türk Kütüphaneciliği* 31 (2017): 11–30.
Al, Umut, Seda Öz, and Zehra Taşkın. "Opportunities of Collaboration with Public Libraries on Government and Governance." Paper presented at the IFLA World Library and Information Congress: 82nd IFLA General Conference and Assembly, August 13–19, 2016, Columbus, Ohio, USA. 2016. http://library.ifla.org/1406/1/179-al-en.pdf.
Anameriç, Hakan. "Osmanlılarda Kütüphane Kültürü ve Bilimsel Yaşama Etkisi." [Library Culture in Ottomans and Its Effect on Scientific Life]. *Osmanlı Tarih Araştırma ve Uygulama Merkezi Dergisi* 19 (2006): 53–78.

Carr, Allison, and Pearl Ly. "'More than Words': Screencasting as a Reference Tool." *Reference Services Review* 37 (2009): 408–420.

Demircioğlu Faydalıgül, Özden, and Bülent Yılmaz. "Türkiye'de Halk Kütüphanesi Hizmetlerinin Yerel Yönetimlere Devri Konusunda Kütüphane Yöneticilerinin ve Kütüphanecilerin Yaklaşımları." [Opinions of Library Directors and Librarians on the Handover of Public Library Services to the Local Governments in Turkey]. Türk Kütüphaneciliği 21 (2007): 414–439.

e-Devlet Kapısı. "Devletin Kısayolu." [Shortcut of Government]. 2017. Accessed June 1, 2017. https://www.turkiye.gov.tr/.

EUROSTAT. "Information Society Statistics at Regional Level." 2016a. Accessed March 15, 2017. http://ec.europa.eu/eurostat/statistics-explained/index.php/Information_society_statistics_at_regional_level .

EUROSTAT. "Eurostat: Your key to European statistics." 2016b. Accessed March 15, 2017. http://ec.europa.eu/eurostat/.

Herkes için Kütüphane. 2017. Accessed June 1, 2017. http://www.herkesicinkutuphane.org/,

ITU. "Percentage of Individuals Using the Internet". Accessed June 1, 2017. http://www.itu.int/en/ITU-D/Statistics/Pages/default.aspx.

KYGM. "Kütüphaneler." [Libraries]. 2016. Accessed March 15, 2017. https://kygm.ktb.gov.tr/TR-131/kutuphaneler.html.

Pektaş, Ethem Kadri. "Türkiye'de Sosyal Belediyecilik Uygulamaları ve Temel Sorunlar." [Social Municipality Applications and Basic Problems in Turkey]. *Akademik İncelemeler Dergisi* 5 (2010): 4–22.

Republic of Turkey Ministry of Development. "Kalkınma Bakanlığı Özel Kalem Müdürlüğü." [Ministry of Development Private Secretariat]. 2014. Accessed June 1, 2017. http://www2.tbmm.gov.tr/d24/7/7-42105sgc.pdf.

TÜİK. "Kütüphane İstatistikleri, 2015." [Library Statistics, 2015]. 2016a. Accessed March 15, 2017. http://www.tuik.gov.tr/PreHaberBultenleri.do?id=21545.

TÜİK. "Kütüphane Türüne Göre Kütüphaneden Yararlanan Kişi, Kayıtlı Üye ve Personel Sayısı." [Number of Library Users, Registered Library Users and Library Staff According to Library Type]. 2016b. Accessed March 15, 2017. http://www.tuik.gov.tr/PreTablo.do?alt_id=1086.

TÜİK. "Hanehalkı bilişim teknolojileri kullanım araştırması." [Household information technologies usage research]. 2016c. Accessed March 15, 2017. http://www.tuik.gov.tr/PreHaberBultenleri.do?id=21779.

Yılmaz, Bülent. "Türkiye'de Halk Kütüphanelerinin Belediyelere Devrine İlişkin Çabalar Konusunda Düşüncelerim." [My Thoughts on the Efforts of the Public Libraries in Turkey to Devote to the Municipalities] *Türk Kütüphaneciliği* 27 (2013): 398–400.

Yılmaz, Bülent, Derya Baklacı, Ömer Çetin, Vuslat Güler, Yelda Güneyoğlu, and Dilek İskenderoğlu. "Türkiye'de Halk Kütüphanelerinin Yerel Yönetimlere Devredilme Süreci Üzerine Ankara Özel İdare Yöneticilerinin Düşünceleri." [Opinions of the Ankara Special Provincial Administration Directors on the Transferring Process of the Public Libraries of Turkey to Local Authorities]. *Türk Kütüphaneciliği* 24 (2010): 471–494.

Irhamni Ali

12 Public Library Development Policy in Indonesia: The Present and the Future

Abstract: Library provision in Indonesia is still below many international standards. This chapter provides an overview of the development and current state of Indonesian public libraries, paying particular attention to the location and distribution of libraries, the status of collections, the levels of staffing and human resource development, and# the nature of services provided. Several information and communication technology (ICT) projects are outlined, including the *PerpuSeru* program, a Bill and Melinda Gates Foundation Global Libraries Initiative, Indonesia OneSearch (IOS), *iPusnas*, a portal project and *ePustaka*, a mobile application. Future policy directions and strategies to provide improvements are suggested, with particular reference to the location and distribution of libraries throughout the country, the improvement of collections and infrastructure, the training and development of library staff and the provision of enhanced services.

Keywords: Public libraries – Indonesia; Library science – Technological innovations; Library planning

Introduction

Indonesia is the fourteenth largest country in the world by land area, comprises more than 17,000 islands and has the world's fourth largest population with over 267 million. The sovereign state is a presidential, constitutional republic with an elected legislature and has 34 provinces (https://en.wikipedia.org/wiki/Indonesia). The Constitution of the Republic of Indonesia aims to: protect the people and the country of Indonesia; promote the general welfare; educate the nation and participate in the establishment of the world order based on freedom, lasting peace and social justice. The Constitution, as well as stating the four pillars, refers to the independence of Indonesia and its formation as a sovereign state based on a belief in the One and Only God, just and civilized humanity, the unity of Indonesia, and democratic life led by wisdom of thought in deliberation amongst representatives of the people, and achieving social justice for all the people of Indonesia. One of the supports for implementing the constitution in educating the nation is constructing the library as a place of lifelong learning and as an education and learning centre. Libraries have been associated with creativity for almost as long as books themselves. Their function is to promote human progress by collecting,

https://doi.org/10.1515/ 9783110533323-015

preserving, and giving access to works of science and imagination. Libraries are the homes of the giants on whose shoulders Newton claimed to stand. Public libraries are at the heart of many communities. They welcome people from all backgrounds; they provide a safe space; and they often are a source of pride for the communities they serve. Throughout history, libraries have been the centre of learning, knowledge-sharing, and personal and social development.

This chapter provides an overview of the background to library developments, particularly in relation to literacy levels. The role of the library in the Indonesian education system is to support the implementation of 12-year compulsory education and elevate the figures for literacy of the population aged 15–44 years of age through the provision of information resources and knowledge so that citizens become avid readers. Library developments in Indonesia are still very far from expectations regarding quantity and quality. This chapter addresses the plight of public libraries in Indonesia with regard to human resources and collections and examines policy development of libraries by the Indonesian government in the present and the future. There are three aspects of policy discussed: access to library services; collection development; and human resource development. Recommendations are made for future improvements and developments in policy.

Literacy Levels in Indonesia

The official language is Indonesian, Bahasa Indonesia, and there are over 700 indigenous local languages (https://en.wikipedia.org/wiki/Indonesian_lan guage). A survey from the Central Connecticut State University in 2016 ranked Indonesia in sixtieth place out of 61 nations in literacy in the world (CCSU, 2016). The survey examines the World's Most Literate Nations (WMLN) and ranks nations not on their populace's ability to read but rather on literate behaviours and their supporting resources. The rankings are based on five categories standing as indicators of the literate health of nations: libraries, newspapers, education inputs and outputs, and computer availability. The multidimensional approach to literacy speaks to the social, economic, and governmental powers of nations around the globe. The literacy ranking survey includes a ranking based on libraries which includes four variables, the numbers of academic, public and school libraries and the total number of volumes held within public libraries. In the library ranking, Indonesia was rated 36.5 of the 61 countries, with China ranking sixty-first (CCSU 2016).

The *Program for International Student Assessment* (PISA) is a system of international assessments allowing countries to compare learning outcomes of students nearing the end of compulsory schooling by measuring the performance of

15-year-olds in mathematics, science and reading literacy every three years. Coordinated by the Organization for Economic Cooperation and Development (OECD), PISA included more than 70 education systems in its 2015 survey (IES NCES 2015). Indonesia was placed at 69 of 75 countries with a score of 397 on reading literacy (https://nces.ed.gov/surveys/pisa/pisa2015/pisa2015highlights_4d.asp) (IES NCES 2015). In 2015, the National Library of Indonesia surveyed reading across Indonesia and found low scores with an average of 25.3 out of 100 (Perpustakaan Nasional RI 2015c). Behind the irony of these poor results, Indonesia has great opportunities as a developing country. The World Economic Forum through its Global Competitiveness Report in 2016 rated Indonesia at 41 in a total of 138 countries. The report notes that its performance remains one of contrasts, performing well in terms of financial development at 42, up seven, but ranking a low 100 in health and basic education (World Education Forum 2016, 29).

Libraries in Indonesia

The library in Indonesia and elsewhere plays a significant part in supporting national education and contributing to the advancement of the community through encouraging superior, intelligent, critical, innovative and evidence-based learning, strengthening the culture and mind-set in line with the Indonesian agenda. Indonesia is headed towards expected growth and transformation involving new ways of thinking and innovative approaches. Indonesia seeks to be a sovereign state, independent politically, economically and socio-culturally through the development of an informed, cultured and well-read society. Indonesia has about 467 public libraries at the district/municipal level and 34 public libraries at the provincial level and the policies of the Indonesian government in the provinces are discussed here. A survey conducted by the Center of Library Development and Reading Habit Enhancement, National Library of Indonesia in 2016 recorded the number of libraries in Indonesia by type, stating that there were some 154.360 libraries in Indonesia (Table 1).

Table 1: Total Number of Libraries in Indonesia.

No.	Library Type	Total
1	National Library	1
2	Public Library	23,611
a.	Provincial Public Library	34
b.	Municipal Public Library	467
c.	District Public Library	600

Table 1: (continued)

No.	Library Type	Total
d.	Village Public Library	21,467
e.	Community Public Library	693
f.	Reading Corner	351
3	**Special Library**	7.132
4	**School Library**	121,187
a.	Elementary School Library	100,000
b.	Junior High School Library	12,000
c.	Senior High School Library	6,599
d.	Religious Boarding School Library	2,588
5	**University Library**	2,428
	Total	**154,360**

The IFLA Library Map of the World (https://librarymap.ifla.org/map/Metric/Number-of-libraries/LibraryType/National-Libraries,Academic-Libraries,Public-Libraries,Community-Libraries,School-Libraries,Other-Libraries/Country/Indonesia/Weight/Totals-by-Country) provides the following data dated 2018 on libraries in Indonesia, with the data supplied by the National Library of Indonesia.

Table 2: IFLA Library Map of the World number of libraries.

Type of Library	Number
National	4
Academic	2,057
Public	42,460
School	13,541
Other	6,552
Total	**164,614**

What is the current government policy in public libraries on access to library services, collection development and human resources development? What are potential actions the Indonesian government might take in the future?

Assessment of Public Libraries

Public libraries have been built on a central ideal: to make available shared, principally print-based, resources that can be used by all members of the community to stimulate imagination and inquiry and nurture the development of culture and commerce. Libraries offer a range of products and services that are open to all and, it is hoped, will benefit those who are least able to afford purchasing similar services. It is the combination of community and choices, provided by publicly supported funding for private benefit, that makes the concept of the public library so special.

There has been strong interest within the library and information science (LIS) community in conducting outcome assessments, which provide valuable information on specific programs and services, and on specific library systems and locales. Nationwide public library surveys (OCLC 2011; Rainie 2014) have focused on the perception and use of public libraries. There are few recent nationwide studies which have examined the ideal form of public libraries. The following examines the ideal form of public libraries from the perspectives of their location and distribution, collections, human resources and services.

Location and Distribution of Public Libraries

One of the clear challenges facing a library in any community is where to locate it and, at some point as the size of the community grows, where to place additional library facilities. A plethora of studies has examined the importance of distance as a factor in determining use of a library. The principal conclusion of these studies is that the impact of distance is not a simple and constant factor; rather, that impact is influenced by the socioeconomic status of the community, the age of the residents, and the characteristics of the library itself and any barriers to access that naturally occur, for example, a river, a freeway, and so forth. The use of a library by children is clearly affected by distance. The closer a child lives to a library, the more likely he or she is to use it, whereas an adult is willing to travel farther, especially if the library is particularly appealing for some reason.

In medium- and large-sized communities, the assumption is often made that a central or main library building is needed. This ignores two very important and fundamental questions that should be asked. First, is a central library really needed? The answer will depend on the needs of the community being served. In addition, it is important to recognize that the library does not exist in a vacuum.

Some communities are surrounded by good public libraries that are located in other jurisdictions. One of the successes achieved by library distributions undertaken by the National Library Board (NLB) in Singapore is that the NLB is responsible for the operation of all public libraries, the National Library and Archives, government agency libraries, and one polytechnic library. In 2000 the

National Library Board began transforming itself by reinventing libraries from the outside in. The mission for the library is to expand the learning capacity of the nation. The service vision is to deliver services that are convenient, accessible, affordable, and useful. The transformation focused on four building blocks: content, services, people, and infrastructure.

The public libraries in Singapore used the transformation opportunity to prototype new facilities and services rather than relying on plain vanilla libraries. The test beds allowed staff to improve on the prototypes, and the successful ideas and concepts were then incorporated into new buildings and rolled out to existing branches. NLB manages twenty-six public libraries. The use of the facilities in Singapore jumped substantially from 2000 to 2006: annual visits increased from 5.7 million to 38 million; circulation went from 10 million to 29 million; and inquiries multiplied, from 50,000 to 2.8 million. Like many library systems, Singapore has built three very large regional libraries of about 120,000 square feet in size that contain a collection of some 500,000 items.

Collections in Public Libraries

Over time, a library will invest a significant amount of money in creating and maintaining its collection, both physical and electronic. Despite the fact that the physical collection is sitting on shelving and directly accessible to the library customer, it can remain, for the most part, an almost invisible resource. The public library, as the centre of information in the community, makes all kinds of knowledge and information available to library users:
- All age groups must have access to sufficient, high quality material relevant to their needs, both current and potential, with respect to literacy, culture, education, recreation, and information
- Collections and services have to include all types of appropriate media and modern technologies as well as traditional materials
- Collections should not be subject to any form of ideological, political or religious censorship, nor commercial pressure (paraphrased from the IFLA/UNESCO Public Library Manifesto, https://www.ifla.org/publications/ifla unesco-public-library-manifesto-1994.

Libraries strive to provide access to a balanced and relevant collection. To achieve this, the library has a collection development policy that covers selecting and withdrawing materials, accepting donations, and addressing challenges to materials. Collection development policies should be reviewed at least every three years. Additionally, community assessments must be carried out regularly to

ensure the collection meets the needs of the community. The collection development policy should be influenced by the following:
- Plan of service
- Population demographics
- Age of collection
- Collection specialties and purchase priorities
- Demand as measured by circulation per capita
- Presence/access to other collections.

Collection size is dependent on the size of population served. However, no matter what size of community it serves, a library should have a base collection of at least 2,500 books. As a general guide, an established book collection should be between 1.5 to 2.5 books per capita. All library materials are kept current with the majority being less than five years old. The periodical collection should be 0.005 to 0.01 per capita for libraries up to 10,000 and 0.003 to 0.005 per capita for 10,000 or more. Smaller libraries may have a higher per capita collection size in order to respond to patron demands. The number of print subscriptions will be impacted by the number of electronic subscriptions available. The non-print collection includes all audio-visual and audio-media collections, such as audio-books, play-away, and DVDs. It might not include any downloadable material. The general rule of thumb is 0.25 to 0.50 per capita.

Human Resources in Public Libraries

It seems so obvious: the future of the library is directly tied to the quality and talent of the library staff. Like most organizations today, the library faces real competition from digital start-up companies who are content providers. People are much more informed because they have access to a wealth of information via their mobile and Internet access. Although attracting top talented librarians is very important, it is equally important to find librarians that work and relate well to other library staff as well as users. Staff is a vitally important resource in the operation of a library. Staff expenses normally represent a high proportion of a library's budget. In order to provide the best possible service to the community, it is necessary to maintain well-trained and highly motivated staff to make effective use of the resources of the library and to meet the demands of the community. Staff should be available in sufficient numbers to carry out the identified responsibilities.

Public libraries should endorse qualified librarians as staff who have undertaken a course of study in librarianship and information studies to degree or postgraduate level. A librarian designs, plans, organizes, implements, manages and evaluates library and information services and systems to meet the needs of the users of library and information services in the community. Activities undertaken include collection development, the organization and exploitation of resources, the provision of advice and assistance to users in finding and using information and the development of systems that will facilitate access to the library's resources.

The number of staff required in each library service will be affected by a range of factors, for example, the number of library buildings, their size and layout, the number of departments within each building, the level of use, the services provided beyond the library and requirements for specialist staff. Where some services are provided or supplemented by a regional or national central agency this will have an impact on the number of staff required at local level. The level of available resources is also a critical factor. Allowing for these and other local differences, the following basic staffing level (excluding support staff) is recommended:

- One full-time equivalent member of staff for 2,500 population
- One-third of staff should be qualified librarians.

These are basic recommended levels, which will be affected by local circumstances. Where reliable population figures are not available, staffing levels can be related to the size of the library, the range of its functions, and the number of users. Another method of developing an appropriate staffing level for a library service is to carry out benchmarking with libraries of comparative size and similar characteristics (Gill 2001).

The Australian Library and Information Association provides guidelines to assist local authorities (ALIA 2012). Included are details on requirements for numbers of staff and their qualifications to encourage consistency of service delivery across the nation. A regional library staffing model should reflect the regional library agreement. One of the Australian states, New South Wales, provides *Living Learning Libraries*, an evidence-based guide to the development of library services in the state. Written in two parts, it provides a practical basis for the comparison among library services, as well as a framework for service assessment and continuous improvement. It states that the distribution of staff across the different councils should be consistent with the distribution of responsibilities (Library Council of New South Wales 2014). Table 3 shows the following standard and staffing for libraries funded through the Library Council of New South Wales.

Table 3: Staffing of Libraries in New South Wales, Australia.

Population	Qualified staffing level		
	Minimum qualified staffing level	Enhanced qualified staffing level	Exemplary qualified staffing level
<50,000	For every 7,500 people or part thereof, one of the full-time equivalent staff should be a qualified staff member.	For every 5,000 people or part thereof, one of the full-time equivalent staff should be a qualified staff member.	For every 4,000 people or part thereof, one of the full-time equivalent staff should be a qualified staff member.
>50,000	For every 10,000 people or part thereof, one of the full-time equivalent staff should be a qualified staff member.	For every 7,500 people or part thereof, one of the full-time equivalent staff should be a qualified staff member.	For every 5,000 people or part thereof, one of the full-time equivalent staff should be a qualified staff member.

Many libraries in Australia, particularly those serving large populations and populations including significant numbers of people from culturally diverse backgrounds, require a higher proportion of qualified staff because the range of programs and special services offered are both more varied and greater in number. Such libraries are likely to exceed the standards. It is acknowledged that many rural libraries have significant difficulties in recruiting qualified staff members. Local authorities are advised to employ the most appropriate mix possible of professional and paraprofessional library staff (Library Council of New South Wales 2014, 9).

The importance of recruiting, training, and involving staff in co-creating a customer-focused library cannot be overstated. In the end, it is staff who will be delivering a set of services, and the manner in which they do this, and their attitudes, will determine in the eyes of the customer whether the library is successful. The public library is a dynamic organization working with other institutions and individuals to provide a range of library and information services to meet the varied and changing needs of the community. To be effective, it requires experienced, flexible and well-trained managers and staff able to use a range of management techniques.

Services Provided by Public Libraries

Libraries reach out to communities in many ways. The make-up of communities is changing, and libraries must make sure they keep up with the changes, with new needs and expectations. Libraries play or have the potential to play an important role in local communities for everyone, but in particular for those who are most vulnerable in deprived areas. One of the difficulties facing a library is that in its desire to provide efficient services to communities, the service itself becomes fairly routine or generic. A generic service is not a good way to differentiate the library from its competitors. The challenge is to design a service encounter that is meaningful and a pleasant experience. A service experience can be great if three things are present: visibility, customer engagement, and positive feelings and perceptions (Matthews 2009).

Public libraries need to be transformed to become much more proactive, interventionist and educational institutions, with a concern for social justice at their core. The specific strategies for such a transformation have been identified as the mainstreaming of provision for socially excluded groups and communities and the establishment of standards of service and their monitoring; the adoption of resourcing strategies which prioritize the needs of excluded people and communities; a recasting of the role of library staff to encompass a more socially responsive and educational approach; staffing policies and practices which address exclusion, discrimination, and prejudice; targeting of excluded social groups and communities; the development of community-based approaches to library provision, which incorporate consultation with and partnership with local communities; ICT and networking developments which actively focus on the needs of excluded people; a recasting of the image and identity of the public library to link it more closely with the cultures of excluded communities and social groups (Pateman 2003).

Libraries must provide services and materials which are targeted to meet the needs of particular customer groups served by the library. Such customer groups may include individuals of all ages who often face barriers to their use of public library services. Barriers may be physical, as in the case of older people, persons with physical or developmental disabilities and those who are homebound or institutionalized or who live in residential care facilities (Library Council of New South Wales 2014, 51). There may be diverse groups which are invisible members of the community. Good planning will identify all of the library's potential constituencies, including individuals with special needs. The library can then develop specific strategies for reaching them and for providing appropriate services, materials and resources. Public libraries should develop over the decades. It is clear that in working with socially excluded groups it is important that:

- Services are targeted towards specific needy groups and individuals
- Services are provided in partnership with local communities
- Staff are given thorough and on-going support and training
- Services are sustainable
- Socially excluded groups have a separate service.

Public Libraries in Indonesia

Location and Distribution

According to the IFLA/UNESCO Public Library Manifesto published in 1994, the public library is the local centre of information, making all kinds of knowledge and information readily available to its users. The services of the public library are provided with equal access to all, regardless of age, race, sex, religion, nationality, language or social status. Certain services and materials must be provided for those users who cannot, for whatever reason, use the regular services and materials, for example, linguistic minorities, people with disabilities or people in hospital or prison. All age groups must find content relevant to their needs. Collections and services have to include all types of appropriate media and modern technologies as well as traditional materials. High quality and relevance to local needs and conditions are fundamental. The materials should reflect current trends and the evolution of society, as well as the memory of the efforts and imagination of humanity. Collections and services should never be subject to ideological, political or religious censure, and much less the pressure of commercial interests.

The IFLA/UNESCO Public Library Manifesto has been adopted by Indonesia in its Library Act of 2007. The Act has declared that libraries should provide community access to information and knowledge; the library is a public service institution required to provide services to the community. People have the same right to obtain services, harness and utilize the library facilities. People in remote areas, isolated or disadvantaged as a result of geographic factors, are entitled to full library services. People who are disabled by physical, emotional, mental, intellectual, or social circumstances have the right to receive library services according to their capabilities and limitations (Perpustakaan Nasional RI. 2007).

Public libraries are situated in the capitals of the 34 provinces and districts as well as in the 416 municipalities, and in the 7,024 districts and 81,626 villages. Public libraries are managed by the respective local governments. Before the autonomy act in 2001, the regional libraries were based on Presidential Decree no. 50/1998 and constituted the National Library in the Province. They became public libraries providing service to all in the community, alongside deposit libraries and local library development, as well as technical assistance in the form of manpower training and library managerial guidance building. In the district or municipal level, many public libraries are managed by district governments, houses of worship, and community effort bodies.

Mobile libraries are organized to support and accelerate public library services, especially for remote rural areas out of reach of conventional library services. They distribute information through mobile vehicles, operating specially designed trucks, mini vans, motorcycles and even bicycles for use on the land, and floating libraries using boats for cruising the rivers in the hinterlands of Riau and Kalimantan provinces. Libraries are located at the mosques, churches, temples, and are also treated as part of the public library because the services and collections are provided for the community. As the effort in developing education in society, especially in the villages, and as reading interest grows in society, the National Library of Indonesia has offered support for rural libraries by giving collections of books to approximately 10,000 out of 70,000 villages, according to the geographical and cultural backgrounds of the villages, providing technical support for the management of rural libraries and giving 259 mobile library vehicles.

Indonesia stretches between the equivalent of London and Tehran, making appropriate distribution of public libraries challenging. A survey in 2016 by the National Library of Indonesia found that the distribution of libraries in all parts of Indonesia was uneven and there were problems in ensuring that communities across the region received adequate library services. The distribution of public libraries in the various provinces can be seen in Table 4.

Table 4: Population and public libraries in Indonesia.

No.	Province	Population	Public Libraries
	Sumatera	**55,272,900**	**8,384**
1	Aceh	5,002,000	1,763
2	North Sumatera	13,937,800	905
3	Riau	6,344,400	522
4	Riau Islands	1,973,000	128
5	Bengkulu	1,874,900	429
6	West Sumatera	5,196,300	344
7	Jambi	3,402,100	1,719
8	South Sumatera	8,052,300	1,710
9	Bangka Belitung	1,372,800	115
10	Lampung	8,117,300	749
	Java	**145,143,600**	**5,881**
11	Banten	11,955,200	445
12	Special Region Of Capitol Jakarta	10,177,900	82
13	West Java	46,709,600	445
14	Central Java	33,774,100	2,382
15	Special Region of Yogyakarta	3,679,200	135
16	East Java	38,847,600	2,392

Table 4: (continued)

No.	Province	Population	Public Libraries
	Borneo	**15,342,900**	**2,038**
17	West Borneo	4,789,600	298
18	Central Borneo	2,495,000	565
19	South Borneo	3,989,800	588
20	East Borneo	3,426,600	140
21	North Borneo	641,900	447
	Celebes	**18,724,000**	**3,009**
22	North Celebes	2,412,100	525
23	Gorontalo	1,133,200	211
24	Central Celebes	2,876,700	573
25	South East Celebes	2,499,500	637
26	West Celebes	1,282,200	188
27	South Celebes	8,520,300	875
	Bali dan Nusa Tenggara	**14,108,500**	**1,478**
28	Bali	4,152,800	204
29	West Nusa Tenggara	4,835,600	328
30	East Nusa Tenggara	5,120,100	946
	Mollucas	**2,848,800**	**694**
31	Mollucas	1,686,500	355
32	North Mollucas	1,162,300	339
	Papua	**4,020,900**	**2,127**
33	Papua	3,149,400	1,589
34	West Papua	871,500	538
	Total	**255,461,600**	**23,611**

In general, the ratio of the numbers of libraries in comparison to the number of residents per provincial average was insufficient and community needs could not be equitably served. Comparison of the distribution of the availability of libraries in each province can clearly be seen in the graph below in Figure 1.

Based on the figures, it appears that the most widely spread availability of the libraries is in the province of Central Java, followed secondly by West Java and thirdly East Java. The least widely spread availability of libraries was in West Sulawesi (Celebes), then North Maluku (Mollucas) and next the new provinces, namely North Borneo. The chart data distribution indicates that the western region of Indonesia, Java and Sumatra, is in the highest position in terms of distribution of libraries. Meanwhile, the eastern region of Indonesia had low numbers. The focus of library development needs to change its orientation, to ensure application of the principles of equity and justice, particularly in eastern Indonesia.

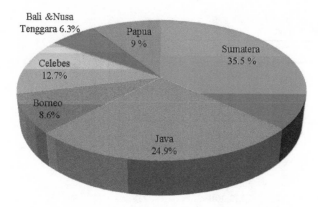

Fig. 1: Public library distribution based on the large islands in Indonesia.

Collections in Indonesian Public Libraries

The various types of public libraries in Indonesia are indicated in Table 1. There are six types: provincial, municipal, district, village, community and reading corner. The public library has two roles, to prepare the community for the future and to transmit the heritage of the past. Selectors of library materials attempt to cover a broad range of formats, subjects, and viewpoints with their selections. Selectors will also attempt to reflect the library's mission when choosing materials for the collection. The library's collection is a constantly changing entity. Various library departments, staff, and users interact with the collection.

A survey of library collections in public libraries in Indonesia in 2016 found there were 76,096,908 copies of books owned by public libraries in Indonesia. The distribution of the largest library collections was dominated by the provinces located in the west area of Indonesia with collections becoming smaller in the east area of Indonesia. The distribution of public libraries in Indonesia is still dominated in the western region of Indonesia and the distribution of the collections owned by the libraries has not been evenly matched against the number of inhabitants in each province. The availability of library materials collections compared to the number of library users served appears in Table 5.

The table shows that all public libraries in Indonesia do not have collection adequacy. The standard adequacy ratio ideal for collections in a public library according to the Public Library Manifesto is 2:1 for the population. Based on calculating the adequacy ratio of the ideal collection by the standards, there is a shortage in the collections of 434,826,292 copies in public libraries in Indonesia. The collections that are currently available at public libraries in Indonesia on

Table 5: Indonesia populations and public library collections.

No.	Province	Population	Collection	Ideal Collection
1	Aceh	5,002,000	1,360,921	10,004,000
2	North Sumatera	13,937,800	2,416,108	27,875,600
3	Riau	6,344,400	688,798	12,688,800
4	Riau Islands	1,973,000	702,593	3,946,000
5	Bengkulu	1,874,900	781,804	3,749,800
6	West Sumatera	5,196,300	1,679,056	10,392,600
7	Jambi	3,402,100	725,936	6,804,200
8	South Sumatera	8,052,300	2,483,881	16,104,600
9	Bangka Belitung	1,372,800	699,242	2,745,600
10	Lampung	8,117,300	1,321,988	16,234,600
11	Banten	11,955,200	1,810,592	23,910,400
12	Special Region Of Capitol Jakarta	10,177,900	748,090	20,355,800
13	West Java	46,709,600	7,257,761	93,419,200
14	Central Java	33,774,100	13,186,604	67,548,200
15	Special Region of Yogyakarta	3,679,200	3,783,581	7,358,400
16	East Java	38,847,600	13,359,485	77,695,200
17	West Borneo	4,789,600	1,123,528	9,579,200
18	Central Borneo	2,495,000	787,449	4,990,000
19	South Borneo	3,989,800	1,850,645	7,979,600
20	East Borneo	3,426,600	1,220,836	6,853,200
21	North Borneo	641,900	221,788	1,283,800
22	North Celebes	2,412,100	298,867	4,824,200
23	Gorontalo	1,133,200	733,149	2,266,400
24	Central Celebes	2,876,700	1,541,569	5,753,400
25	South East Celebes	2,499,500	1,279,313	4,999,000
26	West Celebes	1,282,200	64,170	2,564,400
27	South Celebes	8,520,300	4,577,246	17,040,600
28	Bali	4,152,800	3,753,132	8,305,600
29	West Nusa Tenggara	4,835,600	931,371	9,671,200
30	Esat Nusa Tenggara	5,120,100	2,434,233	10,240,200
31	Moluccas	1,686,500	326,279	3,373,000
32	North Mollucas	1,162,300	1,167,423	2,324,600
33	Papua	3,149,400	344,241	6,298,800
34	West Papua	871,500	435,229	1,743,000
Total		**255,461,600**	**76,096,908**	**510,923,200**

(Perpustakaan Nasional RI, 2015d)

average are still far from what is desired and constitute only 18% of what the collections should be. Public libraries have very serious problems and operate at a significant disadvantage due to limited access to sources of knowledge. There is consequently an adverse impact on the development of literacy levels in almost all parts of Indonesia.

Human Resources in Indonesian Public Libraries

Public libraries are tied to the needs of society in all regions of the country. Public libraries have a powerful and major role to play in delivering services to users with various professional backgrounds, age, gender, social status and economic circumstances. The quality of library service provided affects the perception and the amount of use of the public library as a public space for the community to interact, innovate and gain inspiration. Public libraries are scattered throughout the country and regions, at various levels ranging from village, county/city, province and central Indonesia in Jakarta.

According to the Indonesia Library Act, article 29 states that library personnel comprise librarians and library technical personnel. A librarian is someone who has competencies acquired through education and training in librarianship and who has a duty and responsibility in the management of library services. Librarians' qualifications are ratified by standards set by the National Library. In the management of libraries, librarians are assisted by technical personnel. As for the technical staff of the library, it is primarily non-librarians who provide the technical support and ensure the implementation of library functions; for example, there are computer technical personnel, audio-visual technical personnel, and administrative technical personnel. The quality of library personnel has an important role in enhancing the satisfaction of library users. Users judge the quality of their library visits on the competence and professionalism of library staff. Staff competence and professionalism of the library can be increased by appropriate programs of education and training in librarianship, as well as through the evaluation of library staff through competency testing and certification assessment. The distribution of the number of library personnel in all provinces in Indonesia can be seen in the following table.

Table 6: Indonesian population and librarians.

No.	Province	Population	Librarians
1	Aceh	5,002,000	27
2	North Sumatera	13,937,800	48
3	Riau	6,344,400	41
4	Riau Islands	1,973,000	3
5	Bengkulu	1,874,900	13

Table 6: (continued)

No.	Province	Population	Librarians
6	West Sumatera	5,196,300	14
7	Jambi	3,402,100	30
8	South Sumatera	8,052,300	35
9	Bangka Belitung	1,372,800	14
10	Lampung	8,117,300	12
11	Banten	11,955,200	9
12	Special Region Of Capitol Jakarta	10,177,900	274
13	West Java	46,709,600	49
14	Central Java	33,774,100	86
15	Special Region of Yogyakarta	3,679,200	44
16	East Java	38,847,600	68
17	West Borneo	4,789,600	8
18	Central Borneo	2,495,000	27
19	South Borneo	3,989,800	26
20	East Borneo	3,426,600	17
21	North Borneo	641,900	0
22	North Celebes	2,412,100	26
23	Gorontalo	1,133,200	0
24	Central Celebes	2,876,700	24
25	South East Celebes	2,499,500	19
26	West Celebes	1,282,200	0
27	South Celebes	8,520,300	81
28	Bali	4,152,800	37
29	West Nusa Tenggara	4,835,600	30
30	Esat Nusa Tenggara	5,120,100	16
31	Moluccas	1,686,500	13
32	North Mollucas	1,162,300	0
33	Papua	3,149,400	17
34	West Papua	871,500	0
Total		**255,461,700**	**855**

The data provided in Table 6 records the number of librarians employed in public libraries operated by the government in Indonesia with a total of 855 librarians. There are many librarians who work in the private sector and are not included in the survey. When compared with the number of potential users of public libraries, that is the total population, the number of public library staff should ideally be as many as 102,185 people. The ratio of public library staff to the population according to the IFLA guidelines is 1:2,500. There is a shortage in public libraries of as many as 101,050 people. Public libraries are understaffed across almost all provinces in Indonesia. It is feared that the impact of insufficient staff on the quality of public library service is significant and the library's aims in educating the community cannot be realized.

The Indonesian Government Regulation No. 24 of 2014, concerning the implementation of Library Act article 25, states that librarians, library technical personnel, experts in the field of librarianship and head librarians must have qualifications and competence to perform the various tasks. The IFLA/UNESCO directives for the development of public libraries include a list of the main qualities and aptitudes required of the personnel working in the public library. These include:
- The ability to communicate positively with people
- Capacity to understand the needs of the users
- The ability to cooperate with persons and groups in the community
- Knowledge and understanding of cultural diversity
- Knowledge of the material comprising the library collection and how to gain access to it
- Knowledge of the principles of public service and ability to adhere to them
- The ability work with others to provide effective library services
- Flexible organizational aptitudes allowing for implementation of changes
- Imagination, vision, and openness to new ideas and practices
- The ability to modify work methods to respond to new situations
- Knowledge of information and communications technology.

The numbers of librarians employed in Indonesian public libraries need to be increased and their training and development enhanced if public libraries are to play their appropriate role in the communities they serve.

Services in Indonesian Public Libraries

Public librarians work in their communities to serve all members of the public. They help patrons find books to read for pleasure; conduct research for school-work, business, or personal interest; and learn how to access the library's resources. Many public librarians plan programs for users, such as story time for children, book clubs, or other educational activities. Developing digital trends in public libraries emphasize that the quantity and speed of information, as well as interactive ways of accessing and delivering information, are changing. The service context shows that declining budget support and growing needs for public library services are impacting on the growth and life in local communities. Social interaction exchanges and shares information so that "crowdsourcing enables more uses, sharing, problem-solving through concentrated burst of information sharing" (Bertot 2012).

Public library services play a strategic role in the construction of the social fabric of a country in cultural and educational development. In reality, the mission and objectives of the public library relate to free service, inclusion and the broad base of knowledge covered by the collection, among other things. Other features and tasks of the public library include:

-   Storage, organization, and supply of information contained in any documentary support issued by authorized, reliable sources
-   Making local and global information available that is useful to the community it serves. This suggests that it must face constant challenges regarding access, coverage, breadth and depth.
-   Providing cultural and artistic services that allow the population to acquire, grow and share knowledge for their personal development.
-   The educational function positions the library as a high calibre institution, in that through its services it helps form a better informed, more participative, fair and free society.

Based on the national standards, a public library should have general public services, reference services, serial publication services and Internet services. Nowadays the services are insufficient to serve people in the area. There are some programs that have been carried out throughout the years by the libraries and institutions concerned. However, the impact of such programs is still low and does not touch the grassroots in remote areas which really need such programs to help them in improving their lives. Reading habits are a problem. In other cases, lack of reading material is a problem (Kamil 2003).

Indonesia faces numerous problems in library services. One of its problems is its geographical situation. As already noted, Indonesia is a country with over 260 million inhabitants and 17,000 islands, 8,000 of which are inhabited. More than 25% of Indonesia's people live on remote islands. The role of bookmobiles in Indonesia has already been mentioned. Mobile libraries are often used to provide library services to villages and city suburbs that otherwise do not have access to a local or neighbourhood branch library. They can also service groups or individuals who have difficulty accessing libraries, for example, occupants of retirement homes. As well as regular books, a bookmobile might carry large print books, audiobooks, other media, IT equipment, and Internet access. The floating library service has been mentioned. The National Library of Indonesia (NLI) is giving stimulus donations to seven public libraries to provide a floating library service program. The program has done well, but experienced operational problems because it is a very expensive program. A recommendation from research undertaken is that NLI should seek cooperation between the of Indonesian Navy and the Coastguard to disseminate public library service in isolated islands in Indonesia (Ali and Rachmawati 2013). Besides mobile libraries, the Indonesian government is expanding access to library services to rural areas through stimulating activity with village library programs. These started in 2007 and are carried out through the allocation of funds from NLI. Funds are used to help the village libraries with facilities and infrastructure, as well as collection development and technical guidance.

Delivery of effective village library services has experienced many technical problems. One of the obstacles is the lack of budget at the local level. The main reason is that there is no legal basis for the budget for the village library which has a great impact on development, especially on collection development and human resources. The Indonesian government established the reading garden program to support village libraries in 2005. While there was much enthusiasm about the autonomous reading gardens, it was considered that "community reading gardens are still not successful in carrying out their function as places to increase reading interest and reading culture in the community, especially for new literates, because of several factors. The causes are, amongst others: the managers of reading gardens are not creative enough, they are not skilled enough, not dedicated enough, with the result that the community's desire to read, and to utilize the reading garden, is still not strong enough" (Håklev 2010).

Development of Public Library Policy in Indonesia

Policies put in place by the Indonesian government to strengthen library development in Indonesia have been touched on throughout this discussion. To ensure people can have access to the library, Indonesia is continuing its policy for library development based on collaborative programs involving local government and local community. Some of the collaborations include, from 2008 to 2014, 454 local government grants to the district libraries to develop their collections and provide hardware and software as well as training for librarians and staff. Extensive collaboration has been undertaken with local communities in villages, in coastal and border regions and in religious communities to support the national community program of improving reading habits and to facilitate public information access. From 2007 to 2014, the collaborative village library program supported 21,467 villages from 81,626 villages with books on subjects relevant to their needs, library facilities, and technical training. Collaboration with coastal and border regions since 2009 has supported 160 libraries in remote islands/border regions and 76 libraries in coastal areas. Collaboration with the religious community by the National Library has seen support for 402 religious dormitory school libraries in 33 provinces. Policy development possibilities in collection development, human resources and library services are now outlined.

Collection Development

Policies on collection development ensure the improvement of the quality of library services through the provision of sufficient and appropriate library materials to meet the needs of library users. The library is a mediator or intermediary that brings together the needs of users with a collection available in the library. Libraries should be able to save the cultural treasures of the nation or the community where the library is located, and also increase the value and appreciation of the culture of the surrounding community through the provision of reading materials (Suwarno 2007). Future effective library collection development policies should include:

- Acquiring library materials in conventional and digital formats
- Increasing the availability of collections in the distribution of various types of libraries in the region
- Providing incentives for the translation of foreign works that are important for the development of science and technology in Indonesia
- Providing incentives for publishing important works of Indonesian writers working for the development of science and culture of Indonesia
- Increasing the availability and accessibility of library materials through digital libraries and mobile libraries based on ICT
- Developing a collection of library materials based on social inclusion
- Crowdsourcing building of content based on cultural repository-based social inclusion through archival institutions, private organizations, social media, oral history and local history
- Increasing the provision of digital books
- Increasing assistance to both conventional and digital libraries, especially in the eastern region of Indonesia.

Human Resources

Human resources in the library contribute an important pillar and should develop according to the needs of the library. Developing human resources in a library must be attentive to the needs of the organization, the availability of facilities and infrastructure, costs, materials available, recruitment and selection processes amongst other factors. Economical and practical elements must be considered. Coaching and management skills are required and will affect the morale of employees.

The staff are a vitally important resource in the operation of a library. All staff should have a clear understanding of the policy of the library service, well-defined duties, and responsibilities, as well as properly regulated conditions of employment and salaries that are competitive with other similar jobs. The fundamental qualities and skills required of public library staff have been previously highlighted and can be further defined as:

- Ability to communicate positively with people
- Ability to understand the needs of users
- Ability to cooperate with individuals and groups in the community
- Knowledge and understanding of cultural diversity
- Knowledge of the material that forms the library's collection and how to access it an understanding of and sympathy with the principles of public service
- Ability to work with others in providing an effective library service
- Organizational skills, with the flexibility to identify and implement
- Imagination, vision, and openness to new ideas and practice
- Readiness to change methods of working to meet new situations
- Knowledge of information and communications technology.

Librarians with expertise in specific areas, for example, children's librarians, information officers, and reference librarians, are required to meet the demands of library users. A variety of training and education is required to improve the skills, knowledge, attitudes and images of librarians and ensure appropriate competence with other professions. Professional development of librarians in Indonesia has not been undertaken by the professional association but primarily by the National Library of Indonesia. One of the main tasks of the National Library of Indonesia is to provide human resource development. To do so, the National Library conducts various types of education and training activities, including general library training, library automation, bibliography, and conservation training. The role of the National Library in the field of human resource development is by improving librarians through strengthening functionality and giving credit points as well as providing training to all librarians and library staff in Indonesia.

NLI has increased the number and qualifications of library personnel who have the competence to provide training. Operational steps are performed through:

- Cooperating with relevant institutions including the Ministries of Education, Religious Affairs, Homeland Affairs, and Research and Higher Education, to increase the number and quality of library personnel as required
- Preparation and development of the curriculum and instructional materials
- Accreditation of education and training
- Development of educational and training facilities
- Education and training of library personnel
- Implementation of systems using ICT and training ICT-based library personnel
- Increased competence of the faculty providing training in librarianship.

Another policy taken to increase human resources in the public library is an increase in the number of certified librarians. Operational steps undertaken are:
- Development of guidelines and standards of competence for librarians
- Development of competence and certification schemes for librarians and the assessment team
- Development and popularization of what constitutes a functional librarian
- Coordination of developing the functional librarian program
- Strengthening the librarianship through a grant system assessment
- Selection of librarians' achievements
- Development of data systems librarianship Indonesia
- Facilitating and strengthening assessors and accreditation agencies for librarians at central and local levels.

Services

To ensure nation-wide library coordination and cooperation, legislation and strategic plans must define and promote a national library network based on agreed standards of service. The public library network must be designed around national, regional, research and special libraries as well as libraries in schools, colleges, and universities. Services have to be physically accessible to all members of the community. Excellent library buildings, good reading and study facilities, as well as relevant technologies and sufficient opening hours convenient to the users are required. Outreach services must be available for those unable to visit the library. The library services must be adapted to the different needs of communities in rural and urban areas (Gill 2001). To be successful in fulfilling its goals, the public library service must be fully accessible to all its potential users. Services must be able to adjust and develop to reflect changes in society, for example, variations in family structures, employment patterns, demographic changes, cultural diversity and methods of communication and should take account of traditional cultures as well as new technologies, supporting oral communication as well as making use of ICT. In some countries the services that the public library must provide are defined in legislation.

Library legislation in Indonesia proscribes services to be provided. Article 4 of the Library Act includes emphasising people to read to broaden their horizons and knowledge to achieve a better life. Meanwhile Article 5 points 2 and 3 declare that communities in remote, isolated, or underdeveloped areas are entitled to receive library services as well as people with disabilities. The public library supports lifelong learning, working with schools and other educational institutions to help students of all ages with their formal education. The challenge of providing educational support provides an opportunity for public libraries to interact and network with teachers and others involved in education. The public library provides materials on a variety of topics which will allow people to follow their interests and support their formal and informal education. The library must provide materials to support literacy and the development of basic life skills and study facilities for students who have inadequate or no access to these facilities in their homes.

Some policies in place to increase quality service in the public library are:
–   Improve the quality of services
–   Promote library services
–   Assess library services
–   Repackage information in multimedia formats
–   Develop cooperative library services nationally and internationally
–   Develop services for special needs users with disabilities
–   Converge conventional and digital services
–   Develop library services based on social inclusion
–   Develop library services for users who cannot leave home or are in nursing homes or hospitals due to illness or old age
–   Construct a referral and reference information service, integrating clearing house and call centres.

Future Public Library Policies in Indonesia

There have been suggestions throughout this discussion of future policies and the extension of some already in place. Highlighted now are some current and future activities.

Developing a Needs Based Library Service is not a new concept. It is part of a historical and Indonesian tradition called *gotong-royong* which means cooperation among many people to attain a shared goal. Public libraries are a reflection of *gotong-royong* to educate the poor and disadvantaged. They were not established for the rich or the middle class. They were not intended to be neutral, universal or open to all. They were targeted, focused and pro-poor. They were an early form of positive action. Developing a Needs Based Library Service is a return to this tradition and the values of self-improvement for those who need libraries the most but use them the least. Developing a Needs Based Library Service is primarily about social change, enabling, facilitating, and empowering individuals and communities; giving them the information they need and helping to level the economic, social, and political playing fields of life (Pateman 2015).

The Indonesian Library Act declares that communities participate in the establishment, implementation, management, development, and supervision of the library. NLI is the coordinator of library development in Indonesia and has involved other stakeholders in library development programs, establishing the Government-Private Partnership involving private companies in library development. One of the successful programs initiated by the Ministry of Home Affairs, the NLI, the Coca-Cola Foundation, and the Bill and Melinda Gates Foundation is the *PerpuSeru* program (Safira et al. 2015). It supported new library initiatives and stated that libraries across the nation play an important and strategic role as a source of information as well as providing inspiration for the community, as they seek to improve their lives. It was a nationwide library development project that focused on providing access to ICT, library staff training courses, and advocacy development at 40 district public libraries across Indonesia. A US $5 million grant was awarded by the Bill and Melinda Gates Foundation's Global Libraries initiative, and provided thousands of Indonesians with access to ICT-based learning activities at their district libraries. Coca-Cola Foundation Indonesia acted as the implementing partner in providing support for the empowerment and sustainability of the participating libraries. The support included regular monitoring, advocacy, and contribution of human resources.

In the first phase of the program, *PerpuSeru* partnered with 34 libraries in 16 provinces throughout Indonesia, including 28 libraries at the municipal/city level, one provincial library, three libraries in rural or urban areas, and two community libraries. In the second phase of the *PerpuSeru* program, the project was expanded to include 76 village libraries with 19 libraries at the municipal/city level becoming program partners to *PerpuSeru*, by providing assistance to the library district or city to conduct training and mentoring related to advocacy, how to improve access and use of computers and Internet services by the community, and how to facilitate the needs of the community through activities involving the community. On October 1, 2015, *PerpuSeru* entered a phase of expansion extending the work area to 80 municipal/city libraries (Perpuseru 2015).

The community-based library policies contribute greatly to library development in building the knowledge society through a collective initiative, to foster the tradition and culture in the community (Taylor 2014):

- Community knowledge is part of a critical mass providing a social foundation, to encourage the process of transformation of society towards an advanced life
- Community knowledge is the embodiment of a civilized nation
- A knowledgeable community will always be open, adaptive, willing to accept new ideas derived from anywhere, which leads to change and progress
- People with knowledge can more easily accept diversity and respect plurality and multiculturalism in society as a reflection of cosmopolitan characteristics.

Library information services can provide information quickly, especially in the fields of science, technology, and cultural work. Society has seen a seismic shift, with people using digital technology and the Internet rather than reading a book; and building a culture of reading interest is the most obvious challenge. A survey from the Association of Indonesian Internet Service Providers/Asosiasi Penyelenggara Jasa Internet Indonesia found 88.1 million Internet users in 2014, and in 2016 an increase of 50.5 % to 132.7 million. Unfortunately, the use of the content from the Internet is dominated by games at 44%, social activities at 12%, tools at 9%, photography at 9%, music at 6%, business/productivity at 3%, and reading a book only at 3% (Kompas 2016).

Information technologies have enormous influence on all aspects of life today and use is growing in Indonesia (Wearesocial 2015). The rapid advances in information technology open new opportunities for libraries to convert a collection of conventional formats to digital formats, develop onsite services to online services, and transform conventional libraries into digital libraries. This is consistent with the mandate of Library Act 2007 article 14 paragraph (3), that each library develop library services by the advancement of ICT. The mandate and strategic direction of libraries in Indonesia is to develop collections of all libraries in Indonesia, to establish a national ICT-based information service, to build library infrastructures and facilities and to improve human resource competence in libraries. The library development program was one of the eleven national priority programs within the portfolio of Culture, Creativity and Technological Innovation. Targets to be achieved in the library development programs are:

- Providing reading materials to develop reading habit and culture in the society
- Improving ICT-based library services throughout the country

- Improving the quality and the capacity of libraries throughout the country to support lifelong education
- Preserving and utilizing national intellectual works.

Information technology is driving the acceleration of distribution and access to information in the community. The library can reach library users using ICT. The use of mobile devices is expected to continue to rise in the next few years. Gartner (2015) states "computing everywhere" has become the top trend and will drive the development of digital libraries and enable open access and interoperability among institutions such as libraries, archives, museums, education, publishing and recording, mass media, research institutions, government and private agencies. Interoperability helps people gain wide access library materials and help preserve the culture of Indonesia. Educational content will be enhanced.

The operation of a digital repository ecosystem across national collections will disseminate information. One of the information technology-based services used in Indonesia is OneSearch (IOS) (https://onesearch.id/), a single gateway search of all the public collections of libraries, museums, and archives throughout Indonesia. The portal also provides all registered users with access to international e-resources purchased by the NLI. To join the IOS, each repository must provide an API-based Open Archive Initiative (OAI)-PMH, a metadata retrieval protocol used by 75% of repositories in the world.

The IOS networking innovation centre at NLI is a reference and research centre and an integrated web portal containing bibliographic data and full text of the e-holdings of various libraries in Indonesia and contributes significantly to information access in Indonesia. It also assists with plagiarism, a topical issue among librarians and library users. NLI developed IOS with anti-plagiarism mechanisms to be used by library users to detect plagiarism. IOS is easy for people to search books and articles everywhere, enhancing library materials and information accessibility and use, and improving web rankings.

A mobile app has been developed for use, *iPusnas* (https://ipusnas.id/). It is a form of social media being used to improve the culture of reading in Indonesia. iPusnas acts as a central repository for information but there are obstacles concerning copyright and Digital Rights Management (DRM). An analytic dashboard has been created, so it is possible to see what books are most read, utilization, and other features:

- Collection access: explore thousands of eBook titles in *iPusnas*; select the title, borrow, and read with one's fingertips
- *ePustaka* (http://e-pustaka.com/; http://www.pustaka.co.in/home): access the digital library from a mobile device and gain a portable library in the palm of one's hand

- Feedback and news: view the latest books, books borrowed by other users and other activities
- Bookshelf: virtual bookshelf recording one's borrowing history
- eReader: read ebooks.

ICT innovations can work well but effective implementation faces many problems because of the lack of infrastructure, content and inadequate human resources. There is great potential with increasing Internet penetration in Indonesia and the growing number of increasingly sophisticated mobile devices. All need to develop strategies and plans and come up with new ideas and innovations to shape the digital library.

Conclusion

Indonesian libraries have many problems. There is uneven distribution of facilities; collections are underdeveloped; staff and human resources lack required expertise; and strategic planning is not sufficiently focused. Future library policy in Indonesia must focus on the following:
- Ensure the availability of sufficient different types of libraries distributed evenly throughout the country
- Provide services and collections to the entire region to ensure equitable access and availability of library materials in all types of libraries in all parts of Indonesia
- Ensure the availability and expertise of appropriately qualified library personnel, both librarians and library technical personnel, in various types of libraries and across Indonesia
- Promote the use of libraries and improve access to library services at all levels of society in all parts of Indonesia.

Strategic policies require development to:
- Realize compliance with library standards
- Create a national collection to meet needs of people in all regions of Indonesia
- Implement training and development of library personnel
- Increase the use of libraries and affordability of access to library services.

Future policy development must involve stakeholders. There are many differences in the interests of stakeholders; challenges in the provision of infrastructure; inadequate and poorly trained library staff and lack of uniformity between the approaches of the NLI and its partners. All are major obstacles in nationwide activity. Policy development and implementation in Indonesia need to be enhanced through increased cooperation, intensive coordination between stakeholders and strategic efforts undertaken throughout Indonesia to gain the support, human resources, facilities, infrastructure, and sufficient budget to implement the digital library in public libraries in Indonesia.

References

Ali, I., and T. Rachmawati. "Expanding Library Service through Floating Libraries: Case study on the Republic of Indonesia." *Poster Session at World Library and Information Congress: 79th IFLA General Conference and Council*, August 1–6, 2003.

Australian Library and Information Association (ALIA). *Beyond a Quality Service: Strengthening the Social Fabric: Standards and Guidelines for Australian Public Libraries.* Commissioned by the Australian Library and Information Association (ALIA) and the ALIA Public Libraries Advisory Committee (PLAC). 2nd ed. Canberra: ALIA, 2012. https://www.alia.org.au/sites/default/files/documents/advocacy/PLSG_ALIA_2012.pdf.

Central Connecticut State University (CCSU). *World's Most Literate Nations.* 2016. Accessed September 29, 2016. http://www.ccsu.edu/wmln/.

Gartner. *Gartner's Top 10 Strategic Technology Trends For 2015.* 2015. Accessed September 30, 2016. http://www.gartner.com/smarterwithgartner/gartners-top-10-strategic-technology-trends-for-2015/.

Gill, Philip, ed. *The Public Library Service: the IFLA/UNESCO Guidelines for Development.* In collaboration with the IFLA Public Libraries Section. IFLA Publications Series, 97. Munchen: K.G Saur, 2001.

Håklev, S. "Community Libraries in Indonesia: A Survey of Government-Supported and Independent Reading Gardens". *Library Philosophy and Practice* 2 (2010): 325. https://digitalcommons.unl.edu/cgi/viewcontent.cgi?article=1333&context=libphilprac

Institute for Education Studies. National Center for Educational Statistics.(IES.NCES) *Program for International Student Assessment (PISA).* 2015. Accessed March 28, 2020. https://nces.ed.gov/surveys/pisa/pisa2015/index.asp.

Kamil, H. "The Growth of Community-based Library Services in Indonesia to Support Education". *Information Development* 20, no. 2 (2004):93–96. DOI: 10.1177/0266666904045321

Kompas. Pengguna Internet di Indonesia Capai 132 Juta. Data provided by APJII. 2016. Accessed September 30, 2016. https://tekno.kompas.com/read/2016/10/24/15064727/2016.pengguna.internet.di.indonesia.capai.132.juta.

Library Council of New South Wales. *Living Learning Libraries 2013.* 5th ed. Sydney, NSW: State Library of New South Wales, 2014. https://www.sl.nsw.gov.au/sites/default/files/living_learning_libraries2013.pdf.

Matthews, Joseph R. *The Customer-Focused Library.* Santa Barbara, CA: Libraries Unlimited, 2009.

OCLC. *Meeting the E-Resources Challenge: An OCLC Report on Effective Management, Access and Delivery of Electronic Collections*. 2011. Accessed April 24, 2014. http://oclc.org/content/dam/oclc/reports/pdfs/OCLC-E-Resources-Report-US.pdf.

Pateman, John. *Developing a Needs Based Library Service*. Leicester: National Institute for Adult Education, 2003.

Pateman, John. "Developing a Community-Led Service Culture". *Developing a Community-Led Library Service Network. Blog*. 2015. https://clacommunityled.wordpress.com/2015/04/29/developing-a-community-led-service-culture/

PerpuSeru. 2015. "Transforming Public Libraries to Become ICT-Based Community Learning Centre to Improve Quality of Life". *Workshop Program Perpuseru, October 2015*, 4–9.

Perpustakaan Nasional RI. Undang-Undang RI Nomor 4 Tahun 1990 Tentang Wajib Simpan Karya Cetak Karya Rekam. Jakarta (ID): Perpusnas RI, 1990.

Perpustakaan Nasional RI. Undang-Undang RI Nomor 43 Tahun 2007 Tentang Perpustakaan. Jakarta (ID): Perpusnas RI, 2007.

Perpustakaan Nasional RI. Grand Desain Pembangunan Perpustakaan digital nasional. Jakarta: Perpusnas RI, 2009.

Perpustakaan Nasional RI. Laporan Akuntabilitas Kinerja Pemerintah Perpustakaan Nasional RI. Jakarta (ID): Perpusnas RI, 2015a.

Perpustakaan Nasional RI. Laporan Pengembangan Perpustakaan Digital Nasional Indonesia (e-Library) Tahun 2015–2019. Jakarta (ID): Perpusnas RI, 2015b.

Perpustakaan Nasional RI. Survey Minat Baca di Indonesia. Jakarta (ID): Perpusnas RI, 2015c.

Perpustakaan Nasional RI. Rencana Strategis Perpustakaan Nasional Tahun 2015–2019 Revisi. Jakarta (ID): Perpusnas RI, 2015d.

Perpustakaan Nasional RI. Pusat Pengembangan Perpustakaan dan Pengkajian Minat Baca. 2016. https://www.perpusnas.go.id/organisasi.php?id=Pusat%20Pengembangan%20Perpustakaan%20dan%20Pengkajian%20Minat%20Baca.

Rainie, L. *10 Facts about Americans and Public Libraries*. 2014. https://www.pewresearch.org/fact-tank/2014/01/24/10-facts-about-americans-and-public-libraries/.

Safira, F., C. Saleh, A. Suprapto, J.A. Publik, F.I. Administrasi, and U. Brawijaya. "Implementasi Program Perpuseru Dalam Upaya Meningkatkan Pelayanan Perpustakaan (Studi Kasus Pada Corporated Social Responsibility Coca Cola Foundation Indonesia Di Perpustakaan Kabupaten Sidoarjo)". *Jurnal Administrasi Publik (JAP)* 3, no. 5 (2015): 770–774.

Taylor, N.G., P.T. Jaeger, U. Gorham, J.C. Bertot, R. Lincoln, and E. Larson. 2014. "The Circular Continuum of Agencies, Public Libraries, and Users: A Model of E-Government in Practice." *Government Information Quarterly*, 31, Supplement 1 (June 2014): S18–S25. http://doi.org/10.1016/j.giq.2014.01.004.

Tirta Wirasta. *Evaluasi kepuasan pengguna katalog induk nasional online Perpustakaan Nasional RI*.Bogor. Thesis IPB, 2012.

Wearesocial. *Digital, Social & Mobile In Southeast Asia In Q4 2015: Special Report*. 2015. Accessed September 30, 2016. http://wearesocial.com/sg/special-reports/digital-southeast-asia-q4-2015.

Suwarno, Wiji. *Dasar-dasar Ilmu Perpustakaan: Sebuah Pendekatan Praktis*. Yogyakarta: Ar-Ruzz, 2007.

World Economic Forum. *The Global Competitiveness Report 2016-7*. Insight Report. Geneva, 2016. Accessed September 29, 2016. https://goo.gl/DlrGnQ/.

Part 4: Impact and Evaluation

Anne Goulding

13 The Impact of Evaluation: The Use of Evidence for Decision-Making and Service Development in Public Libraries

Abstract: This chapter explores the role that the evaluation of public library services plays in governance. The link between good governance and evaluation lies in the contribution that the latter can make to improved organisational performance. Evaluation supports the achievement of the goals of the organisation by focusing on accountability, transparency, effectiveness and efficiency. Organisations must have in place sound processes and systems to support and enhance performance, accountability and service development. The results of a study of evaluation activities undertaken by public libraries in New Zealand are discussed to demonstrate the use and value of evaluation in the public library service context.

Keywords: Libraries – Evaluation; Public libraries – Administration; Public libraries – New Zealand.

Introduction

Governance is about establishing the strategic direction of an organisation and ensuring that the necessary arrangements are in place so that intended outcomes for all stakeholders are achieved. For a public library service, addressing the many interests of its various stakeholder communities within the constraints of limited available resources can be a tall order. The balancing act requires the rigorous evaluation of current operations, leading to changes if necessary to optimise the achievement of public purposes. Effective evaluation relies on sound evidence so that managers can identify issues or problems preventing the achievement of planned outcomes, analyse the causes and generate solutions or alternative approaches.

According to Boaz and Nutely (2009), the interest in the use of evidence to support decision-making in the delivery of public services has grown as attention has focused on ensuring more responsible stewardship, the efficient use of resources and stronger accountability. Originating in the health library sector, evidence-based librarianship is now a common feature of scholarly work in the librarianship discipline, emphasising the integration of existing research evidence into practice and decision-making (Eldredge 2016). Library and informa-

https://doi.org/10.1515/ 9783110533323-016

tion science academics advocate strongly for the use by practitioners of research results to inform their work and service development. The focus of this chapter, though, is the use of locally gathered, empirical evidence and the extent to which public library services use evidence gathered through evaluation activities and processes to make decisions which guide service improvements and thus achieve strategic objectives and desired outcomes. The chapter draws on published sources on evaluation, supplemented by selected results of a small pilot project exploring the use of evaluation data in New Zealand's public libraries.

The Evaluation Context

To a large extent, the growth in interest in gathering evidence noted by Boaz and Nutely (2009) is linked to an assessment culture pervasive throughout the public sector and characterised by a focus on efficiency and measurement. Public services once considered public goods are now scrutinised to determine whether they are using public funds wisely and are required to demonstrate the value they provide for their stakeholders. For libraries, a confluence of factors has encouraged closer examination of performance and value. Financial pressures, felt particularly strongly in the wake of the 2008 global financial crisis, have increased demands for accountability, shared with other public services. In addition, technological innovation and increasing user demands and expectations are perhaps felt more keenly by public library services that are often under pressure to justify their continued funding from the public purse in the face of disintermediation and the development of alternative, widely available sources and formats of information and leisure reading material.

A preoccupation with the value of public services generally has been driven by the ideology of New Managerialism or New Public Management (NPM) which emerged in the 1990s and continues to hold some sway in the public sector. With its "emphasis on outputs over inputs; the close monitoring of employee performance and the encouragement of self-monitoring through the widespread use of performance indicators, rankings, league tables and performance management" (Lynch 2014), it has been said that external auditing, accountability and monitoring mechanisms have replaced mechanisms of trust and what Bernstein (2000, 69) calls "inner dedication". He explains that inner dedication "refers to the type of moral commitment, dedication, ethical responsibility and calling to the profession often found in public service fields such as education, medicine and social work". The NPM philosophy replaces autonomy and trust with assessment and top-down regulation. Some in the library field have cautioned against the wholesale adoption of NPM concepts, feeling that "an ideological obsession with the benefits of quantitative measurement to determine service quality" (McMenemy 2007, 446) is unhelpful, not fit for purpose and risks damaging the relationship between professional librarians and their communities. The use of performance assessment is pervasive across public library services, however, and seems here to stay despite a widespread perception that NPM has been largely discredited (Noordhoek and Saner 2005).

In response to demands for accountability, there has been considerable focus across the library sector on finding ways to demonstrate value and impact with the aim of maintaining financial support and the goodwill of stakeholders. In higher education, for example, libraries are currently focusing on collecting learning analytics data to evidence their contribution to the student learning experience (Jantti and Heath 2016). Academic libraries have experimented with the use of the ServQual framework through LibQual surveys (Cook 2002) and the Balanced Scorecard (Self 2003). Public libraries have been slower to adopt performance measurement practices for a number of possible reasons. It is arguably more difficult to demonstrate the impact of library services on the whole community, or even groups within it, than it is to focus on discrete, specific sets of users with defined needs as in higher education libraries. Secondly, as Lakos and Phipps (2004, 351) suggest, "[a] profession that sees itself as 'doing good' is less concerned with outcomes and impacts, since it sees its activities as inherently positive". Here, Lakos and Phipps are discussing libraries in general and their paper focuses predominantly on higher education, but their comments are arguably most relevant for public libraries which, until fairly recently, have been widely accepted by both the public and politicians as "a good thing". Despite evidence that public goodwill towards libraries remains high (Horrigan 2016), the environmental pressures described above suggest that there is no room for complacency and, in response, studies from a range of perspectives have been undertaken to assess the unique impact that public libraries have on their user communities. In Australia, there has been a focus on economic benefits (Australian Library and Information Association 2013), for example, while recent Scandinavian studies have explored the contribution of the library to social inclusion (Aabo and Audunson 2012) and social capital (Varheim 2017).

These examples suggest that has been some shift in emphasis in value studies away from a focus on measurement and efficiency toward one concerned with outcomes, quality and effectiveness. Although a demand for accountability persists, "the obsession with a numbers-driven evaluative framework" (McMenemy 2007, 446) is accompanied increasingly by the search for more meaningful and context-relevant evaluation approaches which attempt to cover a much wider range of concepts. This new approach can be characterised as a move from a summative stance which seeks to evaluate performance against a standard or benchmark towards a formative view where the purpose is to inform service development as well as measure outcomes. Clearly, in an environment where libraries are being required to demonstrate value to justify the financial support they receive, studies like the Australian one cited above which estimated a conservative benefit-cost ratio of 2.9 are vital for demonstrating that public libraries provide a good return on investment. But public libraries should not only seek to prove the value of their services and activities but also to improve them to ensure the best outcomes for individuals, communities and other stakeholders. Such improvement requires what Lakos and Phipps (2004) describe as "a culture of assessment" in which service decisions and planning are based on evidence and analysis. To achieve this, public library services should be constantly evaluating the outcomes of the services they provide, the programmes they offer and the partnerships they build to ensure that service managers have the information required to guide decisions driving service changes and improvements. Decisions driven by an analysis of service outcomes should result in better services for all stakeholders, particularly the local community.

The librarianship literature is replete with reports documenting evaluations of programmes, services, individual library service points and whole library systems. Studies often focus on the evaluation process and provide helpful advice on procedures and issues that should be considered when planning and evaluating programs and services. To give just a few international examples, Barratt-Pugh and Rohl (2016) discuss the complexities of effective programme evaluation using the case study of the *Better Beginnings* family literacy programme in Western Australian public libraries; Brown and Kasper (2013) explore the assessment of video game programmes in public libraries in the United States; and Paberza and Rutkauskiene (2010) describe the development of outcomes-based measurements of public access computing in public libraries in Latvia and Lithuania. Studies like these provide useful frameworks and models that other public libraries can replicate or adapt to their own local circumstances. Similarly, there are guides and toolkits that support library managers to undertake evaluations of programmes and services. Most notably, the American Public Library Association's *Project Outcome* (https://www.projectoutcome.org) provides a range of free resources, advice and support for public libraries seeking to evaluate the impact of their services and programmes.

Evidently, there has been substantial discussion in the public library world about the importance of evaluating the impact of public libraries on their communities of users and a range of methods for doing so have been devised and tested. There has been little discussion of how the data and evidence gathered through impact evaluations are used to inform decisions about strategy and service development, however, confirming Van Dooren and Van de Walle's (2016) assertion that use is a neglected issue in performance evaluation research. There is some scepticism that public library evaluations always have the impact that could be or is anticipated. Matthews (2011), for example, questions the use of impact evaluation using Return on Investment (ROI) measures asserting that, "the evidence to date about the positive impacts of library ROI studies is underwhelming" and quoting a number of library directors expressing the opinion that the "ROI number may not be compelling enough to prevent budget reductions or lead to budget increases" (Matthews 2011, 10). There seems to be a gap in our knowledge of how the results of evaluations are used by public library service managers to inform their planning and decision-making practices to guide continuous improvement and the achievement of public purposes and desired outcomes.

Evaluation of Services and Programmes

For this chapter, evaluation is defined as: "the systematic collection of information about the outcomes of library service programmes, activities, services and facilities to make judgements about them, improve their effectiveness and/or inform decisions about future developments" (based on Patton 1997, 23). This definition has implications for the approach to evaluation. Firstly, the process of making judgements suggests that service managers and other stakeholders have established criteria against which they can determine the merit and worth of the activity being evaluated. The second point about improving effectiveness and informing decisions is underscored in the title of Patton's book from which the definition is adapted, *Utilization-Focused Evaluation*; the emphasis is on deploying the outcomes of evaluation to drive service improvements, with user needs paramount.

A simple overview of the evaluation process is provided in Figure 1. This chapter focuses on the stage at the top left: how evaluation findings are used to make judgements about the success or failure of a library activity, improve effectiveness and/or inform decisions about future activities and operations. Some of the other stages in the figure are also worth considering to clarify the logic of the evaluation process. The first step is identifying the activity to be evaluated and assumes that public libraries are reviewing services and programmes regularly to consider their purpose, design, implementation and overall value for their communities. The planning stage requires thinking through the decisions that will be informed by the findings of any evaluation and therefore clarifying the nature of

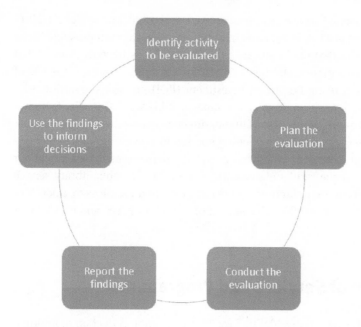

Fig. 1: Evaluation cycle.

the information that needs to be gathered to assist with making those decisions. It also suggests that, as noted above, library service managers have a good idea of the criteria they will use to judge whether or not the intended outcomes of the activity have been achieved so that they can plan the collection of data and information to enable them to make assessments. Library managers should be asking themselves, "What does success look like?". The next stage, conducting the evaluation, is the doing stage, a systematic collection of the evidence necessary to establish how well the service or programme has performed and leads on to an analysis of the evidence against the criteria for success established previously to make judgements about merit, worth or value (Scriven 1991).

At a strategic level, the outcomes of systematic evaluation can benefit library services in numerous ways. Firstly, and probably most importantly, systematic evaluation can help staff understand what is and what is not working, and for whom, among their diverse user groups. In turn, the analysis can drive service improvements by identifying weaknesses as well as strengths and add to knowledge and understanding of what works, with whom, when, how and under what circumstances. The result overall is a reflective approach to service delivery and acceptance of "the need for continuous learning" (Lakos and Phipps 2004, 351). In addition to internal benefits, evaluation can also build or strengthen relationships with stakeholders. Evaluation can help public libraries demonstrate accountability by showing how their services and programmes impact positively on communities and individuals. Hard evidence of effectiveness can result in increased support, whether in terms of funding, patronage or backing.

When considering the purpose of evaluation, Weiss (1998) outlines four uses of evaluation. The first is what she calls "instrumental use" when the outcomes of evaluation activities are used to make decisions about service or programme changes or continuation. Secondly, "conceptual use" is aligned with the points about reflection and learning already noted. Although the findings of an evaluation may not feed immediately into decisions about services or programmes, managers and staff extend their knowledge and understanding of activities and their impact which may lead to changes in policy and direction and eventually to instrumental use. The third and fourth uses both relate to persuasion, internal and external. Weiss explains that the outcomes of evaluation can be used as a form of internal persuasion, to mobilise staff and other stakeholder support for changes to an activity. External persuasion or "influence" in Weiss' terms relates more to advocacy. While she discusses how the collective evidence of programme evaluations can result in "large-scale shifts in thinking" and changes to policy agendas, at a more modest level the results of evaluations can be used to increase public, partners' and politicians' awareness of the value and impact of services in an attempt to influence their decision-making and levels of support.

In the librarianship literature, the focus is often on this last use of evaluations and assessments. Given the turbulent environment outlined, it is perhaps understandable. Thus, in the PLA's *Project Outcome* the section on *Taking Action* focuses on the communication of data and sharing the results of evaluations to explain the value of library services. The section on maximising results gives useful tips for analysing data to identify examples of success, opportunities for improvement and suggestions for new programmes and services. But there is a difference in the use and nature of the information required to improve accountability, on the one hand, and that needed to promote improvement, on the other, and goes back to the points made about formative and summative stances. It is easy to overstate the difference between the two; while the aim of the former, evaluation for accountability, is ultimately to make and communicate judgements of merit and worth of outcomes and that of the latter, evaluation for improvement, is to improve outcomes, conclusions about the value of an activity or service can also lead to their improvement. The next sections consider how public libraries use evaluation data in relation to Weiss' typology of evaluation utilisation, whether, as in the literature, there is a focus on evaluation for advocacy purposes or whether evaluation results are informing service development through supporting decision-making processes.

Motivations for Evaluations in Public Libraries

Under first consideration is the extent to which public libraries evaluate services and programmes to provide information to support strategic planning and operational decision-making. While accounts and case studies of evaluations are reported in the librarianship literature, the prevalence of the practice of evaluation across the public library sector is unclear. A small pilot project examined public library use of evaluation data in New Zealand. The study gathered data through an online survey gaining 20 responses with a response rate of 44%, and five follow-up telephone interviews with public library service managers. The study found that the vast majority of respondents had undertaken some form of evaluation of services, programmes, facilities or space. Just four of the 20 survey respondents indicated that they had not. Asked why not, two respondents selected the pre-selected response of "no demand from stakeholders" while two chose the "other" option. One respondent of these noted "lack of interest" but it was not clear whether the manager or other stakeholders lacked interest. The other explained that s/he was new in the post and had not yet undertaken any evaluations. Interestingly, the options of "lack of time", "lack of expertise" and "lack of resources" did not feature despite evidence in the evaluation literature that time and skills issues frequently deter service or programme managers from engaging with evaluation (Sanders 2003).

The notion, whether real or perceived, that there is a lack of demand from stakeholders is also noteworthy, given the focus in the librarianship literature on the demand for accountability and proof of value and impact from funders and governing bodies. There may be another reason. Sanders (2003) observes that evaluation is not an integral part of operations because of a lack of awareness of its benefits, reinforcing the importance of emphasising the impact of evaluation outcomes on service development. One of the library managers interviewed picked up on the issue of the lack of demand, suggesting that it is the role of library managers to create demand and interest in the service by providing stakeholders with the results of evaluation processes. The implication is that it is important not only to nurture a culture of assessment or evaluation within library services but also within stakeholder groups so that evaluation is considered relevant and expected, thereby raising awareness of service activities and outcomes. A survey respondent made similar remarks in the free text comment box at the end of the survey noting: "Although our Council does not require that we evaluate our services or programmes (outside of the high-level service review, which is undertaken by senior management) I am sure that if we were to do so it would be well-received by management and elected representatives". Figure 2 illustrates why those who had undertaken evaluations said they had done so.

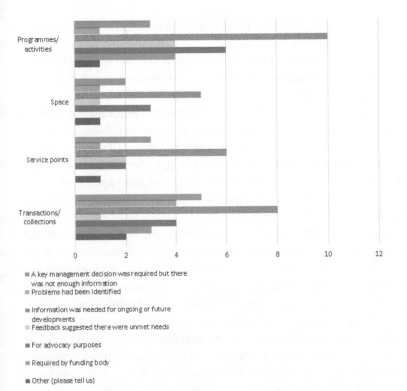

0   2   4   6   8   10   12

- A key management decision was required but there was not enough information
- Problems had been identified

- Information was needed for ongoing or future developments
- Feedback suggested there were unmet needs

- For advocacy purposes

- Required by funding body

- Other (please tell us)

Fig. 2: Reasons for undertaking evaluations.

The data indicate that evaluations are most commonly undertaken in relation to transactional services and programmes or events. While the emphasis varied depending on the target of evaluation, the need for information to support future development dominated overall, aligning with Weiss's (1998) "conceptual use" in which evaluation data and information are gathered for planning and to help managers and staff understand operations in new ways. A survey respondent expressed the point well in a comment:

> We are about to undertake the process of writing our Library strategy and evaluation data is vital for this process as it helps us understand our communities needs now and into the future. It also helps us tell our story and demonstrate the impact and the value of our services in our community.

The use of evaluation in transactional services was captured effectively by one of the interviewees who said that he had reviewed the use of key performance indicators related to collection use in his service to provide "a better picture of what the service is actually doing" in terms of both penetration of library services within the target population and processes. The data collected has given him robust information to report to council and to support planned changes focusing on reaching those not currently served and building collections that better reflect community needs. Turning to other internal stakeholders, sharing the data with staff can also help them see the bigger picture. Another interviewee described the organisational learning that has taken place in her service through repeated evaluations of their summer reading programme which give staff a good overview of what works well and what could be changed. Again, the results are provided to council to provide "enlightenment" (Owen 1992), helping raise awareness of the features of the programme in an attempt to influence attitudes towards the programme and the library service in general.

The first two bars of the charts in Figure 2 represent Weiss' "instrumental" uses of evaluation, immediate tangible use through effective management. Weiss (1984) in fact suggests that little instrumental use takes place and the results of the pilot project seem to corroborate this conclusion, indicating that instrumental use is most common when considering the transactional services provided by library services. Nevertheless, some of the managers gave some good examples. One interviewee described the process as an operational review on an ongoing basis, almost in real time. The information provided through these evaluation processes often supported collection management and development decisions by providing data on subjects or authors issuing particularly well or on areas of stock that are not moving. Use of data in this way is perhaps more akin to performance management than evaluation but it was noted that this type of assessment feeds into and supports other forms of evaluation. The motivation behind the evaluation undertaken is to gather data to enable library managers to make judgements about the success of the library's collection-based services and then to take action to try to ensure better use of those services. One survey respondent noted: "I cannot stress enough the importance of evaluation data to our strategies, tactical approaches and daily operations".

For programming and events or activities held within the library, Figure 2 indicates that conceptual use of evaluation remained dominant but persuasive reasons were rated higher than for the other targets of evaluation in libraries. Using evaluation data in reports of library activities to highlight key outcomes can convince funders and stakeholders to maintain support. One interviewee noted using evaluation data "to persuade people that we need to change". She gave the example of radically altering the layout of one library and then evaluating user response which was positive. She believed that this kind of approach had led to a situation where, "most of the things, if they're well founded, that I'm putting in front of council are getting followed through on". In this case, she is using evaluation data to convince council that they can trust her judgement when it comes to service developments.

Methods of Evaluations

While the results above suggest a strong focus on evaluation in New Zealand's public libraries, the interviews with library managers revealed that the term evaluation was used to cover a broad range of activities, some of which may not conform to more formal definitions of evaluation with their focus on systematic approaches to investigating programme or service effectiveness (Rossi, Lipsey and Freeman 2004). There was quite a marked distinction among interviewees between those who were taking a strategic approach to evaluation and data gathering and others whose main experience of evaluation had been general library or council customer satisfaction questionnaires. While satisfaction is clearly an important aim of public library services, some feedback mechanisms are often too broad to provide useful information to indicate the achievement, or not, of intended outcomes. Responses to questionnaires about satisfaction with public library service tend to be very positive; in the Thames-Coromandel District on the east of New Zealand's North Island, for example, a 2015 customer survey showed that 99% of respondents were satisfied with their public libraries (Thames Coromandel District Council 2016). Results like these can be helpful for advocacy as an indicator of public perceptions and esteem but there is a feeling that people respond positively because of fears about cuts to library services. As one interview participant noted: "I think sometimes people are pleased to have the service and they don't like to say they think it's a very old-fashioned service and the books are all grubby, they don't like to say that because possibly what they've got is better than nothing at all."

Customer satisfaction surveys are unlikely to give sufficient detailed information to drive improvements as the same interviewee noted. She suggested that the exercise in her service had been "a bit of a waste of time" because the survey was not focused on those from whom they ideally wanted information, that is, non-users, and it did not explore reasons for lack of satisfaction in any detail. The importance of evaluations being planned and purposeful cannot be underestimated and, ideally, evaluation should be built into service or programme design. Table 1 illustrates the service managers' responses when asked about the target of evaluations. Respondents could select all that applied.

Table 1: Targets of evaluations (n).

Target	Number
Transactions and/or collections	13
Programmes/activities	11
Whole service points	8
Space within libraries	6

Despite evidence that the number of programmes provided by public libraries and attendance at those programmes have been increasing steadily over the decade (Library Research Service 2011), the results of the survey indicate that evaluations still focus mostly on transactions and collections. This could be because the outputs of such activities are easier to identify and measure through library management systems and associated applications. Identifying the value of other more qualitative outcomes was recognised as difficult. As one interviewee said, "What about the meaningful interactions that are increasing? How the heck do you measure them?". While some detect a shift in public library assessment from measuring outputs to outcomes (Vakkari et al. 2014), there was a degree of frustration expressed by some of the library managers interviewed that their councils "like to see the graphs and the upward trends and things like that".

Nevertheless, other managers felt that, targeted correctly, output data plays a useful role in painting a picture of what the library service is achieving and provides them with rigorous data on which to base collection management decisions. Some managers interviewed were using or considering extending the approach by using proprietary evidence-based performance management tools or adding business intelligence modules to their library management systems to give more detailed information on collection use, enabling them to become more strategic and proactive in the management of their resources.

Uses of Evaluation Data

Although some managers had a very clear view of the kinds of transactional information they found useful to present a picture of library achievements, there is a question about whether much of the output data collected and presented as a matter of routine by public libraries is evaluation in the true sense of the word. As noted, it says little about the impact of the service on users, focusing rather merely on just how much a service or collection has been used. Nevertheless, interviewees thought that the data gathered could be used to inform changes to services to try to improve outreach and performance. This sense was also reflected more generally in the online survey responses as illustrated in Figure 3.

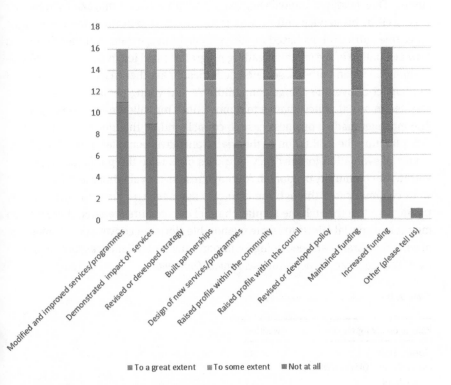

Fig. 3: How have evaluations helped your library service?

Evaluation was considered of most use in an instrumental way, to inform decisions leading to changes and improvements to existing services and programmes. Conceptual uses also featured strongly, with respondents appreciating the clearer picture of services that evaluation provides, leading to better understanding of evaluation outcomes being used to inform future strategy. One survey respondent noted that the service's work on key performance indicators had aimed to: "better inform the council senior management and political body of the scope and impact of library services". Despite the focus in the librarianship literature on communicating the results of evaluation for advocacy purposes, respondents were equivocal about the ability of evaluation data to raise the public library service's profile with key stakeholders and while many felt that evaluations were useful for maintaining funding, a minority indicated that they had led to budgetary increases.

In the interviews and free text comments box at the end of the online survey, library managers gave examples to illustrate some of the responses from the survey. One manager interviewed explained how online magazines were not used well in his service and he was recommending cancelling their electronic magazine subscriptions based on an analysis of usage data. Another described how evaluation of the summer reading programme had led to changes to the programme finale and other associated activities. In another case, an evaluation of the impact of overdue charges on children's and young people's materials has resulted in a trial policy change to remove fines for children and young people. The manager made a business case to council and, at the time of the interview, was planning the evaluation of the trial. None gave examples of the use of outcomes of evaluation for advocacy purposes or to raise the profile of the library within the community or council. Although results of evaluations and monitoring were communicated through the council's management structure and into the political system through the regular channel of committee reports, there was no mention of special efforts to create memorable stories or convey specific message of what the library had been doing for important, core audiences as recommended by library advocacy experts such as *Project Outcome*.

Table 2: Distribution of evaluation results.

People receiving results	Number
Library Staff	13
Other Council Officers/Officials	10
Councillors	9
Library Customers	6
General Public	6
Other Funders	3
Other Partners	3
Other	2

The responses to the online survey about the people receiving the results are shown in Table 2 and indicate that results were shared most often with library staff, suggesting that some services were trying to build an evaluation culture. A couple of managers interviewed talked of involving staff in developing key performance indicators and providing them with the results. One manager admitted that his service was not so good at sharing results with the community, suggesting that, "we tend to fall into the trap that communities think that libraries are a good idea regardless". Although Table 2 indicates that some library services provided evaluation results to users and the general public, it is possible that they were referring to general council surveys, the results of which are often distributed via the council website. There might also be a perception that communities would not find the results of interest, in line with Yang's (2007) assertion that administrators struggle to interest citizens in public service performance management.

As well as considering how the results of evaluations are used and shared by library service managers, it is useful to explore why they are not used. One of the questions on the online survey asked for the percentage of recommendations arising from evaluations that have been implemented. The results given in Table 3 present quite a healthy picture with the vast majority of respondents indicating use of at least half of the recommendations.

Table 3: Percentage of evaluation recommendations actioned (n).

Percentage	Number
100%	1
Around 75%	6
Around 50%	5
Around 25%	1
Less than 25%	0
None	0

A follow-up question asked why recommendations had not been fully implemented. As illustrated in Table 4, lack of resources was considered most problematic.

Table 4: Reasons for recommendations not being full implemented (n).

Reason	Number
Lack of resources	9
Lack of relevance to library service strategy	4
Lack of time	3
Lack of an advocate/chamption with council	2
Didn't agree with results	1
Lack of expertise	0
Other	6

One of the managers interviewed gave an example of an independent whole-service review which he felt had been helpful in taking a long-term view and evaluating aspects such as council spending on libraries and the location of branches, but, he explained, "the suggested changes were quite expensive so it got binned". At council level, politicians and officials have to make decisions about the allocation of limited resources and library managers do so at library service level. One of the "other" reasons given for not implementing suggested changes was "competing tensions across customer groups", reinforcing the point about balancing stakeholder interests and Pollitt's (2006) argument that different stakeholders have different priorities and purposes.

The idea that much of the data provided was too general to be of much use was often mentioned in the interviews and was especially true of the council-wide evaluations but also some library specific ones with managers feeling that they often just confirmed what they knew anecdotally anyway. Perhaps as suggested in both survey and interview data, evaluation was often undertaken ad hoc and not planned systematically. Although some library services appear to be undertaking a lot of evaluation of both services and programmes, it is unclear to what extent the activity is planned and purposeful as discussed in relation to Figure 1. A survey respondent noted, for example: "evaluation of our services is done on an as needs' basis". The importance of planning is emphasised throughout the evaluation literature (for example Owen 2006) to clarify what the evaluation is seeking to achieve, including identifying the key audience for the findings and what they need to know.

One library manager interviewed recognised that, particularly in relation to programming, "you really need to have something built in right from the start for these programmes, rather than trying to add it on ad hoc at the end". If the evaluation is not carefully planned from the beginning, the results are not as helpful in supporting decision making as they could be. In addition, lack of skills and confidence in using evaluation techniques and methods can also mean that evaluations are not collecting useful information for service or programme development. One survey respondent noted: "Our staff lacks practice in the formal preparation, administration and analysis of service evaluations" and a manager interviewed made similar comments, suggesting that they were not getting to the "nitty gritty of what might be problems, or maybe new services that we might want to initiate, or perhaps assess demand or interest or need for those services before we even start on planning". To gain the most from evaluations, library staff require a certain skill set which, as Lakos (2001) notes, has not been readily available within the profession.

Conclusion

The link between good governance and evaluation lies in the contribution that the latter can make to improved organisational performance. It supports the achievement of the goals of the organisation by focusing on accountability, transparency, effectiveness and efficiency. The implication is that organisations require sound processes and systems that support and enhance performance and accountability. At a more practical level, the purpose of evaluation is to establish the effectiveness of a service or programme and take action based on that information. As Powell (2006) notes, evaluation must have a purpose; without the potential for some action there is no need to evaluate.

Public library services in New Zealand are engaging in evaluation activities and in many cases are using the information acquired to plan and make decisions to guide services improvements and to balance and prioritise competing demands within limited available resources. The most rigorous and regular collection and use of evaluation data relates, understandably, to collections and transactions. Public libraries have always collected this kind of data, their systems are set up for it; it is often what their funders require; and collections are a significant asset for public libraries and therefore data that shows how that asset is performing is compelling. Although indicators of collections use and transactions might not be deemed output measures as they indicate what is being used but not how, why or the impact of use, library managers are developing new approaches which may give a better picture of performance both for instrumental and enlightenment purposes. With regard to transactional and collection services in public libraries, evaluations do appear to address Patton's (1997) three questions:

- What? – what does the data tell us?
- So what? – what sense can we make of it?
- Now what? – what do we do now?

While this kind of evaluation information can assist in the analysis of where transactional services are succeeding or have problems, the understanding of the merit and worth of many public library programmes and initiatives is partial at best. As Sally Pewhairangi (n.d.) notes, "All too often libraries are judged and ranked by the number of transactions that occur and not the experiences that make up these transactions". Moreover, if public libraries are moving from transactional to programmatic models as has been suggested, they need to find robust ways of evaluating them to improve outcomes for their communities of users.

Comments from both the survey and interviews in the sample study undertaken suggested that much evaluation of programming, in particular, was limited, informal and based on anecdotal evidence. A key challenge facing public libraries is the difficulty of measuring the outcomes of many of their activities. While most in the public library sector have largely taken on board the importance of evaluating outcomes as well as outputs, that does not mean that it is easy. First, there is the difficulty of identifying and precisely clarifying the desired outcomes

of specific services or initiatives and then of gathering the appropriate information to establish whether or not they have been achieved. It is far more straightforward to measure issue figures of collections than evaluate the impact those
collections have on patrons in terms of increasing knowledge or well-being, for
example.

The importance of making the effort to do so, however, cannot be overstated.
The data and evidence emerging from the processes can inform the way library
services learn from the past and make adjustments for the future enabling them
to redesign and improve systems, approaches and frontline practices to ensure
they remain relevant and continue to meet community needs.

The last word goes to a survey participant who nicely summed up the importance and value of evaluation for public library services:

> Evaluations shed light on dark corners and help curb the enthusiasm of bias with factual
> and anecdotal evidence. In a library service that had been allowed to go to seed, evaluation
> has brought the library service back to life. Partaking in the evaluation has given staff new
> understanding of what we want to deliver.

References

Aabo, S., and R. Audunson. "Use of Library Space and the Library as Place". *Library &
Information Science Research* 34, no. 2 (2012): 138–49

Australian Library and Information Association. *National Welfare & Economic Contributions of
Public Libraries*. Canberra: SGS Economics & Planning, 2013. https://www.alia.org.au/
sites/default/files/Contribution%20of%20Australian%20Public%20Libraries%20Report.
pdf.

Barratt-Pugh, C., and M. Rohl. "Evaluation of Family Literacy Programs: A Case Study of
Better Beginnings, A Library-Initiated Family Literacy Bookgifting Program in Western
Australia". *Library Trends* 65, no. 1 (2016): 19–40.

Bernstein, B. *Pedagogy, Symbolic Control and Identity: Theory, Research, Critique* rev. ed.
Lanham, Md: Rowman & Littlefield, 2000.

Boaz, A., and S. Nutley. "Evidence-Based Policy and Practice". In *Public management and
governance*, edited by T. Bovaird and E. Loffler, 327–342. 2nd ed. Abingdon: Routledge,
2009.

Brown, R.T., and T. Kasper. "The Fusion of Literacy and Games: A Case Study in Assessing the
Goals of a Library Video Game Program". *Library Trends* 61, no. 4 (2013): 755–78.

Cook, C. 2002. "The Maturation of Assessment in Academic Libraries: The Role of
Libqual+™". *Performance Measurement and Metrics* 3, no. 2 (2002): 34.

Eldredge, J.D. "Integrating Research into Practice". *Journal of the Medical Library
Association* 104, no. 4 (2016): 333–7.

Horrigan, J.B. *Libraries 2016*. Pew Research Center, September 2016. https://www.pewresearch.
org/internet/2016/09/09/libraries-2016/

Jantti, M., and J. Heath. "What Role for Libraries in Learning Analytics?" *Performance Measurement and Metrics* 17, no. 2 (2016): 203–10.

Lakos, A. "Culture of Assessment as a Catalyst for Organizational Culture Change in Libraries". In *Proceedings from the 4th Northumbria International Conference on Performance Measurement in Libraries and Information Services*, 311–19. 2001. http://libqual.com/documents/admin/lakos.pdf.

Lakos, A., and S.E. Phipps. "Creating a Culture of Assessment: A Catalyst for Organizational Change." *portal: Libraries and the Academy*, no. 3 (20043): 345–61.

Library Research Service. "Program Attendance at Public Libraries Is on the Rise". *Fast Facts.* ED3/110.10/No. 298. 2011. https://www.lrs.org/fast-facts-reports/program-attendance-at-public-libraries-is-on-the-rise/.

Lynch, K. 'New Managerialism' In Education: The Organisational Form of Neoliberalism". https://www.opendemocracy.net/kathleen-lynch/%27new-managerialism%27-in-education-organisational-form-of-neoliberalism

Matthews, J.R. "What's the Return on ROI? The Benefits and Challenges of Calculating Your Library's Return on Investment." *Library Leadership and Management* 25, no. 1 (2011): 1–14.

McMenemy, D. "Managerialism: A Threat to Professional Librarianship?" *Library Review* 56, no. 6 (2007): 445–9.

Noordhoek, P., and R. Saner. "Beyond New Public Management. Answering the Claims of Both Politics and Society." *Public Organization Review* 5, no. 1 (2005): 35–53.

Owen, J.M. "Towards A Meta-Model of Evaluation Utilization". Paper presented at the *Annual Meeting of the American Evaluation Association*. Seattle, Washington, 1992.

Owen, J.M. *Program Evaluation: Forms and Approaches.* 3ʳᵈ ed. New York: The Guildford Press, 2006.

Paberza, K., and U. Rutkauskiene. "Outcomes-Based Measurement of Public Acess Computing in Public Libraries." *Performance Measurement and Metrics* 11, no. 1 (2010): 75–82.

Patton, M.Q. *Utilization-Focused Evaluation.* Beverly Hills, CA: Sage Publications, 1997.

Pewhairangi, S. (n.d.). *The Library Leadership Manifesto.* https://lianza.org.nz/library-leadership-manifesto.

Pollitt, C. "Performance Information for Democracy: The Missing Link?" *Evaluation* 12, no.1 (2006): 38–55.

Powell, R.R. "Evaluation Research: An Overview." *Library Trends* 55, no. 1 (2006): 102–20.

Rossi, P.H., H.E. Freeman and M.W. Lipsey. *Evaluation: A Systematic Approach.* Thousand Oaks, CA: Sage, 2004.

Sanders, J.R. "Mainstreaming Evaluation." *New Directions for Evaluation* 99 (2003): 3–6.

Scriven, M. *Evaluation Thesaurus.* 4ᵗʰ ed. Newbury Park, CA: Sage, 1991.

Self, J. "From Values to Metrics: Implementation of the Balanced Scorecard at a University Library". *Performance Measurement and Metrics* 4, no. 2 (2003): 57–63.

Thames Coromandel District Council. *Summary of Results for the 2015 Customer Satisfaction Survey.* 2016. https://docs.tcdc.govt.nz/store/default/4213080.pdf.

Vakkari, P., S. Aabø, R. Audunson, F. Huysmans and M. Oomes. "Perceived Outcomes of Public Libraries in Finland, Norway and the Netherlands". *Journal of Documentation* 70, no. 5 (2014): 927–44.

Van Dooren, W., and S. Van de Walle. "Introduction: Using Public Sector Performance Information." In *Performance Information in The Public Sector: How It Is Used*, edited by W. Van Dooren and S. Van de Walle, 1–8. Basingstoke: Palgrave Macmillian, 2016.

Vårheim, A. "Public Libraries, Community Resilience, and Social Capital." *Information Research* 22, no. 1 (2017).

Weiss, C.H." Increasing the Likelihood of Influencing Decisions". In *Evaluation Research Methods: A Basic Guide*, edited by L. Rutman, 159–190. Beverly Hills, CA: Sage, 1984.

Weiss, C.H. "Have We Learned Anything New About the Use of Evaluation?". *The American Journal of Evaluation* 19, no. 1 (1998): 21–33.

Yang, K. "Making Performance Measurement Relevant? Administrators' Attitudes and Structural Orientations". *Public Administration Quarterly* 31, no. 3/4 (2007): 342–83.

David Streatfield, Sharon Markless and Jeremy Paley

14 Measuring Performance and Evaluating Impact of Public Libraries from a Governance Perspective

Abstract: The move towards more strategic public library performance measurement and impact evaluation at international level is traced and the role of the International Organization for Standardization (ISO) is examined from a governance perspective. The shift in library evaluation thinking and the early changes in practice are outlined, drawing on extensive experience working with the Global Libraries (GL) initiative over the past decade. Relevant ideas and innovations from the wider evaluation field are noted. The current and potential roles of the International Federation of Library Associations and Institutions (IFLA) in this work are explored.

Keywords: Libraries – Evaluation; Public libraries – Administration; Performance measurement; International Federation of Library Associations.

Introduction

Why should people involved with the international governance of public libraries concern themselves with performance measurement and evaluation? In an examination of the consequences of twenty-three research projects funded by Canada's International Development Research Centre, Fred Carden (2009) identified three ways in which research can contribute to better governance. They are:
- Encouraging open inquiry and debate
- Empowering people with the knowledge to hold governments or ... institutions accountable and
- Enlarging the array of policy options.

Taking the organization and collection of performance data and impact evidence as an essential subset of organizational research, collection and analysis work is, or should be, important to inform the debate, to provide evidence against which to hold governments and institutions to account, and to guide choices about policy options. Better governance of performance data collection and of impact evidence gathering is critical to the processes.

Secondly, healthy governance of public libraries at international and national levels requires effective evidence collection to show what is changing in the

https://doi.org/10.1515/ 9783110533323-017

world of libraries, how the changes are being effected, and with what impact on the communities served. Having good quality evidence is especially important in the current political and governance climate, when the purposes, relevance, and even the existence of public libraries are increasingly being questioned. What are the main international public library governance roles in relation to collecting performance data and evidence of impact on communities?

Taking performance data first: there is a crucial need for better evidence of public library impact on users and communities, which gives rise to a significant governance issue about the quality and relevance of available public library performance data at national level. In his judicious analysis of statistical standards in global libraries, which includes but is not confined to public libraries, Tord Høivik distinguished between four levels of development at country level. The levels can be summarized as:

- The least developed countries which have no national library statistics. "In a few cases they publish some scattered library data in statistical yearbooks or reports on cultural statistics. But the information is hard to find and hard to use"
- "Countries that try to collect national statistics, but are hampered by uneven and fragmented library systems. The public library sector tends to have greater difficulties than academic and special libraries ... Many Latin American countries are in this group..."
- "Countries with well-developed library systems and some good statistics at the national level, ... Great Britain, Germany and Italy, much of Eastern Europe, the United States, Chile, Singapore and a few others ... The main problem, seen from abroad, is the lack of extensive, user-oriented web publishing of the data"
- "The most advanced countries ... the Nordic group (Finland, Norway, Denmark, Sweden), the Netherlands and New Zealand. Canada (some states) and Australia (some states) could be added. These countries and states take a political interest in measuring library activities and use the web actively to present and disseminate library statistics." (edited from Høivik 2013; direct quotations are shown in italics)

He added that "If we consider continents, Africa faces the biggest problems" and cited Elisha Chiware's observation (https://iflastat.wordpress.com/2010/10/29/library-statistics-in-africa/) that there is: no standard on the type of library statistics to be collected; no shared position on how data must be collected, analysed, presented, and applied; a wide gap in the type and frequency of statistics between technologically advanced libraries and those less fortunate; and no national or regional African database of comparative library statistics available.

These conclusions were strongly upheld in the posts on data collection issues and challenges conducted on the training platform of the African Library and Information Associations and Institutions (AfLIA)(https://web.aflia.net/). Høivik's analysis and governance suggestions will be discussed later in this chapter.

Turning to impact evaluation, the problem appears to be one of lack of governance at country and international levels. With one or two isolated exceptions, public libraries have been slower than education or health libraries to accept the challenge of evaluating services by looking at their impact on library users. The contribution of the Global Libraries (GL) initiative of the Bill and Melinda Gates Foundation is a major exception to the generalization, but one which raises a number of questions about public library governance which are discussed below. The potential role of the International Federation of Library Associations and Institutions (IFLA) in influencing international public library governance is also outlined.

The following pages define impact evaluation; show how measuring performance and especially evaluating the impact of public libraries at international level have become more strategic over the past decade; and examine the role of the International Organization for Standardization (ISO) in influencing and reflecting the discourse. Drawing upon personal experience of working with the GL initiative over the past decade, they then trace and contextualize the shift in thinking and the early changes in practice from an international public library perspective; outline the GL program; describe the change in the governance locus of the program; and highlight some of the consequences. The governance processes involved in creating and then exploiting various common evaluation tools for performance and impact measurement to be applied at country-level are explored and other elements of the GL program examined from a governance perspective. There are final speculations about how the international public library performance measurement and impact evaluation field is likely to develop within a wider international development evaluation context that is increasingly embracing theory-driven approaches. The current and potential role of IFLA in this field is also considered.

Measuring Performance and Evaluating Impact – Story of Change

Defining Impact

The definition of impact used is one borrowed from the educational evaluation field. Following Fitz-Gibbon (1996), impact is defined as "any effect of the service

(or of an event or initiative) on an individual, group or community". The effect may:
- Be positive or negative
- Be intended or accidental
- Affect library staff, senior managers, users/customers, pupils, teachers, parents or other people.

The impact can show itself in individual cases or through more generally discernible changes, such as shifts in:
- Quality of life, for example, self-esteem, confidence, feeling included, work or social prospects
- Educational and other outcomes, for example, skills acquired, educational attainment or levels of knowledge.

The chosen definition is deemed the most useful one to drive evaluation of impact in libraries because it recognizes the complex ways in which libraries can affect and change their users and the wider community. There are many others. The World Bank, for example, defined impact as the difference in the "indicator of interest" with the intervention and without the intervention (White 2010, 154). In this definition, impact is limited to any difference discerned in the indicator of interest that can be attributed to the intervention.

The differences in opinions on definitions reflect a key issue of evaluation governance. What claims are being made? What research methods will be adopted to carry out the evaluation work?

How such questions turn into a governance issue can be seen in the early experience of two of the authors with the Bill and Melinda Gates Foundation (BMGF) evaluation team. Some members of the team at that stage saw impact evaluation as a term reserved to describe attribution studies focused on causal evidence. They would have been happy with the World Bank definition of impact. The GL team was asked to use the term "impact assessment" instead when describing the contribution that libraries can make to individual or community change.

The Foundation now has a more nuanced approach to evaluation, as evinced by the assertion that "We avoid one-size-fits-all prescriptions and strive to make selective, high-quality evaluation an integral part of how we carry out our work". The evaluation policy gives ample scope for flexible governance:

> From the outset of the grant-making process, we work with partners to define the overall results we hope to achieve and the data needed to measure those results. We call this approach outcome investing. To give our partners flexibility in how they achieve results, we do not require them to report on all of their activities. Instead, we focus on purposefully

measuring the most critical metrics of progress that support continued learning, adjustment, and alignment (BMGF 2013).

This flexibility is important when considering the governance of the impact evaluation strategy of the GL initiative.

Performance Measurement and Impact Evaluation; the Changing Picture

Throughout recent history, performance measurement data, usually referred to as library statistics in English-speaking countries, has provided the main service evaluation tool in all types of libraries and especially public libraries. Data collection is often limited to counting book issues, visits to the library, participants at events organized by the library, and other activity indicators and, as already noted, the data collection may not be rigorous or systematic. This is not the whole picture: school library evaluation began to target the contribution of libraries to teaching and learning in schools from the 1980s onwards (for example Didier 1984) and both academic and health libraries began to follow a similar path in the following decade (Wavell et al. 2002; Weightman and Williamson 2005).

With isolated exceptions (such as Holt et al. 1996), public libraries have generally been slower to shift their focus towards the impact of their services on users and academic interest in public library impact only really began to emerge early in this century (for example, Craven and Brophy 2004). However, both performance measurement and impact evaluation in public libraries have recently been positively influenced by the example of the GL initiative, with the work also being promoted, with questionable effect, by the ISO.

Staff of many public libraries around the world collect data on the performance of some or many of their main services. The focus of the library statistics is usually on the amount or frequency of use of particular services, such as the number of loans per year, or the numbers of library visitors or participants at events characterized elsewhere as busy-ness statistics (Markless and Streatfield 2013). Library staff may also collect information on the costs of providing particular services or on the overall operating costs of their libraries.

Whether or not public library staff collect and report performance data is essentially a governance issue: they will normally collect data if they are instructed to do so by people in a governance role, at local authority or national level, and what they collect is likely to be prescribed by the same people. How public library staff collect the data usually depends on whether their leaders at country, provincial or equivalent level specify the data collection requirements, but, as Høivik reported, some countries do not produce national public library statistics and others do not have a commonly shared method of assembling public library data. Many countries do not appear to have a national statistics agency responsible for library statistics. The IFLA website list of national statistics covered only 30 countries in 2017; none was in Africa; one was in Central America and one was in South America, while three were in Asia.

Unsurprisingly, given this picture of public library performance measurement, there was little attempt to accrue evidence of the impact of services on users at country level until the early years of this century. Some individual public library managers began to demonstrate the value of their services from the 1990s onwards (for example Holt et al. 1996) and, in the United Kingdom, a short-lived central government initiative required all local authority services, including public libraries, to engage in a so-called Best Value program of user consultation about services offered (Markless et al. 2000).

International Standards and the Road to Public Library Impact

Despite the patchy activity so far in libraries across the globe, there has been sufficient momentum to encourage people interested in standardizing performance data and impact evidence collection to begin the process. ISO has been active in the library performance measurement field since before 1974 when the first edition of the standard on international library statistics appeared as a four-page note. It was followed in 1998 by the standard on library performance indicators, reflecting a growing but sporadic perceived need for libraries to be able to compare their performance with others and to contribute to the national statistical picture, although this need did not necessarily emanate from the libraries themselves. Last to emerge in 2014 was the first edition of the standard on methods and procedures for assessing the impact of libraries, which, allowing for a time lag between the early efforts to engage with impact evaluation by library leaders and the beginnings of interest in this work at national and international levels, is relatively timely.

In their latest versions, these three ISO publications in particular are still relevant for performance measurement and impact evaluation: they were international library statistics (ISO 2789) and library performance indicators (ISO 11620), both published in 2013, and methods and procedures for assessing the impact of libraries (ISO 16439) which appeared for the first time in 2014. These publications shared some common characteristics: they each offered definitions of key terms and rules or methods for the library and information community when collecting and reporting evidence and all had similar statements recognizing the variable relevance of the Standards because of the differences between types of libraries, in different settings, serving different user groups, and having a range of unique characteristics, such as structure, funding or governance, which was specifically identified as a point of divergence in all three publications.

Perhaps surprisingly, the three publications had different aims:

-   The international library statistics publication (ISO 2789) assumed that if their rules were adopted they would enable: international data reporting; conformity between countries for those statistical measures that are frequently used by library managers, but do not qualify for international reporting; and good practice in the use of statistics for the management of library and information services.
-   The performance indicators document (ISO 11620) aimed to "endorse the use of performance indicators regarding the quality of library services in libraries and to spread knowledge about how to conduct performance measurement".
-   The impact assessment standard (ISO 16439) was a methods guide to the library community on assessing the impact and value of libraries. It was apparently "developed in response to worldwide demand for specifications of library impact assessment", although it is not very clear who created the demand, concentrating on methods "seen to be most heavily used and that have proved most effective for assessing library impact".

But what is the role of the ISO in governance of library performance measurement and impact evaluation? It is hard to judge, because although the more recent editions of the library standards were a little more specific about who prepared them, their link to governance is still unclear. Why is this important? If there is a lack of clarity about the governance of international standards for library evaluation, or for anything else, why should managers and practitioners bother about adopting and applying standards? What are the origins of the most relevant standards?

The most recent editions of the three standards state that "developments in relation to this International Standard will be monitored and additional statistical measures will be incorporated as needed" (ISO 2789). How will this be done and who decides on the need? No details are provided but performance indicators (ISO 11620) say "This International Standard will be maintained by a working group that will monitor developments and incorporate additional indicators as they are tested and validated", leaving speculation about who is on the working group. The people involved with the impact assessment standard (ISO 16439) published most recently in 2014 were much less coy, announcing that "The committee responsible for this document is ISO/TC 46, *Information and documentation*, Subcommittee SC 8, *Quality – Statistics and performance evaluation*". A visit to the ISO website in 2017 established: the names of the TC46 subcommittee secretary and chairman; that there were 25 participating members; and that they were also responsible for the other two standards.

Even with the emergence of the more recent information, governance of standards that affect public libraries remains problematic. It is unclear who decides that library standards are needed, who selects the experts to work on the standards, and on what basis the experts are chosen. Once the process begins, there are further issues about the lack of any consistency in scope and coverage. The clearest part of the picture is around the pricing structure, but who decides how much the standards should cost, and in doing so, who will be excluded from direct access to these publications because of the substantial purchase price?

The issue is compounded by the differences in aims for the three standards. What assumptions were being made about how the standards influence library governance at international and national levels and what needed to be done to encourage widespread adoption of the standards? Renard (2007) attempted to provide a perspective on the usefulness of earlier versions of two of the standards, ISO 2789 and ISO 11620, suggesting that:

> although their aim is not to draw up an assessment framework, they reveal themselves useful for basic operations in such a framework: to define objects and services, and to classify, count and build appropriate indicators. Moreover, as the issue of quantifying and promoting intangible assets becomes a concern in the public sector, these standards can be seen as a first attempt to define library resources and services as such intangible assets. Finally, the challenge of forthcoming evolutions of these standards is the ability to stay up-to-date in a very quickly evolving context.

He concludes that "... the increase in the usability of these standards must be based on an ongoing search for more consistent data and relevant indicators. The question of improvement of the general design of the statistics and indicators standards family should also be addressed". Renard drew attention to the necessarily slow and cautious approach required for standards generation but the apparently opaque governance of production of international standards that relate to libraries, and especially public libraries, does not sit well with "the ability to stay up-to-date in a very quickly evolving context".

The Global Libraries Initiative

Since the beginning of this century, and increasingly over the past decade or so, national and global-level performance measurement and impact evaluation of public libraries were given a significant boost by the Global Libraries initiative

(GL). It was the first program initiated by the Bill and Melinda Gates Foundation and grew out of a series of grants commencing in 1997 to develop public library systems in the US, Mexico, and Chile prior to the establishment of the Foundation. The grants helped to fund the introduction of free public access to computers and the Internet as well as to train library managers and staff to use the Internet. Before the program's conclusion in 2018, GL broadened its role to encompass training library managers and staff in how to help people to search for information on the Internet and how to make the advocacy case for libraries. The GL country grants provided multi-year funds to government institutions or intermediary organizations in countries that had a high need for public access to information and a readiness to implement technology access in public libraries. The grants funded efforts to understand local information and technology needs, purchase equipment for libraries, train library staff, and help libraries build public support for long-term funding. The program focused on developing and transitioning countries. Grants were made to 19 countries, and on a smaller scale, by working through intermediaries, to five more.

The initiative also worked to ensure adequate resources and public policy support for libraries, and to help public libraries, library staff, and the library field measure the impact of public access in libraries and strengthen their advocacy skills, based on a specially developed training curriculum, to try to ensure adequate funding and resources to meet the information needs of their communities. Two authors of this chapter involved with GL as impact consultants since 2007 and the third author was the GL impact planning and assessment specialist (and later a program officer) from 2011 until 2016. The early GL country grantees relied largely on performance data to show their effects, but by the time that the second round of country grants was awarded, from 2007 onwards, it was evident that a stronger focus was needed on changing people's lives, in line with the core aims of the Foundation. The GL efforts to secure this focus for its country grants present an interesting model of governance, involving measurement systems in particular.

The Common Impact Measurement System

In order to tell its story of change to the Foundation, GL needed basic performance data from the grantees who delivered the program in each country, but also impact evidence. At first, the impact emphasis was on collecting country-level evidence to show how the program contributed to change for its users. GL insisted that grantees should employ an impact specialist as part of the program implementation team. GL also employed impact consultants to help shape the

GL approach to evidence-collection based on currently available research and, crucially, to work with potential grantees when they were preparing grant proposals. Once grants were awarded, the consultants continued to work with the country teams and the impact specialists in implementing evaluation plans. In 2009 an impact planning and assessment roadmap for new impact specialists was compiled by the GL team at BMGF, working closely with the existing impact specialists and impact consultants. The resulting document covered both performance data collection, using library performance definitions based on ISO 11620, and impact evidence-gathering for each phase of the country grant cycle: pre-planning and learning; planning; implementation; and applying the findings and embedding impact planning and assessment. The collaborative development approach adopted to produce the roadmap established a governance pattern that continued until the close of the program.

One of the principles underlying the GL approach to development was that each country team should be free to decide where to target its program and how to organize its delivery. This gave rise to the concept of localization of performance and impact indicators and desired impacts at country level in line with the program aims. The concept continued to be important in country grant delivery. At first, the GL team at BMGF was inhibited in its ability to tell the story of change because each country in the program gathered performance data in different ways, largely reflecting existing practice within the countries, and impact evidence was initially collected through a range of methods which allowed little scope for comparisons across countries.

To overcome the problem, GL introduced in 2013 a common impact measurement system (CIMS) based on library user self-reporting of impacts gained from having free public access to computers and the Internet across seven core issue areas: digital inclusion; culture and leisure; education; communication; economic development; health; government and governance. GL country grantees quickly began to use CIMS to quantify the impact of their work on library users. Data collected through CIMS enabled libraries to shift their focus from the services they provided to the impact that the services had on individuals and communities.

By agreeing to report the same measures using common definitions and methods, both the GL team at BMGF and country grantees could use standardized data to inform governance at international and national levels in various ways:
- Aggregate data to show the total impact of GL country grantees and enhance their ability to advocate for the importance of public libraries
- Track data over time to identify and monitor trends in public library use and reach, and incorporate this information into country grant programs and library services

- Compare data across countries to allow them to learn from each other's successes and challenges
- Provide a central, definitive source in communications and advocacy activities, so there is no confusion about where the numbers come from or how they are calculated
- Use the online reporting system to visualize public library data, giving the GL participants insight into dynamic results as they were reported.

Governance and the Common Impact Measurement System

The CIMS outcomes, indicators, and methods were designed in collaboration with the GL staff, evaluation experts, and several members of each country grant team, including program directors and advocacy specialists: in all, more than 50 people shaped the framework over a year-long process. The impact specialists of country teams were most deeply engaged in the design process. They provided critical input on every step of the design of CIMS, from indicator selection to method guideline development.

The stated reasons for adopting a collaborative approach to this element of the GL program were to:

- Promote a sense of shared ownership and familiarity with CIMS among country grantees
- Ensure that the indicators are truly relevant in the context of country grants
- Ensure that the methodology is practical and not a burden on country grantees and
- Enhance country grantee expertise in research, planning, evaluation, and indicator development (Paley 2015, 137, 139).

The first three of the reasons and, implicitly, the fourth one too, continued to underpin the international governance of the GL initiative, as the following two examples of system development show:

- Choosing a set of common performance measures introduced in 2009 and refined in 2013, taking its lead from the Foundation position that "we do not require [grantees] to report on all of their activities" (BMGF 2013), the GL team engaged in extensive consultation with country teams, their impact specialists, and consultants to arrive at a minimum set of performance data, the common performance measurement system, that shows what is happening in each country, and agreed on a set of definitions to ensure that each country reports similar sets of data. Not only was the aim to arrive at a minimum set to help tell the overall GL story of change, but all the impact specialists, both then and since, agreed that the selected data were useful to them for their own evaluation purposes

– The Global Libraries Data Atlas, which began as an online reporting system for the GL grantees to submit data on library performance and community impact. The key players in this phase of development included: GL leaders and staff; other BMGF staff with expertise in analytics, information technology, and software development; grantees, primarily advocacy and impact specialists, but also program directors; and consultants who were library impact evaluation experts as well as analytics and software developers.

A grander ambition to serve the global libraries field was set in late 2015, to connect libraries worldwide through a shared vision of impact and performance metrics, accessible through an interactive website. Work in 2016 focused on outreach to potential users through a pilot project. Both the number of contributors and the consultation process were extended even further. The user requirements gathering process was extended to elicit views from a constellation of other entities in the public library field, comprising representative international bodies including NAPLE, EBLIDA, IFLA, EIFL, regional library associations, and national bodies such as national libraries and national library associations, as well as a variety of people from a broad range of countries: library directors at the local level; system librarians at metropolitan libraries; staff from ministries of culture; and IFLA section leaders. All were consulted to find out what they would want from a library impact data platform, what they would use it for, how it might help them do their jobs more effectively, and how public libraries around the world would benefit. Further consultations continued to guide decisions about creating and developing the Global Data Atlas and to prioritize a set of features for future development. The reporting system was further adapted, developed, and promoted on a world-wide basis through the *IFLA Library Map of the World*.

It is not anticipated that the intensity of consultation will become the norm for shared governance at international level and the final decisions about deploying resources to the Global Data Atlas development were taken by the GL senior management. However, the level of engagement over time demonstrates the GL commitment to shared governance.

Each of these systems represents a distinct link in the GL story of change: the aim is to increase access to information, as measured by the common performance measures and the CIMS, to improve people's lives, and to tell the story across countries using the Data Atlas. The CIMS represents a significant step forward in comparative public library impact evaluation. A full description of CIMS, as well as of the common performance metrics and the Data Atlas, is available (Paley 2015).

Other Global Library Initiatives

Two other GL innovations further illustrate the strength of the collaborative approach to governance of performance measurement and impact evaluation.

A Pan-European survey of attitudes to public libraries in seventeen European Union countries, including five that also received GL country grants, was commissioned from the independent market survey company TNS in 2012. The purpose of the research was to understand the impact that public libraries in the EU have on users' lives, focusing on key areas of the *Europe 2020 Strategy*. The strategy calls for smart, sustainable, and inclusive growth and the research undertaken identified specifically employment, innovation, education, and social inclusion as domains where there is some evidence that ICT access through public libraries can support the implementation of the specific EU 2020 growth, education, and cohesion policies.

The collaborative governance approach was further extended and modified to allow maximum reach for the survey. Key participants included the TNS research team and GL members, GL team members at BMGF, consultants, and the country team impact specialists of the five GL countries in the EU. Selected representatives of the public library field in each of the countries surveyed were introduced soon after the start of the work to provide a bridge between the researchers and public library managers in their countries and later to help with the interpretation of the survey results. The outcome was a survey entailing more than 42,000 interviews with the general public, public library users, and public access computer users in libraries across the seventeen countries.

The complex process was managed through a series of strategy meetings, constant e-mail communication, and a workshop involving key stakeholders to discuss the key priorities for the research. The interaction culminated in a research seminar where participants were joined by other key stakeholders including country program directors and advocacy specialists of the five GL countries to receive the main project report, help interpret the findings, and decide what to do with the results. In addition to the main project report (Quick et al. 2013), TNS prepared comparative reports for each country and a further report comparing the five GL countries with the other twelve. Documents are available at the University of Washington TASCHA website: http://tascha.uw.edu/publications-resources/. Advocacy work based on the survey is being pursued with EU policymakers through a strategy led by the Reading and Writing Foundation (Cottrill et al. 2015; https://publiclibraries2030.eu/resources/eu-library-factsheets/).

Learnings about the GL evaluation and evidence-based advocacy work have been published in reports of progress and innovative evaluation and advocacy work has been made available in peer-reviewed journals. Impact specialists in country teams are encouraged to make conference presentations and to publish accounts of their work. In order to attract attention for this work, GL has taken over two special issues of the journal *Performance Measurement and Metrics* to tell the evolving GL story of evaluation and advocacy. The first of these was published in volume 13, issue 1 in 2012. The more recent issue was volume 16, issue 2 in 2015 and consists of four papers, introduced by the GL Director. The papers report on GL impact planning and assessment progress (Al et al. 2015); describe the evolution of GL measurement and evaluation systems (Paley et al. 2015); outline the GL approach to advocacy (Cottrill et al. 2015); and identify some innovations, for library evaluation, measurement, and impact work (Streatfield et al. 2015). Later papers offered a further progress report (Streatfield et al. 2019a) and updates on innovative evaluation (Streatfield et al. 2019b).

The papers were written by various combinations of country team directors, impact and advocacy specialists, GL team members and consultants, and national library staff. One paper has 17 authors! Looking at the GL approach to performance measurement and impact evaluation described from a governance perspective, it is clear that GL is setting and driving the strategy but sharing the international governance of the program, and largely devolving responsibility for the country-level delivery, evaluation, and reporting of the program to the country teams. The approach works if there is a strong hand at the centre to decide between conflicting points of view and offers the most productive way forward even if more compromise is needed to achieve satisfactory progress.

The GL collaborative approach proved effective because all the participants had a shared commitment to making the program work and because adequate funding was available to bring people together when required as part of their normal work commitment. Although a collaborative approach to governance looks like the only viable way to fully engage a critical mass of public library leaders in international performance measurement and impact evaluation, there are obvious potential issues about the commitment of key players and their competing work priorities as well as challenges in achieving and maintaining a common focus and shared understanding of objectives. However, the approach offers a potential solution to the current ISO problem of how to get countries to adopt common standards for public library performance measurement. It also offers a tested model which could be adapted for the governance of evaluation tool development and other international evaluation initiatives in the library world and beyond.

Unfortunately, the GL initiative ended in 2018 after more than 15 years of generous funding by the Bill and Melinda Gates Foundation, but the GL evaluation story does not end there. Three legacy partner organizations are continuing aspects of the envisaged GL work. They are organizations that are seen to be core contributors to the library sector and will continue to do strategic work, aided by GL grant funds, for much of the next decade. One of these, IFLA, also has a potentially important governance role for performance measurement and impact evaluation which is examined in the next section.

Another GL initiative, the International Network of Library Innovators (INELI), is training future public library leaders from emergent and developing countries across the globe. Through INELI, future leaders are being exposed to performance measurement and impact evaluation issues and approaches which should equip them to take on strategic roles in influencing future international governance of public library evaluation.

Measurement and Evaluation in Public Libraries: Future Governance

What are the governance issues and challenges for future public library performance measurement and impact evaluation at national and international levels? As Høivik (2013) shows, some countries still have no national statistics for libraries and the precise number of functioning public libraries in some countries, such as India, is not known even before moving into considering the thorny areas of defining a public library or collecting data consistently. How can the gaps be addressed? Renard (2007) has shown the limitations of a top down approach to encouraging standards for public library performance measurement, especially when the approach is led by armchair experts.

The GL initiative may provide a useful model. In some GL grant countries such as South Africa and India, starter-level workshops are being provided for library staff to help them to understand the importance of having good library data. The aim is to prepare the way for new data collection processes, ensuring that the data are collected and reported more carefully, and to encourage library staff to draw attention to interesting stories of change amongst their users. A combination of awareness-raising about the importance of being able to demonstrate the value of public libraries, specific training such as just described, and giving greater attention to the transparency of international standards creation, are needed if real progress is to be made.

Learning from International Development Evaluation

Future governance of national and international evaluation is not happening in a public library bubble. International development and education evaluation, from which most ideas about impact evaluation are drawn, are steadily evolving. Over the past two decades, there has been growing disillusion with the simple logic model of evaluation in these fields because the model does not represent either the complexity of an intervention or of the environment in which it is operating. The simple logic model leaves out other factors that might contribute to observed outcomes, including the implementation context; it assumes a stable environment and predictable outcomes. The disillusion has led to a gradual movement towards program-theory approaches (Rogers and Weiss 2007). There are several variations on program-theory driven evaluation but they all share some key factors:

- Acceptance of the argument that complexity is now the norm and that complex situations and initiatives require flexible, agile evaluation approaches to deal with multiple factors, relationships, and layers. Complexity, in this context, describes situations where the paths from action to impact are complex, with disproportionate relationships in which, at critical levels, a small change can make a big difference and emergent impacts, which cannot readily be specified at the outset.
- Central importance is given to rigorous and systematic early articulation of the ways in which the program or service expects to bring about clearly identified changes in individuals and communities at a range of different levels and identify the assumptions lying behind expectations and the barriers to change. These are all usually distilled into a Theory of Change
- Using the Theory of Change to carefully focus data collection activities, increasingly by using mixed methods which combine several qualitative and quantitative research methods to provide evidence of change (Greene 2008; Patton 2011).

The more advanced public library services appear to have all the characteristics required for the complex logic model, but to date there has been more discussion than action in addressing the issue. A fuller discussion of the relevance of program theory to a library context is addressed by Markless and Streatfield (2017).

More Inclusive Evaluation

The international development evaluation literature is advancing another important idea that is relevant to the governance of public libraries, that of a more inclusive and democratic evaluation embracing a wider range of stakeholders, including marginalized groups, and involving them in designing the evaluations and in interpreting the findings (for example, Mertens 2003; Greene 2006; Patton 2012). Central here is the idea of preventing qualitative evaluation from becoming just another way of enforcing the existing power relationships between organizations and their people. In public library evaluation this idea can take various forms, ranging from consultation with users about the impact areas for evaluations and forming evaluation partnerships with stakeholders to establishing panels of library staff and users to review impact evidence and take editorial decisions about the presentation of results.

The Role of IFLA

With the conclusion of GL funding, who else can lead the international governance of public library evaluation? The most likely candidate is IFLA and there is already evidence that IFLA is renewing its interest in collecting national public library statistics and beginning to engage with impact evaluation.

Two of the authors have been involved in advising IFLA about evaluating the impact of three of their international programs. By describing these briefly in chronological order of engagement, it is fairly easy to see how the strategic IFLA view of evaluation is changing.

Freedom of Access to Information and Freedom of Expression (FAIFE)

FAIFE (https://www.ifla.org/faife) is "an initiative to defend and promote the basic human rights defined in Article 19 of the United Nations Universal Declaration of Human Rights, by furthering freedom of access to information and freedom of expression ... related to libraries and librarianship." The FAIFE Committee has adopted a top-down approach to creating an impact evaluation framework, with consultancy help from the authors, but largely delegated implementation of the evaluation to country teams and individually to a centrally-provided team of core trainers.

Building Strong Library Associations (BSLA)

With BSLA (https://www.ifla.org/bsla), the governance of the program evaluation evolved as the program itself developed. The evaluation framework for the first phase of the program was again created by a planning group, with help from the authors, who were then asked to adapt the framework for small projects, and for assessing impact at the regional level by country or regional teams during phase two. Finally, they were asked to conduct a summative evaluation for phase two of the program. Since the authority, decision-making, and accountability within the program were all diffuse, it is not surprising that BSLA lacked a strong Theory of Change. The omission resulted in a situation where it was clear from the summative evaluation that the program was a big success. However, it was difficult to describe the precise intervention method that brought about success and in which circumstances this occurred, because the core trainers who acted as change agents for the program interpreted and carried out their roles in different ways.

The International Advocacy Program (IAP)

IAP (https://www.ifla.org/ldp/iap) is a new capacity-building program designed to promote and support the role libraries can play in the planning and implementation of the UN 2030 Agenda and the Sustainable Development Goals (https://sustainabledevelopment.un.org/sdgs). This time, the consultants have been asked to help construct a Theory of Change to drive the program evaluation, as well as to provide evaluation materials and guidance for people involved in evaluating the program at country and regional levels (Streatfield and Markless, 2019).

By continuing to use their development programs to encourage people at country and regional levels to engage in systematic performance measurement and impact evaluation, IFLA can make a major contribution to raising awareness about the importance of gathering evidence of change and using it to advocate on behalf of public and other types of libraries.

Today the World

IFLA has made earlier attempts to gather comparative library statistics with mixed results, but has now re-entered the fray by taking over, extending and developing the *GL Data Atlas* concept and launching the *IFLA Library Map of the World*.

It is a representative source of basic library statistics and a robust tool providing country-level data and a worldwide comparison of different library performance data by global region. It features all types of libraries, including national, academic, public, community, school, and special libraries. The initial set of performance metrics include number of libraries, number of libraries providing Internet access, number of staff and volunteers, number of registered users and visitors, and number of loans.

The Map is not just a library statistics tool. It is being expanded to include stories of change relating to the UN Social Development goals. Picking up on the shared governance theme, the *IFLA Library Map of the World* is being created in partnership with data and story contributors including national library associations, national libraries, library support organizations and other institutions, from around the world. Reliable global library statistics is our shared vision". By late 2017, the map covered 99 countries and had 110 contributors (https://librarymap. ifla.org/).

It is strongly hoped that people involved in national and international public library governance will work to ensure that their libraries engage more systematically with impact evaluation in coming years. If this happens, there should be scope to make the collection of stories of change more systematic and to build on the example of CIMS to add a dimension of comparative impact evidence to the global public library picture presented in the IFLA Library Map of the World.

References

Al, U., P. Andrade Blanco, M. Chiranov, L.M. Cruz Silva, L.M., L.N. Devetakova, Y. Dewata, I. Dryžaite, F. Farquharson, M. Kochanowicz, T. Liubyva, A. López Naranjo, Q.T. Phan, R. Ralebipi-Simela, I. Soydal, E.R. Streatfield, R. Taolo, T.T.T. Trần, and Y. Tkachuk. "Global Libraries Impact Planning and Assessment Progress". *Performance Measurement and Metrics* 16, no. 2 (2015): 109–31. https://doi.org/10.1108/PMM-05-2015-0015.

Bill and Melinda Gates Foundation (BMGF). *How We Work: Evaluation Policy*. Seattle, USA: BMGF, 2013. https://www.gatesfoundation.org/How-We-Work/General-Information/Evaluation-Policy.

Carden, Fred. *Knowledge to Policy: Making the Most of Development Research*. Ottawa: Sage/IDRC, 2009. https://idl-bnc-idrc.dspacedirect.org/handle/10625/37706.

Cottrill, J., F. Letelier, P. Andrade Blanco, H. García, M. Chiranov, Y. Tkachuk, T. Liubyva, R. Crocker, M. Vanderwerff, .G. Cistoviene, I. Krauls-Ward, E. Stratilatovas, D. Mount, and A. Kurutyte. and Triyono. "From Impact to Advocacy: Working Together Toward Public Library Sustainability". *Performance Measurement and Metrics* 16, no. 2 (2015): 159–76. https://doi.org/10.1108/PMM-04-2015-0008.

Craven, J., and P. Brophy. "Evaluating the Longitudinal Impact of Networked Services in UK Public Libraries: The Longitude II Project" *Performance Measurement and Metrics* 5, no. 3 (2004): 112–7. https://doi.org/10.1108/14678040410570139.

Didier, E.K. "Research on the Impact of School Library Media Programs on Student Achievement: Implications for School Media Professionals". In *School Library Media Annual*. edited by S.I. Aaron and P.R. Scales, 343–61. Littleton, CO: Libraries Unlimited, 1984.

Fitz-Gibbon, C.T. *Monitoring Education: Indicators, Quality and Effectiveness*. London: Cassell, 1996.

Greene, J.C. "Evaluation, Democracy and Social Change". In *Handbook of Evaluation: Policies, Programs and Practices*, edited by I.F. Shaw, J.C. Greene, and M.M. Mark, 312–317. London: Sage, 2006.

Greene, J.C. "Is Mixed Methods Social Inquiry a Distinctive Methodology?" *Journal of Mixed Methods Research* 2, no. 1 (2008) 7–22. https://doi.org/10.1177/1558689807309969.

Høivik, Tord. "Improving Practices: Statistical Standards in Global Libraries". Paper presented at: IFLA WLIC 2013 – Singapore – Future Libraries: Infinite Possibilities in Session 177 – Committee on Standards. 2013. http://library.ifla.org/229/.

Holt, G.E., D. Elliott, and C. Dussold. "A Framework for Evaluating Public Investment in Urban Libraries". *Bottom Line 9*, no. 4 (1996): 4–13.

International Organization for Standardization. *ISO 2789: Information and Documentation: International Library Statistics*. 5th edition. Geneva, Switzerland: ISO, 2013.

International Organization for Standardization. *ISO 11620: Information and Documentation: Library Performance Indicators*. 3rd edition. Geneva, Switzerland: ISO, 2014.

International Organization for Standardization. *ISO 16439: Information and Documentation: Methods and Procedures for Assessing the Impact of Libraries*. 1st edition. Geneva, Switzerland: ISO, 2014.

Markless, S., and D.R. Streatfield. *Evaluating the Impact of Your Library*. 2nd edition. London: Facet Publishing, 2013. http://www.facetpublishing.co.uk/title.php?id=8125.

Markless, S., and D.R. Streatfield. "How Can You Tell if It's Working? Recent Developments In Impact Evaluation and their Implications for Information Literacy Practice." *Journal of Information Literacy* 11, no. 1 (2017): 106–119. https://doi.org/10.11645/11.1.2201.

Mertens, D.M. "The Inclusive View of Evaluation: Implications of Transformative Theory for Evaluation". In *Evaluating Social Programs and Problems: visions for the new millennium*, edited by S. I. Donaldson and M. Scrivens, 87–105. Mahwah, NJ: Lawrence Erlbaum Associates, 2003.

Paley, J., Cottrill, J., Errecart, K., White, A., Schaden, C., Schrag, T.,Douglas, R., Tahmassebi, B., Crocker, R., and Streatfield, D.R. "The Evolution of Global Libraries' Performance Measurement and Impact Assessment Systems". *Performance Measurement and Metrics* 16, no. 2 (2015): 132–58. https://doi.org/10.1108/PMM-04-2015-0010.

Patton, M.Q. *Developmental Evaluation: Applying Complexity Concepts to Enhance Innovation and Use*. New York, NY: The Guilford Press, 2011.

Patton, M.Q. *Essentials of Utilization-focused Evaluation*. Thousand Oaks, CA: Sage, 2012.

Quick, S., G. Prior, B. Toombs, L. Taylor, and R. Currenti. *Cross-European Survey to Measure Users' Perceptions of the Benefits of ICT in Public Libraries: Final report*. London: TNS and BMGF, 2013. https://tascha.uw.edu/publications/cross-european-survey-to-measure-users-perceptions-of-the-benefits-of-ict-in-public-libraries/.

Renard, P.-Y. "ISO 2789 and ISO 11620: Short Presentation of Standards as Reference Documents in an Assessment Process". *LIBER Quarterly* 17 (2007): 3–4. http://doi. org/10.18352/lq.7885.

Rogers, P.J. "Using Programme Theory to Evaluate Complicated and Complex Aspects of Interventions". *Evaluation* 14, no. 1 (2008): 29–48. DOI: 10.1177/1356389007084674.

Rogers, P.J., and C.H. Weiss. "Theory-based Evaluation: Reflections Ten Years On: Theory-Based Evaluation: Past, Present, and Future". *New Directions for Evaluation* 114 (2007): 63–81. http://dx.doi.org/10.1002/ev.225.

Streatfield, D.R., and S. Markless. "Impact Evaluation and IFLA: Evaluating the Impact of Three International Capacity Building Initiatives". *Performance Measurement and Metrics*, 20, no. 2 (2019):105-122. https://doi.org/10.1108/PMM-03-2019-0008

Streatfield, D.R., P. Andrade Blanco, M. Chiranov, I. Dryžaite, M. Kochanowicz, T. Liubyva, and Y. Tkachuk. "Innovative Impact Planning and Assessment through Global Libraries". *Performance Measurement and Metrics* 16, no. 2 (2015): 177–192. https://doi.org/10.1108/ PMM-04-2015-0011

Streatfield, D.R., R. Abisla, U. Al, V. Bunescu, Y. Dewata, C. Garroux, D. Sharma, D. Greeb, A. Maister, J. Paley, S. Sharma, T. Sharma, I. Soydal, and T.T.T. Trần. "Global Libraries Impact Planning and Assessment Progress: part 2" *Performance Measurement and Metrics* 20 no. 2 (2019a): 85-104. https://doi.org/10.1108/PMM-03-2019-0007

Streatfield, D.R., S. Markless, N. Cookman, D. Herbert, S. McCulloch, and R. Swan. *Best Value and Better Performance in Libraries*. Library and Information Commission Research Report 52. Twickenham, Middlesex: Information Management Associates for the Library and Information Commission, 2000.

Streatfield, D.R., R. Abisla, V. Bunescu, M. Chiranov, C. Garroux, A. Maister, L. González Martín, J. Paley, and S. Rae-Scott. "Innovative Impact Planning and Assessment through Global Lbraries: Sustaining Innovation during a Time of Transition", *Performance Measurement and Metrics* 20 no. 2 (2019b): 74-84. https://doi.org/10.1108/PMM-03-2019-0010

Wavell, C., G. Baxter, I. Johnson, and D. Williams. *Impact Evaluation of Museums, Archives and Libraries: Available Evidence Project*. Prepared by the School of Information and Media, Faculty of Management, Robert Gordon University, 2000.

Weightman, A.L., and J. Williamson. "The Value and Impact of Information Provided through Library Services for Patient Care: a Systematic Review". [Work conducted on behalf of the Library and Knowledge Development Network (LKDN), Quality and Statistics Group]. *Health Information and Libraries Journal* 22, no. 1 (2005): 4–25.

White, H. "A Contribution to Current Debates in Impact Evaluation". *Evaluation* 16, no. 2 (2010): 153–64. http://evi.sagepub.com/content/16/2/153.

Jan Richards
15 Public Libraries – A Global Vision

Abstract: While the core values for public libraries remain constant, the environment is constantly evolving, and public libraries must change in response. The International Federation of Library Associations and Institutions (IFLA) has played a crucial role in the development of public libraries across the world, and particularly in their governance. Following consultations in 2017 as part of the IFLA *Global Vision*, the IFLA Public Libraries Section recognised the core value of public libraries as including social inclusion, free and open access to information, and a force for democracy. The need to challenge current structures and behaviours and to step outside the comfort zone if public libraries are to remain relevant in today's society was affirmed. Increasingly there is a recognition of the need to work collaboratively and internationally to expand the capacity and influence of the public library. This chapter highlights public library achievements in relation to the IFLA *Global Vision*.

Keywords: Globalization; Library cooperation; Organisational change; Public libraries; International Federation of Library Associations and Institutions

Introduction

Writing in the *Library Journal*, Rebecca Miller editorialized "I have long thought of libraries as a network that, despite largely local governance, transcends borders of all types to make up a global community" (Miller 2018). The concept of a connected community of interest is reflected in the *IFLA Library Map of the World*. In 2017, there were an estimated 345,660 public libraries worldwide (405,455 in 2019) with 533.5 million registered members and 3,720.8 million physical visits. These numbers are extremely conservative as the country data from much of the developing world is yet to be included but it provides an indication of the breadth and reach of the global public library community (IFLA Library Map of the World 2018).

As part of IFLA's *Global Vision* process (https://www.ifla.org/node/11900) examining future directions, IFLA sections held discussions and addressed issues in 2017 and 2018. Following consultations in 2017, the IFLA Public Libraries Section prepared a report on how a united library field might tackle the challenges of the future (IFLA Public Libraries Section 2017). The report identified the core values of public libraries as:
- Social inclusion

https://doi.org/10.1515/ 9783110533323-018

- – Free and open access to information
- – A force for democracy
- – Centre for life-long learning
- – Promoting reading and literacy.
- –

While public library core values remain constant, the environment is constantly evolving and the vision, values, role and activities of public libraries must change accordingly. This chapter presents a snapshot of the public library environment in the second half of 2018. The fact that it will unquestionably alter reflects the rapidly evolving operational setting where the only certainty is that change is inevitable. What is important is how the sector moulds and adapts to change to meet the needs of society and addresses the specific needs of the community.

Think Global Act Local

Originally coined in the context of environmental challenges the expression, Think Global, Act Local, mirrors the attitude of the international public library sector which has a highly collaborative, flexible and nimble approach. At the global level, IFLA's Public Libraries Section is a very active unit with a wide geographic reach. The highly experienced Standing Committee comprises 25 elected members from 21 countries across five continents. The Section is committed to ensuring that the world's communities have free and equal access to information and public library services and it provides a forum and network for the development and promotion of public libraries. The Section also represents mobile libraries.

During 2017, IFLA embarked on a journey to bring together the international library community in a series of workshops and online discussions, to explore the challenges and opportunities that face us all. Branded as the *Global Vision* the project focused on how to strengthen ties within the library field, the identification of future challenges and opportunities, and priorities for actions that the library environment could take in response to the fast-pacing changes in society. *Global Vision* presented the opportunity to look to the future and agree on a shared way forward. The Public Libraries Standing Committee used the process as a chance to engage in a robust discussion about the future of the sector. The Committee's detailed responses have formed the basis of much of the content of this chapter. While Committee members' individual views have been formed by individual experiences and circumstances, the Committee as a whole was unanimous in the assessment that in the twenty first century public libraries are still relevant for society, but they must be really inclusive, adapt to new challenges and constantly re-define their role.

In March 2018, the findings of the global discussions were released at the IFLA President's meeting in Barcelona, Spain. The *Global Vision* develops *Our Vision, Our Future* (IFLA 2018a) and the *Report Summary* (IFLA 2018b) brings together the findings of 185 workshops across 190 UN member states on seven continents attended by 9,300 individuals. The Summary identifies ten interlinked highlights and opportunities to consider and explore in moving towards a collaborative future. The highlights, and the opportunities, provide a sound basis on which to reflect on the current position and future direction of public libraries and are used in this chapter to outline global developments:

1.   We are dedicated to equal and free access to information and knowledge/We must be champions of intellectual freedom
2.   We remain deeply committed to supporting literacy, learning and reading/We must update our roles in the digital age
3.   We are focused on serving our communities/We need to understand community needs better and design services for impact
4.   We embrace digital innovation/We must keep up with ongoing technological changes
5.   We have leaders who see the need for strong advocacy/We need more and better advocates at all levels
6.   We see funding as one of our biggest challenges/We need to ensure stakeholders understand our value and impact
7.   We see the need to build collaboration and partnerships/We need to develop a spirit of collaboration
8.   We want to be less bureaucratic, inflexible and resistant to change/We need to challenge current structures and behaviours
9.   We are the guardians of the memory of the world/We need to maximise access to the world's documentary heritage
10. Our young professionals are deeply committed and eager to lead/We must give young professionals effective opportunities to learn, develop and lead (IFLA 2018b).

Free and Equal Access to Information

The first highlight refers to free and equal access and the public library's role in supporting an informed, engaged and democratic society is enshrined in the *IFLA/UNESCO Public Library Manifesto* (IFLA 1994). Freedom, prosperity and the development of society and of individuals are fundamental human values. They will be attained only through the ability of well-informed citizens to exercise their democratic rights and to play an active role in society. Constructive participation and the development of democracy depend on satisfactory education as well as on free and unlimited access to knowledge, thought, culture and information. The public library, the local gateway to knowledge, provides a basic condition for lifelong learning, independent decision-making and cultural development of the individual and social groups. While the *Manifesto* is dated 1994, the findings of the 2017 *Global Vision* process confirmed that a commitment to equal and free access to information and knowledge is universally accepted by the profession as the most highly rated value.

Internationally, public libraries in many countries are supported by legislation, which enshrines these principles. As society changes, the frameworks need to be assessed for relevance and adapted to meet community needs and expectations. In the past few years the Nordic countries of Finland and Norway have identified the need to review their respective legislation to strengthen communities. Based on the principles of equity and democracy, the Finnish Library Act was first established in 1928 and, in the intervening years, has been revised on a number of occasions. A combination of social changes led to the development of a new Act which came into force at the beginning of 2017. The new Act promotes active citizenship, democracy and freedom of expression grounded in principles of commonality, diversity and multiculturalism (Finland 2016). The concept of active engagement is key to amendments in the Norwegian Public Libraries Act of 2014 (Norway 2014) "...to promote the spread of information, education and other cultural activities through active dissemination... Public libraries are to be an independent meeting place and arena for public discussions and debates" (Somby 2017). The Finnish and Norwegian legislation recognise the role played by the extensive public library networks in both countries, and the importance of the library as the third place, a non-judgemental community and collaborative space that is available to everyone. Similarly, in Mexico the role of libraries in helping citizens to access public information and promote active participation in public decision-making is preserved in law (Mexico 2016).

While legislation plays an important role in facilitating free and equal access to information, positive and proactive action is required. Public libraries pride themselves on offering a safe, non-judgemental environment that is open to everyone; however, the processes and conventions in place often inhibit this. If public libraries are to guarantee that everyone is welcome and equally able to obtain information, lateral thinking and a fresh approach to problems from a different perspective are needed. Administrative requirements and societal attitudes often mean that homeless people have limited access to services provided by

public libraries. Among the possible barriers identified by the American Library Association as hindering use of the public library by this target group, the following rank the highest:
- Membership policies requiring a permanent address
- Prohibitive fines and fees
- Prejudices of staff and other library members
- Limited programs or resources that address people's experiences or current situations (American Library Association, 2019).

If the profession is to uphold the concept of free and equal access, library staff need support and permission to be adaptable and to consider services from the user perspective. This in turn requires awareness and a new way of thinking as outlined in the IFLA Guidelines for Library Services to People Experiencing Homelessness (IFLA 2017). Prejudice and barriers must be identified and overcome.

Zagreb City Libraries' award winning A *Book for a Roof* program provides services for the homeless including IT and creative workshops and engages with homeless people by utilising their skills in a volunteer capacity. "Our homeless citizens are not only users but also creators of the program, they become students who adopt new information and teachers who share knowledge and experience. We also started free art workshops for homeless people with the purpose of animating creative expressions. All this helps them to be included" (IFLA Public Libraries Section 2014).

Libraries throughout the world have a strong history of responding to natural disasters and humanitarian crises. They provide a welcoming environment, a place of refuge for body and soul, and a source of information. In December 2015, the Public Libraries Section brought together examples of public library initiatives that were being rolled out across Europe to support the refugee crisis. The result, *Responding! Public Libraries and Refugees* (IFLA 2015) demonstrated how flexibility and lateral thinking helped to position libraries as key to the relief effort. Simple measures such as reassessing the strict requirements for membership which included a permanent address for users, negotiating contracts with e-content providers and offering services outside the confines of the physical library all combined to ensure that libraries made a difference to people's lives.

Sadly, in some parts of the world, gender discrimination denies women the same free and equal access to information as men, and consequently many women are uneducated, illiterate and unskilled. For example, in some parts of Asia, women must often seek permission from their husbands to leave home for reasons other than childcare or farm work. Rural Education and Development (READ) Global (https://www.readglobal.org/) is a non-profit organization working in rural Asia to build community library and resource centres, READ Centers, that serve as platforms for education, community development, and women's empowerment. Through the work of READ Global, libraries have been positioned as safe, neutral places that women and girls can access independently and use to engage in practical courses and discussions. The recognition of barriers that prevent the free flow of information to all sections of the population is the first step in developing meaningful ways of overcoming them and creating an inclusive educated society.

A New World Supporting Literacy, Learning and Reading

Management of today's public library is a finely tuned balancing act. The community shows no sign of requiring less of the traditional services offered; at the same time, it is demanding new services, products and programs. Even the customary staple, the book, comes in new formats that force a reconsideration of the manner in which distribution and promotion are undertaken. All of this provides challenges, but also enormous opportunities to curate services designed specifically for community needs and to attract new audiences. Public librarians have adopted a flexible and inventive approach to meet changing user expectations and societal norms. Literacy has long been a core service provided by libraries but the definition of literacy has greatly expanded and now incorporates digital, cultural and financial literacy as well as other aspects. The Free Library of Philadelphia's Culinary Literacy Center (https://libwww.freelibrary.org/programs/culinary/) is a commercial-grade kitchen that serves as a classroom and dining space for the city. It supports a number of literacies in a fun, practical and interactive way through measuring, reading recipes, and observation. Classes have been designed for all ages and skill levels. A similar experience awaits the community at Barcelona's Bibliotecca del Fondo which, in addition to providing literacy programs, encourages the rich cultural heritage of the local cuisine (Domingo 2017).

Public libraries worldwide have increasingly focused on empowering their communities through the introduction of digital literacy programs. The field strongly agrees on the essential role of digital innovations in realising libraries' potential to enrich society, regardless of how extensively they already can and do use technology.

Hutt City Libraries in New Zealand runs Clubhouse13, an after-school program for 10–18 year olds, in two of its highly deprived communities. It is a free program, run by library staff and volunteer mentors. The program has social advantages and engages with disenfranchised communities. Attendees have learnt Photoshop, completed basic electronics projects with makey-makey kits, mashed up circuitry with fashion design, made and edited films, taken part in robotics competitions, completed graphic design jobs for community clients, formed a band, recorded tracks, and created start-up businesses (Australian Public Libraries Alliance 2017, 17). In the south of Sweden, Vaggeryd's joint public and upper secondary school library is the site of the first makerspace in Sweden. Opened in 2013, over the last four years makerspace programs have evolved to meet the technical skills needed in a community where furniture making is the main industry. There are workshops on robotics, lessons in CAD drawing, and the library is home to an upholstery machine that has enabled asylum-seeking unaccompanied minors to learn upholstery and carry out furniture repair as a social enterprise (Australian Public Libraries Alliance 2017, 20).There is a recognition that outreach is an important component of accessing hard to reach communities. In the northern Netherlands province of Fryslan, a mobile lab facility Fryslab has been used to bring 21ˢᵗ century technology skills to primary and secondary students in this rural area (De Boer 2014).

A Community Focus

Opportunity three in IFLA's *Global Vision Report Summary* provides a reminder that community needs must be better understood and services designed for impact. Expanding library outreach will enhance links with local partners, engage new and underserved sections of the community, and have a measurable impact on peoples' lives. Public libraries universally strive to ensure that the needs of their actual and potential users are addressed, and employ community-specific strategies to ensure that opportunities are maximised.

Community engagement is as an integral part of planning for library buildings and services. The best practice, Danish *Model Programme for Public Libraries* (Denmark 2015) places great emphasis on a well-planned user engagement strategy in the design of new or refurbished spaces and provides guidelines for how to achieve this. The IFLA/Systematic Public Library of the Year Awards (https://www.ifla.org/node/29023) were an outcome of the Model Programme and require strong evidence of how applicant libraries interact with local surroundings and culture. Those libraries which have been successful in the awards since they were instituted in 2014, have been able to satisfactorily demonstrate this.

The Model Programme highlights Narok Library, located about 150 kilometres from Nairobi in Kenya, which plays an important role in informing and bringing together the community. The population consists mainly of Maasai herdsmen who, at times, visit the Library with their flocks of cows and goats. Enclosed lands have been established around the Library to enable the herdsmen to read as they look after their herds. The Library works closely with the Ministry of Agriculture to give technical advice on livestock farming to help the Maasai people (Denmark 2017). In many countries where government funding is not available, communities and community organisations are actively engaged in developing and delivering public library services.

In Brazil, the number of public libraries does not meet the demand of the population. To address the issue, the Brazilian Institute for Studies and Community Support/Instituto Brasileiro de Estudos e Apoio Comunitário (iBeac) (http://www.ibeac.org.br/) has been instrumental in developing community libraries which meet identified needs in different parts of the country. iBeac has a particular focus on working with young people and assisting them to become a resource for their families and leaders within their communities. An example of the approach is evidenced in the creation of the Community Library Paths of Reading in Parelheiros, a low socio-economic, mostly rural district in Sao Paulo. Established in 2008 after community consultation, the Library initially occupied space within a health facility. When the space was no longer available, everyone mobilized to find a new location for the library. The solution was a gravedigger's house inside a cemetery. What could have been a cause for embarrassment became a source of pride for the young people who have continued to deliver literacy projects to children, young people and adults within their communities; and work with government and other agencies to improve educational, cultural and environmental policies (Ferrari 2016).

Recognition of community needs extends to the provision of services to remote communities where flexible and creative solutions are required to address specific situations which extend beyond traditional housebound and mobile services. One innovative example is the Ideas Box (https://www.librarieswithout borders.org/ideasbox/), a mobile pop-up multimedia centre and learning hub that provides educational and cultural resources to communities in need, including refugees and displaced persons in camps around the globe, and underserved communities in developed countries. Conceived by Libraries Without Borders following the devastating 2010 earthquakes in Haiti, the Ideas Box is highly durable, energy-independent and easy to set up. Each box contains technology, books, board games and arts and crafts materials and a stage for music and theatre. Each box is customised to meet local needs. Since its introduction to the library community, the Ideas Box has been employed in about 20 countries worldwide and its flexibility has allowed it to be used in a variety of ways, addressing local needs. It has been effective in reaching people in remote, rural populations in Columbia most affected by war (Libraries Without Borders 2017) and, at the same time has been used in Detroit in the US as a means of highlighting the importance of literacy, numeracy and digital fluency (Gullickson 2015). If public libraries are to secure and maintain support, including funding, there is a need to ensure that stakeholders, particularly decision makers, understand the value and impact of public libraries.

During March 2019 the Islamic Republic of Iran was affected by extensive flooding with extensive damage in 28 of the country's 31 provinces. Against the background of this national disaster, the Iran Public Library Foundation and the public library sector worked with the community to support the citizens of Iran. Under the banner Spring Kindness, a program was launched to distribute books, games and toys to children in flood ravaged areas with libraries acting as deposit stations and the library infrastructure being used to deliver the items. Libraries were seen as places of safety for at risk groups, in particular children and young people, and in some centres, schools operated out of public libraries (Iran Public Library Foundation 2019).

Advocacy and Value

"While there is a general recognition of the vital contribution public libraries make towards the social capital, educational and recreational development of local communities, there is increasing pressure for libraries to clearly demonstrate their contribution in terms of value". This introductory statement in *Enriching Communities: The Value of Public Libraries in NSW* (Library Council of New South Wales 2008, 3) describes the necessity for public libraries to be able to articulate their worth and to adapt the argument to suit the audience.

There have been many international studies about the social and economic value of public libraries and many of these are detailed on the IFLA Public Library Section's website with a page devoted to the value of libraries (https://www.ifla.org/node/9011). While each study varies in approach, collectively they provide a compelling argument to support public libraries. Recent initiatives in library assessment include tools to assist public libraries in analysing their communities and measuring outcomes. One initiative is the PLA *Project Outcome* toolkit (Public Library Association 2018), which gives libraries worldwide free access to a suite of resources that can be used to gain a greater understanding of library effectiveness.

Working Collaboratively

While public libraries have long been active in the partnership space, increasingly there is a recognition that working collaboratively will expand capability and influence. In a global world, public libraries have many potential competitors, and while public libraries argue that they are best placed to deliver effective services to their communities, a realistic approach must be taken to build on support by creating alliances. The evidence of successful partnerships can be found across library networks and includes all aspects of service delivery. Partners include: other libraries; the Galleries Libraries Archives and Museums (GLAM) sector; government agencies and non-government organizations (NGOs); charities; educational institutions; the media; and heritage organisations. The possibilities of working together with others are limited only by the imagination of the participants.

An example of lateral thinking in this regard is the award-winning project Library in the Tram – Tram to the Library from Brno in the Czech Republic, a partnership between the library and the city's public transport network. Designed to promote library use, the customised tram is equipped with special library displays and QR codes for downloading free eBooks. Throughout the year, the library mounts thematic reading campaigns, and library volunteers riding the tram give small gifts to reading passengers. Reaching about 1,000 passengers a day, the tram service demonstrates innovative thinking (IFLA Public Libraries Section 2014). *Building on the Bookends Scenarios,* an examination of future trends in the NSW Australia public library network, suggested that libraries shift "slightly from places full of interesting and useful stuff to places where interesting and useful stuff happens" (State Library of New South Wales 2015a, 32), potentially encompassing alliances with arts-based organisations to attract new audiences. An example of such a program is the livestreaming of Sydney Symphony Orchestra's (SSO) performance of Verdi's *Requiem* across regional areas of the state as part of 2018 Make Music Day. The locations chosen for participation would not normally have access to live performances by the SSO and the partnership confirmed the Library's place as central to the cultural life of the community (State Library of New South Wales 2018). Also in Australia, ScreenWest (https://www.screenwest.com.au/) works with the State Library of Western Australia to support digitising some of the Library's most at risk films, which they then broadcast on large outdoor screens in the Perth CBD (State Library of Western Australia 2018).

Public Libraries in England have worked with The Reading Agency and the Wellcome Institute to develop their Universal Health Offers (https://www.libraries connected.org.uk/universal-offers/health-wellbeing) which help people better understand their health and wellbeing. Through the Health and Wellbeing Offer, libraries promote healthier, happier, connected living providing self-management support and engagement opportunities for children and adults supported by welcoming spaces, effective signposting and information to reduce health, social and economic inequalities. The programs provided build on the concept of the library as a trusted community space, which offers assisted digital access, health information, resources and services, and volunteering and recreational opportunities (Libraries Connected 2018).

In Kiberia, an informal settlement in Nairobi, Kenya, the Kenya National Library Service has partnered with NGO Practical Action and Berkley Foundation in the UK to establish a community library. With over 500 visits a day, the Library supports the 30 educational institutions that surround it. One of the Library's key projects is Kids on the Tab, an initiative that encourages learning through the lending of tablets with pre-loaded educational content. There have been demonstrated improvements in educational achievements, motivation and confidence resulting from the approach (IFLA Library Map of the World 2018).

Professional networks and associations have a key role in promoting and enabling a collaborative approach. Some public library associations have a long and proud history. Others are evolving as public librarians gain a voice within their country. In India, 111 years since the first public library system was established, the Indian Public Library Movement was registered as an independent and legal entity in October 2018 as a result of sustained effort by local and international partners to achieve the vision of creating an enabling environment with multi stakeholder engagement. It operates under the auspices of the NASSCOM Foundation (https://nasscomfoundation.org/iplm/; https://www.facebook.com/nasscomfoundation1/).

Change and Stepping Outside the Comfort Zone

If public libraries are to remain relevant in today's society, current structures and behaviours must be challenged. One might cringe at the stereotypical portrayal of a librarian, and yet maintaining a bureaucratic and inflexible approach because that is the way it has always been runs the risk of alienating public libraries and librarians from their stakeholders. Rethinking the context and environment involves reflection on how best to maximise opportunities and consider how current practices might limit outreach and goal achievement. Examples of how some restrictive administrative practices such as membership prerequisites impact on service delivery have already been mentioned, while others such whether or not to impose overdue fines continue to be debated. A bigger discussion revolves around the public libraries' place in the world of anywhere and anytime. Do libraries continue to operate within set hours from fixed locations or is it timely to move beyond and truly engage with communities?

The concept of the 24/7 library has expanded to encompass not just the online, but also the physical environment. Increasingly libraries are responding to community expectations that entrance to library spaces and collections will extend beyond the traditional staffed opening hours. This builds on the experience of the academic world where information commons accessed by swipe cards have been standard practice for some years and reflects commercial models of practice such as 24-hour gyms. Incorporating extended, unstaffed hours into the library model requires a consideration of service delivery that includes a perceived relinquishing of control. The successful introduction of new operational initiatives is based on sound risk management, the effective use of technology and a cost/benefit analysis.

The model is well-established in in Scandinavia where libraries opening in an extended mode are also known as open libraries. Experience demonstrates that visitation and loans have increased and there is greater community ownership of the facility (Larsen 2013). Building on the concept of the public library as the new community living room, extended opening hours offer potential for a welcome civic space in high density living. Ørestad Bibliotek in Copenhagen is the cultural heart of a new, high rise, residential area with a high percentage of children under 12. Planned and built in 2012 as an open library with increased, unstaffed opening hours, it provides a place for young families to go and interact seven days a week (Denmark 2018).

By comparison, the 24/7 service offered since 2016 by Parkes Shire Library in the small farming community of Tullamore in Australia, with a population of 424, is very low tech and demonstrates a practical approach to the problem of limited resources. Before moving to a 24/7 model the library was open for only 4.5 hours a week providing limited access for residents, which has a high proportion of school-aged and older people. It had been a constant challenge to determine the most appropriate use of library access. The arrangement for 24-hour access was kept simple with library members who requested it being given a key to the door. The self-checkout station is used to return and borrow and a CCTV camera provides a level of security. A notepad beside the self-check provides a line of communication between library members and library staff. Since launching the service, membership and loans have almost doubled (Pearce 2017).

The 1990s first saw discussion about libraries without walls, mostly referring to the development of electronic collections and web-based services. Increasingly libraries are extending beyond the walls and going where people are. While the outreach may be in the form of a traditional mobile library service, increasingly it will be a more flexible form of service delivery that meets the needs of a specific community, or is linked to an event. Pop-ups, express libraries, deposit stations, vending machines and mail delivery services all have specific requirements and demand a thoughtful approach (State Library of New South Wales 2015b). One outreach example is the book-lending machine installed by Warwickshire County Council in the UK at the George Eliot Hospital in the town of Nuneaton in February 2013. The project was the result of a partnership agreement between the Council's Library service and the local National Health Service Trust, which runs the hospital. With a workforce of 1,800 staff and a throughput of 245,000 patients a year, plus visitors, the George Eliot is a busy 24-hour operation with a community much larger than many Warwickshire villages. Consequently, the Library made the decision to install the book-lending machine, which provides a 24-hour book loan service to local people, hospital staff and patients. It serves multiple audiences in a non-library setting, attracts new and lapsed members, and extends library services with no extra staff while supporting the Council's wider health and wellbeing agenda. The hospital has added a library card to the list of things incoming patients should bring with them (Khan 2014).

The Keepers of Local Memory

The public library community is actively involved in securing cultural heritage and creating a sense of place through the creation and curation of locally relevant collections, ranging from extensive digitisation programs where historic and sensitive collections are made available online, to projects that capture local stories and assist citizens in the creation of local content. In an increasingly globalised and connected world, the public library's role in safeguarding, and sharing local content is crucial. It is also each library's point of difference, actively connecting the library to the community in which it is embedded. Emphasising local connections and connotations is a powerful link in strengthening the library's profile and attracting key stakeholders, including politicians, media and volunteers. The appeal of local should never be underestimated.

As a key component of the program to commemorate the Centenary of World War I in the Australian city of Orange, staff at Central West Libraries developed a blog and related wiki where the stories of the men and women who served in the war are told, and details of the impact of the War on the district are related. The online resource is a combination of official records and personal reminiscences and is intended as a permanent memorial to the men and women involved in the First World War. The project has an active community engagement component, and has helped to position the Library as a key as a key source of quality assured information and content creation (Richards 2016).

San Javier-La Loma is a mixed working class and farming neighbourhood of about 25,000 people on the outskirts of Medellin, Colombia's second largest city. Homes are close together; roads are narrow and some places are accessible only on foot. The Public Library San Javier-La Loma, a branch of the Medellin public library network, was eager to offer services to the community which focused on its needs. But they ran into a problem. There was no recent map of the area: the last official map was dated 1971. Modern San Javier-La Loma was invisible to Colombia and the world. Librarians found a solution in the concept of community mapping, a process through which communities decide what to include in maps to create maps of their own neighbourhoods. Over 400 residents of San Javier-Loma are involved in the library's project, bringing memory, photos and stories about their day-to-day experience to the mapping process. The new maps are online, and the members of the community can constantly update them to reflect changes in their location and lives. San Javier-La Loma is now mapped in more detail than any other part of Medellin. Access roads and footpaths, markets and businesses, statistics, farms and factories, historical, religious and cultural sites, schools and social services are all included in their living online maps (EIFL 2014).

The EU-project, A Million Stories, demonstrates the importance of contemporary collecting and the power of cooperation and collaboration in curating local content. Public libraries in Cologne, Germany; Malmo, Sweden; Roskilde, Denmark; and Future Libraries, Greece, offer refugee people a forum to document and publish their personal experiences and stories. Operating for twelve months from 2018 – 2019, the project built an intercultural and multimedia collection of stories about life including childhood, background, education, desires and hopes, but also distress, grief, flight and uncertainty (http://refugeelives.eu/).

Looking Towards the Future

The tenth and final point in the *Global Vision Report Summary* focusses on supporting emerging leaders and equipping them with the necessary skills to navigate the ever-changing environment. In looking to the future, for many, librarianship is a second or even third career choice which brings a far greater breadth of professional and life experience. Correspondingly, as libraries expand the range of services and programs on offer, the capabilities and attributes required of the leadership team also need to be expanded. Future leaders may be recruited from a non-traditional library background. In Finland, for example, the change in thinking is reflected in the new Library Act, which reversed the previously strictly defined professional qualifications required, instead placing emphasis on knowledge and experience. While leadership programs for the wider library and information profession are offered in many countries, those targeted at the public library sector are fewer in number and not necessarily sustainable.

One continuing example, the PLA Leadership Academy in the US, recognises that specific abilities are needed to provide public librarians with the skills for the future (http://www.ala.org/pla/education/inperson/leadershipacademy). The program has been designed to empower participants with the knowledge necessary to be innovative and successful leaders of change and to shift their thinking from an internal, operational focus to one that is reflective of community needs. The PLA model has been replicated in Africa where middle management public library leaders are afforded the opportunity to attend the AfLIA Leadership Academy (AfLAC) which has been developed in partnership with PLA (https://web.aflia.net/call-for-applications-aflia-leadership-academy-cohort-3/; https://web.aflia.net/webinar-library-leadership-and-management-building-todays-african-public-and-community-library-leaders-for-tomorrow/) .The Carnegie Library Lab in the UK is a program aimed at supporting and developing innovation and leadership in the public library sector. In addition to a tailored learning program, networking and mentor support, participants are funded to develop and deliver a pioneering, practical program within their own library service. These experiences are shared online and provide inspiration for colleagues worldwide (Carnegie Trust UK, 2018).

The International Network of Library Innovators (INELI) (https://en.unesco.org/creativity/policy-monitoring-platform/international-network-library), supported by the Bill and Melinda Gates Foundation operated globally across seven regions. With a vision of building a worldwide network of innovative public library leaders, INELI aimed to identify, nurture and develop innovative, emerging leaders and to foster partnerships and collaboration of stakeholders in the respective regions. Funded for a specific time period, the challenge for the future is to ensure that the momentum and enthusiasm generated by the programs are not lost.

It is important to recognise the role of sector specific, professional development that understands the need to support public library staff in gaining, maintaining and expanding their knowledge base. In Australia, the Australian Library and Information Association (ALIA) has recognised the need for specialist professional development opportunities for public library practitioners in order to maintain currency of professional knowledge and practice. The Public Library Specialisation delivers a diverse range of topics and is divided into streams encompassing contemporary fields including: Aboriginal and Torres Strait Islanders; Accessibility; Child/Youth; Community Engagement; Cultural Diversity;

Digital Literacy; and Local studies and Genealogy (https://membership.alia.org.
au/pdinfo/specialisations/alia-pd-scheme---specialisations).

At an international level, the IFLA Public Libraries Section actively promotes
engagement of public library practitioners with each other and with leaders in
the sector through a program that builds on IFLA's mid-term meeting and satellite conference structure. Working with colleagues in host cities, the Section has
facilitated professional development opportunities that encourage participation
by local library staff, expanding their exposure to contemporary thinking, best
practice and networking opportunities. Recent events in Cape Town, Birmingham, Malmo, Barcelona, Sydney and Bergen have attracted significant involvement and demonstrated the benefits of working collaboratively.

Conclusion

The public library sector is a reflection of the world today. There are examples
of magnificent, state-of-the-art buildings with a dizzying array of resources and
services. At the other end of the spectrum, there are simple spaces with minimal
collections that bear the name of library. Wherever they are located and whatever they offer, public libraries occupy an important place in the psyche of their
communities. They are places that are safe, non-judgemental and provide a route
to knowledge, skills, escape and enjoyment. They reflect and support the community in which they exist. Public librarianship affords a real chance to make a
difference in people's lives. Increasingly, public libraries are thinking beyond the
established way of delivering services and are personalising resources, programs
and activities to meet local needs. While local is paramount, never has global
been more important. The ability to share ideas, concepts, successes, and failures
has never been easier. Working together, the international public library community can ensure that the global vision for a united field that supports the value
and role of libraries is met.

References

American Library Association. "Libraries Respond: Services to Poor and Homeless People".
   August 19, 2019. Accessed April 7, 2020. http://www.ala.org/advocacy/diversity/
   librariesrespond/services-poor-homeless.
Australian Public Libraries Alliance (APLA). *How Public Libraries Contribute to the STEM Agenda
   2017*. Canberra, ACT: Australian Library and Information Association, 2017. https://www.

alia.org.au/sites/default/files/How%20public%20libraries%20contribute%20to%20 the%20STEM%20agenda%202017.pdf. Accessed May 13, 2018.

Carnegie UK Trust. "Carnegie Library Lab". [2018]. Accessed April 6, 2020. https://www. carnegieuktrust.org.uk/project/library-lab/.

De Boer, Jeroen. "Mobile Fab Lab Brings New Skills to Rural Areas", *Opensource.com*. 2 June 2014. Accessed May 13, 2018. https://opensource.com/education/14/5/mobile-library-fab-lab-brings-new-skills-rural-areas.

Denmark. Agency for Culture and Palaces. "Model Programme for Public Libraries: Intro". 2015. https://modelprogrammer.slks.dk/en/about-the-programme/intro/

Denmark. Agency for Culture and Palaces. "Model Programme for Public Libraries; Case: Narok". 2017. https://modelprogrammer.slks.dk/en/cases/inspirational-cases/ narok-library/

Denmark. Agency for Culture and Palaces. "Model Programme for Public Libraries: Case: Ørestad Bibliotek". 2018. Accessed May 13, 2018. https://modelprogrammer.slks.dk/en/ cases/inspirational-cases/oerestad-library-copenhagen/

Domingo, Mariona Chavarria "A Kitchen in the Library: the Espai Cuines del Món at the Biblioteca del Fondo (Santa Coloma de Gramenet)", *BiD: textos universitaris de biblioteconomia i documentació*, no. 38 (June 2017). Accessed November 1, 2018. http:// bid.ub.edu/en/38/chavarria.htm .

EIFL. "Creative Use of ICT: Innovation Award: Public Library San Javier-La Loma Puts this Colombian Community on the Map" [2014]. Accessed April 6, 2020. https://www.eifl.net/ eifl-in-action/creative-use-ict-public-libraries-5.

Ferrari, Adriana Cybelle. "Community Libraries in Brazil" *IFLA Public Libraries Section Blog*. 1 October 2016. Accessed May 13, 2018. https://blogs.ifla.org/public-libraries/2016/10/01/ community-libraries-in-brazil/.

Finland. "Public Libraries Act". FINLEX, 2016. Accessed November 3, 2018. https://www.finlex. fi/en/laki/kaannokset/2016/en20161492.

Gullickson, Joel "The Ideas Box Brings Tech and Education Access to Underserved Neighborhoods". *Daily Detroit*. December 1, 2015. http://www.dailydetroit. com/2015/12/01/ideas-box-brings-tech-education-access-underserved-neighborhoods/

IFLA. *Global Vision Report Summary: Top 10 Highlights and Opportunities*. The Hague: IFLA, 2018b. https://www.ifla.org/files/assets/GVMultimedia/publications/gv-report-summary. pdf

IFLA. *IFLA Guidelines for Library Services to People Experiencing Homelessness*. Developed by the IFLA Library Services to People with Special Needs (LSN) Section. The Hague: IFLA, 2017. https://www.ifla.org/files/assets/lsn/publications/ifla-guidelines-for-library-services-to-people-experiencing-homelessness.pdf

IFLA. *IFLA/UNESCO Public Library Manifesto*. The Hague: IFLA, 1994. Accessed March 13, 2018. https://www.ifla.org/publications/iflaunesco-public-library-manifesto-1994.

IFLA. *Responding! Public Libraries and Refugees*. The Hague: IFLA Public Libraries Section, 2015. Accessed March 13, 2018. https://www.ifla.org/files/assets/public-libraries/ publications/library-service-to-refugees.pdf.

IFLA. *Our Vision, Our Future: A Strong and United Library Field Powering Literate, Informed and Participative Societies*. The Hague: IFLA, 2018a. Accessed May 5, 2018. https://www.ifla. org/node/11905.

IFLA. Public Libraries Section. *Global Vision Discussion: How a United Library Field Can Tackle the Challenges of the Future: Report of the Public Libraries Section meeting*. 2017.

https://www.ifla.org/files/assets/gvsr/GV%20Report_IFLA%20Public%20Libraries%20 Standing%20Committee.pdf

IFLA. Public Libraries Section. "Library in the Tram – Tram to the Library". *IFLA Public Libraries Section Blog*. 11 April 2014. Accessed May 13, 2018. https://blogs.ifla.org/public-libraries/2014/04/11/library-in-the-tram-tram-to-the-library/#more-454.

IFLA. Public Libraries Section. "With Book to a Roof over the Head". *IFLA Public Libraries Section Blog*. 10 February 2014. Accessed April 16, 2020. https://blogs.ifla.org/public-libraries/2014/02/10/with-book-to-a-roof-over-the-head/.

IFLA Library Map of the World. The Hague: International Federation of Library Associations and Institutions. [2018]. Accessed March 13, 2018. https://librarymap.ifla.org/.

IFLA Library Map of the World. "Library in Kibera, Africa's Largest Informal Settlement, Improves Access to Education". Contributed by Knls Kibera Community Library. 31 July 2018. https:// librarymap.ifla.org/stories/Kenya/LIBRARY-IN-KIBERA,-AFRICA'S-LARGEST-INFORMAL-SETTLEMENT,-IMPROVES-ACCESS-TO-EDUCATION/123.

Iran Public Library Foundation "The Best Safety for Children and Adolescents in Flooded Areas". 2019. Accessed April 16, 2020. https://www.iranpl.ir/news/21335

Khan, Ayub "Hospital Book Lending Machine: a Different Way to Provide Library Services". *IFLA Talk Transcript*. [2014)]. Accessed October 11, 2018. https://www.ifla.org/files/assets/ public-libraries/publications/ayub_khan_.pdf .

Larsen, Jonna Holmgaard. "Open Libraries in Denmark". *Scandinavian Library Quarterly* 46, no. 3 (2013). Accessed April 6, 2020. http://slq.nu/indexfd9c. html?article=volume-46-no-3-2013-5.

Libraries Connected. "Universal Health Offers: Health and Wellbeing". 2018. https://www. librariesconnected.org.uk/universal-offers/health-wellbeing

Libraries Without Borders. "Building Peace through Libraries in Colombia". Projects. 20 December 2017. Accessed April 6, 2020. https://www.librarieswithoutborders. org/2017/12/20/building-peace-libraries-colombia/.

Library Council of New South Wales. *Enriching Communities: the Value of Public Libraries in New South Wales*. Sydney, NSW: State Library of New South Wales, 2008. Accessed May 20, 2018. https://www.sl.nsw.gov.au/sites/default/files/Enriching%20Communities%20 -%20the%20value%20of%20public%20libraries%20in%20New%20South%20Wales%20 Full%20Report.pdf.

Mexico. *Federal Law of Transparency and Public Access to Information*. The United Mexican States, 2016. Accessed May 18, 2018. http://www.dof.gob.mx/avisos/2493/SG_090516/ SG_090516.html.

Miller, Rebecca. "This Library World: Editorial". *Library Journal*, 17 April 2018. Accessed May 2, 2018. https://lj.libraryjournal.com/2018/04/opinion/editorial/library-world-inspired-greater-global-perspective-editorial/#.

Norway. "Act Relating to Public Libraries (The Public Libraries Act)". 2014. Last amended: LOV-2013-06-21-95 on 1 January 2014. Accessed April 6, 2020. https://www. culturaydeporte.gob.es/dam/jcr:e7981b2e-6e6a-47ff-ae34-9a1c116de609/norway%20 public%20libraries%20act%20english.pdf.

Pearce, ·Melanie. "Tiny Town of Tullamore Experiments With 24 Hour Library". *ABC News*. 11 May 2017. Accessed April 26, 2018. http://www.abc.net.au/news/2017-05-11/24-hour-library-boosts-reading-in-regional-town/8411206.

Public Library Association. "Project Outcome: Measuring the True Impact of Public Libraries: Outcome Measurement Made Easy for Public Libraries: Resources and Tools to Create

Surveys and Analyze Outcome Data. 2018. Accessed November 2, 2018. https://www.projectoutcome.org/.

Richards, Jan. "A City Remembers". IFLA World Library and Information Congress, Columbus, Ohio. 2016. Accessed June 4,2018. http://library.ifla.org/1448/1/108-richards-en.pdf.

Somby, Marit Andersen. "Transforming Norwegian Public Libraries". *IFLA Library Buildings and Equipment Section Blog.* August 8, 2017. https://iflalbes.wordpress.com/2017/08/08/transforming-norwegian-public-libraries/

State Library of New South Wales. "Sounds of Music in the Library". *State Library of New South Wales: Public Services: Blog.* June 22nd 2018. Accessed November 2, 2018. https://www.sl.nsw.gov.au/public-library-services/blogs/sounds-music-library.

State Library of New South Wales. *Building on the Bookend Scenarios: Innovation for NSW Public Libraries 2014 to 2030.* Sydney, NSW: State Library of New South Wales, 2015a. Accessed May 13, 2018. http://www.sl.nsw.gov.au/sites/default/files/building_bookends_scenarios.pdf.

State Library of New South Wales. *Mobile and Outreach Services.* Sydney, NSW: State Library of New South Wales, 2015b. Accessed April 12, 2018. http://www.sl.nsw.gov.au/sites/default/files/mobile_outreach_services.pdf.

State Library of Western Australia. "Screenwest Partners with the State Library to Revive Heritage Western Australian Film". *State Library of Western Australia. News.* 2 May, 2018. Accessed April 6, 2020. https://slwa.wa.gov.au/news/screenwest-partners-state-library-revive-heritage-western-australian-film-0

Contributors

Abbott-Halpin, Edward
Principal Orkney College, University of the Highlands and Islands, and Professor of Social and Human Rights Informatics, University of the Highlands and Islands. Edward Abbott-Halpin is an experienced professor and lecturer with a demonstrated history of working in the higher education industry and management experience at several levels. He describes himself as a political scientist, with experience in governance, child rights, human rights, peace and conflict and the use of information and ICT in these areas. He has a Ph.D. from Leeds Metropolitan University focused on the use of information and technology for human and children's rights and a Master's degree in public policy from the University of Central Lancashire. He joined the Board of Human Rights Information and Documentation Systems, International (HURIDOCS) in 2009 and was its Chair from 2009–2016. He is a Visiting Professor in the governance and citizenship research area at the Open University, UK.

Al, Umut
Chair, Department of Information Management, Hacettepe University, Turkey. Umut Al received his Ph.D. in information management from Hacettepe University in 2008. He teaches courses on scholarly communication, information brokerage, and research methods. His research interests include information retrieval on the internet, marketing of information services, university libraries, and bibliometrics. He has published numerous papers in professional journals, including *Aslib Journal of Information Management*, *JASIST: Journal of the American Society for Information Science and Technology*, *Journal of Librarianship and Information Science*, *Library & Information Science Research*, *Libri* and *Scientometrics*. He is a member of professional associations, including the Turkish Librarians' Association and the Association of University and Research Librarians. Between 2013–2018, he worked as an impact assessment working group leader at Librar-e Turkey and Libraries for Everyone, programs of the Global Libraries Initiative of the Bill and Melinda Gates Foundation. He also worked as a project manager and researcher in several national projects and as a researcher on European Union projects.

Ali, Irhamni
Chief Library Program Analyst and Reporting Subdivision, Strategic Planning Bureau, National Library of Indonesia. Irhamni Ali finished his Bachelor in Library and Information Science degree from the University of Indonesia in 2005 and continued to the Master's program in Information Technology for Libraries at the Computer Science Department of Bogor Agricultural University in 2011. His thesis title was: *Evaluation and E-government Design of Legal Product Repository System as the Implementation of Deposit Function at the National Library of Indonesia*. He is an active member of the Indonesian Library Information Scholars Association, and the Board of Directors of the ASEAN Public Library Information Network (APLiN).

Anstice, Ian
Public Library News Editor and Locality Librarian, Cheshire West and Cheshire Council. Ian Anstice has spent his career working in public libraries, working first frontline in Cheshire and then in various management roles. He started the *Public Libraries News* website in 2010 to chronicle the changes to the sector within the UK. Ian has won several awards, including the British Empire Medal, an honorary fellowship in the Chartered Institute of Library and Information Professionals (CILIP)

https://doi.org/10.1515/ https://doi.org/10.1515/ 9783110533323-019 and Information Professional of the Year, as well as twice being recognised for providing the best customer service in the town where he worked. He divides his time between working full-time for Cheshire West and Chester public libraries during the day and spending time in the evenings and weekends on *Public Libraries News*, various minor community roles, including pantomime appearances, and of course his family.

Black, Alistair

Professor Emeritus, School of Information Sciences, University of Illinois at Urbana-Champaign, US. Alistair Black is the author of *A New History of the English Public Library* (1996), *The Public Library in Britain 1914–2000* (2000) and *Libraries of Light: British Public Library Design in the Long 1960s* (2017). He is co-author of *Understanding Community Librarianship* (1997), *The Early Information Society in Britain, 1900–1960* (2007) and *Books, Buildings and Social Engineering* (2009). With Peter Hoare, he edited Volume 3, covering 1850–2000, of the *Cambridge History of Libraries in Britain and Ireland* (2006). He was Chair of the Library History Group of the UK Library Association (1992–1999) and of the IFLA Section on Library History (2003–2007). He served as editor of the international journals *Library History* (2004–2008) and *Library Trends* (2009–2016). His recent research has focused on the design of US Carnegie libraries and information management in the Intelligence Branch of Britain's War Office before 1914.

Bossaller, Jenny

Associate Professor and Program Chair of Library and Information Science at the iSchool at the University of Missouri, US. Jenny Bossaller researches the intersections of the public, ethics, policy, and history. She is co-author of: *Introduction to Public Librarianship*, 3rd ed. She has served as a member-at-large in the Missouri Library

Association and is past chair of the Library History Round Table of the American Library Association (ALA). She has been Principal Investigator and Co-Principal Investigator on Institute of Museum and Library Services (IMLS) grants focusing on education for librarianship in public library leadership (PuLL) and healthy communities through the Collaborative for Universal Health (C4UH). Jenny has worked in public and academic libraries, and as a systems librarian for the MOBIUS consortium. She is a passionate and creative educator who has led initiatives in service-learning and international studyabroad to deepen students' understanding of librarianship and information provision.

Dolan, John

Consultant in Libraries and Regeneration, Birmingham, UK. John Dolan is an adviser on libraries with over forty years' experience in public libraries in the UK. As Head of Libraries in Birmingham, he also managed Early Years Education, the Youth Service and Adult Education. He led on the business case and concept development for the Library of Birmingham. John has always been at the forefront of public library developments in community information and librarianship, lifelong learning, and children's services. He was Project Leader for the People's Network strategy for Internet access in every UK public library. He was Head of Library Policy at the Museums Libraries and Archives Council and has advised on many UK library projects while supporting national strategies in Bulgaria, India and Ireland. John has worked on British Council libraries modernisation, including a regional digital library, across South Asia and in Zimbabwe and public libraries in Bangladesh. Latterly he helped create a research library in the new Basrah Museum, Iraq. John was a Board member and Chair of CILIP, honoured by the award of an Order of the British Empire (OBE) and is a member of the Council of the Shakespeare Birthplace Trust.

Goulding, Anne
Director, Research Degrees Programme,
School of Information Management, Victoria
University of Wellington, New Zealand.
Anne Goulding is Professor of Library and
Information Management. Her research
interests lie primarily in the area of the
management of library and information
services and her main focus is on the
management of public libraries. She has a
particular interest in how GLAMR, galleries,
libraries, archives, museums and records,
organizations demonstrate the impact of their
services, activities and programmes. She
teaches in research methods and is involved
in the continuing professional development
of librarians and information workers. Her
professional interests are considerable
and she is Editor in Chief of the *Journal of
Librarianship and Information Science*. She
has published widely in refereed journals
and edited works, and has given conference
presentations internationally based on her
research.

Irwin, Bill
Associate Professor, Huron University,
Ontario, Canada, where he instructs in both
the Bachelors of Management and Organizational Studies program and Governance,
Leadership and Ethics. Bill Irwin holds
a standing appointment in the Local
Government Program at Western University,
Ontario, where he has instructed since 2007,
and also currently instructs in the School
of Policy Studies at Queen's University,
Kingston, Ontario. With many decades of
public sector practice, his expertise focuses
on the areas of: leadership, policy, program
development and evaluation, performance
measurement, and community engagement.
His research interests centre on issues
of policy, leadership, and community
engagement. He is primarily interested in
the interaction between institutions and
community; the interplay between policy and
practice.

Kammer, Jenna
Assistant Professor of Library Science,
University of Central Missouri, Warrensburg,
MO, US. Jenna Kammer has a doctorate
from the University of Missouri in the
School of Information Science and Learning
Technologies. Her research interests are
related to critical theory as applicable in
libraries, including issues of equitable
access and societal improvement. She has
collaborated on several works related to
private interests in public learning spaces,
including universities, schools and libraries.
In addition, Jenna teaches information
literacy, reference, technology and action
research to school librarians and integrates
the importance of critical librarianship as a
tool for the reflective practitioner.

Kargbo, John Abdul
Associate Professor and Dean, Faculty
of Arts, and Specialist Assistant to the
Deputy Vice Chancellor at Fourah Bay
College, University of Sierra Leone. John
Abdul Kargbo holds a Master of Arts degree
in Library and Information Studies from
the University of Sierra Leone. Before
being elected Dean of Faculty, John was
the Director of the Institute of Library,
Information and Communication Studies at
Fourah Bay College for close to a decade.
As a professional teacher, he taught in
a number of secondary schools in Sierra
Leone before proceeding to his Master's
Studies at Fourah Bay College. John is a
prolific writer in library and information
studies and is currently contributing to
over twelve international journals. He is the
proud winner of the R.D. Macleod Award for
Excellence (2000) and is a member of the
Literati Club. John teaches at the Institute
of Library, Information and Communication
Studies at Fourah Bay College. His research
interests include knowledge management,
research methodology, records management,
bibliographic control, librarianship and
information management.

Koren, Marian

International library expert. Marian Koren has studied international law and Swedish, and received her Ph.D. cum laude: *Tell Me! The Right of the Child to Information* in 1996 from the University of Amsterdam. She has longstanding experience based on working at the Netherlands Public Library Association, in various capacities such as Head of Policy Staff and Head of Research and International Affairs. She was a researcher at the Research and Development Department of the National Library of the Netherlands in The Hague and served as its policy adviser on professional issues from an international perspective. As Director of the Netherlands Library Forum (FOBID), she extended her international work and involvement in IFLA, serving in the Library Theory and Research and Management of Library Associations Sections and the Governing Board: and in the European Bureau of Library, Information and Documentation Associations (EBLIDA) in Expert Groups and its Executive Committee. Her work includes international lectures and publications on library advocacy, policies and innovative programs, especially related to human rights in library services. She took early retirement in 2017.

McMenemy, David

Lecturer and Deputy Director for Postgraduate Teaching, Department of Computer and Information Sciences, University of Strathclyde. Glasgow, Scotland. David McMenemy's research interests encompass information law and ethics, including intellectual freedom and freedom of expression, freedom of access to information, privacy, and the philosophy of information. He has also extensively researched around public library policy and development in the UK. He is author of *The Public Library* (Facet, 2009) and co-author of *Librarianship: An Introduction* (2008) and *A Handbook of Ethical Practice: A Practical Guide to Dealing with Ethical Issues in information and Library Work* (2007).

Markless, Sharon

Senior Lecturer in Higher Education, King's College London, and a Senior Associate, Information Management Associates. Sharon Markless divides her work between teaching and research, where she focuses on information literacy and library impact evaluation. She has been an impact consultant to the Bill and Melinda Gates Foundation and has conducted impact consultancy work for the Global Impact Study, focusing on the impact of public access computing in the developing world, as well as for IFLA and the UNDP in Bulgaria. She was until recently a member of the UK National Health Service (NHS) Knowledge for Health Workforce Planning Group. In 2009 Sharon was awarded a National Teaching Fellowship from the Higher Education Academy and she is an Honorary Fellow of the Chartered Institute of Library and Information Professionals (CILIP).

Öz, Seda

Ph.D. candidate, University of Delaware, Department of English. Seda Öz received her B.A. degree in English Language and Literature from Istanbul University in 2012, and her M.A. degree in British Cultural Studies from Hacettepe University in 2015. Alongside her academic studies, she volunteered in NGOs, including Greenpeace Mediterranean and Unite for Literacy. Between 2013–2016, she worked as a project expert at Librar-e Turkey and Libraries for Everyone programs of the Global Libraries Initiative of the Bill and Melinda Gates Foundation. Currently, she is working on adaptation studies with a special emphasis on transnational film remakes.

Paley, Jeremy

Senior Program Manager, Bill & Melinda Gates Foundation. Jeremy Paley has fifteen years of experience in the design and measurement of philanthropic and international development initiatives. As a program officer for the Bill and Melinda Gates Foundation's Global Libraries initiative, he developed and managed a portfolio of grants to support public library development programs in Indonesia, Bangladesh, and Eastern Europe. In an age when economic, educational, and social opportunities increasingly depend on access to information, the programs helped public libraries acquire the tools and skills to offer new services relevant to their communities' needs. Jeremy commissioned research on usage of public libraries, managed portfolio evaluations, and oversaw measurement technical assistance to grantees. He also led the collaborative development and implementation of a common impact measurement system used by grantees and across the wider public library sector. In addition to Global Libraries, he has worked on the Foundation's central monitoring and evaluation and nutrition teams and worked as a researcher for Mathematica Policy Research's global philanthropy practice.

Pateman, Joe

Ph.D, candidate, University of Nottingham, UK, studying politics with a specific interest in the disciplines of Marxist political theory and international political economy. Joe Pateman has written several essays from the Marxist perspective, on topics such as globalization, inequality, poverty, international relations, political strategy, racism and hegemony. Joe is currently writing a dissertation that analyses the relationship between Leninism and democracy, and he is planning on specialising within this area whilst pursuing an academic career in politics. He studied overseas as an exchange student at the University of Hong Kong during the midst of the protests in 2014. Joe has visited the Democratic People's Republic of North Korea as a student ambassador, and is interested in bringing the North Korean philosophy of *Juche* into mainstream western academic discourse.

Pateman, John

Chief Librarian and Chief Executive Officer, Thunder Bay Public Library, Thunder Bay, Ontario, Canada. John Pateman has worked in public libraries for 42 years in various roles ranging from Library Assistant to Chief Librarian. He was Chief Librarian of three library systems in the UK: Hackney, a diverse inner London borough; Merton, a multicultural London suburb; and Lincolnshire, a large rural county. John was part of the research team which produced *Open to All? The Public Library and Social Exclusion (2000)*, which informed the Working Together Project (2004–2008) in Canada. He is the author of *Developing a Needs Based Library Service (2003)*, *Public Libraries and Social Justice* (2010, with John Vincent) and *Developing Community-Led Public Libraries* (2013, with Ken Williment). His latest publication is *Managing Cultural Change in Public Libraries* (2019, with Joe Pateman). John writes a column "Open to All?" for *Open Shelf*, the Ontario Library Association (OLA) online journal, which explores barriers to library use and how to reduce or remove them. He is the Director of the Cuban Libraries Solidarity Campaign and received the National Culture Award from the Cuban government for his work in support of Cuban libraries. He is a Fellow of the Chartered Institute of Library and Information Professionals (CILIP) and a founding member and editorial collective member of Information For Social Change. He is a member of the Canadian Federation of Library Associations (CFLA-FCAB) Indigenous Matters Committee, the CFLA-FCAB National Forum Planning Committee, the Progressive Librarians Guild Co-ordinating Committee, and the Centre for Free Expression Working Group.

Rankin, Carolynn

Senior Lecturer and Researcher, with twenty years of experience as an information management specialist before moving into professional education in 2000. At Leeds

Metropolitan University, Carolynn Rankin was Postgraduate Course Leader in the School of Information Management and in the School of Applied Global Ethics. She is currently a member of the teaching team for the M.Sc. Library and Information Management course at Ulster University and a senior adjunct lecturer at Charles Sturt University in Australia. Carolynn has interdisciplinary research interests, exploring the connections between civil society, social justice and access to literacy and learning via libraries. She has a Ph.D. from Leeds Metropolitan University focused on the role of the public library in supporting the development of communication, language and literacy in children and their families. Current professional activities include the role of External Examiner for the Chartered Institute of Library and Information Professionals (CILIP) Professional Registration Board, and Assessor for CILIP Accreditation for Learning Providers. She has also served as a member of the IFLA Library Theory and Research Section Standing Committee and corresponding member of the IFLA Children and Young Adults Standing Committee. Carolynn has co-authored and edited several books including *Library Services from Birth to Five – Delivering the Best Start* and *Library Services for Children and Young Adults – Challenges and Opportunities in the Digital Age* both published by Facet Publishing.

Richards, Jan
Manager, Central West Libraries, New South Wales Australia. Jan Richards is an active member of the Australian library community and a past President and Fellow of the Australian Library and Information Association (ALIA). She currently chairs the Australian Public Library Alliance and is a member of the Library Council of New South Wales. In 2017, Jan was awarded Membership of the Order of Australia, AM, for her contributions to librarianship. She was also awarded the H.C.L. Anderson award

by ALIA in recognition of her outstanding service to the industry domestically and internationally. Jan is a strong advocate for the International Federation of Library and Information Associations (IFLA) and is former Chair of IFLA's Standing Committee on Public Libraries, and Committee on Standards. She is currently Information Coordinator for IFLA's Literacy and Reading Standing Committee.

Robinson, Simon
Professor of Applied and Professional Ethics, Leeds Beckett University. Educated at Oxford and Edinburgh Universities, Simon Robinson became a psychiatric social worker before entering the Church of England priesthood in 1978. He entered university chaplaincy in Edinburgh and Leeds, developing research and lecturing in areas of pastoral care, medical ethics and business ethics. In 2004 he joined Leeds Metropolitan (now Beckett) University as Professor of Applied and Professional Ethics, and at Leeds Business School founded the Centre for Governance, Leadership and Global Responsibility. He focuses on business and professional ethics, the nature and practice of responsibility, responsibility and pedagogy, governance, and leadership ethics across all sectors. Running throughout is a concern about the meaning of responsibility, focused in virtues, culture and critical dialogue. He is ethics advisor to the UK Northern Region Police Code of Ethics Committee, and has worked with many businesses and professional bodies, including Nestlé, the Royal Academy of Engineering and the Institute of Civil Engineering, on the development of ethical codes and culture. He has written or edited many books the latest of which are: *The Practice of Integrity in Business* (2016), *The Spirituality of Responsibility* (2017), and *Nursing and Healthcare Ethics* (2021).

Streatfield, David
Principal, Information Management Associates, a research, training and

consultancy team formed in 1991 and focused mainly on evaluating the impact of libraries. David Streatfield recently completed a decade as an independent impact consultant to the Bill & Melinda Gates Foundation, where he advised the team managing the Global Libraries Initiative and worked with the impact specialists and country teams supporting impact development in Brazil, Colombia, Jamaica, South Africa and Turkey, as well as various countries in Eastern Europe and South Asia. His other impact consultancy clients have included the International Development Research Centre (IDRC), the US Public Library Association and the International Research and Exchanges Board (IREX). He recently completed the programme evaluation for the IFLA International Advocacy Programme and previously performed in this role for the IFLA Building Strong Library Associations programme as well as advising IFLA's Freedom of Access to Information and Freedom of Expression (FAIFE) evaluation work.